*This book is dedicated to those who have taught and inspired me
to become a professional helper—
my parents, mentors, clients, colleagues, friends,
and my partner.*

CONTENTS

PREFACE

My high school Latin and English teachers would, no doubt, be surprised to see that I took their lessons to heart. I wasn't the student voted most likely to put Latin (or even English) to good use. Nonetheless, I remembered their lessons about launching any new undertaking with a definition of one's subject matter. So when I began teaching the course that became the impetus for this textbook, I sought out the origins, history, and current usage of the words *professional, helper,* and *helping.* While the *Oxford English Dictionary* (1989) goes on at length about each of these words, understanding their essence may assist readers. Such understanding assisted me as I created this book.

The word *professional* comes from the Late Middle English *professe* and from the Latin *profess,* meaning "to claim to have knowledge of or skill in some art or science" or "to declare onself an expert or proficient in such skills." A professional is someone who follows an occupation otherwise engaged in as a pastime, who reaches a particular standard or has the qualities expected in a specific profession. Someone who is trained and skilled not only in the mechanics, but the theory or science of an occupation is said to have "raised the dignity of a trade to a 'learned profession'" and is referred to as a professional.

A *helper* is someone engaged in the process of *helping,* or "adding one's own actions or effort to those of another so as to make something more effectual." Helping is the process of furthering action or purpose, being of service or use, or making something easier.

For many people, perhaps even most people, helping others is a normal part of everyday life. We add our actions or efforts to those of others with the goal of making life easier or more effective or furthering a specific purpose. What sets helping professionals apart is that we make our living by helping others; we receive training in the mechanics, science, and theories of helping; and we define standards that identify expert practice. Psychologists, therapists, social workers, counselors, and human services workers each declare a unique perspective about helping. At the same time, the different helping professions all share the common aim of adding our efforts to the efforts of our clients to make it easier or sometimes possible for the client to accomplish her or his goals. One result of our common aim is an overlap in some training essentials that prepare us for our professions. This textbook is about the skills, theories, science, and ethical values that lay a foundation for effective professional helping.

I decided to write this book after reviewing textbooks in the fields of psychology, social work, counseling, and human services while preparing to teach a course about the theory and practice of professional helping. Most texts addressed either microskills or theory, but not both. I took an opportunity to lament (some overhearing that conversation might have said, "complain about") the lack of an integrated text to T. Gregg Bell, the Allyn and Bacon district manager. He courageously responded, "Well, then, write one." So, surprising even myself, I did.

Microskills and Theoretical Foundations for Professional Helpers is intended for those who are training to be professional helpers. My purpose was to offer readers both microskills and theory in one text with enough depth to frame common activities of professional helpers and to support additional training in their disciplines. I designed it to be used as a primary text for advanced undergraduate and beginning graduate courses in therapy, counseling, and interviewing. Administrators or trainers in human services or human resources agencies may also find the book helpful in training entry-level employees.

My approach to this topic grew out of my many years as a clinician, teacher, and trainer, working with beginning helping professionals to establish a sound foundation from which to advance in the skills of our profession. In the course of any helping relationship, professional helpers must make myriad decisions quickly and spontaneously. Students are often disappointed at the lack of definitive guidelines about what to do when facing these decisions. Human interactions are too complex to make it possible to detail the responses or answers to all of the situations that a helping professional may encounter. Instead, just as a strong foundation supports a building, a strong foundation can support the structure of solid helping decisions. I look at microskills and theories as the bricks and mortar of helping. The strategies used in helping are held together by the relationship and together microskills and theory provide a strong foundation for furthering a client's purposes. So, although microskills and theories will not answer every question that arises or determine everything that could be done in that setting, they should offer a foundation from which to determine such answers.

This book begins with an introduction to helping as a profession. Students often want to know what it takes to become a helping professional, so I begin by outlining the types of training and education that different helping professionals receive. The introduction also explores the nature of the helping relationship and how it is distinguished from personal help that people provide regularly for each other. Common themes in the ethics of professional helping are explored briefly. Ethics are standards of conduct derived from personal values, but each helping profession also endorses standards that form the basic value structure of the profession and the basis of many helping decisions. Personal and professional ethics shape the professionals who make these decisions. Finally, the introduction explores the different roles that microskills and theory play in forming the foundation of helping.

Following the introduction, the book is divided into three parts. Part One introduces the microskills of helping. *Microskills,* a term coined about twenty-five years ago, refers to those skills common to helping professions. With slightly different emphases, each of the microskills are integrated into most existing theoretical frameworks and most professional helping activities. This part of the book systematically guides students through the development of the microskills of helping, from very basic nonverbal skills that include the proxemics, kinesics, and time perspectives that create synchrony with a client and then through the process of building empathy through reflecting a client's content and feeling. Part One ends by framing more complex skills such as confronting, self-disclosing, immediacy, and information-giving in an ethic of advancing a client's goals.

Part Two introduces the theories that form the foundation of different approaches to helping. By exploring both traditional theoretical influences on helping and more contemporary schools of thought, this part of the book begins the process of facilitating students' development of a personal philosophy and theory about change and helping. Whenever possible, I present each theory in parallel construction with the others so that students can compare and contrast the different approaches. Each theory chapter includes history and background, key concepts important to understanding the theory, some variations within the theory, suggested helping strategies arising from the particular theory, research that supports the theory, and critiques of the theory.

Part Three offers two further applications of the skills and theories addressed in the book. The first applications chapter introduces students to the application of helping skills to crisis theory and intervention. Internships and graduates' first employment experiences in professional helping often include crisis intervention work. Drawing from the Chinese characters for *crisis,* signifying both opportunity and danger, I present basic crisis theory, outline specific and commonly encountered crises, and guide beginning helpers through the process of effective crisis intervention. Crisis helping is also compared to and contrasted with brief and longer-term counseling and therapy.

The second applications chapter is designed to give students a glimpse of ways in which interviewing and helping skills may be applied to research designs. Qualitative research is beginning to gain the same foothold in the fields of psychology, counseling, and women's studies as it has had for several decades in sociology, social work, education, nursing, and anthropology. Many helping professions now require more accountability than in the past. Basic and applied research (e.g., outcome effectiveness research) are improved by professionals who are at least aware of quantitative and qualitative methods of answering questions about helping. Raising awareness of how interviewing techniques may be used as research methods exposes students of professional helping to the cutting edges of several academic disciplines and offers a new lens through which to consider these skills. I explain how the same techniques that are used in effective helping can be used as effective research methods and explore some of the similarities and differences in using these techniques for individual or group interviews for research purposes.

In writing this text, I have worked not only to include microskills and theories that form the foundation for professional helping across multiple disciplines, but also to ground each in supporting science. My own training is in psychology and I understand human beings from this scientific perspective. Readers will find that I support my general approach to helping with psychological research. In addition, my personal and professional ethics about appreciating differences are woven into the fabric of the text much as the differences clients themselves bring are woven into the rich fabric of everyday life.

ACKNOWLEDGMENTS

This book found its shape through the professional and personal skills of friends and colleagues. I want to take this opportunity to acknowledge those who added their efforts to my own to make my writing easier and, in some cases, possible. T. Greg Bell (Great Lakes District Manager) and Judy Fifer (former Editor) from Allyn and Bacon believed in the project from its infancy. Patricia Quinlin (Editor), Annemarie Kennedy (Editorial Assistant), Anna Socrates (Editorial Production Administrator), and Lauren Shafer (Editorial Production Services), also of Allyn and Bacon, ushered the project through what was for me an unfamiliar process, offering much-needed words of encouragement. Jim Larson (Professor of Psychology), at University of Wisconsin–Whitewater, mentored and encouraged me when my resolve was weakening. Meg Cole constructed the first draft of the glossary, helped track the references, and showed me the book through a student's eyes. Micael Kemp (Associate Director of Career Services), at University of California–Santa Barbara, and Susan L. MacQuiddy (Senior Psychologist), at Colorado State University, both of whom have taught helping theory and microskills courses for many years, reviewed critical chapters and confirmed that I was on the right track. My thanks extend as well to reviewers Delores Dungee-Anderson, Virginia Commonwealth University, and Doug Fleischer, Walla Walla College.

Finally, I want to acknowledge Susan Simmons, a professional editor and writer and my partner of fifteen years. Her countless hours of listening (in her own natural helping style) regularly enhance my helping skills and gave me the early and ongoing confidence I needed to propose and then implement this project. I am grateful for her skillful editing as well as for her professional and gently offered advice.

INTRODUCTION

Helping is the process of adding one's own actions or efforts to another's actions or efforts to make them more effectual; furthering the action or purpose of something; being of service or use; and making something easier to do. This book is about the process of professional helping and brings together two critical components of that process: **microskills** and **theories.** The process of helping is comprised of the helper, the basic values and standards that guide helping processes, the microskills and theories of helping, and perspectives about how and when to use helping tools. This chapter introduces the different helping professionals and examines the helping relationship in terms of its component parts: ethical standards, microskills, theories, and the stages of helping relationships.

I begin with a description of the professionals in helping occupations who establish and then constantly strive for the standards and quality expected in their work and who are trained and skilled both in the theory and science of their occupation and in its applications. This is then followed by an overview of the microskills or mechanics of the relationship, the theories or science of helping strategies, and the stages in the helping process. Microskills are at the heart of developing an empathic relationship—the most crucial element in helping. Once a firm foundation of interchangeable empathy is established, theories of helping create the foundation on which strategies to facilitate client goals are based. When goals have been met, microskills again guide helpers through the process of empathic closure of the relationship. Forging and enveloping specific strategies born of differing theoretical perspectives, relational microskills are the context of helping. Finally, an outline of the basic professional and ethical values that guide helping is examined.

PROFESSIONAL HELPERS

This book was written for students planning on becoming professional helpers and for beginning professional helpers. Neither this book, nor

1

the course or training the book will likely be used for, will prepare someone to engage in professional helping. Additional training is needed and each helping professional undergoes specific training to add to his or her own helping efforts. Although all have a common aim, each professional helper also brings a unique perspective to effective helping from his or her background and training. The educational backgrounds, typical practice activities, and typical practice settings of different helping professionals both overlap and vary.

Psychiatrists

A psychiatrist is someone whose primary training and credentials are in medicine. A student who aspires to be a psychiatrist usually has an undergraduate education in pre-medicine, biology, or chemistry. After graduating, those who want to pursue a career in psychiatry first go to medical school and receive a general medicine doctorate. Following this, they intern in general medicine before completing three years of residency training, specifically in psychiatry. Both a medical internship and residency training are supervised apprenticeships with seminar courses, assigned reading, and ongoing discussions about what they are learning. The amount of formal coursework varies from residency to residency, but at the core of each residency training is supervised treatment. A very small number of those who have trained and interned in general medicine and completed a residency in psychiatry go on to get additional training in psychoanalysis.

When they complete psychiatric residency training, psychiatrists engage in a variety of practice activities. Most psychiatrists assess patients or clients for psychiatric disorders and determine whether and how much psychotropic medication would help make life easier. Psychiatrists also consult with others about medication intervention. Psychologists and social workers, who do not have prescription privileges, may still see clients who can benefit from psychotropic medication. Some psychiatrists also provide therapy, some teach in medical schools, and some become clinic administrators.

The settings in which psychiatrists commonly practice include hospitals, clinics, managed care organizations, and private practices, and those who teach are likely to do so in universities or medical schools. In general, psychiatrists enjoy prestige among many helping professionals because of their background in medicine, although among medical professionals, their prestige and status is considered lower.

Psychiatric Nurses

A psychiatric nurse is someone whose primary training and credentials are in nursing. He or she may have an associate's degree or a bachelor's degree in nursing that includes an emphasis on courses in biology and chemistry as well as in nursing practice. To become a psychiatric nurse, students complete a bachelor's degree in nursing and then a master's degree program specializing in psychiatric nursing. In some states, people with psychiatric nursing degrees may also pursue additional training in psychopharmacology to earn prescription privileges.

Once their educational training is complete, psychiatric nurses most frequently engage in collaborations with other helping professionals, like psychiatrists and psychologists, to implement treatment plans. Psychiatric nurses are often involved in medication education. Medication education is a follow-up activity for patients who are taking prescription psychotropic medications. It involves instruction about the nature, dosage, appropriate administration, and side effects of the particular medication the patient may be taking. Sometimes this is done individually and sometimes in a group. Other activities that psychiatric nurses engage in include case management, **triage,** and psychotherapy. Psychiatric nurses may also become administrators of clinics, and some choose to teach in university, college, or hospital nursing programs. Psychiatric nurses most often practice in clinics, managed care organizations, and hospitals.

Social Workers

A social worker is someone whose education and professional credentials are in social work. Those who aspire to be social workers usually complete an undergraduate degree program in social work, sociology, or psychology. In some states, those with an undergraduate degree may be certified as social workers. More commonly, people who wish to practice as social workers go on to complete a master's degree program in social work (M.S.W.). This includes foundation courses in interviewing; field experience; working with individuals, groups, families, and communities; research methods; working within diverse client communities; and various aspects of social work policy and practice (e.g., case management, administration of social programs). Beyond the foundation courses, social work students specialize their programs to the settings in which they wish to work (e.g., human services organizations, children or family services, schools, mental health clinics) or the types of activities in which they hope to engage (e.g., case management, therapy, child protection). Some social work graduate programs offer an emphasis on psychiatric social work.

Once they have completed their training, social workers may find jobs in various human services, social services, welfare, mental health, school, and other institutional settings. Social workers also practice in hospitals, clinics, private practice, and university health centers. Some social workers choose to teach in university or college settings.

Social workers engage in a broad variety of activities. They may manage cases; engage in psychotherapy; interview clients' employers, relatives, and teachers; and match and refer clients to appropriate vocational, living, and social programs. Of all of the professional helpers, social workers probably have the most intense involvement in the everyday living and stresses of their clients. They are the professional helpers most likely to make home visits or work-site visits.

Psychologists

A psychologist is a person whose training and professional credentials are in psychology. There are several different types of psychologists who apply psychological principles to the professional practice of helping. Clinical psychologists, counseling psychologists, and school psychologists receive training and credentials that are slightly different, but they share a common background in the psychological foundations of behavior (e.g., learning, development, personality, social, biological). As undergraduates, those who intend to go on for advanced training in psychology most often complete a bachelor's degree in psychology, although some complete degrees in related fields like biology, neuroscience, social work, or special education.

If you were to compare the advanced training, practice activities, and professional settings of the three largest of the applied psychology fields (i.e., clinical, counseling, and school psychologists), you would find overlapping similarities and distinct differences. In addition to offering advanced courses in the learning, developmental, personality, social, and biological bases of behavior, most graduate programs in the applied areas of psychology also offer courses in research methods, assessment and diagnosis, consultation, clinical supervision, and theories of psychotherapy. Both master's degree programs and doctoral programs in clinical, counseling, and school psychology also offer courses unique to each specialization. Clinical psychology programs offer a slightly greater emphasis on diagnosis and treatment of mental health disorders. Counseling psychology programs offer a slightly greater emphasis on problems in everyday living and development and life transitions that, while not diagnosable, still require professional help (e.g., career development, assessment, counseling). School psychology programs offer a greater emphasis on facilitating the educational process of students through consultation with teachers, parents, and school administrators, and working to assess the personal and academic difficulties that create barriers for students.

Most graduate programs in applied areas of psychology also require an internship, and many students (particularly those in clinical psychology, counseling psychology, or neuropsychology) also complete an optional two-year residency or postdoctoral training. Most states license those with doctorates in psychology for practice, and some states offer a modified version of this license for those with master's degrees in applied areas of psychology.

Psychologists engage in diagnosis and assessment, psychotherapy, clinical supervision, consultation, research, teaching, and administration. Psychologists may practice in clinics, managed care organizations, private practices, hospitals (including both psychiatric and general hospitals), schools (especially K–12 for school psychologists; university health services for counseling psychologists; medical schools for counseling and clinical psychologists), correctional facilities (especially for clinical psychologists with forensic training), and nursing homes. In addition, some clinical psychologists complete specialized training in pediatric, forensic, or health psychology that prepares them to work with different populations and with different emphases.

Counselors

A counselor is someone whose training and credentials are primarily in counseling, education, or counselor education. As undergraduates, those who plan to pursue graduate training in counseling complete degrees in psychology, education, or special education. Graduate programs in counseling are usually housed in education departments and offer core courses in assessment, counseling, research, theories of counseling, ethics, and diverse client populations that prepare students to assess personal issues related to client problems; collect and analyze information in determining appropriate counseling interventions; employ appropriate facilitative techniques; and prepare documents such as counseling-related reports and treatment plans. Some programs in counseling offer emphases in guidance counseling focused on academic development; community counseling, which emphasizes preventive and ecological approaches to client problems; or marriage and family counseling, which focuses on problems and solutions within a relational context. Counselors generally complete a master's degree (M.S. or M.Ed.) or a doctorate (Ed.D.) and are licensed as counselors by each state. Counselors practice in high schools (if their emphasis is guidance or higher education), clinics or managed care facilities (if their emphasis is marriage and family or community counseling), and private offices.

Human Services Workers

Psychiatric aides or attendants, psychiatric or mental health technicians, group home workers, probation and parole officers, human resources personnel, day care aides, battered women's shelter and rape crisis center advocates, and crisis telephone workers are all examples of human services workers who may receive specialized training from the facilities or organizations in which they work. They generally have undergraduate degrees in psychology, sociology, social work, human services, or education. Some community colleges offer more specialized training and associate degrees in fields like psychiatric or mental health technician or child care. These generalists often provide the day-to-day work of the various human services and, in institutional and clinical settings, may actually have more continuous contact with clients than do other helping professionals.

THE HELPING RELATIONSHIP

Whether professional helpers have completed training and received credentials in psychiatry, nursing, psychology, social work, counseling, or general human services, each must establish a relationship with clients that will facilitate the clients' growth and development, change, or progress toward a goal, and each draws from a theoretical foundation to guide additional strategies in helping. This book takes the position that developing an empathic relationship provides the foundation for any helping process. Empathy results from an ability to put oneself in another's place, to see the world from her or his perspective, and to feel what another's experiences have been like for her or him. In this text, I use the phrase *interchangeable empathic foundation* to describe the kind of relationship in which the helper listens to the client so carefully and understands the client's experiences, behavior, and feelings so thoroughly that she or he can offer the client a nearly interchangeable reflection of these factors.

This book is divided into two main parts: the microskills of helping and the theoretical foundations of helping. The microskills included in the first part are the mechanics of how to build such empathy in a helping relationship. They include nonverbal skills (proxemics, kinesics, and paralinguistic aspects of the helping relationship) and verbal skills (paraphrasing, clarifying, reflecting). The second part of the text focuses on some of the many specific strategies of helping processes that have evolved from and are guided by different theories of helping. The theories included in this text provide a sort of map, guiding other helping strategies once a helping and empathic foundation has been established. Microskills and theories each bring different perspectives and different materials from which to build a helping relationship.

The Role of Microskills in Professional Helping

Microskills, a term coined about twenty-five years ago, refers to the basic skill components that together form the common communication behaviors critical to professional helping and to building an effective helping relationship. With slightly different emphases, these skill components or microskills are integrated into most existing theoretical frameworks and professional helping activities.

Successful communication requires specific skills. While these skills can have a nearly magical effect, they are neither magic nor entirely elusive. People are not born with these skills. They are not uncontrollable. They are a part of everyday communication that many simply do not pay particular attention to. It is possible to focus on and learn these skills. Microskills are specific behaviors that require awareness and attention on the part of the helper and much practice to ensure that they are not only well developed, but become a natural part of a helper's approach to clients. In other words, it is not just important to hear or believe that communication is important, a professional helper must learn and practice the skills well enough that they become part of a natural listening style.

The opposite to the view that communication skills are "magic" is that "anyone can communicate, so why teach it?" I think of communication skills and professional helping in somewhat the same way that I think of driving as a recreation or means of transportation and professional driving. While I was in graduate school learning to be a professional helper, I drove a bus to support myself. I was initially amazed that there could be any training for a bus driver. After all, I reasoned, we already had driver's licenses. We clearly knew how to drive. What was the big deal? But since the city paid for my time to attend driving classes, I went. In the process, I learned to attend to many things I had never considered while driving for recreation or personal transportation and to intentionally behave in ways that maximized my own and my passengers' safety and well-being. Being a professional in any field means learning all of those job requirements that allow you to do something with more consistent skill and expertise than nonprofessionals may have.

It is no different for professional helpers than for professional drivers. Most human beings communicate both verbally and nonverbally. Professional helpers are those who study and understand the process of communication and consciously practice the most effective skills in order to consistently and expertly understand clients and build empathic relationships. Learning and practicing these skills is easier if the skills are broken down into their component parts. In this way, the "magic" of communication is demystified, the skills become less overwhelming, and professional helpers can more specifically concentrate on learning each skill more competently.

Part One of this textbook systematically guides students through the development of the microskills of helping, beginning with the most fundamental of all communication skills: nonverbal communication. Because they convey so much information, several dimensions of nonverbal communication are considered most important to helping relationships: kinesics (body movements, including movements of the face), proxemics (the social and personal use of the physical space and interpersonal distance between helper and client), paralanguage (the "how" of a message, like voice qualities, silent pauses, even errors in speaking), and time (perceptions and use).

After detailing the various components of effective nonverbal communication and how to use nonverbal skills to match a client, Part One continues by focusing on the process of feedback. Whether given to clients or to classmates who are learning helping skills, offering effective feedback is a skill that returns an observation to someone. Feedback may take a positive form or it may take the form of a suggestion for improvement. Giving and receiving both positive and negative feedback are important skills.

Building empathic helping relationships also involves basic verbal listening skills that begin with a helper showing a desire to comprehend a client's perspective or frame of reference. This interest is demonstrated in attempts to discuss what is important to the client and to understand the content that a client conveys so well that the helper can restate it using his or her own words. Paraphrasing involves restating the client's message in the helper's own words to ensure that both client and helper have an opportunity to reflect on that understanding, while summarizing requires the helper to collect several paraphrases and offer them to the client in a condensed form. Summarizing assists clients in identifying themes or linking thoughts together. Both focus on developing and communicating an empathic understanding of the content of a client's reports.

Reflection refers to the process of returning to a client an image of her- or himself; it is the process of mirroring a client's feelings so that she or he may observe and explore them more fully. Reflecting is to feelings what paraphrasing is to content. Both paraphrasing and reflecting convey empathy for a client by communicating an understanding of what the client's experience and world are like. After establishing an empathic foundation, many helping relationships prepare clients to take action. Preparation involves facilitating client clarity about the personal meanings of life experiences or behaviors, and self-assessment of strengths and limitations, and goal-setting. Finally, Part One addresses common skills helpers use to advance client goals that involve information-giving. These include complex skills like giving advice, instructing, directing, confronting, interpreting, immediacy, and self-disclosure.

The chapters in Part One define each of the microskills, describe what each skill involves and how it may be used in helping, and offer specific directions on the mechanics of best practices. After the microskills have been described and their uses and mechanics have been explained, the theories that form the foundation of helping are described and briefly explored.

The Role of Theory in Professional Helping

The word *theory* comes from Latin and Greek words meaning "to look at, speculate, examine, or contemplate." While originally it meant a mental viewing or contemplation and indicated a plan or speculative method for doing something, the word *theory* has evolved to indicate a systematic statement of the underlying principles or the relationships between observed phenomena that have been verified to some degree (*Webster's Unabridged Dictionary*, 2001). It often refers to the branch of an art or science that focuses on knowledge about principles and methods rather than on the application or practice of such methods. Sometimes theory is contrasted with practice; sometimes with empiricism; sometimes with certainty. Theory is often seen as a set of statements used to help explain data or observations (Marx & Goodson, 1976).

In the case of helping, theory refers to consistent perspectives on human behavior, psychopathology or problems, and the mechanisms of change (Norcross, 1985). A theory of helping, then, systematically examines the underlying principles and relationships of a given approach to helping and outlines observations that have been verified to some degree. Several professional helping disciplines study theories of helping, focusing on the principles and methods of helping advocated by a particular theorist or group of theorists (sometimes referred to as a "school of thought"). When professional helpers talk about their theoretical orientation, they are referring to the theory that they generally use as a sort of compass or reference point when looking at people and the problems they present.

The microskills of helping that are examined in the first part of this text facilitate the initial creation of relationships among helpers and clients. Theories of helping, on the other hand, include the underlying principles that guide strategies and tools that helpers use to establish the specific kind of relationship activities they believe will be helpful. After establishing a relationship, or in addition to the focus on developing the relationship, helpers must make decisions about how to proceed. All helping interventions follow directly from a helper's underlying conceptions about human nature, the development of problems, and what constitutes health. Each theory also makes assumptions about the helping process: its goals, the role of the helper, how assessment is viewed and implemented, the techniques unique to the theory, and the process of helping. Finally, each theory is supported by research about how effective that theory and its strategies may be for helping with different problems.

No one theory is universally considered the best. Each theory is evaluated critically by those who subscribe to it and those who study it. Without theoretical foundations, helpers would face hundreds of pieces of information, impressions, observations, and decisions in a single session without much guidance. I think of a theoretical framework or orientation as a sort of compass or map. If you had no particular destination in mind or even if you knew that you wanted to get to Chicago, you could get into your car and just start driving. It would be an adventure and you could decide that whatever you found along the way was fine with you. If, however, you wanted to be sure to get to Chicago, you would probably want something that gave you some direction when you faced spontaneous decision points in your travel. The path to psychological solutions, while not as easily mapped as the roads to Chicago, requires something more than a sense of where you are going. Helpers must determine which questions are most important to ask or whether to ask questions at all. We make decisions about when and if we should reflect feelings or content, confront, interpret, or remain silent. We have to know when or if it is time to move into action-plans and what form those plans could take. It is theories that facilitate limiting the information to what is most relevant to attend to and when and theories that help us to organize myriad information and then integrate it into meaningful knowledge of our clients and their journey. Theories prioritize both helper and client focus, and they direct treatment plans. They do not tell us as neatly as a map can when to take a specific turn, but they give helpers a clearer idea of the direction in which helping should proceed.

Students beginning to study professional helping often complain about the idea of studying theories of helping. They are usually contrasting theory with practice when they do so. Students complain that they have heard enough theory and they are ready to get out and practice what they have been learning. They do not want to wait for the "how to's." I remember my own impatience pretty well—I looked for graduate programs with a lot of experiential learning based on that same kind of thinking. Looking back, I now understand that I did not see the connection between theory and practice, and that I wanted to get my feet wet with "real" problems and "real" clients. I did not understand as I do now that as soon as I encountered real clients who spontaneously interacted, I would need something to help guide and focus me on what was most critical to attend to. If I had had it my way, we could have ended up in Boston while on our way to Chicago.

Sometimes students are also intimidated at the thought of adopting a theory of their own. Fears about not knowing enough to have a theory have some truth to them. Knowing about the many theories of helping can seem overwhelming to even the most seasoned helper. Raymond Corsini (1981) lists 241 different systems of psychotherapy. Others suggest there may be more than 400. I think there may actually be as many theories of helping as there are helpers. However intimidating that may sound, it may be important to remember that each helper comes to the practice of helping with what Barbara Okun (2002) calls a **theory of use,** and that textbooks offer students a glimpse of others' ideas to provide a platform from which helpers can develop a stable theoretical orientation of their own.

A theory of use includes beliefs and assumptions each of us has about behavior. These beliefs and assumptions operate daily and affect our own interpersonal behavior (Okun, 2002). Theories of helping are an outgrowth of each helper's worldview and are influenced by our gender, ethnicity, socioeconomic and family backgrounds, past experiences and opportunities, and our temperaments, self-awareness, and exposure to different schools of thought. In the second part of this text, my objective is to enhance helpers' exposure to different schools of thought about how people and specific behaviors develop, what motivates people, how people think and learn, how patterns in humans develop, how groups impact individual behavior, and how behavior, emotions, and thoughts change. It is not designed to take the place of additional texts or courses in personality or development. The idea is to offer students glimpses of different maps and compasses in the belief that when added to theories of use, helpers will fashion more effective guides.

When I teach classes about professional helping, I often begin the part of the course that focuses on theories by helping students examine existing theories of use. Many exercises can help students think about their own theories of use. I often guide their introspection with a number of questions about the nature of human existence, problems, change, and individual differences. I also suggest that students brainstorm characteristics of effective helpers that they believe may facilitate change processes in others and then identify those that they believe they themselves possess. Each of these exercises is designed to facilitate exploration of those theories students begin with in their practice of helping. Of course, as the course progresses, I expect that students will add to their own perspectives by drawing from the additional exposure to the theories that I teach.

Eclecticism.   Sometimes the wish to remain flexible and not foreclose prematurely on helpful ideas or strategies concerns novice helpers. Maybe it is reassuring to note that having an identifiable theory need not mean setting it in concrete for all time. Neither does a preference for one theoretical framework preclude using strategies from another theory. In fact, the last 20 years have seen not only a proliferation of theories but also many efforts to integrate those theories (Prochaska & Norcross, 1999). Efforts to combine, integrate, or blend together several theories or strategies is referred to as being **eclectic.** Allen Garfield and Sol Bergin (1994) found that between one-third and two-thirds of all professional helpers identified themselves as eclectic.

Eclecticism itself takes on fairly eclectic forms. Helpers who identify themselves as eclectic seek to integrate the key concepts of several theories. According to James Prochaska and John Norcross (1994), almost 20 percent of helpers engage in this kind of theoretical integration. In my own graduate programs in clinical psychology and counseling psychology, I was encouraged to integrate theories in comprehensive exams in which I presented my theory of helping followed by a case example to illustrate how the principles of my theory directed my methods and techniques. Most of my colleagues and I had our own perspectives about others' theories and blended together two or more to create our unique approach to the process of helping. Many theories that students reading this text will study are extensions of or an integration of two or more other theories.

In addition to those who attempt to integrate theories of personality and change, approximately one-third of all helpers practice **technical eclecticism** (Prochaska & Norcross, 1999). This term refers to at least two different approaches. In one approach, helpers who identify themselves as technically eclectic draw from a theoretical view selected for a specific client or for a specific problem. For example, some therapists who would choose a psychodynamic approach with a particular client or problem do not identify themselves as psychodynamic in their general orientation to helping. They would simply choose this approach with a particular client or problem because they believed it would be beneficial to the client.

Helpers may also use many techniques drawn from many theoretical orientations without necessarily subscribing to the theories from which they are drawn. For example, a helper may decide to interpret a client's resistance to helping without necessarily claiming psychodynamic theory—from which the concept of interpreting resistance evolved—as their primary theoretical identification. Arnold Lazarus began developing an approach called *multimodal therapy* in the late 1970s that is a good example of this second type of technical eclecticism. Lazarus advocates (1981/1989) assessing seven basic modalities through which clients experience the world and themselves: behavior, affect, sensation, images, cognition, interpersonal relationships, and drugs and biological functioning. Treatment goals combine the basic modalities, and Lazarus advocates an approach to treatment that "tracks" the priority given to each modality and the current modality of each client in selecting techniques from different theoretical traditions.

Some who write about eclecticism (e.g., Prochaska & Norcross, 1999) take what is called a **transtheoretical approach** to integrating theories. After examining many different theories, Prochaska and Norcross have attempted to select those conceptual and technical factors that effective helping approaches have in common. Their change model is based on client readiness for change, the type of problem that needs changing, and processes and techniques shown to be effective in bringing about the specific change.

Most helpers make thoughtful plans about integrating helping methods, though some are eclectic by default. Rather than systematically examining the assumptions of different theories and techniques, they simply borrow strategies liberally from any theory depending on the needs of each client. On the face of it, this pragmatic "whatever works" approach appears to customize helping to the unique needs of each client; however, it can pose some difficulties. Without examining the assumptions of a given strategy, helpers may find unexpected results. The results may be helpful, but they may also be harmful to clients. In my opinion, this is yet another compelling reason to study theories and the assumptions each makes about human behavior and change. Helpers not only have the power to influence clients but also a responsibility to know how and why and in what way they will influence clients.

Whether a professional helper chooses one theoretical orientation or an integrative approach, helping requires knowledge of the many different perspectives about development, behavior, and change. Decisions about what theories to draw from, what techniques may apply, under what circumstances the use of a specific technique or theory might be beneficial, and which clients might benefit from a particular approach require knowledge of each and require that helpers have some guiding principles. The guiding principles are not fixed and rigid, but serve as a frame of reference from which decisions can be made. Helpers must use systematic and critical thinking to support their reasoning about applying specific techniques or theories.

Some helpers are trained to understand the science of constructing theory. Psychologists are a good example. Graduate and undergraduate training in psychology emphasizes the science behind psychological constructs. Regardless of whether a helper has formal training in the science of knowledge construction about people and problems, all professional helpers are ethically bound to be at least good consumers of theory by understanding the underlying principles and assumptions on which a theory is based. Adopting an approach because it is popular or the one most easily understood is like buying an expensive product because others have it or because it is easily available, but without actually knowing what you will use it for or whether it may be useful at all. It could as easily turn out to be useful, a waste of money, or harmful. So, whether or not a helper is formally trained as a scientist, a helper must be willing to think as a scientist would, continually testing hypotheses to determine whether, when, and how well an approach is working.

Theories of Helping.   Although there are many theories of helping, perhaps even as many as there are helpers, most of the helping theories can be grouped into several categories. Psychodynamic theories include early psychoanalytic, later neoanalytic, object-relations and self theories, and the most recent self-in-relations theories. Psychodynamic theories initially emphasized the importance of inborn drives, conflicts, and unconscious processes in determining the structure and development of personality and problems. Later followers of this tradition, while not challenging the usefulness of inborn drives, conflicts, and unconscious processes, placed more emphasis on human adaptations to the environment, early relationships between mother and child, and developmental changes in being absorbed with oneself at the expense of meaningful relationships with others. Self-in-relations theories, a sort of hybrid psychodynamic and feminist theory about helping, emphasize empathy and mutuality developed in early and subsequent relationships that lead women to a connected rather than an autonomous view of self represented by the hyphenated term *self-in-relation*. While they share some common features, psychodynamic theories are not a singular approach but several perspectives from which to examine people and problems.

Person-centered theories, which grew out of humanistic, existential, and phenomenological philosophies, have been best articulated by Carl Rogers. While existential, humanistic, and phenomenological philosophies are difficult to understand, Rogers's emphasis was on the client and her or his view of the world and involved skills readers of this text will probably recognize readily. Rogers focused on the relationship between client and therapist in which genuine caring and unconditional acceptance were not only the antidote to barriers in self-actualization, but the basis for the active listening skills that became what most helpers now study and call the "microskills of helping." These skills enable helpers to understand the clients' experience from the clients' perspective and communicate that understanding in a way that fosters trust and change. Each client is held responsible for actualizing her or his own potential and eliminating the conditions that initially posed barriers. Each is also held responsible for changes made in her or his life.

Behavioral theories of helping are based on psychological principles of learning and conditioning developed through countless experiments with animals and human beings. Behavioral theories emphasize the application of these basic learning and conditioning principles to both the development of problems and solutions to those problems. Rather than being determined by unconscious motives, relationship templates, or individual decisions, behavioral theories emphasize that behaviors are learned by association, by events that follow behaviors, through imitating models, and through *socialization,* the process by which people are taught social expectations. Both functional and problematic behaviors are thought to be learned through the same mechanisms. The good news is that if a problem is learned, it may be unlearned and others learned in its place. The challenge is that unlearning a behavior that has been learned in many and varied ways is difficult and replacing it requires putting all of those mechanisms in play in a different way. Behavioral therapies involve modifying learning by modifying multiple environmental influences.

Cognitive-behavioral theories are, as the name might imply, an outgrowth of behavioral theories that take into account cognitive or thinking processes that include individual decisions. Research demonstrates that human beings think about, remember, consider, imagine, and plan behaviors. These cognitive processes that precede, occur during, and follow a given behavior affect that behavior. Identifying, challenging, and changing problematic cognitions that result in problematic behaviors and feelings is the focus of cognitive-behavioral theories of helping.

Unlike the preceding theories whose emphases are on individual development, growth, and change, some theories examine the role of social systems (e.g., families and even whole societies) in creating individual differences and problems. Family systems theories view the family as a social system, and changes in functioning and relationships necessarily take place within the family. Some family systems theories focus on the multigenerational influence of families; some emphasize the ways in which family members relate to each other in the immediate moment. Some look at how to rally the family's abilities to solve the problems of each individual family member, while some examine the different constellations of relationships within the family in an effort to challenge the structure of those relationships and impact change. All emphasize the family as the unit of attention in helping.

Sociocultural theories, like feminist and multicultural theories, look at families as one of many social agents that influence individuals. Both feminist and multicultural theories are social and psychological views that emphasize the impact of expected social roles and social power differences in shaping individuals and characteristic problems. Both feminist and multicultural theories have spawned the development of similar models of helping to capture the challenges people in subordinated groups face in developing a positive identity in the face of institutionalized oppression. Feminist theories specifically examine role expectations and power differences related to gender, whereas multicultural theories look more specifically at the role of race and ethnicity, and to some extent class expectations and power differences, in shaping individuals and problems.

There are theories about helping that do not draw from the Western model of talk as a means of influencing changes in behavior and feeling. While an examination of these theories is beyond the scope of this text, it is important to note that body therapies, psychodrama, hypnosis, and creative arts therapies are approaches used by many helpers either in conjunction with or instead of the traditional approaches on which this text spends more time.

Part Two Objectives. The second part of this textbook focuses on theories and facilitates exposure to each of those schools of thinking about helping. At the end of each Part Two chapter, students should be able to:

- identify the historical, cultural, and philosophical context that influenced each theory.
- identify how each perspective views human nature and defines health, problems, and problem-solving.
- identify the goals of each approach to helping.
- identify the approach to assessment that each theoretical perspective takes.
- identify contemporary research about each theoretical perspective.
- critique each theoretical perspective.

I encourage students to make charts like the one shown in Figure I.1 to organize the key concepts, goals, assumptions, approaches to assessment, unique techniques, biases, and key criticisms for each theory. Students report that this is helpful in studying for exams—often their initial impetus for doing this—but also in organizing a lot of information into manageable chunks. Of course, it is still a great deal of information, but seeing it organized in this way can make it easier to compare, contrast, and see connections between the theories and help students not only remember them but integrate them. In the same way that a number of different routes to Chicago may get you there, seeing them all clearly may allow you to make more informed decisions about which one you want to take.

Stages in the Helping Process

Many models conceptualize the process of helping differently, although virtually all acknowledge that, as is true of any relationship, helping has a beginning, a middle, and an ending. The beginning of a

FIGURE I.1 Contemporary Models and Assumptions

Model	Assumptions			
	Humans as:	*Health*	*Problems*	*Treatment*
Biological	Physical systems	Normal biological functioning	Injury, illness, and defect	Drugs, surgeries, and procedures
Psychodynamic	Energy system; structures in conflict over energy distribution	Availability of energy	Investment of energy in symptoms and defenses	Releasing energy; encouraging insight
Behavioral	Learners	Adaptive behavioral pattern and habits	Maladaptive behavioral patterns; faulty learning	Unlearning and relearning behaviors
Cognitive	Information-processing systems	Adaptive cognitive patterns; habits	Maladaptive thought patterns; faulty learning	Changing thinking
Humanistic-Existential-Phenomeno-logical	Choice-makers; architects of our own behavior and existence	Self-fulfillment; realizing potential; congruence	Barriers to self-actualization	Choosing to live authentically; actualizing potential
Family Systems	Products of family forces	Healthy homeostasis within family; functional norms	Family disturbances; dysfunctional norms	Changing status quo in the family
Sociocultural	Products of social and cultural forces	Absence of stressful social conditions; functional social norms	Stressful life events; stigma; status-related oppression; dysfunctional social norms	Changing social and cultural conditions

helping relationship is characterized by building a strong foundation of interchangeable empathic responses. It is the process of nonverbal and verbal communication that establishes an empathic connection between helper and client. Building such a relationship takes time and careful attention to hearing and understanding a client's thoughts, feelings, behavior, and experiences and conveying that understanding to the client. Once an empathic bond has been established, communication can shift from those skills that build empathy to those skills that focus on deepening the clients' understanding of their difficulties and personalizing the meaning of their strengths and limitations, and establishing goals. Once goals are personalized and established collaboratively, information advances client exploration, and strategies borrowed from one or more theoretical foundations help clients make changes in thought, feeling, behavior, experience, or identity to meet those goals. Ethically, in the context of the helping relationship, helpers also discuss benefits and risks involved in any of the strategies being considered.

Helpers then implement chosen strategies and remain open to modifying them based on client needs or differences and ongoing evaluation. Helping ideally draws to a close when goals are achieved, but, since the onset of managed care and insurance coverage for mental health services, often the end of professional helping is predetermined by the limits of insurance coverage. Nonetheless, the process of ending effectively is at least as important as empathy-building was to the beginning of helping. Regardless of how the relationship draws to a close, helpers can facilitate additional growth for clients by focusing time and attention on the meaning of closure for each client and using similar communication skills and the empathy built early in the relationship to help clients explore feelings and thoughts about: (1) where they were when they began; (2) where they are as they come to the end of the present helping relationship; and (3) where they would still like to go. The final question is particularly important if the client's work is not yet finished. Focusing on the current and other endings in the client's life can help facilitate ongoing exploration of other relationships as well as planning for future goals and objectives. Often helpers plan a follow-up session at some future point to check in on client progress or the stability of client changes. This can provide a sense of reassurance for clients and reinforce the idea that goals continue to be achieved or that work is ongoing.

ETHICS

Regardless of their training and credentials, their theoretical orientation, their communication skills, or theories, all helping professionals are also guided by ethical standards. The word *ethics* comes from the Greek *ethikos* and the Latin *ethicus,* meaning "a standard of conduct or morality." In the case of professional helping, ethics are standards of conduct or morality as prescribed by each profession. These standards include behaviors that each profession considers right and wrong in the practice of the profession. Each profession has its own standards of conduct set by professional organizations within the profession, although there is considerable overlap. The American Psychological Association (**APA**) sets ethical guidelines for the ethical behavior of psychologists, the National Association of Social Workers (**NASW**), for social workers, and the American Counseling Association (**ACA**), for professional counselors. The National Organization of Human Services Employees (**NOHSE**) sets the ethical standards for human services workers. The American Medical Association (**AMA**) sets ethical guidelines for psychiatrists. Each organization regularly publishes updates on ethical standards.

At the heart of each professional helping organization's ethical standards is primary consideration for the welfare of patients or clients. Moreover, although not always stated directly, most ethical standards are generally based on two principles called *maleficence* and *beneficence.* The word *maleficence* refers to wrongdoing or harm-causing injury; when used to refer to ethical principles, the maleficence standard says "first do no harm," which cautions professional helpers to ensure that policies and practices will, at minimum, not result in harm to the clients they serve. Beneficence is the general standard that directs professionals to "help if you can." This principle suggests that if it is possible to do so, helping another is a moral or ethical thing to do. So, a client's welfare is considered primary, and professionals are directed to avoid or minimize harm; not to mislead or exploit others; and to be helpful if possible. In addition, most ethical guidelines consider what is included in a client's basic rights, what is just and fair, and what is considered compassionate practice.

Recently, professional helping organizations have instituted ethical imperatives directing helpers to gain knowledge, sensitivity, and awareness of individual and group differences between clients with respect to differences in age, gender, race and ethnicity, national origin, religion, sexual orientation, disability, language, and socioeconomic status (e.g., APA, 1993). Such guidelines offer more specific direction to professionals to be aware of research pertinent to the populations they serve; recognize culture and ethnicity as important aspects of human experience; respect the role of religious and spiritual beliefs and of families and communities; interact in the language requested by the client; be aware of and work to eliminate biases, prejudices, and discrimination; and take note of such culturally relevant factors as number of generations and years in the country, fluency in English, family supports, community resources, education, and acculturation stresses (APA, 1993).

Most ethical guidelines for professional helpers expect that helpers will practice within the boundaries of their competencies as determined by training and supervised and professional experience and advise practitioners to undertake new areas of helping only with additional and ongoing training. Most also promote professional integrity by cautioning against false or misleading statements about qualifications, services, products, and fees, as well as awareness of beliefs, values, needs, and limitations. Most professional organizations expect that their members will uphold the ethical standards of the profession and consult with others in the profession to prevent unethical conduct.

Professional helping organizations generally propose client rights that are remarkably similar in content: privacy, confidentiality, self-determination, and autonomy. Finally, most professional helping organizations expect social responsibility in terms of awareness of the community in which we live and work as well as compliance with laws and social policies. In keeping with the expectation of social responsibility are standards that encourage professional helpers to offer a portion of professional time for little or no personal gain.

Ethical Dilemmas

Ethical dilemmas may be created when one ethic and another seem to demand contradictory action, when an ethical standard and the law seem to contradict, and when personal and professional ethics seem to be in conflict. I usually teach students the following model for resolving the ethical dilemmas they may face.

Ethical Decision-Making Model
- Identify the problem.
  - Ethical
  - Legal
  - Professional
  - Clinical
- Apply the ethical guidelines of your profession.
- Determine the nature and dimensions of the dilemma and seek consultation.
  - How can I best promote client independence and self-determination?
  - What actions have least chance of bringing harm to the client?
  - What decisions will best safeguard the welfare of the client?
  - How do I create a trusting or therapeutic climate where clients find their own solutions?
- Generate possible courses of action.
  - Brainstorm as many options as you or others can think of.
- Consider the possible consequences of all options and determine a course of action.
  - Evaluate each option for its consequences to each party.
- Evaluate the selected course of action.
- Implement the course of action.

SUMMARY

This book is intended to provide an introduction to the communication microskills and theoretical foundations of professional helping. Together, the microskills and theories in this text form the foundation of the professional helping practices of psychologists, social workers, counselors, psychiatrists, psychiatric nurses, and human services workers. Although each profession has different training, credentials, practice activities, and settings common to their work, they also share in drawing from both microskills and theories to create effective helping.

Microskills are basic communication skills broken down into component parts that help to build a relationship in which the helper comes to understand a client's thoughts, feelings, behavior, and experiences so well that she or he could offer a virtually interchangeable picture of the client's perspective.

Theories form the sort of road map that guides the strategies helpers use in the middle stages of helping. While there may be as many theories as there are helpers, most can be categorized into four main groups based on the forces they emphasize in understanding human behavior. Psychodynamic theories share a belief that behavior is determined by biological energy as a force. Behavioral theories share a belief that it is experience that determines behavior. Humanistic theories posit that individual choice determines behavior. Sociocultural theories focus on the role that social and cultural forces play in determining human behavior.

In addition to various communication skills and theories, helpers also draw from ethical standards to guide helping behavior. Ethical standards are set by each helping profession, but there is considerable overlap between them. All emphasize the welfare, rights, and respect for individual differences of clients and the competencies, integrity, responsibilities, and social obligations of helpers.

This introduction offers a brief look at the ways in which the main parts of this text can be integrated into the process of helping. Looking at helping as having a beginning, a middle, and an ending requires different skills from helpers. Communication microskills form the foundation of the helping relationship and promote empathy. Theories guide decisions about strategies chosen in the middle of helping to facilitate client goals. Finally, microskills and an examination of the current relationship and its impact on the client help promote effective endings to helping relationships.

PART ONE

Microskills of Helping

CHAPTER

1 Nonverbal Communication

Research on interpersonal communication has estimated that at least two-thirds of human communication involves nonverbal interaction (Birdwhistell, 1970; Okun, 2002). At its simplest, nonverbal communication includes any communication that is not talking. Many people do not recognize how much "not talking" is involved in interpersonal communication. Students are generally surprised at the amount of nonverbal interaction that interviewing, counseling, and therapy entail. Even when teaching helping skills, we tend to place much more emphasis on dialogue than on listening, although research in the helping field indicates that a wealth of information is conveyed nonverbally by and to clients (Ekman & Friesen, 1969; Knapp, 1978).

When students are asked to imagine what therapy or counseling involves, they often report a picture of the skillful therapist or counselor making clever interpretations or initiating provocative confrontations. (I remember that was my ambition early in my education!) Famed psychoanalysts Sigmund Freud and Frederick "Fritz" Perls, as clever as they were at the interpreting and confronting skills they are remembered for, still used those particular skills far more sparingly than those of nonverbal communication. The bulk of their communication with clients was nonverbal. For professional helpers, a great deal of time goes toward conveying that they are listening to and hearing their clients (Cormier & Cormier, 1991; Hill & O'Brien, 1999a). More than the specific words the professional helper chooses, this basic attending is accomplished through nonverbal responses.

Nonverbal skills, even one as simple sounding as silence, are difficult for many if not most people to master. Reserving talk is a skill that involves more than simply waiting your turn to speak. Nonverbal skills require attending and following so closely to what another is saying that you can see at a glance what they are experiencing or even what they may be about to communicate verbally. Later, this book focuses on verbal skills like paraphrasing the content important to clients, hearing what clients are feeling and identifying correctly what those feelings are, offering them a glimpse of themselves through your eyes, and helping them to see part of what they are saying in a new or different way. To begin with, though, a powerful way to communicate to someone that she or he is being heard is through nonverbal behaviors, such as facial expressions and gestures, voice volume and tone, fluency of speech, appropriate silences, how close to sit, when to look at a client, and how to view and treat time. If this sounds like a lot to pay attention to, it *is* a lot at first—but it soon becomes second nature.

Consider facial expressions as one example of nonverbal communication. My deaf friends and students have taught me more successfully than any of my formal training the value of facial expressions as an important part of nonverbal communication. American Sign Language (ASL) and other sign languages rely on facial expressions to convey the intensity of a particular word (Shroyer & Shroyer, 1982). This is not unique to signing, however. People, in general, convey more information with their facial expressions than by their words alone. Well-known studies about emotion suggest that humans can correctly identify any number of emotions by simply observing body posture or a face (Izard, 1977). A discrepancy or inconsistency between someone's verbal message and facial expression is confusing and will cause the listener to reconsider what message is really being given. Further, when people are confronted with discrepant information between verbal and nonverbal messages, most of us believe the nonverbal message. Think about the last time someone said, "I'm not angry!" with observable venom in her voice or anger on his face. Which message did you believe? Probably everyone has watched television newscasters announce the sadness of a death with no change in facial expression and tone of voice from the prior good-news report about the new playground equipment at the local park. Did you believe they were really saddened? Do you think they were even paying attention to what they were saying? Facial expressions are one of many complex dimensions of nonverbal communication that can have an impact on helper and client communication.

Some disagreement exists about how to identify all of the possible topics of nonverbal communication, but most classify and organize these topics into several key dimensions for the purposes of studying nonverbal communication (e.g., Harper, Wiens, & Matarazzo, 1978) and teaching professional helping (e.g., Cormier & Cormier, 1991; Hill & O'Brien, 1999a). Because they convey so much information, four of the dimensions of nonverbal communication that are most important to helping relationships are introduced here. The first dimension is *proxemics,* or the social and personal use of the physical space and interpersonal distance between the helper and the client. This includes touch. The second dimension is *kinesics,* or body movements, including movements of the face. The third dimension is *paralanguage,* or the "how" of a message, like voice qualities, silent pauses, and even errors in speaking. The fourth dimension is the *perception and use of time.*

Proxemics includes both the use of space in the room in which helping takes place and the environmental characteristics of the space. When considering proxemics, we look at the physical distance between client and helper (did the client choose a seat as far from the helper as possible?), their position in the room (is there a desk between them?), and their use of touch (did the session begin with a handshake?). Furnishings, seating arrangements, and touch all convey information.

At its most overt, kinesics includes the study of eye-contact or movement, facial expressions, head and body movements, and gestures (Cormier & Cormier, 1991; Knapp, 1978). (Did the client slip deeper into the chair when talking about the death of her friend?) However, those physical characteristics that remain relatively unchanged, like physique, height, weight, and general appearance (Birdwhistell, 1970), as well as visible cues about ethnicity, sex, orientation, and disability, are also part of kinesic nonverbal communication and important in a helping relationship.

Paralanguage includes consideration of the voice level and pitch of a message as well as the fluency of someone's speech. Voice level refers to the volume of someone's speech, whereas pitch indicates intonation determined by the frequency in the verbal sound waves. A high-pitched voice or intonation—like that of a soprano—is actually vibrating many more times per second than a low-pitched voice—like a bass or baritone. Most people with what we call "normal hearing" can identify sounds within a range between 20 Hz and 20,000 Hz per second, but it is hearing the constancy or variations in pitch from each person that signals possible changes in their internal experience. (Did the client's voice grow higher when saying something wasn't really

---

E X E R C I S E 1.1

Observing a Good Listener

Think for a minute about the people in your life who you consider to be good listeners. Good listeners are ones who encourage and even facilitate continuing communication and even risk-taking in self-disclosure and who engender confidence in their communication. What is it that they actually do that makes it easy to risk telling them about yourself with some confidence? What convinces you that they are listening well to you? If this is hard to imagine, then consider giving yourself this homework assignment: Go to someone you consider a good listener and talk to him or her for 5 minutes. While you talk, pay careful attention to what he or she is doing. After your conversation, write down what you observed in the communication. You may begin finding that your listener has developed or refined some of the same skills you will need for effective helping.

---

very important?) Fluency of speech includes elements like hesitations, errors, rates of speech, and silences.

Finally, how the helper and client use time and their perceptions about time are important elements in their nonverbal communication with one another. Time can have a great deal of impact on the helping relationship. (Does the client become petulant when it's time to end a session, but always show up late for the appointment? Do you have trouble remembering your appointment book with one particular client?) Concepts of time vary among cultures, among genders, and among orientations. Differences in timeliness or the amount of time given to different activities can raise questions about what is really important to us or about power dynamics in our relationships.

Before looking at some of the actual skills involved in nonverbal communication, I offer helpers a word of caution about universality or, rather, the absence of it. As with all of the skills involved in helping, helpers are expected to adjust to their client's culture, ethnicity, gender, and orientation. Helping in a multicultural context means learning what is appropriate for specific clients based on their backgrounds and expectations. Each of us learned the rules of our own culture(s) about nonverbal communication without paying particularly close attention to them. Cultural rules for nonverbal behavior are typically outside of a person's awareness (Hill & O'Brien, 1999a), so students often wonder how they will ever learn all of the specific cultural differences in terms of even the most basic listening skills. The answer is, you won't. Most professional organizations (e.g., NASW, APA, ACA, NOHSE) have made it an ethical imperative for helpers to attend to, respect, and celebrate differences among clients, but this does not mean helpers will know every culture or background as well as they know their own. It does mean that part of the profession of helping is defined by the requirement to be aware of clients' individual backgrounds as they influence needs and preferences. It means paying attention and noticing how a client presents her- or himself and adapting accordingly. Specific examples of this type of attending are given as each of the four dimensions of nonverbal communication is reviewed.

PROXEMICS: SPACE AND DISTANCE

Clients do not immediately notice a helper's amazing wealth of information, incisive problem-solving, or insightful interpretations. The first things clients note are a variety of physical aspects about the space in which helping takes place. Because clients look at the space, professional helpers should review the physical arrangements of the room or space in which interviews, counseling, or therapy takes place. Professional helpers can be thought of as the *stimulus screeners* for their clients (Mehrabian, 1976). In a sense, our offices screen out what is less relevant to our purposes in order to make way for what is more relevant. Offices communicate fundamental information to clients about the nature of the helping relationship and the task at hand. Points to consider include the setting, the helper's physical position relative to the client, the physical distance between the helper and the client, the seating arrangements, and touch between the helper and the client.

The Setting

A carefully considered physical setting can begin the process of establishing a helping environment. Like the backdrop in a play, the setting gives instant clues to the client about the helper and what to expect. Settings should either convey something important to the helper or to his or her philosophy of helping, or they should show something fairly ambiguous. One way to view physical surroundings is by evaluating how they fall along a continuum from high arousal (stimulating) to low arousal (subduing). A setting that fosters low arousal and mild pleasure results in client comfort and relaxation; however, upping the arousal to a moderate level may be necessary to encourage more activity. Clients need to feel comfortable enough to self-disclose and share their concerns, but perceive enough energy to feel invited to explore their problems or themselves (Mehrabian, 1976).

A second important consideration is to match the setting to the tasks the helper intends to accomplish or the process into which the helper intends to invite the client. For example, the setting for an intake interview with a lengthy list of prescribed questions and a tight time limit will look different from a setting planned for possible conversations of intimate and threatening content. A setting conducive to the first situation may include a table and straight-backed chairs, with few accessories (pictures, pottery, memorabilia) so as to curtail distractions and maintain focus on the task at hand. Cool colors and a limited palette would support this goal.

A setting congruent with the second situation may include a conversational grouping of comfortable furniture in warm colors, earth tones, and a more expansive palette. Pictures and other decorations should be carefully chosen to reflect the helper's philosophy of helping or, if the helper prefers clients to concentrate on the conversation, to be unprovocative so as not to claim a client's attention. Furniture should be comfortable enough to allow a relaxed posture, but not so comfortable as to encourage lounging. Furnishings chosen and arranged in this way signal intimate conversation, and the setting conveys safety and comfort to the client preparing to take on the hard tasks often involved in helping.

Lighting also sets the stage for the interaction that will take place. Natural light or soft, incandescent lamps cast a warmer light and to many people indicate that a warmer interaction will take place. Overhead lighting can cast harsh shadows and may cause clients to feel like they are being interrogated. Flourescent lighting, common in business or institutional settings, is a cooler shade and may indicate a cooler, more distant connection. Neon lighting enhances the festive atmosphere at bars, concerts, and parties. It is rarely chosen to light interview, counseling, or therapy settings, because it is used to draw attention to the recreational nature of an environment.

The Helper's Physical Position Relative to the Client

Equally important to the physical arrangement of the space in which the helping will occur is the position of the helper and client. Sitting face to face makes it easy to observe a client's facial expressions and is common in some cultures. It can also indicate a confrontational stance. In some cultures, sitting face to face is considered threatening and predicts an adversarial relationship. In others, it is considered impolite or disrespectful. Add a desk between the helper and the client and it may indicate that this is business. However, it may also suggest distance or authority and may project a subordinate status to clients. Sitting at right angles to a desk often indicates a collaborative interaction in which both helper and client may be working on something together. Sitting at right angles in more comfortable chairs often indicates that a more intimate conversation will take place.

Although the words "comfortable," "intimate," and "collaborative" have a socially desirable ring to them, it is more important to consider the specific objectives of the helping relationship and client preferences than to make this fit some stereotype of "best" practice. Most people consider congruence in communication very important. In this case, congruence refers to the match between intention and communication. If the point of an interaction does not include collaboration, why communicate collaboration in one's physical setting? The contradiction may simply confuse or anger clients. Likewise, instant intimacy is unrealistic and may even be threatening to some. Regardless, if intimacy is not what the process will involve, conveying intimacy through the physical setting will be incongruent.

The Physical Distance between Helper and Client

Finding a comfortable physical distance between helper and client is important because distance has both relationship and cultural implications. Physical distance between two people can shape and reflect their interpersonal distance. The distance the helper and client choose communicates the distance expected in the relationship. Helpers need to pay attention to the usually nonverbal negotiation process they go through with their clients to arrive at a comfortable and appropriate

distance. Sitting or standing close to each other may indicate the expectation of more interpersonal closeness than the helper or client is comfortable with. It may also indicate warmth and empathy. Such an expectation may feel threatening in one interviewing, counseling, or therapy situation, whereas in another it may feel welcoming.

It is equally important to note any change in physical distance once a mutually acceptable distance has been established. Just as the distance negotiation can shape the relationship between helper and client, it can also reflect the emotional closeness of the relationship. If the client begins choosing a seat that is closer to or farther from the helper, the helper should take a look at what that change may indicate, as a change in physical distance often parallels emotional or relationship changes. If the helper finds her- or himself escorting the client to the door when that was not part of the usual routine, the helper should take a look at that, too. In some family therapies, seating and spatial arrangements are an important part of the assessment and therapy process as the helper pays attention to how far apart family members sit, who sits next to whom, and who stays closest to the therapist. These choices provide information about family rules, alliances, roles, and relationships and assist the helper to address the family's concerns. Again, any changes in physical distance to an arrangement or routine that everyone has become accustomed to may also provide valuable information about other changes taking place.

Keep in mind that people of different cultural backgrounds and different experiential backgrounds have different expectations about physical space. In some cultures, close physical distance is considered appropriately friendly, in others, it indicates an aggressive and disrespectful posture. Adult, middle-class, European Americans often find 3 or 4 feet of personal space least anxiety-provoking and most productive, whereas Asian Americans prefer somewhat more space and African Americans somewhat less (Lecomte, Bernstein, & Dumont, 1981). Heterosexual women often tolerate less personal space than gay or heterosexual men do, especially when interacting with other heterosexual women (Harper et al., 1978). Lesbians often prefer slightly more space than heterosexual women. However, it would be a gross overstatement or stereotype to say that all European Americans, Asian Americans, African Americans, heterosexual women, lesbians, or gay or heterosexual men express these preferences.

Expectations about physical space also differ depending on the kind of interaction or the activity. Clearly different comfort levels and cultural practices exist between new and old relationships, between and within age groups, and between and within genders. Proximity is more or less acceptable if the activity involves a business, school, or social engagement; family or strangers; dining at home or eating out; sports like basketball versus cross-country skiing. The list is endless.

How, then, can a new helper (or an experienced helper, for that matter) establish a comfortable working distance without running in and out of the room to consult a cultural handbook? How can a helper hold a conversation with a client without paying so much attention to shaping their relationship or to multicultural correctness that the real reason for the interaction falls by the wayside? The guideline is one that is basic to all interviewing, counseling, and therapy interactions: Pay attention to the distance that is comfortable for *this* helper and *this* client and demonstrate respect for the client's, and your own, preferences. Helpers should remember that differences exist and attend to what clients may be communicating in making their nonverbal choices and remain aware that physical distance is negotiated, may be renegotiated, and may provide information about the relationship or interaction.

The Seating Arrangement

Many professional helpers provide a number of different kinds of seating in their offices. In my office, I try to provide different types of chairs and couches, and different configurations when there is room. To respect my clients' preferences, I simply offer my clients a seat and take my lead from them. If they sit on one side of my desk, I sit on the other. If they sit on the couch, I sit in a nearby chair. If I notice them squirming or backing up, I adjust my distance accordingly.

I am amazed at how often clients choose to sit in my favorite spot. (Of course, when that happens, I admonish them harshly and refer them to an associate with extremely uncomfortable chairs!) Other professional helpers have mentioned the same curious tendency in their practices. I have come to realize that my favorite chair is often the most appealing to others, too, and for similar reasons. If a client chooses your favorite chair, just choose another chair without any delay or reaction.

Close and intimate connections are often made in counseling or therapy, but they cannot be rushed by closing the physical distance gap too quickly. A client who chooses to sit on one side of the desk may simply have done what he or she thought was expected in a counseling or therapy setting. Then again, the client may have needed to feel the presence of a big solid piece of furniture between us. Either way, a suggestion early in a helping relationship, whether verbal or nonverbal, that the client sit in a more comfortable chair or move to the side of the desk is likely to be disrespectful of or even threatening to her or his choice. At the very least, it will be premature. Initially, I think it is most important to simply respect the client's preference and sit down.

Further down the road, helpers may wish to establish the meaning behind a client's choices in many respects, including the preferred seating arrangement. One element of an effective relationship is noticing how others prefer to interact with you. When the relationship is more advanced, knowing why may provide an additional puzzle piece to understanding who a client is.

Touch

The last element of proxemics to be considered is touch. Although a very powerful nonverbal stimulus, the effects of touch in helping relationships have rarely been examined scientifically. Some people are very comfortable touching others while interacting. Others, because of their backgrounds or experiences, are not. In some cultures, touching sporadically or regularly is considered a sign of casual, friendly contact. In others, touching is considered disrespectful or may be perceived as having sexual overtones. Touching may also have the effect of making some clients feel dangerously powerless—an intrusion they have no control over. So, although some studies have shown that handshakes and touches to the arm or back can have a positive effect on clients (Alagna, Whitcher, Fisher, & Wicas, 1979) or on the client's evaluation of counseling (Hubble, Noble, & Robinson, 1981), decisions about touching must include a number of ethical and professional considerations.

The question of touching can be a tricky one for a new professional helper, because humans also use touch as a way to offer comfort. New professional helpers often want to comfort and reassure clients. Perhaps the best way to illustrate the possible negative impact of well-intentioned touching is to consider the clients for whom touching has often meant physical or sexual abuse. I have met many clients for whom this is true. For that man or woman, touching has been associated with harm and the powerlessness to control even the most basic of human dimensions—their own physical boundaries. This client may find a simple welcoming touch aversive or dangerous, not merely uncomfortable. Helpers have a responsibility to become aware of the meaning of touch to their clients so as not to repeat even an appearance of the victimization clients have encountered. In this instance, asking the client directly for his or her sanction could create an additional infraction. Abused clients' sense of powerlessness often extends to a feeling of discomfort when they deny someone they perceive as an authority—including professional helpers—what they think the authority wants. In this client example, in fact with all clients, show your respect for the importance of a client's experiences and their consequences by reserving touch until the client has made it clear that touch is acceptable or welcome. Acceptable body parts to touch include clients' hands, arms, back, or shoulders.

KINESICS: BODY LANGUAGE

Body movements are not random. Most body movements have some meaning, although they do not have a specific universal meaning. They are culturally learned. From an early age, humans appear to try to synchronize body movements and speech sounds, and some even believe that a lack of synchrony may be evidence of mental health problems. A lack of synchrony in helper-client kinesics can indicate an absence of listening (Condon & Ogston, 1966). It is important to convey with body posture, gestures, eye-contact, and facial expression that the helper is open to hearing, can empathize with the client's experience, and has heard clearly what a client has to say. Even when a helper's words are distracting or inaccurately capture a client's message, a helper who demonstrates a relaxed body posture and direct eye-contact will be seen in a more positive light (Fretz, Corn, Tuemmler, & Bellet, 1979). This may serve to reassure the beginning helper who struggles to master the words of professional helping.

Body Posture

Starting with one of the simplest of the kinesic elements, I recommend that helpers adopt an open body posture. An open body posture means that arms and usually legs are unfolded and settled comfortably in a resting position. Avoid the two extremes of squirming, rocking, or tapping versus sitting erect and stiff on the edge of the chair. Your hands should be visible and not shoved into your pockets—you will need your hands available to make gestures that illustrate your meaning. Keeping in mind the need to maintain a respectful distance, position yourself so that you face the client clearly, if not squarely. You should be easily in each other's line of vision.

By leaning forward slightly toward the client, a number of positive effects may be accomplished. This posture conveys open attention to communication. Sitting up and leaning into a conversation conveys interest. Of course, the helper must still be cognizant of the distance, so leaning in too closely can be as uncomfortable as leaning away. Alter the angle of your "lean" to effect an appropriate distance. Studies show that leaning slightly forward is generally perceived as more attentive than sitting up straight (Cormier & Cormier, 1991; Hill & O'Brien, 1999a).

Gestures

In general, gestures and other body movements should also convey interest in and attention to the client's reports. Gestures can be used to emphasize a point, to create an image, to give information about topics that cannot best be understood with words, and to regulate or maintain interpersonal interactions. Taking a position near the door indicates leave-taking (Cormier & Cormier, 1991), and raising an index finger while also straightening and tightening posture is associated with requests for a turn to speak (Knapp, 1978). Persistent fussing and body-touching is perceived as a preoccupation with oneself or discomfort with the other (Freedman, 1972). Attending to breathing and changes in breathing is another, perhaps more subtle, body movement that may indicate level of comfort, feelings, and significant issues. In each case, body movements like gestures or breathing can be powerful indicators of client or helper experience.

Eye-Contact

In many Western cultures, visual contact is considered a crucial element during an interaction, and professional help is no exception. In general, natural and direct, mutual eye-contact conveys that someone is engaged in the interaction, is willing to interact, or has a desire to continue talking (Cormier & Cormier, 1991). One's gaze can communicate interest, intimacy, dominance, or submission (Kleinke, 1986). Eye-contact should remain relatively constant, but you should avoid staring or glazing over.

Physically maintaining eye-contact can be viewed as a metaphor for maintaining an emotional connection, indicating that one is present and accessible. Breaking eye-contact not only signals anxiety or discomfort, but a wish not to maintain a connection or communication with the other person. Averted gazes may also indicate shame (Cormier & Cormier, 1991). Interruption in eye-contact is generally expected when there is a break in the discussion or when someone is thinking or processing information.

Time spent in eye-contact is usually negotiated nonverbally and norms vary. Although in general, eye-contact is correlated with emotional involvement and comfort, the amount of eye-contact maintained and the nature of the helper's eye-contact is another element of nonverbal communication that is influenced by differences in background.

Cultural backgrounds influence the nature and maintenance of eye-contact. White, middle-class Europeans and European Americans often prefer direct and somewhat sustained eye-contact when speaking, but averted glances when listening (La France & Mayo, 1976). Even among European Americans, there are gender and orientation differences in eye-contact. For example, studies show that heterosexual European American women prefer to look directly for a briefer period of time and then avert their glance, while European American lesbians have a tendency to sustain direct eye-contact. European American men tend to sustain eye-contact longer than European American women. Eye-contact customs of clients with ethnic backgrounds that are non-European American will not necessarily follow these findings. For example, among some Native Americans, particularly men and women raised on a reservation, there is a tendency to look downward in the company of those they respect as an authority or elder (Brammer & MacDonald, 1996). Other indigenous peoples avoid eye-contact when speaking of serious topics (Ivey, 1994).

Once again, the point of this information is not to intimidate a beginning helper by demanding constant political or multicultural correctness. Nor is my aim to send would-be helpers running to the library stacks before making any response to a client from a different cultural or ethnic background than the helper. What is important to acknowledge and remember, however, is that messages are conveyed nonverbally as well as verbally, that eye-contact is one way in which we communicate, and that these messages can be interpreted differently based on disparities in background.

Helpers generally do not ask clients for direct instruction about which eye-contact is appropriate. Just as with seating arrangements, I pay attention to clients' duration and use of eye-contact as an expressive form of communication and then follow their lead. Matching communication styles is a component of many cultures and so, for many helpers, developing this ability is not as difficult as it sounds. One example of verbal communication that I regularly alter may give a clearer idea about how matching nonverbal communication styles works. I am comfortable using swear words for emphasis and often find it colorful and expressive in others. People have different views on the suitability of swearing, so I modify my language based on the setting I am in (e.g., classrooms, houses of worship) and the background of the person I am speaking to (e.g., those who consider swearing ill-mannered, disrespectful, or immoral). I do not require direct instruction to accommodate differences; I simply "read" the common expressive style of those around me, adapt accordingly, and eliminate swearing from my vocabulary during those interactions.

As with swearing, eye-contact modification involves paying attention to clients and how they themselves maintain eye-contact. If a client has a tendency to look away quickly, adjust your gaze and look away more frequently than might feel natural to you. If prolonged eye-contact feels rude to you, but your client seems to use it to indicate respectful attention, increase the duration of your eye-contact. Basically, you are trying to establish a comfortable, welcoming environment so the client can focus on the task at hand.

Facial Expression

Students often argue that facial expressions cannot be controlled. What they usually mean is that this element of nonverbal communication is difficult to develop an awareness of and difficult to practice without appearing insincere. However, facial expressions, too, are a part of the nonverbal skills that can be taught and practiced. Many languages use facial expressions to convey the tone, intensity, or affective (emotional) part of a message. Facial expressions have similar meanings in many cultures (Ekman & Friesen, 1969), but people from different cultural backgrounds still may equate different facial expressions with different emotions.

Helpers who convey to a client that they are following and matching what a client is feeling build the rapport and empathy critical to professional empathy (Maurer & Tindall, 1983). While tracking a client's story, accomplished professional listeners follow along and match the client with not only their body posture, but their eyes, their gestures, and even their facial expressions. When a client's eyes tell of their sadness, the helper's eyes are sad, too. When the client's whole face lights up with the joy of an experience, so does the helper's. This process is called *synchrony* (Cormier & Cormier, 1991).

Synchrony must be distinguished from *mimicry*. Mimicry is copying another exactly and often includes an element of ridicule. (How many older brothers and sisters have been annoyed to tears by a "copy-cat" younger brother or sister?) For example, if someone continuously swipes at a strand of hair fallen across his or her forehead, a mimic will do the same. Helpers practicing synchrony match and reflect clients' voices, body postures, gestures, or facial expressions to express harmony with and understanding of their meaning. The more patterns being matched by the helper, the more powerful the effect (Cormier & Cormier, 1991). Trying to attend to all aspects of synchrony at once may feel overwhelming to the new helping professional. To make it easier, focus on one aspect of a client's nonverbal communication at a time and try to synchronize your nonverbal style with his or hers.

Matching a client's affect is one way to effect synchrony. Affect refers to emotional expression. Every interchange has an emotional tone set by both what is being said and how it is being said (paralanguage). When people are really hearing what someone is saying, it is not uncommon for them to feel the other person's feelings right along with the person as she or he speaks. This shows in their face as they match the emotional tone being set by the other.

Just as a helper's eyes follow a client's movement, a helper's facial expressions can follow a client's emotion to create synchrony. Some people do this naturally; most need feedback to learn and refine this skill. When children first learn to brush their teeth, the mirror offers valuable feedback as they watch carefully to see that they don't jam bristles into their gums or overshoot their mouths entirely. They already know where their hands and teeth are, but they are seeking feedback to improve a specific behavior. This is the same kind of

EXERCISE **1.2**

Practicing Matching

Videotape yourself listening to someone for 5 minutes. Replay the tape and observe your face at various points during the conversation. Are you following the other person's conversation? Are you following his or her emotions? Does your face match the feelings that the person is having or reporting? Does your body posture match his or hers? Do your gestures match any gestures that he or she is making?

feedback that beginning helpers often find useful in learning about facial expressions and matching a client's affect.

Other kinesics like body posture can also be matched to create synchrony or dyssynchrony with a client. Dyssynchrony occurs when client and helper are not matched in their nonverbal communication. Many beginning helpers believe that they should smile to appear pleasant and nonthreatening to clients. The smile will appear incongruous, however, when a client recounts a sad event or something about which he or she feels ashamed. Despite the goal of appearing pleasant, give up the smile and match the client. Anything else can be off-putting.

PARALANGUAGE

Voice volume, intonation, rate of speech, and fluency of speech as well as pauses and silence are a part of the paralanguage of nonverbal communication. Paralanguage, also called paralinguistics, is the "how" of a message. Vocal cues help client and helper negotiate taking turns in listening and speaking. For example, decreased pitch generally indicates turn-yielding, whereas increased volume or rate of speech is associated with turn-maintaining or holding the floor. Second, voice characteristics convey information about the client's or helper's emotional state. A person speaking softly may be tentative, reluctant, shy, or ashamed, whereas one who speaks loudly may be angry, happy, or aiming to dominate the conversation.

As with other nonverbal communication, a person's background influences paralanguage. For example, both loud and soft volume may indicate hearing impairment and say absolutely nothing about the person's emotional state. North Americans are known for speaking more loudly than people from other countries (Sue & Sue, 1990). First-generation immigrants to the United States may speak more softly because they come from a culture that values gentle or quiet speech patterns, not because they are reluctant, shy, or hesitant.

Silence

Silence is more than the absence of speech or sound. It is also the presence of a specific kind of listening skill. Excellent listeners are those who know when it is time to use this skill and how to use it to facilitate helping communication. Silence is a way of making room for something to occur. Without silence, the verbal space in an interaction is said to be filled, and filling verbal space is often associated with anxiety and discomfort (Knapp, 1978). Filling verbal space may also indicate aggressive or dominating speech patterns.

Beginning helpers are anxious to do well and often believe that they are only helping if they are saying something. They often strive to fill pauses or spaces in the conversation, which then prevents clients from filling those same spaces with something of interest or concern to them. It is the interchange between helper and client that provides help, and this interchange includes both the speaking and the silences.

Many clients report that well-timed silence gives them an opportunity to collect their thoughts, consider something more carefully, or reflect back on a previous experience (Duncan, 1972, 1974). A client's silence may also signal a client's need to reflect or consider something previously said or done. Silence can communicate a client's desire to avoid a topic, or it can be a client's way of slowing down the pace of a particular exploration. There are times when silence simply means that a client or helper has nothing to say about a recent comment. Sometimes, when a helper has said something that was not an accurate reflection of a client's report, the client will respond with silence.

A helper's silence may communicate any of the same things conveyed by a client's silence, but it can also indicate self-consciousness about what to say or confusion at not having tracked the client's last report. With experience, helpers tend to get more comfortable with silences and learn how to use them to enhance helping. Much can be said and done with silence.

Minimal Verbal Responses

So far, this chapter has focused on the elements of communication that do not involve talking, but I would like to turn to a sort of gray area of paralanguage's nonverbal communication. **Minimal verbal responses** are the verbal equivalent to a head nod (Okun, 2002). They are those miniscule utterances made by a person who wants someone else to continue with her or his report. They include "mm-hmm," "uh-huh," "yeah," "nah," and "oh?" On the one hand, these utterances are simple, often overlooked responses, and on the other hand, they are critical to helping the client continue her or his reports with minimal interruption or distraction.

Studies show that minimal verbal responses act as reinforcers for continuing whatever topic is being addressed (Benjamin, 1987), or they can actually reinforce the use of a specific word or discussion of a particular topic (Hackney & Cormier, 1994). In other words, minimal verbal responses enhance the possibility that the client will repeat or continue the topic. Clients are often conveying difficult stories. They are not always convinced even when they are speaking that they want to continue and may be equally uncertain that the helper wants to know what they fear to tell. So, if a helper wants a client to continue, she or he will interject the barest of responses so as not to interrupt the flow, giving the client an opportunity to reevaluate the decision. The idea of a minimal verbal response is to communicate as simply as possible, "I'm still here and listening intently. Please continue on with what you're saying; it's very important to me." What could be a less intrusive or distracting way to say all of this other than, "Uh-huh," coupled with a nod?

TIME

Perceptions about the nature of time can certainly influence the helping relationship. A client or helper who views time as a commodity to be used, wasted, managed, or saved has quite a different approach compared to the person who views time in a cyclic fashion. Many

Native Americans (including my own partner) have a concept of time as an infinite, ongoing process that cannot and should not be controlled by humans. This is a nonlinear conception of time. When asked when something will be finished, my partner often responds by saying, "When there is nothing left to do." This is not intended to be sarcastic, but rather a clear communication about my partner's concept of time. Coming from a more task-oriented Anglo-European background, I have a more linear view of time. I am more likely to respond to the same question by saying, "I can have that to you tomorrow after two o'clock," indicating my view that time is measurable and that tasks can be measured by these time units. Regardless of the specific content of the communication about time, much may be communicated in the observation of how time is approached. Being "on time" may be very important to the client who has a structured view of time and being late may convey disrespect. Others may see time in a less linear or structured way and are not annoyed when sessions start late.

A second aspect of time that has an impact on helping relates to the timing of helper responses. This is true of both verbal and nonverbal responses. Prompt reactions may indicate attention and interest to clients' statements, whereas delayed reactions may indicate self-consciousness or convey inattention to their reports. The "gold standard" for assessing timing, whether in verbal or nonverbal communication, is still being in synchrony with the client.

DO ALL OF THIS AND RELAX, TOO?

Research demonstrates that helpers who are more relaxed and comfortable tend to act as models of relaxation for their clients (Mehrabian, 1976). Relaxing is not a matter of denying the often intense problems that clients present in a helping situation or the intense feelings that the helper who is following may be sensing or feeling. It is rather another nonverbal way to communicate that the interaction is one in which someone can feel comfortable being themselves, whatever that may include, and that the helper will remain calm with whatever a client may present. That is not to say that clients do not present difficult challenges or that clients will not present things that upset helpers. They do and they will. A relaxed helper is telling the client that "you can trust that I'm going to do my best to stay here with you wherever this interaction takes us and to handle calmly whatever comes up."

It is probably hard to picture how you can attend to so many details while meeting with a client and still remain relaxed. Just trying to implement all of these instructions designed to raise a helper's awareness about communication must seem like an immense expectation. You're not going to put it all together at once, so relax with that idea right away. Helpers are not usually very relaxed when they first begin to work with clients, and experienced helpers will not be relaxed with all clients, all of the time. Nonetheless, it is important for helpers to cultivate a relaxed approach in a helping interaction because it conveys a vital message to the client. Of course, relaxing may also benefit the helper.

EXERCISE 1.3

Making a Videotape and Self-Assessment

Videotape yourself while you listen to someone you know for 5 minutes. Next, videotape yourself while you listen to someone you do not know for 5 minutes. Observe yourself and all of your nonverbal communications. Critique your performance according to the Rating Guideline offered below. Be honest. There is very little point to deceiving yourself about this skill. It is impossible to improve without at least giving yourself accurate feedback. Next, give the videotape to a classmate to review and critique.

Rating Nonverbal Skills

A number of rating systems exist to give beginning helpers rapid information about which responses are effective and which need improvement. The easiest is to assign a number to the various kinds of responses that could be made. The rating system suggested in this text was developed by Robert Carkhuff (1978), used by many others since (e.g., Doyle, 1998; Ivey, 1994), and focuses on the degree to which a helper's responses effectively allow the client to continue or distract the client or helper from the task of communicating. The system will later be described more fully when helpers are reflecting content and beginning to assess in more detail how accurately this is done. For now, a brief introduction is made to give beginning helpers a way to evaluate nonverbal skills.

The system ranges from 1 to 4 levels. A 3 indicates that the helper's response allowed the client to continue speaking. Although that may sound simple, it is one of the skills that will be practiced over and over again. Helpers may also respond in a way that distracts the client somewhat or significantly from telling her or his story. These numbers are indicated by 2 or 1 respectively. A helper can respond in a way that allows clients to add something somewhat or significantly beyond what they had initially thought or told the helper. This is done later in the helping relationship by adding some of the more advanced skills of helping. A 3 is the rating to which helpers should generally aspire. Many beginning responses will be somewhat to very distracting for clients. This is to be expected. Beginning helpers tend to try too hard to "do," when "being" may be more important. Helpers distract someone somewhat by making a response that is not quite with the client or distract significantly by not following what the client is saying or by responding to or launching a topic that is well outside of the topic (or range of related topics) that the client is addressing. It is important to remember that even when a helper's response is clever or insightful, if the client is not ready to address the topic raised, the response is still a distraction from the topic being discussed. So, this rating system does not evaluate the cleverness of a response made; cleverness may not be helpful. It is, in a sense, a way to assess whether the helper remembered that the focus of helping is on the client.

Level 1. Indicates kinesics, proxemics, paralanguage, or dyssynchrony that is distracting.

Level 2. Indicates partial attending (e.g., tonal quality or gestures that are somewhat dyssynchronous or eye-contact that does not quite follow the client).

Level 3. Indicates at least some evidence of clear and definite eye-contact that is neither staring, nor off-task; well-placed minimal verbal responses; tolerance of silence; and gestures, facial expressions, or body posture that matches the client's (synchrony).

Level 4. Indicates maintaining appropriate eye-contact and physical attention throughout the interchange; very well-placed silences and minimal verbal response; gestures, facial expressions, and body posture that follow the client and match his or her affect (synchrony) and reflect a hint of the helper's own style as well, or that invite the client to consider an alternative without imposing one.

EXERCISE **1.4**

Observing and Assessing Nonverbal Listening

Form a triad to practice this exercise. Two of the three people will be communicating and one will be observing. Ask a classmate to watch your nonverbal listening style and rate it over a 5-minute period. Change positions and watch a classmate's nonverbal listening style. The checklist below was shortened and adapted from William Cormier and Sherilyn Cormier (1991) and may help you focus on specific nonverbal skills as you observe each other.

Checklist for Nonverbal Listening

Kinesics
- ☐ Eyes
- ☐ Face, mouth, and head
- ☐ Body movements, posture, and gestures

Paralanguage
- ☐ Continuity or change in voice level, pitch, rate of speech
- ☐ Minimal verbal responses emphasizing particular topics
- ☐ Silence initiated by helper
- ☐ Silence initiated by client

Proxemics
- ☐ Environmental characteristics (e.g., furnishings, color, light)
- ☐ Distance (e.g., continuity or shifts)
- ☐ Use of appropriate touch (e.g., handshake; brief, gentle touch to arm; pat on the back)
- ☐ Reserved use of touch

Timing
- ☐ Meeting started on time or late
- ☐ Promptness or delay in responding to client communication
- ☐ Continuity or change in pacing

Synchrony
- ☐ Helper synchrony or dyssynchrony (e.g., facial expression doesn't match other body movements or posture)
- ☐ Helper-client synchrony/dyssynchrony (e.g., helper's facial expression does or does not match client's facial expression)

Overall Assessment of Session
- ☐ Based on your observations, those conclusions you might draw about: the helper; the client; the relationship.

CHAPTER

2 Feedback

When learning new skills, **feedback** is critical. Feedback can be understood by looking at the electronic process in which a signal is returned to its source. Musicians and their sound engineers are familiar with this kind of feedback, as is anyone who has ever sat in the audience while a novice turned on a microphone without paying attention to the direction it was facing. When an electronic signal is returned to its source, the resulting sound can be quite unpleasant as the signal is amplified.

Therapists use a process called biofeedback to return information (*feedback*) about a bodily function (*bio*) to the source of a behavior—the client exhibiting the behavior. Biofeedback employs a device that offers information concerning a bodily function about which the client exhibiting the behavior is usually unaware. Through biofeedback, clients can pay attention to functions they are not usually aware of and modify functions over which they do not usually feel a sense of control. Studies have shown this to be an effective way to modify heart rates, breathing, vascular activity, temperature, and even brain wave activity (Miller, 1975; Roberts, 1985, 1988; Sterman, 1996).

When learning the microskills of helping, feedback also refers to the process of returning information to the source of a behavior with the intention of offering that person an opportunity to observe, improve, or refine a particular behavior. In this case, the person is a student of professional helping and the behavior is communication behavior.

WHY LEARN TO GIVE AND RECEIVE FEEDBACK?

Learning to give and receive feedback serves the initial purpose of assisting students in learning the microskills of effective helping and the later purpose of helping clients to realize their goals. Feedback may include information about behaviors students are unaware of or behaviors students have identified and wish to modify or improve. Self-evaluation is not sufficient to develop effective helping skills. For example, well-intentioned helpers want to look engaged or interested when interviewing a client, but won't have a clear idea whether or not they are successful without input from others. Behaviors that are not usually in our awareness, like facial expressions, are difficult to modify. Achieving effective modifications becomes more likely if someone describes how the behaviors are being perceived—in effect, metaphorically holding up a mirror. Communication is another example of a helping skill that can be more easily improved with feedback.

EXERCISE **2.1**

Understanding the Process of Feedback

Imagine you were going to dress up like a clown for a young child's party. Buy an inexpensive tube of lipstick and white eye shadow or grease paint. Without using a mirror, put the lipstick around your mouth to exaggerate the size of your mouth and the white eye shadow clear to your eyebrows and down to your cheek to exaggerate the size of your eyes. How did you do? Now try it with a mirror. How did you do?

What does this exercise in putting on makeup have to do with feedback?

EXERCISE **2.2**

Understanding the Process of Feedback

For this exercise, you will need a partner. Find a blindfold that makes it impossible to see; put that blindfold on one partner. The blindfolded partner now tries to leave the room and building that the two of you started in. It is fine to pick a place that is somewhat familiar to the person being blindfolded. The partner who is not blindfolded offers information about position, number of steps, and so on to assist the blindfolded person in finding his or her way. Does this have any parallels to feedback?

Offering feedback is actually a fairly advanced microskill and will be addressed again (see Chapter 7). To include the advantages of feedback in the training process, however, the rudiments should be learned early. A class environment can be a safe and supportive context in which to practice the skill of giving feedback and good preparation for the much greater challenge of offering feedback to clients. Clients are more likely to be vulnerable to or defensive about feedback than a classmate usually is. There is less likelihood of harm as students learn skills by practicing with one another.

THE PURPOSE OF FEEDBACK

If you tried Exercise 2.1 or Exercise 2.2 and put on grease paint or found your way around blindfolded, you may have discovered or confirmed your understanding of the value of feedback. When learning microskills, feedback can allow helpers (and clients) to (1) develop a behavior that they do not ordinarily engage in or are not ordinarily aware of; (2) observe their own behavior and its impact; (3) improve or modify a behavior that is not effective; or (4) refine a behavior that is satisfactory but not exceptional or consistent.

According to behavioral learning theories (see Chapter 9), anything that follows a behavior can increase or decrease the probability that the behavior will be repeated. So, feedback can act as a reinforcer for helping behaviors. Comments that result in an increased incidence of a particular helping behavior would be viewed as positive reinforcers. Comments that result in a decreased incidence of a particular helping behavior could be considered punishment. Withholding comments about a helping behavior may well result in the extinction (disappearance) of that behavior. If the comments result in the receiver avoiding situations in which he or she would receive additional comments, the comments could be thought of as negative reinforcers. Developing, learning, and refining the microskills of helping depend on receiving effective feedback, not just any feedback. Feedback should be focused on the specific behavior a person is trying to learn or improve, increase the possibility of effective helping behaviors, and decrease ineffective helping behaviors. When I teach helping microskills, I encourage class feedback that does not result in classmates avoiding future feedback situations.

WHAT FEEDBACK IS *NOT*

Many people find it easier to comment about the pleasant aspects of another person's character than to offer feedback. Colleagues or friends who say, "You're a very nice person," or, "You are someone I admire," are not offering feedback. Comments indicating that someone values a particular trait or thinks of another as nice or admirable are important to developing a relationship but do not fall within the definition of feedback. Some people think that giving feedback means making a negative comment. Comments such as "You're sure in a rotten mood" or "You're an unpleasant person" are not offering feedback. For a comment to fit the definition of feedback, it must focus on offering specific information about a specific behavior. Terms such as *nice* or *admirable* or *unpleasant* are traits made up of many behaviors, not information about a specific behavior. Whether complimentary or uncomplimentary, terms that are too broad and vague cannot be used to modify or refine a behavior.

HOW TO MAKE FEEDBACK USEFUL

Useful feedback begins with statements about observable behavior. Determining what is an observable behavior can be tricky. Consider a videotape camera as one tool that records observable behaviors. That which can be seen or heard is observable. Intentions, motives, traits, values, and assumptions are not observable on camera. Even though it may be possible to form an impression, have an intuition, or make educated guesses from what is observed, the impressions, intuitions, and guesses are still based on observations.

Providing others with feedback based on observations is important so that specific behaviors can be continued, modified, or eliminated. Comments like "I thought you did a good job" make the recipient feel great but do not include enough specificity to be useful. Beginning helpers who are studying nonverbal communication would have a clearer idea about the good job they just did if the feedback took the form of "I noticed that you leaned forward when I spoke." The specificity of this comment allows the helper to observe him- or herself through the eyes of the person giving the feedback and prompts continuation of the behavior—in this case, leaning forward. Another example of a general and a specific comment applies to a behavior often difficult for beginning therapists to master—the art of being silent. Comments like "I thought you used silence well" do not offer the same specificity as "I noticed that you remained silent for a moment after the client spoke." The latter comment would be more useful because it allows helpers to see when and where they accomplished the behavior and they can thus continue it. In both of the examples given, feedback involves making a statement of ownership of the observation by using the word *I,* following that with a word indicating a form of observation, specifying the behavior, and identifying the time frame in which the behavior occurred. If you are someone who likes to think in terms of formulas, the formula for effective feedback would look like this:

Effective Feedback
"[I] + [observation word] + [specific behavior] + [time frame]"

Following a comment about specific behavior with a comment about its impact may also be useful. Whenever giving information about the personal impact of a behavior, it is important to remember to use statements that begin with "I" and indicate that the impact is not forever, but has or had a temporary effect. For example, "I noticed that you leaned forward when I spoke; I felt like you were really listening to me when you did that," is a useful piece of information to the student of microskills. After the specific behavior is described, the impact is described in terms of its immediate personal effect on the feedback-giver. The formula for effective feedback with a statement of impact is more complex and would look like this:

Effective Feedback with Statement of Impact
"[I] + [observation word] + [specific behavior] + [I] + [felt/thought] + [specific feeling or thought] + [time frame for behavior]"

Thinking of feedback as a type of self-disclosure may help facilitate recognition that some risks are involved in giving feedback. This way of thinking about feedback may also recognize that offering feedback is not just useful to the recipient but may be valuable to the giver and to the relationship. Shared perceptions and risked disclosure are the basis of most relationships. A helping relationship is no exception.

FEEDBACK THAT INCLUDES SUGGESTED IMPROVEMENTS

Many students and beginning helpers find offering feedback that suggests an improvement an uncomfortable and therefore difficult process. Students are often loathe to give one another this type of feedback. Whether because of the fear of hurting another's feelings or because of identifying with the person trying hard to learn something new or because of personal experience with feedback that was too harsh, it is hard for many students to feel at ease saying anything less than positive.

Thinking of this as negative feedback—not unlike the painful screech that comes from a microphone turned to face the source of its signal—will not be useful. There can be no guarantee that the receiver's feelings will not be hurt. A feedback-giver always takes a certain amount of risk when offering feedback, more so when it includes a suggestion for improvement. Students taking a course in the microskills of counseling, therapy, or interviewing are likely to be trying hard to do their best. A suggestion for improvement can feel as if that effort is being denied or devalued. Many people lack skills at giving feedback or are not invested in giving gentle or constructive feedback, so most of us have been on the receiving end of feedback that was too harsh at one time or another. But just because giving feedback can be difficult to deliver, or receiving feedback can be difficult to hear, does not eliminate its necessity. Even experienced helpers can benefit from suggestions for improvements, but students and beginning helpers need the advantage of suggestions even more. Remember that your well-crafted suggestion for improvement may be the most valuable suggestion your classmate will ever receive. In the process of offering feedback with suggestions for improvement to your classmates, you will be practicing techniques for offering feedback with suggestions for improvements to your future clients.

The basic principle of suggested improvement feedback is the same as any other—to offer a person information about a specific behavior. The crucial difference here is that information is being offered about a behavior that needs improvement or refinement. Some ways of offering feedback about improvements are more helpful than others. Begin by keeping in mind that everyone can make improvements. That is only realistic and human. Students of counseling, therapy, or interviewing are not expected to know this or any other material upon its introduction; that would make the course and this book unnecessary! Directing the feedback toward a very specific behavior is more likely to be well received than offering a general statement about character traits. Offering the feedback in a tentative rather than absolute way is generally received more favorably. Offering a specific time frame in which the behavior occurred helps the receiver to understand that they are not forever flawed—something very specific about them could use improvement. Informing tends to be more helpful than demanding.

Using a format for tentatively offering a suggestion may make this type of feedback less aversive, focusing on a specific behavior and time frame gives an opportunity to change the behavior, and informing someone about a behavior leaves them feeling empowered to do something in the situation. A comment like "Wow, that was really bad" hurts the receiver's feelings and is not even considered feedback for the same reason that "You did a great job" was not considered feedback. Neither are useful when learning microskills because the comment is not specific enough to enable someone to change the behavior. Feedback that sounds more like "Maybe you could try looking away more often" offers a suggestion about a specific behavior that allows a chance to change it and is unlikely to result in anyone's death from humiliation. Tentativeness is often equated with gentleness and a collaborative relationship.

Another way to enter comfortably into giving suggestions for improvement is to begin with a global positive (there must be some place that all of those vague, global comments about someone's character can come in handy) and then proceed to offer a suggestion. "I really admire your being able to risk going first today . . . [pause] . . . Maybe you could speak more slowly next time; it felt too rushed to me" is an example of prefacing a suggestion with the recognition of a positive trait. The recipient's bravery is not the focus of the lesson they were working to learn, but recognizing it gives valuable credit where credit is due and cushions the specific behavioral suggestion related to the lesson itself. A similar technique is to structure the sequence of feedback so that specific behaviors done well are recognized before offering suggested improvements. "When you leaned in to hear her as she got quiet, I thought you looked really interested and caring . . . [pause] . . . maybe next time, you could even scoot your chair over to be closer then" is an example of first acknowledging something done well and then offering a suggestion about how to improve it.

OFFERING FEEDBACK WILL SEEM PHONY

As with any new skill, first attempts feel stilted, not very genuine, and unreal. Remember first bike-riding attempts? The bike itself felt foreign. It certainly did not feel like it could be controlled by anything the rider did. However, as time went by, the bike nearly became one with most bike riders, and turning was so automatic it required not much more than a thought of which direction to go. So it is with different communication skills, too. Initially, they will feel contrived and foreign, maybe even insincere. With practice, these skills become so much a part of helpers that they are automatic and require little thought to be a genuine response. Giving feedback using these formulas or maps will feel initially foreign, not very genuine. After you have practiced giving feedback using the map, giving feedback will become integrated into how you communicate. You will set the map aside, and the feedback will require little thought to produce. This style of offering feedback will have become genuine.

CHECKING ON THE IMPACT OF FEEDBACK

Once feedback is given, the feedback-giver has a responsibility to check its impact on the receiver. Simply asking a direct question like "How did you feel when I said that sitting with your arms folded seemed to

EXERCISE **2.3**
Giving Feedback on Communication Skills

After listening to a classmate try out his or her microskills for a few minutes, offer feedback about how he or she performed. Check in with your classmate to see what effect your feedback had. Try to focus on at least one thing you would like to see him or her continue to do and one thing you would like to see some improvement in. This format will be continued throughout assignments that involve classmates.

indicate disinterest?" can get the job done. It offers the recipient of the feedback an opportunity to tell about the impact of the feedback. The impact of the feedback is important information for the feedback-giver, because offering feedback is itself a skill that may be improved and refined. Just as it is important to give feedback information that is specific rather than general, it is important to frame the question about impact so that specific behaviors and time frames are shown to be the expected information. Beginning the question with phrases like "How did you feel . . . ?" or "What did you think . . . ?" specifies (and limits) whose feedback is important and helps responders limit their feedback to that which they observed themselves rather than making a universal response. If you were to create a formula, it would look like this:

> *Checking the Impact of Feedback*
> "[open question about feeling or thought] + [time frame] + [specific behavior]"

RECEIVING FEEDBACK

Helpers receive a great deal of feedback while in training. In fact, helpers continue to receive feedback even after they enter professional practice. I have sometimes wondered whether the reason we call it "being in practice" is because we are expected to continue getting feedback and practicing our skills over and over so we can improve and refine them during our entire careers. Feedback usually takes either the form of offering someone a glimpse of something done well so that it can be repeated or offering a glimpse of something that needs improvement so that it can be modified. Students and professional helpers alike can often benefit from improving how we receive one or both kinds of feedback.

Receiving Positive Feedback

When I listen to my 3-year-old niece and 5-year-old nephew respond to a compliment, what I often hear is something that sounds like "Yeah, I know." When I hear my students' responses, what I often see are caricatures of cartoon people shuffling their feet and looking down at their shoes. What is it that happens to us as we mature that we can go from unassuming assurance to bumbling, sheepish diffidence?

Discounting positive feedback is common, and students often receive complimentary comments with shy reserve or minimization. Some people do it by blushing, looking down, and shuffling like the cartoon characters. Others may say, "Oh, do you think so? I thought I really messed it up!" or, "It was just luck." Many people have been taught that to think too much of themselves is arrogant. Some have been told to be modest about accomplishments. Some do not believe that they have done a noteworthy job until it is perfect. Regardless, helpers-in-training have a tendency to shrug off feedback that offers them a glimpse of a behavior someone thought of as positive or helpful.

Discounting feedback has a couple of possible effects for both the giver and receiver. When feedback is discounted, the person giving the feedback may feel discounted and may repeat the comment. Sometimes, having the positive feedback repeated was precisely the recipient's goal when they hemmed and hawed about it. The feedback-giver may soon tire of having to repeat her- or himself, and it may begin to feel like playing a game, which it is. In addition, the feedback-giver may not want to offer the comment again if it has been rendered unimportant or shrugged off or if the feedback-giver feels manipulated into convincing the receiver of the value of the comment or the worth of the receiver.

Perhaps the greatest loss, however, is that receivers who discount feedback are often unable to use the feedback to reinforce and continue the complimented behavior. If they cannot take it seriously or take it in at all, then they cannot utilize it. For all of these reasons, learning how to effectively receive positive feedback is a useful and necessary skill.

Receiving Suggestions

Receiving suggestions graciously is at least as difficult as offering them, perhaps even more so. It is difficult to hear that hard work or an intense wish to do well has not resulted in exquisite performance. Nonetheless, effort is not always equated with excellence. Excellence generally comes with practice. Further, perfect performance can sometimes be repeated, but making mistakes is often the best way to learn something new or different. Even when we know all of this to be true, suggestions are often difficult and uncomfortable to hear.

Even the most well-delivered suggestion can result in protective behavior on the part of the receiver. Most people do not want to feel bad about who they are or the effort they gave something, and so they will want to protect themselves from these feelings. Cultivating responses and internal dialogue to assist with this type of feedback will make receiving suggestions for improvement less threatening.

What to Say When Receiving Feedback

Developing a kind of formula to respond to those types of feedback that are most difficult can enhance feedback receiving skills. As with feedback-giving, this formulaic response will not feel genuine at first. It is a considered response, not a spontaneous response. It has been designed to reflect the values and beliefs of the recipient, precisely because they believe that what comes more naturally or spontaneously needs improvement. A formula like cautioning oneself to pause for a moment and then saying, "Thank you," before proceeding can begin a response on a more positive footing whether the feedback received is positive or negative. Considering the importance of the skill being complimented or the improvement being suggested could follow. "Thanks, I think of nonverbal listening as important; I'm glad you thought I did it well" or "Thanks, I think of nonverbal listening as important; I'll try that" both recognize the feedback-giver's role in facilitating the learning process, comments on a value shared by both recipient and giver, and keeps the focus on behaviors being learned rather than on the whole character being evaluated. If recipients themselves are able to stay focused in this way, they are also more

---

E X E R C I S E **2.4**

Practicing Receiving Feedback

Set up a time to discuss something with a friend or classmate for 5 minutes. Instruct your friend to watch how you are speaking and then say, "Maybe next time you could . . . ," to several things in the course of your discussion. Practice responding by saying, "Thanks, I think that's important, I'll try to. . . ."

Set up another time with a friend who tells you that you have just done something very well. Explain that she or he should be specific about a behavior. Practice saying, "Thanks, I think that's important, and I'm glad you thought so, too."

likely to use the feedback. The formula for receiving feedback then, looks like this:

> **Response to Feedback**
> "[Thanks] + [statement of value about the behavior being observed] + [statement of future intention if a suggestion
>
> OR
>
> statement of appreciation of the other's feedback if positive]"

NONVERBAL FEEDBACK

Not all feedback is given verbally. Just as a large percentage of any communication is nonverbal, a substantial portion of feedback will also be nonverbal. Nonverbal feedback is any information given to the source that is not spoken. Learning how to recognize and receive nonverbal feedback is an important helping skill. Students and clients may hesitate to offer feedback directly, may still be formulating their thoughts about what to say, or may not even be aware of a reaction, but often facial expressions, voice tone and inflection, or posture can give important feedback. Take for example the following interchange between client and helper:

> HELPER: "How are you feeling about what I just said?"
>
> CLIENT: "Oh, fine" (said while slouching into chair, looking down, and speaking slowly and with little affect).

This helper just received valuable, albeit nonverbal, feedback about something he or she has said. Even though the helper asked directly for the feedback, and the client directly stated that the intervention was fine, additional and perhaps contradictory nonverbal feedback was also given. The client's word was *fine*, but the behaviors said, "I didn't like it very much," or may even have said, "I'm feeling pretty ashamed right now." (In Chapter 7, I will address in more detail how a helper might point out this discrepancy in ways that advance client goals.) Clients are not responsible for giving helpers feedback that facilitates the helpers' learning. (The exception, of course, would be the client who is there to specifically work on learning how to give feedback more directly.) The helper is the one who is responsible for receiving nonverbal feedback, too, and giving it the same importance as verbal feedback, making sense of it, and allowing it to enhance his or her helping skills.

The client who slouched and spoke slowly offered the helper feedback that the helper could utilize immediately to improve her or his work with this client. Clients who feel very strongly that a helper's skills should have been different may simply choose not to return. Addressing more difficult or complex nonverbal feedback, like not keeping the next appointment or refusing to participate, is an advanced skill not addressed in this text. For now, there is plenty to remember about giving and receiving feedback.

SUMMARY

To recap briefly, feedback is returning to someone a glimpse of something observed. Giving and receiving feedback is one of many tools used by helpers when learning the microskills of helping that are also used in professional work. It is important for helpers to practice both giving and receiving feedback, because many of the microskills require feedback for effective learning to take place. Feedback given and received may take a positive form when the skill being observed was accomplished, or it may take the form of a suggestion for improvement when the intended behavior was not achieved. A number of formulas may be useful to consider when responding to and giving feedback.

Effective Feedback
"[I] + [observation word] + [specific behavior] + [time frame]"

Example: "I noticed that you leaned forward when you were listening."

Effective Feedback with Statement of Impact
"[I] + [observation word] + [specific behavior] + [I] + [felt/thought] + [specific feeling or thought] + [time frame for behavior]"

Example: "I noticed that you leaned forward when you were listening; I felt really heard when you did that."

Request for Feedback
"[open question about feeling or thought] + [time frame] + [specific behavior]"

Example: "How did you feel when I said that?"

Response to Positive Feedback
"[Thanks] + [statement of appreciation of the other's feedback]"

Example: "Thanks, I think leaning into a conversation is important; I'm glad you noticed."

Response to Suggestion
"[Thanks] + [statement of value about the behavior being observed] + [statement of future intention]"

Example: "Thanks, I think leaning into a conversation is important; I'll try that."

While these formulas and the ways of responding will feel very stiff initially, they will feel more genuine as they become more familiar. Feedback about communication skills will help students learn and refine those skills that will be invaluable in professional helping. Who knows? The same skills may even enhance the interpersonal lives of the professional helpers. They certainly won't hurt!

CHAPTER

3

Restating Content

A critical component of professional helping is being able to verbally and nonverbally demonstrate an empathic understanding of what another person is saying. A brief discussion of empathy may be useful. In its original usage, empathy referred to the tendency of observers to project themselves "into" that which they observe. Hilary Lipps (1905, 1926) adopted the term for use in psychological contexts, applying it to the process by which we come to know other people. Lipps argued that witnessing another's emotional state prompts observers to covertly imitate, albeit more weakly, another's emotional cues. The process of empathy is an active one in which the observer purposefully steps outside of her- or himself and into the experience of another. Some have argued that empathy involves understanding the feelings of another (Kohler, 1929; Stotland, 1969; Stotland, Sherman, & Shaver, 1971) or feeling in a congruent manner with another (Barnett, 1978; Batson, 1991; Gruen & Mendohlson, 1986; Wispe, 1986, 1991), while others suggest that empathy involves more cognitive skill, like taking on the role of another (Mead, 1934), decentering (Piaget, 1932), or creating an accurate image of another's viewpoints (e.g., Chapin, 1942; Kerr & Speroff, 1954). Still others suggest that the process of empathy is both cognitive and affective role-taking (Eisenberg, 1986). Mark Davis (1980, 1983, 1999) added to Douglas Hoffman's (1984, 1987) early framework by suggesting that empathy encompasses cognitive role-taking, personal feelings of distress created by another's distress, and feelings of sympathy or concern for another. Finally, the theorists at the Stone Center for the Development of Women (Jordan, Kaplan, Miller, Stiver, & Surrey, 1991) define empathy as a capacity to share in and comprehend the momentary psychological state of another that involves both affective arousal and cognitive structuring. For the purposes of this text, I define empathy as both a cognitive skill and an affective skill that involves seeing the cognitive and affective world of others from their perspectives.

Empathy may be communicated in a variety of ways (Cormier & Cormier, 1991; Hill & O'Brien, 1999a). Empathy may begin with nonverbal synchrony and continue with a helper showing a desire to comprehend a client's perspective or frame of reference. This interest is demonstrated in attempts to discuss what is important to the client and to understand the content and feelings that a client conveys so well that the helper can restate it using his or her own words.

Empathy is not conveyed in one response, but rather in several accurate representations of a client's experience. Empathic understanding involves, in part, being able to see things from another's perspective (Cormier & Cormier, 1991; Davis, 1996). Seeing things from a client's perspective does not mean that a helper loses her or his own perspective. Instead, empathic understanding is a complex process of knowing your own perspective and temporarily suspending your frame of reference while looking at another's world through her or his eyes (Jordan et al., 1991). Without judging or evaluating a client's story or perspective, helpers convey this understanding to clients using a variety of nonverbal and verbal tools.

This chapter focuses specifically on two verbal tools that demonstrate empathic understanding of the content of what someone is saying. The chapter begins with the more basic content skill of paraphrasing and then proceeds to the more complex skill of gathering several accurate paraphrases to summarize themes being observed by the helper. **Paraphrasing** involves restating the client's message in the helper's own words to ensure that both client and helper have an opportunity to reflect on that understanding. **Summarizing** is a skill that requires the helper to collect several paraphrases and offer them to the client in a condensed form. Summarizing assists clients in identifying themes or linking thoughts together. Both skills focus on developing and communicating an empathic understanding of the content of a client's reports.

PARAPHRASING

The word *paraphrase* comes from two Greek words. *Para-* is a Greek prefix, meaning "alongside," "at the side of," or "along with but just beyond." *Phrase* comes from the Greek *phrasien*, meaning "to speak." To paraphrase someone in helping, then, is to literally walk alongside their words with your own words and is another way to convey empathic understanding to a client. The word *paraphrase* has come to mean conveying a single thought in a few, well-chosen words. A paraphrase is a brief comment used to restate the content of a client's message. This restatement has several objectives. A paraphrase can help clients articulate their ideas or help them focus on a particular situation, person, object, or idea by drawing attention to the content. A paraphrase also conveys to clients that the helper intends to walk alongside them. Finally, a paraphrase conveys understanding of the client's content.

Four steps help create an effective paraphrased response. The first of these is to recall the message. To do this, helpers must attend to their clients and often covertly repeat or restate the message to themselves. Second, the content part of the message must be identified. Once clients begin to fill the verbal space in the room with words, it may be difficult to focus on the essential content of the stories being told. Often helpers find it useful to ask themselves the same types of questions that good reporters are advised to ask, such as "Who are the key players in this story?" "What is the situation being described?" "When did this take place?" "Where was all of this happening?" and "How did this happen?" An equally useful question is "What idea is she or he trying to express?" when a client is stating an idea or belief. Helpers then check in with themselves to see if answers to these questions are missing or confusing. If so, a clarifying question may be in order. (See Chapter 5 for a discussion about clarifying questions.)

Once the helper is clear about the content of the client's message, the third step involves translating the content into the helper's own words; then in the final step, this translation is suggested to the client for his or her consideration. The helper must learn to restate the main idea without adding or changing the meaning of the statement but must still avoid parroting the client's comments. A statement like "Sounds like you think . . ." or "Seems like you are seeing . . ." can be captured in a formula that involves a tentative stem followed by a helper rephrase of what the client just said.

Paraphrasing
"[tentative stem] + [helper rephrase]"

The client determines the accuracy of the helper's paraphrase, and client feedback about accuracy is usually immediate. Clients may give helpers verbal or nonverbal feedback. A wince probably communicates that the paraphrase is off the mark. Hesitation or a pause in the client's reports may indicate that the paraphrase was either just beyond what was said or did not really capture it. Nodding, whether slowly or rapidly, most likely conveys a client's sense of being understood.

Effective paraphrases can also be followed by verbal confirmations, like "Yeah," and the client continuing to elaborate on the theme or story. Ineffective paraphrases are most often followed by a statement, like "No, not really," which then may be followed by clarifying remarks by the client. If it seems to the client that her or his content was not understood, the client may simply respond, "Huh?" All of these responses to the paraphrase serve as immediate feedback to the helper about the accuracy of the paraphrase.

The first few attempts to paraphrase when developing this skill quite often miss the target. Beginning helpers may be reassured to know that even if paraphrases are inaccurate, they can still be quite

EXERCISE 3.1

Paraphrasing

For this assignment, you will need a partner. Together with your partner, select a topic about which it is nearly impossible to not have an opinion. Something like abortion, same-sex marriages, euthanasia, slavery reparations, and so on would work well for this exercise. Nearly everyone has an opinion about these controversial issues. After selecting a topic, select someone who will be the first speaker. The first speaker's assignment is simply to tell her or his opinion about this subject. The first speaker should offer about a paragraph's worth of opinion. (I know that you may have more, but for this exercise, your opinion is just a vehicle to practice paraphrasing.) When finished, the listener should attempt to paraphrase what was said and establish that the paraphrase is correct before going on to the next step. The next step is for the person who was listening to give her or his opinion about the topic. The listener (who was the first speaker before) is now required to paraphrase and receive confirmation that the paraphrase is correct before continuing to offer more opinions about the topic. This process can continue until all opinions have been aired and heard correctly or until you run out of time or energy for the process.

useful in furthering the interaction. So although some helpers may be embarrassed about not paraphrasing accurately, remember that both accurate and inaccurate paraphrases can be helpful. Either the client elaborates on the story being told or clarifies that the helper did not understand her or him fully. Either way, the paraphrase draws attention to the content of what has been said and facilitates further discussion and exploration of the client's perspectives.

To summarize, the process of paraphrasing involves recalling the client's message, identifying the content, translating the content into the helper's own words, and then offering those words in a brief statement to the client. Once the paraphrase is offered, the helper attends to the client's responses to determine whether the paraphrase accurately captured the content.

SUMMARIZING CONTENT

After a number of interchanges have taken place in which a helper has accurately paraphrased what a client is saying, it may be appropriate to summarize an overarching theme found in the statements. The word *summarize* comes from the Old French *sume* and *some* and the Latin *summa*, a superlative form of *superus*, indicating "that which is above or beyond." To sum up means to add up or collect things into a whole and then to condense them or put them into a few words or briefly review them.

In the case of professional helping, the things being gathered are the helper's paraphrases. Summarizing is a microskill that involves gathering together several paraphrases and offering a client a condensed version of a broader theme that may connect them. This review of what has been said allows both the helper and the client to identify themes and to tie together or link multiple elements of the interaction. It can provide organization for clients by giving a concise, accurate, and timely overview of the topics discussed. It can also serve to focus a client who is feeling overwhelmed after rambling or reporting on a number of topics. Summarizing can provide clients with a source of feedback by creating meaning and organization from a number of vague or ambiguous messages. Finally, summarizing responses are used to begin identifying common themes and patterns that become apparent after several interchanges or meetings. Identifying common themes and patterns facilitates both helper and client recognition of the general topics, issues, or difficulties on which the client needs to focus during subsequent conversations.

As with the paraphrase, the first step in summarizing is to attend to client messages. With the summary statement, however, helpers appraise both client messages and their own accurate paraphrases over a period of time before selecting the critical dimensions of a client's statements. Then the helper is in a position to identify the common themes in the messages. Once these factors are considered covertly, the helper is ready to summarize.

Summarization offers an abridged version of the recapitulated or restated messages or themes for the client to review. By offering this abbreviated version of the interaction to the client in a tentative form, the client is empowered with the final say about the accuracy of the meaning. I recommend choosing informally worded stems like "So taken altogether, it sounds like . . ." or the even shorter "So, sounds like . . ." to summarize. Using the word *so* to introduce your thoughts creates a bridge between the client's stories and explanations and your recap of what has been said. The tentative use of the phrase "sounds like" leaves room for the client to feel comfortable confirming, clarifying, or disagreeing, as needed. The formula for summarizing then would look like this:

> **Summarizing**
> "[bridging word] + [tentative stem] + [brief review of theme(s)]"

To summarize, after attending to, clarifying, and paraphrasing a number of client messages, the helper may be able to identify and recap themes from the interaction. The helper offers a brief summary of themes to the client using a simple tentative stem and the helper's synopsis of what has been said.

RATING HELPER RESPONSES TO CONTENT

Listening to content can be variously effective. When a helper listens most effectively, accurate paraphrases and summaries will communicate understanding and an ability to focus on what is most relevant.

In addition, the client will recognize that the helper not only hears the major message, but also can go behind the words to capture the underlying meaning. Listening to content can be rated using a 4-level scale similar to the one for nonverbal listening (see Chapter 1). In the case of listening for content, rating the responses pivots on the accuracy and timing of the helper responses.

Level 1 Response. This level indicates that the client's messages have been glaringly misinterpreted. This can occur when the response reveals little awareness of the content about which the client is speaking or when a helper response is given at an inappropriate time.

Level 2 Response. This level indicates responses that partially capture the content about which the client is speaking. Partial understanding can occur if the helper only caught part of the story or only part of the importance of what was said, or if the response is a superficial restatement of a client's story.

Level 3 Response. This level is a component of what is called "interchangeable empathy" (Carkhuff, 1977) or "primary empathy" (Egan, 1994). It indicates that the helper's responses accurately captured the messages conveyed by the client and that the helper briefly and succinctly communicated them back to the client. The client response confirms either verbally or nonverbally that the helper's responses are accurate enough to allow continued reporting.

Level 4 Response.   This level indicates responses that demonstrate precise accuracy and even go a bit beyond what has actually been said to capture the meaning behind the actual statement. Robert Carkhuff (1969) called this "additive empathy"; Gerald Egan (1994) referred to it as "advanced empathy." A restatement that is additive or advances a client's meaning must first be met with confirmation not only of accuracy, but of precision (e.g., "Exactly!"). It then results in a client adding more or a different angle to their report, like "you know what else . . ." or "I hadn't thought of it before, but now that you say it, I think it might be true." Clients not only continue to tell their story with this type of response but examine new or previously unmentioned aspects of the idea or experience. According to Carl Rogers (1977), a helper who can enter a client's private world may not only be able to clarify the messages of which the client is aware, but even those messages just below his or her level of awareness. This may sometimes enable helpers to add inferences to clients' statements or to draw implications from what was said.

As an example, suppose a client says, "I don't want to just pick a major so that I have one. But there's so much to think about. Like what if I don't like it. True, I need to graduate, but if I don't like it, I'm not gonna stick with it. And what if I can't get into the program I want, then what?" Helper responses to each of the four levels on the scale might sound like this:

> *Level 1 Example.* "Get a grip! You don't have to like your major to graduate with it." This response ridicules the client, shows a lack of compassion about the difficulty of choosing the major, and ignores the client's meaning. The client did not ask for a quick fix to the problem of finding a major; the client indicated that he had been overwhelmed by all of the things to consider in choosing a major.
>
> *Level 2 Example.* "If you don't know what some of your options are, you might want to check with someone in the career counseling department." This response still offers advice about fixing without conveying an understanding of the situation or the importance of the situation to the client. The response does nothing to involve the helper with the client's concerns or to convey an understanding of the client content.
>
> *Level 3 Example.* "It sounds like you are looking for something that will not only allow you to graduate, but that you'll also like." This response attends to the surface content and supports the client's search as valuable. It shows openness to further dialogue about the situation.
>
> *Level 4 Example.* "Now that you can see graduation ahead, it sounds like you've been considering a number of questions, like whether you'll find a major that you can enjoy and also one that you can qualify for." This response goes beyond the statement by attempting to pay attention to the underlying message and identifying the context, tone, and implications of the statement.

The process of attending to, listening for, restating, and summarizing the content of a client's reports is an important part of communicating empathy to a client. Chapter 4 focuses on developing an empathic understanding of a client's emotional experience.

EXERCISE **3.2**

Listening for Content

Audiotape a lengthy conversation (about 20 minutes) with someone during which you listen to the content of what is being said and attempt both paraphrasing and summarizing kinds of responses. Afterward, transcribe your audiotape and evaluate your responses using the 4-level scale. Type the number next to each response that best indicates its level of effectiveness. Next, type in brackets, next to each of your responses, what you thought you were demonstrating or not demonstrating in your response.

In addition to scoring and marking the transcript yourself, make a copy of it with your evaluation and rationale deleted or erased. Give a clean copy to a classmate to rate your responses and give a rationale for the rating chosen. Your classmate will serve as a previewer. After she or he has previewed your transcript, offered you feedback on the assignment, and been thanked by you, hand in this assignment and get feedback from the professor about your responses and ratings.

CHAPTER

4 Reflecting Feelings

Empathy is demonstrated by attending to and matching clients nonverbally, by being able to restate the essence of a client's content, and by reflecting a client's feelings. The word *reflection* comes from the Latin prefix *re-*, meaning "to return," and *fleciere,* meaning "to bend." To reflect is to bend back as in reflecting light, sound, or heat. A mirror is an object designed to reflect images that allow people to see themselves or their surroundings. In helping, reflection refers to the process of returning to a client an image of her- or himself. Reflecting is also used to refer to the process of mirroring a client's feelings so that he or she may observe and explore them more fully. Reflecting is to feelings what paraphrasing is to content. Both paraphrasing and reflecting convey empathy for a client by communicating understanding of what the client's experience and world is like. Verbal responses that focus on and convey awareness of client feelings and then name or label the feelings accurately are sometimes called *interchangeable empathy* (Carkhuff, 1977) or *primary empathy* (Egan, 1994).

The ability to build a foundation of content that has been accurately restated in the helper's own words and of accurately labeled feelings can be thought of as laying an interchangeable base of responses (Carkhuff, 1977) or building a foundation for the helping relationship. While Chapter 3 emphasized the skills necessary to convey an understanding of the content of a client's message, this chapter focuses on listening to, understanding, and reflecting the affective state or feelings someone has about what she or he is saying and the personal meaning the experience has for the client. Several listening skills associated with understanding feelings are included.

The chapter begins with a comparison of paraphrasing and reflection, outlines basic reflecting skills, and continues with descriptions of more complex skills. Accurately selecting the general category and intensity of a client's feeling from a feeling word vocabulary and then conveying that choice to a client facilitates the **interchangeable responses** that allow the helper to gain access to the client's feeling experience. Adding the content from paraphrasing is more complex than reflecting a feeling word alone, but it begins the process of putting the client's affect into a context. Finally, finding the personal meaning in what the client is saying involves zeroing in on what a client is saying about her- or himself in her or his reports.

THE DIFFERENCES BETWEEN REFLECTING AND PARAPHRASING

Before proceeding to the skills of reflecting, it is important to understand the similarities and the differences between reflecting and paraphrasing. The portion of a client's reports that conveys information, describes an event, or contains references to events, people, objects, or ideas is the content or the cognitive part of the message. Another part of the message concerns the client's feelings about the content. This is referred to as the affective or feeling part of the message or, in a more concise term, as the client's *affect.* So, paraphrasing attends to the content or cognitive part of a client's reports, while reflecting attends to the feelings or affective part of the client's experience.

EMPATHIC RESPONSE

Both paraphrasing and reflecting are important elements in communicating interest and concern for the well-being of a client. Both facilitate a client's perception that she or he is being understood. To the extent that the helper's nonverbal and verbal tone, pacing, and word selection match that of the client, clients are more likely to perceive helpers as empathic (Maurer & Tindall, 1983). Empathy is a complex cognitive and emotional state in which one person is able to know her own perspective, while at the same time perceiving what another person perceives. This perspective is so clearly perceived that one feels it as the other person would and imagines responding as the other person's perspective or values would dictate (Jordan et al., 1991).

Helpers who know themselves and their worldview well, yet suspend it momentarily while seeing the world from the client's perspective—in a sense juggling both worldviews—achieve empathy. Putting oneself into someone else's place, even if only for a brief period of time, and seeing and feeling another's perspective is both a powerful and an empowering skill. Demonstrating empathy for another builds rapport, elicits information, and fosters self-exploration that allows clients to see themselves more clearly and to assign value to what they see or to change it.

Reflection validates and reinforces a client's feelings and encourages a focus on the affective part of a client's experience. The timing of reflections can make the difference between a client feeling more depressed and a client recognizing depression and feeling like they can cope with it effectively. Reflections can also be threatening and intrusive to clients who are reserved or reluctant to express emotions. Incisive and ill-timed reflections may actually serve to push a feeling further from a client's awareness and facilitate a client's containment rather than expression or exploration of her or his feelings. Carefully considered and timely reflections can serve to help even the most reserved client move through developmental stages in the feeling process (Ivey, 1994). It is important to recognize the need to move with the client, to recognize individual, gender, and cultural differences in affective expression, and to proceed slowly and tentatively in reflecting feelings. Before offering a tentative reflection of a client's feelings, the helper goes through several steps of observing and attending to the feelings, matching a client's affect, and selecting accurate feeling words. Each of these steps is addressed in this chapter.

OBSERVING AND ATTENDING TO FEELINGS

Whereas clients may convey at least some content directly, feelings are often expressed nonverbally, may be out of the client's conscious awareness, or may be purposefully contained by the client. Reflection is used to encourage clients to articulate feelings, to experience feelings more intensely so as to facilitate change, or to become more aware of the feelings they may be ignoring. Effective reflection begins with observing the nonverbal behaviors that can offer clues to a client's feelings. A client's facial expression, posture, and tone of voice tell part of a story while their words tell another part. The first step in reflecting feelings then is to use the nonverbal skills described in Chapter 1 to attend to the client's nonverbal communication and the listening skills described in Chapter 3 to attend to the content of what the client is reporting.

MATCHING A CLIENT'S AFFECT

In addition to observing a client's nonverbal communication, many effective helpers begin to mirror the client's communication in their own facial expressions. It is not uncommon for helpers to begin feeling what clients may be feeling by this mirroring. Research shows that facial expressions both reflect feeling states and shape them (Izard, 1977). The extent to which helpers can reflect the facial expressions of the client may be the extent to which they offer another clue about the client's feeling experiences. In other words, trying on the facial expressions of another can actually assist helpers in identifying the other's feelings. Matching a client's affect or emotional expression is also another way to nonverbally communicate that the helper is right there alongside the client.

Once the helper pays attention to the content and the nonverbal communication of the client and begins to move nonverbally with the client, helpers can exercise their cognitive skill at both looking inside themselves and putting themselves into the client's place. "If I had experienced this or my body and face showed these things, what would I be feeling?" is the complex question effective helpers ask themselves next.

SELECTING ACCURATE FEELING WORDS

Selecting a feeling word that accurately reflects a client's experience is no small task. Most adult humans have large general vocabularies but far fewer words to describe affective states or emotional experiences (Rogers, 1957). Luckily, the process of identifying feelings accurately can be broken down into several smaller steps. The first step is to pick a general category into which the feeling belongs. Those who research and practice professional helping often identify basic and auxiliary categories of feelings (Carkhuff, 1977, 1979; Hill, Seigelman, Gronsky, Sturniolo, & Fretz, 1981; Ivey, 1994). As presented in Figure 4.1 (see pages 76–77), I use ten basic categories: happy, caring, depressed, inadequate, fearful, confused, hurt, angry, lonely, and guilty/ashamed

FIGURE 4.1   Vocabulary of Feelings

Levels of Intensity	Happy	Caring	Depressed	Inadequate	Fearful
Strong	delighted ecstatic elated enthusiastic euphoric excited exhilarated fantastic great marvelous overjoyed sensational terrific thrilled	adoring affection for attached to captivated by cherish devoted to enamored of idolize infatuated loving prize worship	alienated barren bleak dejected depressed desolate despairing dismal empty gloomy grief grieved grim hopeless	crippled emasculated finished good for nothing helpless impotent inferior like a failure powerless useless washed up worthless	desperate dread frightened horrified intimidated panicky paralyzed terrified terror stricken vulnerable

Moderate	aglow
	cheerful
	elevated
	glad
	glowing
	happy
	in high
	  spirits
	jovial
	lighthearted
	neat
	riding high
	serene
	up
	wonderful
		admiration
		caring
		close
		concern for
		fond of
		hold dear
		prize
		regard
		respectful
		taken with
		trust
		warm
		  toward
			awful
			demoralized
			discouraged
			distressed
			downcast
			horrible
			lost
			melancholy
			miserable
			pessimistic
			rotten
			sorrowful
			tearful
			terrible
			unhappy
			upset
			weepy
				defeated
				deficient
				immobilized
				incapable
				incompetent
				incomplete
				ineffective
				inept
				insignificant
				lacking
				no good
				overwhelmed
				small
				unable
				unfit
				unimportant
				whipped
					afraid
					alarmed
					apprehensive
					awkward
					defensive
					distrustful
					jittery
					jumpy
					nervous
					risky
					scared
					shaky
					threatened

Mild	contented
	fine
	good
	gratified
	pleasant
	pleased
	satisfied
		friendly
		like
		positive
		toward
			bad
			blah
			down
			glum
			low
			sad
				inefficient
				lacking
				  confidence
				uncertain
				unsure of
				  oneself
					anxious
					doubtful
					embarrassed
					hesitant
					ill at ease
					self-conscious
					shy/bashful
					uncomfortable
					unsure/timid
					worried/
					  uneasy

Confused	Hurt	Angry	Lonely	Guilty/ Ashamed
baffled	abused	bitter	abandoned	degraded
befuddled	anguished	burned up	all alone	disgraced
bewildered	crushed	enraged	cut off	exposed
confounded	degraded	furious	forsaken	horrible
full of	destroyed	galled	isolated	humiliated
questions	devastated	hatred/hateful		mortified
in a dilemma	discarded	indignant		sick at heart
in a quandary	disgraced	infuriated		unforgivable
perplexed	forsaken	nauseated		
puzzled	humiliated	outraged		
trapped	pained	pissed off		
	rejected	seething		
	ruined	vengeful		
	tortured	vicious		
	wounded	violent		
adrift	belittled	aggravated	alienated	ashamed
ambivalent	censured	agitated	alone	crummy
at loose ends	cheapened	annoyed	apart from	demeaned
disconcerted	criticized	antagonistic	others	guilty
disorganized	debased	belligerent	estranged	lost face
disturbed	defamed	exasperated	isolated from	regretful
embroiled	discredited	hostile	others	remorseful
flustered	disparaged	irritated	left out	to blame
foggy	exploited	mad	remote	
frustrated	invalidated	mean		
going around	laughed/	offended		
in circles	scoffed at	resentful		
helpless	mistreated	spiteful		
in a bind	mocked	upset with		
lost	overlooked	uptight		
mixed up	ridiculed	vexed		
troubled	scorned	vindictive		
uncertain	slammed			
	used			
bothered	minimized	bugged	aloof	at fault
uncomfortable	neglected	chagrined	distant	blew it
undecided	overlooked	cross	excluded	embarrassed
unsure	taken for	disgusted	lonesome	goofed
	granted	dismayed		in error
	unappreciated	impatient		lament
		irked		responsible for
		miffed		wrong
		perturbed		
		ticked off		

E X E R C I S E   **4.1**

Building a Feelings Vocabulary

This exercise will help you develop and enhance your feeling word vocabulary.

1. Make a graph with the ten feeling states categories along one axis and the three intensity categories along the other axis.
2. For each category of feelings, generate ten feeling words. Make sure that not all of your words fall into one intensity.
3. Distribute the words you think of throughout the intensity dimensions. For example, under *angry,* you might have *irritated* and *annoyed* under mild intensity; *pissed off* under moderate intensity; and *furious* or *enraged* under strong intensity.

To help you expand your feeling word vocabulary, try to come up with words other than the ones used as examples in the text. Think in terms of the various language forms clients may use. A client who uses a large and complex vocabulary may be able to identify with a feeling word like *morose;* someone who uses a simpler vocabulary might find a feeling word like *sad* a better fit. The object is to match the intensity of a client's experience in the tone and language of the client.

---

to begin this categorization of feelings. The helper's next step, then, is to select a general feeling state in which the emotional experience of the client can be categorized.

Take "Gary," for example, a student who is slouched in his seat, eyes downcast, voice slow and soft, who reports that he is pretty down. He and his girlfriend are having problems; his schoolwork is slipping and seems not to matter to him anymore. Life just seems too hard right now. Could you generally characterize his affective state? Of course, he is sad. That is a good start but not all there is to know to understand what life is like for Gary right now. It is also important to understand the intensity of his sadness.

Sad is one of the general categories used to facilitate understanding of feelings, but within each category are a number of words to describe feelings. One way to further catalog these feelings is to group them by intensity. Intensity indicates the strength of the feeling. Initially you may find it useful to think of the intensity of feelings in

terms of strong, moderate, or mild. Of course, there are other grada-
tions, but this is a start.

SELECTING WORDS AND PHRASES THAT CAPTURE FEELINGS

Once you have attended to the content and the nonverbal elements
of a report and then categorized the general feeling state and intensity
of the feeling, it is possible to formulate a response that captures the
feeling in a word or phrase. It is important to offer this to a client in a
succinct yet tentative way. The response should be succinct so that the
focus remains on the client and not the helper. To the extent that
helpers fumble with a not-quite-fully-baked response, they remove
the focus from the client. The response must also be tentative in order
to empower the client to explore and modify the reflection rather than
to assume that the helper necessarily knows what the client is feeling.

Effective reflection of feelings begins with the selection of an
accurate feeling word, but conveying this to a client begins with a
tentative stem. The simple formula for this type of response is made

---

EXERCISE 4.2

Identifying Feelings

This exercise will help you practice describing feeling states.

1. Pick a television drama that you ordinarily enjoy and pair up with a
   partner in your class who agrees to watch the same show. Sitcoms do
   not work as well in this exercise, because the aim of the actors is
   generally to bring out the comedy of a situation, a comedy that often
   revolves around misunderstandings in verbal communication.
2. Select one member of your dyad to watch the show with the sound
   off, seeing only the nonverbal communication of the actors. Identify
   the communications by feelings category and intensity at different
   points in the show. Have the second member of your dyad watch the
   show with the sound on and identify the feeling states and intensity
   of the feelings of the characters at different points in the show. You
   may wish to consult with your partner ahead of time to decide if you
   will compare notes after 5 minutes, or after a commercial break.
3. Meet to compare notes and rate your perceptions.

up of two parts: a group of words conveying the tentative nature of the helper's reflection of feeling that I call a **tentafier,** plus a feeling word. To this basic formula other, more complex elements of listening for feelings can be added:

Reflecting Feelings
"[tentafier] + [feeling word]"

For several reasons, tentative words are often used to preface or conclude observations, reflections, and paraphrases. It is rare in any relationship that the listener is more knowledgeable about someone else's experience than the reporter is about her- or himself. This is true in helping as well. In addition, it is important to offer a client the opportunity to think about what the helper is saying and correct or modify the statements in order to give the most accurate picture of her or his experience (Hill & O'Brien, 1999a). Both of these premises empower clients. Tentative stems include:

"It sounds like you're feeling . . ."
"It looks like you're feeling . . ."
"So, you've been feeling . . ."
"Did I hear you correctly?"
"I wonder if you're feeling . . ."

It is helpful to use the sensory mode that the client tends to express her- or himself in most frequently (Cormier & Cormier, 1991). Some clients are more auditory in their orientation and tend to speak in terms of "hearing what you said." Others are more visual and speak in terms of "seeing what you mean." A part of matching a client is paying attention to their usual mode of expression and creating a parallel response (Cormier & Cormier, 1991).

RATING HELPER REFLECTIONS OF FEELINGS

Just as it was possible to rate helper performance in the skills involved in observing, attending, and listening for content, it is possible to rate a helper's skills in reflecting feelings. The underlying expectation in this rating system is for helpers to achieve an interchangeable response with a client's feeling states. An interchangeable response is one that correctly identifies the general category and specific intensity, selects an accurate word to capture the experience of the client, and then delivers it while matching the client's affective tone and language tentatively enough for the client to continue reporting or to modify the helper's reflection. That is a lot to remember. The text and practice assignments are designed to facilitate a step-by-step development of these skills, while the rating system is designed to help you measure your progress in this development.

Level 1 Reflection. This level indicates that the helper has selected a feeling word that is not in the general category of the client's feelings. The helper has misread the nonverbal cues or misheard the content of the client's story, or both.

Level 2 Reflection. This level indicates that the helper has selected a feeling word that is in the general category of the client's feeling state but either has not correctly identified the intensity, has offered a word or phrase that does not exactly capture the feeling, or has offered it in a way that does not capture the affective tone of the client.

Level 3 Reflection. This level indicates that the helper has selected a feeling word that is in the general category of the client's feeling state, has identified and matched the intensity of the feeling correctly, and has used a tentative stem with the feeling word to reflect this to the client.

Level 4 Reflection. This level indicates that the helper was matching the client's nonverbal communication, appropriately timed the reflection, selected a feeling word response that reflected both the general category and intensity of the client's reports, and then reflected it to the client using a tentative stem and feeling word

---

EXERCISE **4.3**

Practicing Reflecting Feelings

Practice listening to a classmate and identifying feeling words and their intensity, using the basic formula for responding to them. Ask a third person to observe you and rate your responses as indicated in the rating system. Discuss why each rating was given and what could be done to improve your skills.

that matched the client's language, affective tone, and the implications of what the client said.

ADDING TO THE BASIC FORMULA FOR REFLECTING

Once helpers have begun to be able to identify feeling states and the intensity of those feelings accurately, it is time to contextualize the feelings. Giving feelings a context is done by adding the content to the reflection. The formula for this is:

Contextualizing Feelings
"[tentafier] + [feeling word] + [brief content paraphrase]"

Returning to Gary, the student mentioned earlier, an example of a response using all of these elements might be "It sounds like you're feeling pretty sad about how your life is going right now." Adding what the feeling is about gives a reason and context for the feeling. He is not just feeling sad, he is sad about something. Clara Hill and Karen O'Brien (1999a) suggest using a similar format of tentatively identifying the feeling and adding "because . . ." to offer meaning and context to the client's feeling. Determining either what the sadness is about or the reason for the sadness helps the client to perceive the feeling state in a more specific and circumscribed way. The feeling state is less likely to feel overwhelming if it has a context and some boundaries around it. It also conveys that the helper understands the client context and meaning.

Part of the context of a feeling is identifying the tense of a feeling. Is the client reporting a situation about which she or he had a feeling? Is she or he currently having a feeling or expect to have a feeling? Of course, the tense of a feeling can be more complex than past, present, and future differentiations, but again, accurately identifying feelings begins with the more simple distinctions and proceeds to more complex ones. When beginning to practice reflecting feelings, some recommend focusing on present feelings to allow clients to immerse themselves in their immediate experience (Hill & O'Brien, 1999a).

Another critical part of identifying a context for the client's feelings may be understanding her or his background and development and how each influences affective experience and expression. In *Intentional Interviewing and Counseling: Facilitating Client Development in a*

Multicultural Society, Allen Ivey (1994) discusses a developmental approach to affective expression that recognizes some of the individual, gender, and cultural differences in affective expression from a developmental perspective. Some of Ivey's ideas about multicultural developmental counseling are discussed more fully in Chapter 14, but it may be useful to briefly consider his developmental approach to affect.

It is important to be able to distinguish how a client's feelings vary in intensity and expression in order to better understand her or his world. Ivey (1994) organizes these variations into four emotional orientations:

> *Sensorimotor.* Clients whose orientation to emotions is sensorimotor can access the real and immediate experience of being sad, mad, glad, or scared at the moment it is occurring. Their emotional experience is primary, and there is limited separation of thought and feeling. They experience the emotions, rather than reflecting on them or exploring them. This client's challenge may be in being overwhelmed by too much emotion.
>
> *Concrete.* The client whose orientation to emotions is concrete can name the feelings she or he is having and even add an understanding of the reasons for the feeling. This moves clients away from direct experiencing, which may minimize the possibility of being overwhelmed by the feelings but may also be used to avoid feelings.
>
> *Formal-Operational.* Clients whose orientation to emotions is formal-operational can see the repetitive pattern to emotions and identify some of the **dominant themes** in their emotions. Their challenge is to allow themselves to experience the emotions as they are occurring.
>
> *Dialectic/Systemic.* Clients whose orientation to emotions is dialectic/systemic are very effective at analyzing emotions and the complexities of their emotions within the context. They have a strong sense of the reason for emotions but may move further away from directly experiencing their feelings.

No one orientation should be viewed as the goal or the most positive orientation. Each orientation is valuable, and each has limitations. Clients bring different strengths to exploring their emotional experience and may require different approaches from the helper to realize the limitations in their own orientation. The helper who can recognize a client's usual orientation can also begin to gently challenge the client to expand this orientation by focusing on modes less frequently used.

In addition to a general orientation to emotions that may influence clients' expression and needs in a helping situation, culture and background will influence clients' expression of emotions and needs with respect to their affective experience. A good friend of mine is an excellent example. She comes from a family in which one parent is Japanese and one parent Chinese. Both parents had emigrated to the United States from their respective countries as adults, and my friend grew up enveloped by the cultures of the United States, China, and Japan. My friend explained to me that in terms of emotional expression, she had been educated in the rationale that social order does not require or even appreciate extensive consideration of personal, individual, or inner feelings. Rather, meaning is derived from the social group and the role one has in it. For centuries, little emphasis had been placed on individual feelings; how one behaves in harmony or disharmony with the social group has been more important. This is not to say she was devoid of emotion. My friend did not convey her feelings as European Americans did. This was problematic for the European American faculty in the graduate program where she was studying to be a professional helper. While they espoused diversity and multiculturalism in theory, it seemed difficult for them to realize what this might look like in practice. Although Chinese and Japanese American, she was supposed to look and sound like European Americans if she was to become an effective counselor.

Open, public expression of feelings is not common among many Native Americans nor Latino, African American, or European men (Ivey, Ivey, & Simek-Morgan, 1997). Many women also resist sharing emotions, particularly with a male helper. Lesbians who have had to protect themselves against the ubiquitous wish to change their orientation may find sharing emotions with both men and heterosexual women leaves them too vulnerable (Falco, 1991).

From my personal life, I offer a second example. My partner and I grew up with very different backgrounds. No surprise to most that our expressions might also be different. In British and in Native American families like that of my partner's, anger is often expressed in a reserved way, while in my Anglo-European family, I felt free to express anger loudly and with much passion. I will always remember discovering, after an event that angered us both, that in my partner's quiet "I am so irritated by this," and in my shouting "Gawd, I'm so pissed!" (while gesticulating wildly), we were actually communicating the same reaction to the event with the same intensity of inner feeling. Before we knew to clarify this with one another, I would have used my background to interpret "I am so irritated" as not really angry at all, while my outburst would have been conversely interpreted as enraged to the point of frenzy. Neither would have been true. We were both equally angry about the event. By clarifying with each other what was meant and confirming the intensity, we came to better understand each other's feelings about that specific event but also about the feeling vocabularies we each used and our individual ways of expressing feelings. Our different word usage did not necessarily mean a lack of agreement.

With so many differences possible in emotional orientation and expression, should a beginning helper just give up now? My point is not to intimidate helpers. My point is to caution beginning helpers that real empathy requires that helpers both know themselves and their background and natural way of responding. Helpers need to learn how to temporarily suspend judgment about another's approach, while perceiving experiences through their worldview. It is important for helpers to recognize the strengths and limitations of their clients' approaches as well as their own strengths and limitations. To be effective means both knowing yourself and allowing yourself to know others in their context. Evaluating another from your frame of reference as though that were the absolute measure of worth is not empathy, it is judgment. Judgment is certainly important in certain contexts and at certain times. The initial stages of a helping relationship is not the time, nor is the helping relationship the context, for this type of judgment.

LIFE AFTER INTERCHANGEABLE RESPONSES

So, what happens after the helper is able to reflect feelings in an interchangeable way? For those who have seen tapes illustrating the beginning stages of helping, it often seems that reflecting simply goes around and around without aim or direction. That is partially correct.

The aim of laying a foundation of interchangeable base responses is to be able to build a dense foundation of empathy between helper and client before directing the conversation anywhere else. This foundation or base is important to the development of the helping relationship because it is unlikely that a client who does not feel fully understood or who cannot feel a helper's empathy will allow that helper to influence her or him in the direction to be taken in life. Nor should they. Imagine what it says about someone who is willing to let another influence her without being fully understood from her own frame of reference. It may seem gratifying to a beginning helper to feel so powerful and necessary, but this is certainly not a self-empowered stance for the client, nor would this prove to be an empowering stance for the helper in the long run.

An interchangeable empathy takes some time to establish. One or two accurate reflections do not build a foundation sufficient to support much weight. Many beginning helpers err by rushing too quickly into planning for action or problem-solving (Hill & O'Brien, 1999a) in the mistaken belief that helping is "doing." Carl Rogers (1957) reminded us that empathy is a state of being that puts one in tune with another.

Following the establishment of an interchangeable base of empathy, helpers begin to zero in on the personal meaning a client attaches to their own reports (Carkhuff, 1978). What are the clients saying about themselves in their statements? Helpers then begin to identify dominant themes in clients' reports, create a more complete picture of the personal context of clients' affective worlds, and set the stage for more advanced helping skills that facilitate changes.

PERSONAL CONTEXT

A client's personal context is comprised of her or his ethnic, ability, gender, and orientation backgrounds, as well as the difficulties, limits, and problems a client perceives in her or his current approaches and goals. In other words, clients have both a background that reflects and shapes where they have been and where they are and a picture of where they wish to go. After building an interchangeable base of a number of responses in which the helper correctly identifies the client's feelings and the reasons for those feelings, it is appropriate for the helper to accurately state the client's problems and goals in her or his own personal terms. Chapter 5 will focus on this next step in listening to and understanding a client, which begins the process of initiating further action.

EXERCISE **4.4**

Reflecting Feelings and Self-Assessment

This exercise will give you practice in reflecting feelings and in self-analysis.

1. Audiotape yourself reflecting feelings first with someone you know and then with someone you do not know as well. While you are listening, reflect the affective state of the person you are listening to at least six different times, illustrating your ability to lay down an interchangeable base.
2. Transcribe your tape and identify each of the reflections that you attempted by writing "feeling reflection" next to it. Rate each attempt on the scale from 1–4. Explain briefly why you think the rating is appropriate (e.g., "client response [nodding and saying "yeah" with emphasis] seemed to confirm the timing and appropriateness of my reflection" or "client response seems to indicate this was premature or off base").
3. Give the transcript to a classmate for feedback about your reflections and your self-ratings.
4. Turn the assignment in to your professor for additional feedback.

CHAPTER

5 Asking Questions

The role of the client in a helping process involves offering information about internal and external experiences that may be confusing, vague, or ambiguous for both clients and helpers. When a client's experiences, thoughts, or feelings are unclear, asking for more information is certainly useful to the helper. Sometimes exploring an experience, a thought, or a feeling further can be useful to the client as well.

The process of gathering more information from clients has been referred to with various words—*question, probe,* and *clarification* are the most commonly used. Although these words have been used almost interchangeably to refer to the process of requesting more information, each word has a slightly different connotation from the others that may be interesting to consider. Question and **inquire** have similar and overlapping roots. The word *question* comes from the Latin word *questos,* for "seeking" (as in a truth) or "an inquiry." The word *inquiry* comes from the Latin word *inquirare.* It is a compound word made up of the prefix *in,* meaning "into," and *quirare,* meaning "to seek" or "to search." Inquiry literally means "to look into." Both inquiring and questioning refer to the process of seeking information through asking.

Probe is a verb taken from the Latin *probare,* meaning "to test" or "to prove." To probe, then, is to search or investigate with great thoroughness in order to test or prove something. Some authors (e.g., Okun, 2002) use the word probe to indicate any open-ended effort to obtain more information that does not include a question. Interestingly, the noun *probe,* also based on the same Latin origin, is an instrument used to poke around in a wound in order to investigate. So the connotations of the verb *to probe,* while indicating thoroughness or depth of investigation, also appear to indicate more intrusion than the verbs to inquire or to question.

"To clarify" comes from the Latin *clarificere,* which is a compound word made up of *clares,* meaning "bright" and "clear," and *ficere,* meaning "to make." A clarifying response, then, is one that is designed to make clear the client's narrative. It may be used to check helper perceptions (Brammer & MacDonald, 1996), to establish what topic or focus is most important to a client, or to request further information or elaboration. Picturing a metaphor derived from the physical world may help to illustrate this concept. Windows in a building allow people to view what is inside or observe the world outside. If the windows are not clean, you may still find it possible to see vague shapes but difficult to distinctly observe some of the details. Washing the windows (or breaking them!) will create a clear, bright, easy view; however, as anyone who has ever washed windows will tell you, glass often requires a second and sometimes even a third washing before all the streaks are removed and the outside world is clear. In a sense, clients' stories, reports, or narratives are windows into the worldview that makes them who they are. It is not reasonable to assume that only one look through the window or looking through an unclean window would allow the helper to see a client's world or perspectives distinctly. Realistically, it may take a couple of tries before the story of a client's world is apparent. Clarifying responses are one way that helpers begin to make the perspectives of the clients clearer and brighter. While making things clearer and brighter for the helper, this process often makes things clearer and brighter for the client as well.

Whether seeking information by asking, probing in order to test or prove something, or hoping to see a client's world or perspective more distinctly, asking for more information is a very important skill for helpers who want to understand a client's experience. The most common way to ask for more information is through questioning or making direct requests. Questions can encourage clients to:

- clarify their experiences,
- check out unclear helper perceptions,
- focus on a topic most important to a client or focus a session according to client expectations,
- encourage depth or intensity of exploration of feelings that may lead to the release or expression of emotion,
- help clients hear what they are saying so they can identify thoughts and perhaps even map a different way of thinking, and
- request further information or elaboration (Brammer & MacDonald, 1996; Cormier & Cormier, 1991; Hill & O'Brien, 1999a; Okun, 2002).

The process of asking questions in helping, although important, is not without risks. The risks revolve around two problems. Many people have negative experiences with questions, and many who ask questions have poor skills. A poorly asked question will easily elicit defensiveness, guilt, or anger. This is a matter of skill-building and often what helping focuses on is overcoming past experiences and reclaiming new uses of old processes. Maybe an even more difficult risk in question-asking is the challenge of using a skill in which one person gets to ask questions and the other person is expected to respond. Many view the process of helping as involving an uneven distribution of power in a relationship (e.g., Jordan et al., 1991; Miller, 1982; Rawlings & Carter, 1977; Sturdivant, 1980) with particularly serious implications for those who have been historically disempowered like women; gays and lesbians; and people from ethnic, cultural, or religious minority backgrounds (Ivey, 1994). So, before continuing with the usefulness, precise skills, and reasons for asking questions, I consider briefly the issue of power and question-asking.

QUESTIONS AND POWER

The person asking questions in any interaction is controlling the conversation, at least for that moment. He or she is controlling the topic being addressed and often the parameters of what constitutes a satisfactory answer. In fact, asking questions can be a purposeful attempt to exact control over another person or a group of people. Most of us can picture someone who dominates the verbal space at, let us say, a family gathering by asking many questions. While annoying at a party, there are occasions when this type of question-asking can benefit clients. For example, if a client is feeling or behaving in an out-of-control fashion, asking questions, even *many* questions, can be used to provide structure to the interaction, which may then feel less overwhelming to the client. Still, helpers are cautioned about using too many questions or conducting sessions using questions primarily (Hill & O'Brien, 1999a).

A helper who asks too many questions or conducts whole interactions using questions primarily is going to be perceived by a client as controlling. Some clients will respond to this by passively awaiting helper direction; others will get angry about it. Still others will accommodate the helper's control of the session and then resist the helper more indirectly when the opportunity arises. While helping relationships are by nature uneven in the distribution of power, if one purpose of helping is to empower clients, it is important to challenge the use of any strategy that takes control away from the client. This does not mean that helpers should not ask questions. Rather, helpers should be mindful of the unevenness of the helping relationship in general and pay attention to the number of questions used in any given client meeting in particular.

The disempowering nature of questioning aside for a moment, the reality is that often helpers need more information in order to be helpful to, to empathize with, and even to empower their clients. At their best, questions, inquiries, and clarifying or probing comments are employed to obtain more information. They can be used for a variety of purposes, such as (1) to begin an interview; (2) to invite or encourage clients to discuss topics that are relevant to them; (3) to explore different parts of a topic or a concern, or to add information; (4) to encourage clarification or focus; (5) to elicit examples of specific behavior so that the helper can better understand a client's experience, situation, thoughts, or feelings or so the helper can better assess a client's overall functioning or problems; or (6) to ask for or encourage expressions of feelings. After a brief examination of the types of questions generally used by professional helpers, each of these uses will be considered.

TYPES OF QUESTIONS

Questions can be thought of as either open or closed. A **closed question** is one that limits the possible responses a client may make. In quantitative research, it is useful to limit the range of responses someone can give to a particular stimulus so that responses can be summarized across many participants and an aggregate statement made about how many people believed this or experienced that. In assessment processes based on such research, questions may limit client responses for comparative purposes. It is often helpful to know whether a client's behavior falls within or outside the limits of what others do. In general, closed questions are used when a very specific, brief fact is the objective. For the purposes of a helping relationship, closed verbal questions are used infrequently because, in general, helpers are seeking more elaborate information, rather than less, and

seeking information relevant to the unique experiences and circumstances of clients, rather than comparisons between that client and a
group norm.

An **open question** is one that invites clients to tell more and
encourages clients to tell it in their own way. Beginning a question
with "what" may establish various facts and details. "How" questions
request information about people, procedures, or processes. "When"
and "where" questions are seeking information about a context for the
report. "Who" clearly indicates that the helper would like more
information about the people involved. Examples include "What can
you tell me about that experience for you?" "How would that be for
you?" "How would you feel about that?" "When I said that, what were
your reactions?" "Where were you when that took place?" and "Who
were you with?" The following are examples of closed and open
questions about the same event.

- Closed question: "Did you get a decent grade on that exam?" (This
question can easily be answered with "Yes" or "No.")

- Open question: "How did you do on the exam?" (This question
requires that someone give more information about his or her performance.)

- More open question: "What did you think about that exam?"
(This question invites clients to give information that could include
their performance or their opinion of the exam process, content, or
maybe even the course.)

One gauge for a beginning helper of whether a question is open
or closed is the length and depth of a client's response to the question
being asked. If the client can find a way to respond with only a yes or
no, chances are the question was closed or relatively closed to other
responses. Studies have shown that clients rate open questions as
moderately helpful and believe that this type of question can lead to
exploration and experiencing (Elliot, 1985; Hill et al., 1988).

"Why" questions can be open questions, but they tend to elicit
defensiveness (Hill & O'Brien, 1999a). They are used to establish
reasons for thoughts, feelings, or behavior, and they come with a
hidden expectation that clients will justify themselves or an action.
In fact, "why" question are often suggestions, judgments, or approval
in disguise. Consider, for example, the question "Why did you [do/

EXERCISE 5.1

Opening Up Closed Questions

Closed questions limit or even end a dialogue, assume a "correct" answer, and convey judgment. Practice opening up closed questions by reframing the following closed questions as open ones:

1. "Aren't your parents helping you with school?"
2. "Do you always argue with your roommate?"
3. "Do you try to help out at home?"
4. "Surely you love him/her?"
5. "Really, you want to leave home?"
6. "Do you enjoy being with that type of person?"
7. "You've never married?"
8. "Have you stopped fighting with your husband/wife/partner?"
9. "Shouldn't you consider what your family might think?"
10. "Do you want to do something about your problems?"

---

think/feel] that?" If this question were made into a direct statement, it would be clearer that it is actually being used to suggest that you should not have done that. "Why do you think that?" communicates that the questioner probably does not agree and that the recipient of the question had better be prepared to argue their position. "Why do you feel that way?" can also convey that you should not feel that way or that you should be feeling another way. Since feelings are fairly spontaneous and uncontrollable (even though the behaviors associated with them are controllable), critiquing them is seldom useful for a client. For all of these reasons, "Why?" does not serve a very useful purpose, but particularly in helping situations, there is little point to enhancing a client's defensiveness or asking that they justify themselves.

QUESTIONS THAT BEGIN AN INTERVIEW

Although many clients will simply enter a helping situation and begin talking, others require a prompt or a signal from the helper, who represents authority, to give them permission to begin telling their stories. In these situations, a generic, nonthreatening opening question can serve as such a prompt. "What brings you here today?" was my standard until a particularly concrete client responded, "The bus." That interchange gave me enough pause to consider other options. Other options can include questions like, "How is it going?" "What's going on for you today?" "What can I help you with today?" In each case, the helper is making a request. Clients, of course, can refuse this request and some do. Sometimes in the helping process, a useful question to have at hand is one that not only opens the discussion for the session but also promotes exploration of client expectations about the session. Questions like "What would you like to have happen in this session?" or "What feelings are you having about coming in for help?" may elicit the client's perceptions about her or his interest and involvement in the helping situation (Hill & O'Brien, 1999a).

QUESTIONS THAT OPEN RELEVANT TOPICS

When running a bath or heating a bottle of formula for a baby, wise caregivers test the temperature so as not to burn the child. Many clients "test the water" in helping situations. They will dunk a general or somewhat ambiguous statement into the helping waters to see if the topic is something that the helper is willing to discuss. Asking a question can help the client know that it is. For example, when a client says, "Well, my family is kinda weird," a responsive question from the helper—"How are they weird?"—invites further information. Another possible response from the helper would be "Tell me more about your family." Although not framed like the other questions illustrated under the previous heading, statements like this one are considered in the same category because they ask for and elicit the same type of response. Both questions and statements request more information or exploration from the client. In this case, each helper response offers the client an opportunity or invitation to explore the topic of family "weirdness" more fully.

CLARIFYING QUESTIONS

Clarification involves gathering enough information about what the client is saying to make sure the helper is not confused about the content. While most of us use words to convey what we are experiencing, feeling, believing, and thinking, words alone do not facilitate understanding. For understanding to take place, listeners must grasp the meaning of what is being said as well. To grasp the meaning, helpers must first be clear about what a client has said. It is not the client's responsibility to be clear; rather it is the helper's job to clarify those things in a client's statements that are confusing or require confirmation. Making assumptions about meaning is not safe. The helper's best bet is to clearly establish that what is meant by a client is what is understood by the helper.

Beginning helpers often believe that a professional helper must understand everything being said and when they do not, the "fault" lies somewhere with them. Some new helpers are reluctant to admit to being unsure or confused. Professional helpers with more experience are quick to point out and admit that hearing the words a client says and actually understanding what a client means requires not only careful attending, but often some discussion to arrive at a shared meaning (Okun, 2002). In addition to clearing up confusing and missing parts of a client's story, helpers often need to confirm what they thought they heard. To accomplish any of these objectives, helpers use what are called clarifying responses or questions.

The first step in the process of clarification is to identify the content of the client's nonverbal and verbal messages (Cormier & Cormier, 1991). This identification has been addressed in more detail in Chapter 1 and Chapter 3. Before clarifying, the helper is encouraged to ask her- or himself briefly, "What has the client told me?" The second step is then to identify the part of the message that is unclear, confusing, or that simply requires confirmation (Cormier & Cormier, 1991). This sounds easy enough, but often may be quite difficult. Figuring out the presence of what you do not know exists in the first place can be daunting. A good way to start is for helpers to take a moment to stand back from what the client is saying and check whether the pieces fall together to form a complete picture or whether some parts of the picture are murky and indistinct. If there are none, select another type of helping response. If, however, some parts of the story are unclear, vague, or ambiguous, decide what needs clarification.

Once the part of the message that is confusing is identified, an appropriate clarifying response can be constructed. A clarifying response usually begins with a response stem like, "Do you mean . . . ?" or "Are you saying . . . ?" After the stem, the helper fills in the blank with a rephrase of that part of the message that was unclear or about

---

E X E R C I S E **5.2**

Clarifying Content

While listening to a friend, find something that is not clear to you and practice using one of the clarifying responses. Follow up with efforts to arrive at a shared understanding of what is being reported.

---

which they wanted confirmation. In a sense, then, clarifying combines a question with a paraphrase. Examples of clarifying responses are "Do you mean you would rather spend your vacation at the lake than stay at home?" or "Are you saying that you don't like that class?"

The approach of presenting a clarifying response as a tentative question has a couple of benefits. First, it conveys that the helper believes that it is the client who best understands her or his own meaning. Second, adding the rephrase of what was just said communicates that the helper was listening to the content. Demonstrating careful listening may be particularly important if the helper is about to indicate that the client's meaning was unclear. Together, the tentative question and the rephrase then create an opportunity to arrive at meanings understood by both client and helper.

In summary, the process of clarifying involves identifying the confusing or unclear part of the client's message and then rephrasing it for the client in a tentative way. A helpful formula for conceptualizing a good clarifying response is:

> *Clarifying Response*
> "[tentative stem] + [rephrase of confusing content]"

QUESTIONS THAT ELICIT EXAMPLES

Clients and helpers often negotiate the meaning of a particular report. When a client makes a statement that is not understood or that is idiosyncratic, it can be useful to inquire about the meaning that the client has attached to that statement. For example, I could not figure out the meaning of "the bomb" as a positive adjective applied to people or experiences. Coming as I do from a generation rife with peace activists, describing anyone or anything as a "bomb" would certainly not have been a positive judgment. While helpers can wait to see if they will get any clues from the context, they may also make mistakes from a misunderstanding. Asking a question like "When you say bomb, what do you mean?" invites and encourages examples that often result in a better understanding of the client's ways of viewing and describing the world.

In my area of specialization, I have learned that clients often refer to someone as having a "bad temper" when what they mean is that the person regularly abuses them. I have learned from these clients that understanding how they see the abuse, as well as getting a clear picture of what has been going on, is best served by asking for examples. A question that will elicit examples resulting in a more detailed picture of the actual behaviors included in "bad temper" is "What does that look like?" To get an even clearer picture of what is going on, assessment tools that utilize a number of open questions are available. In the example of clarifying the client's phrase "bad temper," an assessment tool such as Murray Strauss's Conflict Tactics Scale (1977) may add to the helper's understanding.

If a client says, "I'm gonna have to try to change this," a question like "What would a change look like for you?" is likely to result in not only more specific information for the helper but may facilitate a more detailed examination of the cognitive map a client has for how to go about making such a change. In a sense, then, asking a question that encourages more detail or examples about vague or ambiguous statements may enable both the helper and the client to clarify client thoughts and map out changes.

QUESTIONS THAT ENCOURAGE MORE EXPRESSION OF FEELING

Many people have learned to control the expression of their emotions or do not spontaneously express how they are feeling about a particular report. Sometimes helpers want to invite clients to talk about feelings or experience their feelings more deeply. Some theories of helping even suggest that helping clients to experience their feelings more intensely will enable them to solve their own problems (e.g., person-centered theories). In such instances, it may be useful to ask a question like "How did you feel when . . . happened?" or "How are you feeling right now?" or to make a statement like "Tell me what feelings you had about that." Each of these focuses clients on a specific experience that the helper wants them to tell more about.

These questions are also invitations to express the emotion associated with an experience and an opportunity for clients to explore what they felt.

Asking this type of question can be a powerful mechanism, particularly if it was not safe for the client to examine a particular feeling at the time they experienced it. For example, in my practice, I have found that people who are abused are often rightly frightened by the prospect of expressing any anger at the abuse or the abuser. They have accurately assessed the expression of anger to be dangerous. However, never expressing their anger about the abuser or their fear about expressing their anger, or expressing other anger has problematic consequences. Anger can act as a gauge of violation and as a motivating influence for change. Asking for an expression of the angry feelings in the presumably safe context of a helping relationship can allow recognition of the violation and permit the client to identify changes.

QUESTIONS THAT ADVANCE ASSESSMENT AND DIAGNOSIS

Questions can be used to assess problems in more detail or to help establish a diagnosis. Both formal and informal lists or inventories of interview questions are available that can be used to clarify such information as the nature, type, and frequency of behaviors. The Conflict Tactics Scale (Strauss, 1977) mentioned earlier is a series of structured interview questions in which the helper asks questions that clarify the nature, type, and frequency of different kinds of abuse. Welfare workers, for example, ask a series of questions designed to determine eligibility for government subsidies and needs for social services. Advocates in battered women's shelters ask a number of questions to help identify not only eligibility for housing, but also other legal services that may be helpful. To help decide on a course of action, crisis workers ask specific questions that establish whether a client's suicidal thinking is likely to result in lethal behavior. This is referred to as assessing suicidal lethality. Assessment in a helping context is the process of evaluating individual differences. It may involve interviewing, observation, or testing (Goldstein & Herson, 1984). Psychometrists focus more on testing as a way to assess, but the focus of this text is on verbal questions used to assess a client's experience, behavior, thoughts, or feelings.

In addition to assessing the nature, type, and frequency of various mental health and social problems, some professional helpers will be in the position of making diagnoses. The mental status exam is one example of a number of dimensions along which various questions are designed to facilitate broad diagnostic impressions. Helpers often ask many other questions to further differentiate one kind of mental health problem from another. For example, a number of structured interviews like the Structured Clinical Interview for *Diagnostic and Statistical Manual* (SCID) (Spitzer, Williams, Gibbon, & First, 1992) are patterned after the Decision-Trees Differential Diagnosis from the American Psychiatric Association's diagnostic and statistical manuals.

Just consider for a minute that many clients come into a therapy or counseling situation reporting that they are feeling depressed. Depression can take many forms and some forms require different responses from helpers or different responses from different types of helpers. Depressions following the death of a loved one, depressions due to a difficult life transition like going away to college, depressions that include hallucinations or delusions, and depressions that involve oversleeping or lethargy to the point of not getting up, not eating, and recurrent suicidal thoughts are different and may demand different responses on the part of the helper. It is important to be able to gather enough information to make assessments that differentiate between these types of depression. Such distinctions guide helper or client action and problem-solving. Questions are one tool that helpers use to make these assessments. Certainly other tools are available and can also be used for these purposes (e.g., listening for content and feelings; mental status exams; psychological tests or inventories).

GUIDELINES FOR ASKING EFFECTIVE QUESTIONS

Some clients are people of few words who can find a way to respond to almost any question with a yes, no, or short phrase. In most instances, however, a helper can elicit more information through skillful inquiry. This guideline gives ten suggestions for creating effective questions:

1. *Keep the questions short and simple.* This limits the intrusion and keeps the focus on the client.

2. *Avoid multiple-choice questions.* They are really just a variation on the yes or no response and they limit a client's responses. Well-designed multiple-choice tests can establish whether someone knows material well enough to select correct information from a number of options. In helping others, the aim is not to test whether clients can figure out the correct answer from among a limited set, but to offer opportunities through talking to explore the past and try out what could be in the future. Opening doors will be much more effective than closing them.

3. *Avoid questions for which a specific desired answer is sought.* If the helper has an opinion to offer the client or already knows the answer to a question, it is more direct and respectful to simply state that than to ask a question that begs for a specific answer. Questions like "Don't you think that your drinking has gotten out of control?" actually reflect a helper's opinion that the drinking has gotten out of control. Some questions in which the helper already has an answer in mind, but is hoping the client will say it, place clients in the position of "playing student" to the helper's "teacher." Waiting for a client to guess the right answer can easily be perceived as patronizing. Often it is.

4. *Avoid asking questions that satisfy helper curiosity alone.* A client's role does not include satisfying helper curiosity. The interested helper can use other references to gather more information, and asking questions out of curiosity alone runs the risk of being, what a professor in one of my graduate classes called, an "auditory voyeur." While initially offended by his accusation, I thought very carefully about this perception and what it might mean to me as a professional helper. His words gave me a clear and graphic picture of the possibility of a helper exploiting another's experience for her or his own pleasure or compulsion. Taking the role of an auditory voyeur, as with any exploitation, creates mistrust of a helper.

5. *Ask for detail necessary to clarify an idea or a picture but avoid excessive detail-seeking.* Requesting more detail than necessary conveys the message that the helper is primarily interested in the "what" of a client's life and not the client her- or himself.

6. *Watch the tone in the delivery of a question.* Even a well-intentioned, well-designed question can create problems if delivered in an abrupt or disinterested fashion.

7. *Timing is important.* Questions asked before a client is ready to elaborate can result in the client shoving the topic into unconscious oblivion for her or his own protection. The response to a poorly timed question will be "I don't know."

8. *Even clever, insightful, incisive, and well-timed questions should be used sparingly.* Insightful questions may facilitate focus and offer clients the opportunity to explore a relevant and useful topic in greater depth. However, they may merely serve to highlight the helper's brilliance. Too many questions that point out an area removed from the client's awareness can foster dependency on the helper's skills, rather than enhance the client's abilities. This will ultimately backfire since the overall purpose of any helping is actually to eliminate the need for help.

9. *Keep the number of requests for more information in any interchange small.* A large number of questions can be overwhelming to clients. In some cultures and among some people, asking too many questions can result in distrust of the helper (Ivey, 1994).

10. *If a client is already exploring a thought, feeling, or experience, there may be no need to question or ask for more.* Listen carefully and respond appropriately.

RATING QUESTION EFFECTIVENESS

The skillful use of questions is a function of several elements, such as (1) the relevance of the questions, (2) the depth of the questions, (3) the pacing and timing of the questions, and (4) the warmth, respect, and genuineness associated with the question (Doyle, 1998). These dimensions can be used to rate the effectiveness of questions on a 4-level scale.

> *Level 1 Questions.* Questions that are irrelevant, antagonistic, or accusatory; questions that satisfy the curiosity of the helper; leading questions; voice quality or body movements that communicate abruptness, authoritarianism, or disinterest. These types of questions usually distract the client from telling more about themselves or the topic being explored.
>
> *Level 2 Questions.* Questions about related but unessential information; poorly worded questions; multiple-choice questions.

These questions are likely to interrupt, if not distract, the client from conveying more information.

Level 3 Questions. Relevant, open, well-phrased questions, timed so that the client appears ready to answer them (one way to verify this is to note whether the client actually does answer the question). Voice tone shows concern and interest in the client. These questions are likely to be met with the client offering more information.

Level 4 Questions. Sparing questions that are phrased in a way that encourages going beyond the stated, superficial message and result in exploration of a different angle on a theme being examined by a client.

EXERCISE **5.3**

Using Questions Effectively in an Interview

Audiotape an interaction between you and someone you know. Illustrate an appropriate use of questions by:

1. Using a question to open the conversation.
2. Asking a question that opens a relevant topic.
3. Asking at least one open question that is followed by additional client information.
4. Asking a question that clarifies something about the other person's experiences, thoughts, or feelings.
5. Asking a closed question that results in a limited response.
6. Asking a "why" question that might be appropriate.
7. Asking a "why" question that elicits defensiveness.
8. Asking a question that elicits an example.
9. Asking a question that encourages more expression of feeling.

Transcribe your interaction, and beside each of your responses, place a mark to indicate your assessment of what you were attempting and how successful you thought you were in achieving your intention. Give the transcript of your tape to one of your classmates and ask her or him to review your effectiveness at illustrating each of the elements of this assignment. Turn in the assignment to your professor for additional feedback.

6 Preparing for Action

Prepare comes from the Latin *preparare* and the French *priparer*, both made up of the prefix *pre-*, meaning "before," and the root *parer*, meaning "to set in order; to be ready as for a specific action." Before taking other helping actions, the helper must facilitate preparation for these actions. Until now, the discussion of helping skills has focused on laying the foundation of empathy for a strong helping relationship. To ensure that clients are understood and that empathy and a strong helping relationship are established, helpers observe, follow, and match client's nonverbal messages, paraphrase and clarify the content of the client's reports, and reflect the client's feelings about his or her experiences. Once a solid, empathic helping relationship is established, it may be time to help clients prepare for action to solve problems. This chapter focuses on the skills used to lay the remaining groundwork needed before helpers begin the process of facilitating the many different actions clients can take to solve problems.

To set the stage or prepare for taking action, helpers must ensure mutual understanding of the client's assessment of her or his limitations and what the client wants to do about it. They must help the client's transition from content and feelings exploration to more focused exploration of dominant themes, to identifying points of empowerment, and finally to mapping a plan. In other words, before a client can launch an effective plan of action, both client and helper should be certain about what the client sees as the problem and what the client wants to do about the problem. Helpers who become too anxious to "do" often believe they know the way without this mutual understanding. Proceeding without client agreement can have difficult consequences.

I am reminded of the old story about the child who asks a parent where she came from. The conscientious parent, taking a deep breath, launches a detailed explanation of human reproduction, being careful to scale down the language for the child to understand. When finished, the parent, quite proud of his accomplishment, asks if the child has any questions. The child responds, "No, Johnny said he came from Boston and I was just wondering." In this story, the consequence of assuming clarity was perhaps amusement or embarrassment. In interviewing, counseling, and therapy, the stakes are often higher.

A number of advanced skills can be used to facilitate solutions to the problems clients encounter. Helpers may comment on their own previous experiences, their immediate observations, inconsistencies they have observed, or their interpretation of clients' behaviors. Some helpers offer guidance, advice, or evaluation of clients' behaviors. Each of these skills, however, requires client preparation and begins with a clear understanding of the client's perspective about what is needed. Research shows that clients who are more invested in the solutions are more likely to implement them (Goldfried & Davison, 1994).

Helpers who are going to empower clients to resolve difficulties and limitations themselves find it important to prepare for action by understanding the personal meanings, strengths, and limitations clients bring to their difficulties and what the clients themselves consider appropriate solutions. Helpers effect this preparation by unpacking clients' perceptions about themselves, their strengths and limitations, and where they want to go (goals). This assists clients to better understand the nature of their own situation and to develop resolutions that they perceive to be appropriate and valuable. The skills that follow involve listening for the personal context of the client's experience and identifying dominant themes, facilitating identification of the client's perceptions of her or his difficulties, and identifying the goals or where the client wants to go next.

LISTENING FOR PERSONAL CONTEXT AND IDENTIFYING DOMINANT THEMES

After laying a foundation of empathy in the helping relationship, the helper is in a position to listen even more closely to the personal context of a client's reports. This exploration of a client's personal context prepares the helper to find dominant themes, complete with the client's perspectives about her or his difficulties or limitations and what the client sees as her or his goals.

Summarization is the process of finding an overall theme in the content of client reports (see Chapter 3). Identifying a dominant theme calls on the helper to have listened carefully to both content and feelings and to have begun to recognize the themes that reveal what a client may be saying about her- or himself. These themes will not be found in one client report but must be determined over the course of a number of interactions. When a theme stands out, helpers call it a dominant theme.

A theme can dominate because of its recurrence or because of the intensity of the reports attached to it (Carkhuff, 1979). Once a helper observes a dominant theme, the theme can be covertly noted for future reference or it can be conveyed to the client and then checked out in much the same way used in summarization. Using a tentative approach allows clients to verify, modify, or disconfirm the theme. Reviewing the previous summaries allows both client and helper to see the emotional foundation of the relationship and the content foundation for distilling previous summaries into this particular theme. Checking out the identification allows clients to assume ownership of the theme. The formula for identifying a dominant theme then would look like:

> ### Identifying a Dominant Theme
> "[tentative stem] + [review of summaries] + [distillation of a dominant theme] + [checking out the accuracy of the helper's understanding of the dominant theme]"

An example of this kind of reflection might be "We seem to have been talking about this from several different angles: [summary 1], [summary 2], [summary 3]. Seems like all of the angles have revolved around [dominant theme]. Does that sound like what you've heard?" Take Jennie, for example, a student who has been regularly meeting with the professor to discuss her limitations as a beginning counselor. After several conversations, the professor might reflect, "We seem to have been talking about the challenges of this course from several angles: you're feeling discouraged with yourself for not getting these skills more easily, believing that this comes more easily to others, and wanting a career in which you can excel. Seems like all of these revolve around wishing this could be easier. Does that fit?"

EMPOWERING: IDENTIFYING CLIENTS' PERCEPTIONS ABOUT THEIR DIFFICULTIES AND FACILITATING OWNERSHIP OF GOALS

After identifying the dominant theme or themes, whether the helper chooses to reflect it to the client or hold it as an internal observation, the next step in the process is helping clients find their own points of personal power in the situation. Taking care not to blame the client for the difficulties they are experiencing, it is important to help the client find those actions that are within their control. This may sound like a subtle distinction, but it is a very important one to consider. In the theory section of this text, you will find a discussion of those theories that hold the client responsible for virtually anything and everything in her or his experience, and others that look almost exclusively to the social, political, and interpersonal milieu of the client to find the responsibility for problems. One thing that each helping theory could agree on, though, is the need for helpers to assist clients in finding those actions that, if taken, would enable them to feel more powerful and less limited. To do so, the helper actually begins by helping clients assess their limits or difficulties and then moves on to helping the client take personal ownership for solutions.

The type of response that may help a client begin to explore her or his perceived limitations or the personal meaning behind her or his perceived limitations combines a tentative stem, a feeling word, and a restatement of the client's perceived limitation (actually a specific type of paraphrase). The formula for this response is:

> ### Exploring Limitations Response
> "[tentafier] + [feeling word] + [perceived limitation]"

It takes the form of: "It sounds like you are feeling . . . because you cannot. . . ." The "you cannot" brings the client back to themselves to explore perceived difficulties and limits. This line of interaction then is focused on those ways in which the client feels powerless or limited in his or her power to effect change and will further set the stage for the client to see possibilities for action that may enhance a sense of personal power or efficacy in the situation. Let's return to Jennie. Each time they have met, the professor has found that their focus has been on Jennie's limitations, perceived limitations, or problems. The professor has been reflecting Jennie's

---

EXERCISE 6.1

Empowering Practice

Practice finding the personal meaning, limitations, and goals without attempting any resolution.

---

frustrations with this and summarizing the content of those frustrations. Today, the professor wants to help Jennie focus on how she is seeing herself and her limitations. To do this, the professor says, "You know your frustration with these skills has come up over and over again, and it sounds like you are feeling discouraged with yourself for not getting this more easily." Then the professor checks in with Jennie to see how this new route has fit the client's experience by asking questions like "Does that make sense to you?" and "Does that seem to fit for you?"

FACILITATING CLIENT GOAL-SETTING

After establishing where the client is now and her or his perceived limitations in a situation, the final step in preparing for action is to help empower the client to see where she or he wants to go next or what she or he wants. One way to do this is to combine the use of a tentative feeling and the perceived limitation with a tentative goal in a formula like:

> *Goal-Setting Response*
> "[tentafier] + [feeling word] + [perceived limitation] + [possible goal]"

This kind of response would look like "It sounds like you are feeling . . . because you can't . . . and you want to. . . ." So, if we go back to Jennie, our beginning counselor, the response from the professor might go something like "It sounds like you have been pretty harsh with yourself for not getting these things more easily and you want to feel better about your skills," or, if the emphasis is on competence instead of self-esteem, "It sounds like you've been getting discouraged with yourself about not getting these skills more easily, and you'd like to be able to." Once the client has recognized her or his limitation, assessed the personal difficulties in the situation, and conceptualized a goal, the client can begin to initiate action.

MAPPING A PLAN

By attending and responding to the client's experiences and reports, a helper prepares to understand her or his client's experience, and this understanding enables the helper to explore the experience in enough depth to understand the client's experience. Seeing the world through the eyes of the client or understanding her or him through the client's own frame of reference allows the helper to determine those behaviors that the client perceives to be a limitation or difficulty and which ones the client wants to see developed. Next, the helper begins to help a client initiate action or map a plan. Initiating action does not mean that the helper will be acting for the client, rather it means that the helper begins assisting the client in determining the next direction. Think of taking a trip across the country to a place you have never been. While it may be nice just to head out with little sense of where you may be going or when you will get there, if you want to be sure you are going to get there, you would probably consult a map and decide on a plan. The direction this trip takes should not be of the helper's making. It may be flattering to be thought of as the map maker, but if the helper has been listening to the thoughts and feelings of the client fully, the directions should emerge from the client's input and will therefore be in keeping with the client's perspectives.

Borrowing from learning principles and behavioral interventions, the next steps in this mapping process could be called (1) operationalizing the goal, (2) mapping the steps involved in meeting the goal and scheduling the time frames for the goal, and (3) identifying events, thoughts, and feelings that might enhance the possibilities of maintaining a newly learned behavior. Each of these steps is addressed in order.

OPERATIONALIZING THE GOAL

Operationalizing is a twenty-dollar word that in this case means knowing in very specific terms how to measure success or how particular actions serve to realize a specific goal. Recently, managed care organizations like HMOs have proliferated to the point of dominating professional mental health helping settings, and consumers have demanded more cost-effective services and greater accountability from professional helpers. As a result, it has become even more important for helpers to conceptualize a client's difficulties in small, attainable steps that can be concretely evaluated and reinforced. This holds the helpers accountable for their helping and also requires that helpers and clients begin to see the "how to" of achieving various helping goals. The question asked of clients takes the form of "How will we know when you've reached this goal?" If this were a trip you were taking, you would know you had arrived when some sign announced it. In helping, both helper and client have to figure out what the sign will say, but the principle is the same. Put into other words, the goal is operationalized when it is broken down into specific, observable, and measurable actions.

Returning to Jennie, the student who wanted to either feel better about her competencies or develop competencies more easily, the question for the helper becomes "How will I know when her goals are being met?" This can be posed as a question to the client, as in "How will we know when you've begun to get the material more easily?" or "How will we know when you feel better about yourself?"

Operationalizing Goals Response
"[how will we know when you have] + [statement of goal]?"

Once the client has been invited to specify those behaviors or events that will be operating to show achievement of the goal, this, too, can be paraphrased to enhance the client's sense of being understood and checked out with the client. So, assume for a moment that Jennie has identified her goal as feeling better about her competencies. One possible operationalization could be phrased as "It sounds like you want to be able to recognize your own competencies better, and this could be shown by the percentage of times that you mention competencies rather than limitations." The helper has now assisted the client in making the goal much more concrete. But the task is not yet complete. While the goal is more concrete, the client may still not see how to achieve it. I can know that I want to get to Chicago and still have no idea how to get there.

IDENTIFYING FIRST STEPS AND SETTING UP A SCHEDULE

The next steps toward preparing the way to action include helping clients to identify the first steps toward the goal and setting up a schedule for achieving those. To better understand these steps, consider examples of physical skills development. Many people find it easier to conceptualize the steps necessary for concrete physical actions than emotional or psychological changes. Just for a moment imagine that you are a parent who wants to help a child (Matthew) learn to walk. Matthew is not finished because he wants to be walking. He must begin to learn all of the steps involved in walking and then map a plan that allows learning each of the steps. The wise parent is not going to start the child off by standing him up and saying, "Okay now, walk!" For several reasons, Matthew's parents will first help him stand, then support him physically as he moves along with them, and then they will fade out the use of their hands. Matthew's parents would probably have him make small steps using the supports of walls and various household objects as he learns to support himself. Later, his parents would probably have Matthew—who at the same time was watching others doing the same thing—practice increasingly more steps until he could begin to take steps without supports.

As with any behavior, helping actions also follow a similar pattern of learning the steps to a particular goal, practicing the steps, then practicing increasingly more complex steps before the goal is reached. Regardless of the theoretical framework a specific helper uses, this pattern necessary to learning new behaviors is remarkably similar and borrows heavily from the psychology of both human and animal learning and conditioning.

Helping is not and should not be parental, and in the case of professional helping, unlike learning to walk, both helper and client can identify the next steps toward a goal. I recommend that both engage in a brainstorming exercise of determining the first steps. The helper can initiate the exploration by asking an open question like "I wonder what the first step toward that might be?" or "What do you see as the first thing to do?" Time lines can be set in a similarly negotiated fashion with direct, open questions. "How long do you think it might take before you could try that?" or "When should we check in on that?" are ways to ask the client to identify the time frame for accomplishment. Once the client actually takes the first step toward a change in behavior, the helper's role then shifts somewhat toward identifying and facilitating ways to maintain changes.

MAINTAINING CHANGES

Helpers may prompt or support clients through the beginning steps of learning new behaviors, but once a client has begun taking the steps involved in reaching his or her goals, it is important, as it is in any new learning, that the helper help the client create her or his own reinforcements for achievements. Newly acquired behaviors must be continually reinforced at first to help establish them as patterns. Once the new behavior has been established, it is possible to fade out the reinforcements to a more natural (i.e., intermittent) schedule (Sarafino, 1996).

Returning to the example of teaching a child to walk, when children are first learning, parents physically support them, then later encourage them to use walls or objects. Parents also often coo over every step the child first makes. As walking becomes the child's more established mode of getting around, parents comment on their child's abilities more sporadically, and the child begins finding things in walking that they themselves may not have discovered crawling. This can serve to increase the likelihood that the child will continue walking. These self-reinforcements serve to maintain the behavior much more effectively than a parent's constant comments about how wonderful walking is. Parents cannot always be handy to do this, and walking is not only beneficial to the parents, but to the child. But, before the child can find these self-reinforcing events, they must take the first steps, and someone often must help shape the behavior and then observe and applaud them for exhibiting it. The same thing holds true for clients. At first, the helper may encourage and offer words that applaud client accomplishment. Since one objective of professional helping is to empower clients and essentially work our way out of a job, it is important to help clients find ways to maintain changes for themselves.

To the helper who is already familiar with some of the theories of changing behavior, this past section must certainly sound like behavioral therapies. Actually, this is common to nearly all forms of counseling and therapy and many other helping professions.

Helping a Client Prepare for Action

In this exercise you will practice having an interaction that includes a difficulty and requires you to help the "client" prepare for action.

1. Ask a classmate to work with you. The classmate should be prepared to discuss an experience that includes a difficulty. Here are several sample difficulties, which are suggested to offer new helpers some practice without overwhelming your competencies:
   - Uncertainty about plans after graduation
   - Lack of clarity about graduation requirements
   - Uncertainty about a major
   - Problems with a boss
   - Problems with a work schedule
   - Roommate difficulties
   - Time-management challenges at school or work
   - Minor relationship difficulties with partner, date, or spouse
   - Struggles to be independent from family

   (*Note:* Avoid topics that involve traumas (like abuse), topics about which the person may feel ashamed, topics that include serious relationship conflicts, or topics that involve drug or alcohol dependency/abuse. Beginning helpers should have more practice before taking on these more complex issues.)
2. Audiotape yourself demonstrating an extended conversation in which you lay a foundation of numerous paraphrases and reflections; help the client find the dominant themes and personal meaning in the client's reports, and help explore the client's perspectives about the personal limitations or difficulties she or he is encountering; identify where the client wishes to go to resolve them.
3. Ask your classmate to offer feedback about the following:
   - How strongly did the foundation support the transition to identifying the dominant theme?
   - How accurately did the dominant theme reflect the problem?
   - How skillful was your transition in identifying the personal limitation or difficulty?
   - How well did you reflect the client's perceived goal?
4. Transcribe the part of this interaction that transitions from the content to the dominant themes, from empowering the client to mapping a plan.
5. Give your self-analysis to a classmate and ask her or him to review it for you.
6. Turn in the assignment to your professor for feedback.

WHAT IS NEXT?

Once the client has an action plan identified that includes (1) an operationalized goal, (2) the steps involved in reaching the goal and a schedule for achieving the steps, and (3) some things that would serve to increase the likelihood that they will continue the new behaviors, there are a number of more complex skills that helpers may use to assist the client in achieving his or her goals. These skills include immediacy and self-disclosure, confrontation, interpreting and evaluating, advising, and problem-solving. The next chapter fully describes these skills, which include advising, instructing, directing, suggesting, problem-solving, evaluating, immediacy, self-disclosure, feedback, interpreting, and confronting.

CHAPTER

7 Advanced Helping Skills

The word *advance* offers a sound foundation from which to construct additional, complex helping activities. Advance derives from the Old French words meaning "to forward" and the Latin words literally meaning "away from before." To advance, then, means to move further to the front, to bring forward, to promote, to improve or make better, to accelerate, to bring into view, and to furnish or supply for others. Helpers are asked to consider that the skills described in this chapter are not just skills that require a previous helping foundation, though they do. Neither are they simply more complex skills involved in professional helping, though they are. Rather, these skills also illustrate the specific direction of the client being guided or the process being facilitated by the helper. Each of the skills described in more detail in this chapter either brings into view, accelerates, moves further into the foreground, promotes, or furnishes for the client something that she or he has identified as a goal. In a very real sense then, it is not the helper's state of developing more complex skills that is referred to in the title of this chapter, it is the process of *advancing the client's goals* that guides the use of these next skills.

INFORMATION-GIVING TO ADVANCE A CLIENT'S GOALS

A component common to each of the more complex skills and critical to their implementation is implied. The helper must have established a pattern of interaction in which clients perceive themselves, their experiences, and their behaviors, ideas, values, and beliefs to have been understood and must have created the foundation upon which the actions being planned can be built. However, the insightful reader will quickly notice that in each of the more complex skills is another common critical component—the skill is used in the service of advancing the client's goals. However brilliant, insightful, experienced, or knowledgeable a helper imagines her- or himself to be, it is advancing the client's goals that remains the purpose of any helping.

So, once a helper has established an interchangeable foundation of empathy (e.g., through nonverbal listening, paraphrasing, and reflection) and understood what the client wishes to work toward (e.g., through personalizing the meaning or preparing for action), additional helping goals can take place. This additional helping may take many different forms. This chapter describes a number of different ways to advance a client's goals through information-giving. Other advanced skills unique to each brand of psychotherapy and counseling are also added to these in Part Two of this text.

Information-giving skills may be thought of as falling into three categories based on the source of the information. Some involve information based on expertise (advising, instructing, directing, suggesting, problem-solving, evaluating); some, information based on the helper's reactions, similar experiences, or perceptions (immediacy, self-disclosure, feedback, and interpreting), and one involves information based on observed discrepancies or inconsistencies (confrontation). Regardless of the source of the information, in order for information-giving to be helpful, a strong foundation must be established in which a client is clearly understood. Even when a strong foundation of empathy has been built in the helping relationship, information-giving skills are used sparingly to ensure that the focus of helping remains on the client's own experiences, behavior, goals, and feelings and on the client's empowerment. Regardless of the source of the information, the skills in this chapter are called advanced skills because it takes additional training to implement them; because they are not used unless a foundation has been laid that permits the client to feel understood from her or his own perspective; and because they must be implemented in the interest of advancing a client's own goals. In addition, these are skills that involve some risks, discussed in this chapter.

INFORMATION-GIVING BASED ON EXPERTISE

Helping that involves giving information based on expertise can take several forms and can be glimpsed through: the helper's expert opinion (advice); a reaction to something occurring in the helping relationship at the moment when it is occurring (immediacy); the helper's life outside of the helping relationship (self-disclosure); how the helper views or evaluates the client's experiences, behaviors, or feelings (feedback and evaluation); and/or what the helper believes to be an appropriate way to address a problem the client has identified (problem-solving) (Ivey, 1994). Advising, instructing, directing, suggesting, problem-solving, and evaluating all involve the helper offering a client specific information about how to go about developing a particular behavior or resolving a specific difficulty based on specific expertise of the helper. Each is slightly different and each shares the common aim of offering information based on the expertise of the helper. Each also involves some risks in a helping relationship since they each assume the helper to be the expert.

Giving information based on the presumed expertise of the helper assumes that the giver has more expertise than the client. Of course, if the helper does not actually know more than the client, it would be foolish to offer information. Further, it is generally considered disempowering to offer information on a topic that a client could be expected to acquire for themselves. Information-giving may make the giver feel more necessary and useful, but it may also convey the message that the client is not capable of finding the way themselves. Under the best of all circumstances, giving information in a helping relationship is risky. The information-giver or one who is sought for information is often perceived to be or recognized as an authority. Because of this, offering information holds the possibility of disempowering the client. It may foster dependency on the helper to figure out a problem that the client is capable of figuring out, in which case it tells the client indirectly that the helper believes they are not capable. It can remove responsibility for achieving something that clients themselves could do and may therefore send the message "I don't think you'll take care of this; you're not responsible." As each of these is counterproductive to helping clients, it is important to offer information only with these risks in mind and to do so rarely. In general, I prefer to offer information in the spirit of collaboration rather than to advise or direct a client to do something. I believe that this way offers the greatest chance of empowering the client.

Advising

Advising is an informational process in which a helper, recognized to have had certain experience or expertise in a particular area or topic, shares that expertise to advance a client's goals. A good example of appropriate advice-givers are academic advisors. Academic advisors have usually obtained advanced training in the discipline or major that the student wishes to pursue. In addition, they have usually received extra training about the specific curriculum in which the student is enrolled or wishes to enroll. They are therefore in a position to offer information about how to go about doing that which they have already achieved. Consider the student who comes to see her academic advisor because she wants to major in psychology and become a therapist and wants information about what is involved in this path. The student could not be expected to know the path to becoming a therapist as she has not traveled that path before. However, an academic advisor whose training and experience are as a therapist may be positioned to give information about how to get there. Although the advisor may have personal biases about this path, she or he would be expected to advance the student's goals by giving the information at her or his disposal.

On a smaller scale, the same could be said of the information I give students about wearing a suit when they present papers or posters at national conferences. There is no reason to assume that a student would know this without the benefit of hearing from someone who had been there before them and every reason to assume that as someone who has presented papers and posters at a number of conferences, I would be expected to know this. Though they could find out by trial and error, offering them advance information may save them from feeling uncomfortable. Even in these cases where a clear and legitimate request is being made by a client, phrasing the advice in collaborative terms can be most useful and avoids the disempowering effect of presuming to be "the expert." In my experience, using phrases like "In my experience . . . is usually helpful because . . ." assigns ownership of the information to the helper without presuming that the helper knows all and still empowers the client to choose to adopt the behavior.

Another way to offer advice is by checking to see if clients can imagine giving someone else advice and then use the same advice themselves. For example, I've had clients who are very unsure of themselves who want me to tell them what I think they should do. When they ask me what to do in a given situation, I often respond by asking, "If someone came to you seeking advice about that, what would you tell them?" This strategy invites clients to exercise their expertise in the situation and to arrive at advice they may need without relying on the helper to provide it. Another strategy that invites clients to advise themselves is to encourage clients to tell helpers what other advice they have heard and then evaluate it for themselves.

Making effective referrals to other helping professionals often calls for direct advice-giving. Take, for example, the client who is actively hallucinating. Although talking with clients who are hallucinating may be helpful in many ways, it is generally accepted that psychoactive drugs will facilitate understanding by reducing the incidence of hallucinations so that the client can hear more accurately what the helper is saying (Nolen-Hoeksema, 2001). An example of direct advice that still conveys empathic understanding of client experiences and ownership of helper perceptions about the possible benefits of medication might be a statement like, "It sounds like the voices you've been hearing are disturbing to you; I would recommend a psychiatric evaluation to see if medication could help control the voices."

Another example of a situation in which advice-giving is expected and appropriate, but may still be handled with attention to empowering the client, is the case of abuse reporting. Most helpers are mandated to report suspicions of child or vulnerable adult abuse. It would be misleading to present this as a situation in which the client holds the power to decide to report or not based on their own assessment of the situation. Even so, the reporting event can be more or less empowering to the client based on how the helper approaches this. There is a big difference between saying, "This has to be reported; I'd advise you to call them yourself," and, "You've told me some things that I think suggest abuse, and I'm required to protect your child's safety by involving protective services. Let's figure out a way to report this that also respects you in this process." While the helper must still make the report, it is within the helper's control to frame it in terms of collaborating with the client, advancing the client's goals, and conveying respect and concern for the client.

Instructing

Instructing, similar to advising, assumes that the helper is someone who has additional training in a specific area in which a client, student, or trainee wants further training. The key difference between advice-giving and instruction is that the how to of instructing usually involves a longer, more intensive and extensive series of interactions in which the helper is offering information and often involves some kind of assessment of the client's mastery of ideas or behaviors. The course you may be taking that uses this text is a good example of instructing. Typically, the person teaching such a course has advanced training and usually experience in professional helping of some sort. That person devises a plan, based on their background, then offers a step-by-step method for achieving the student goals and a way to measure when and whether the goals have been met. Instructing may involve the instructor setting goals she or he knows to be associated with the client or student goals. Another good example of the way that instructing may be used in professional helping can be found in cognitive-behavioral theories of helping. In cognitive-behavioral theories, helpers advance client goals by instructing the client about the specific mechanisms by which a client can change feelings and behaviors by changing thoughts. The helpers then work collaboratively with the client to experiment or practice these approaches with specific examples from the client's life.

Directing

Providing direction or issuing a directive is another information-giving mechanism that involves helper influence. Directives indicate that the helper is deciding where to go or what to do next. Directors in media productions tell actors how to act, where to stand, how loudly to speak, and what tone or inflection to portray. Often, it is the director who interprets the author's intent and then conveys this to the actor, who is someone skillful at portraying specific character traits, emotions, and behaviors. In the same way, when a helper is **directing,** she or he is telling the client how to and perhaps when to engage in a particular behavior. When I tell students to begin studying for the GREs at least six months before they plan to take them, I am directing them. This is not a series of directions as in instruction or in offering them the advantage of my expertise—I didn't do that well on the GREs—I am telling them to take action in a particular way or at a particular time in order to advance their goal of going to graduate school. Whether they did poorly or well, there is general agreement among those who study such things that this type of standardized test requires more preparation than can be effected in a day, week, or month.

Direction, as with any influencing response, runs the risk of either fostering dependency or resistance depending on the personal power the client wishes to maintain. As such, directives should not be given lightly. I usually reserve direction-giving for specific homework based on a collaboratively arrived-at assignment. So I might use direction-giving for a situation in which a client and I just established that she doesn't seem to do very well at taking time for herself and needs some specific practice at this. After she decided that she wanted some homework about this, I would give a specific direction like "I want you to take ten minutes each day until we meet again just to do something for yourself."

Suggesting

Suggesting is the process of offering possible options that a client may choose to pursue. Take, for example, the client whose goal is to go to graduate school to become a therapist and who also reports that he really dislikes math, statistics, and anything to do with numbers but is quite competent when it comes to words or social skills. After listening, reflecting, and paraphrasing to arrive at the meaning all of this has for the client, I would probably suggest that two options, social work programs and counseling programs, might be a better fit than coun-seling psychology, clinical psychology, psychiatry, or nursing, even though any of these disciplines could prepare someone to do therapy. The client is offered information and encouraged to consider options that advance his goals based on a full understanding of the content and meaning of the reports. This may even be followed by a suggestion that one option would be to look at the curricula of several such programs to see if it fits what he hopes to study. Offering suggestions rather than directions is usually considered less likely to take away clients' power to control what they do, but this method still has some of the same pitfalls of disempowerment.

Problem-Solving

Perhaps more helpful than advising, directing, or suggesting is engag-ing the client in collaboration to solve problems they are encountering. **Problem-solving** is the process in which both client and helper engage to modify the behavior, correct the difficulty, or develop skills to offset limitations that the client is experiencing or perceiving in the advancement of the client's goals. It involves helpers observing the difficulty or limitation and then asking clients' input about how they think the problem can be solved or wondering aloud how together they can address the problem. If clients could solve the problem, they may already have done so and even collaboration about solutions may be limited without exploration or additional skills. Nonetheless, problem-solving is another type of collaborative information-giving tool that may be used to further a client's goals.

Evaluating

Evaluation is a specific blend of information-giving and self-disclosure that involves a helper commenting on the value she or he places on a particular behavior or idea. Because of the power clients attribute to the values a helper holds and because of the power a professional helper holds in the helping relationship, this type of disclosure is used even more sparingly than other advanced skills in helping. Evaluations are generally synonymous with value judgments and may be risky to render in the context of a helping relationship.

Most people have had the experience of being evaluated. Often it is associated with criticism, though criticism and evaluation are different. When helpers evaluate a client's behavior, thoughts, or feelings, they are placing a value based on their own experiences of or perspectives on the client's behavior, thoughts, or feelings. While "good" and "bad" are the simplest evaluative statements that can be made, often more complex evaluations are made. In fact, it is useful for helpers to be able to offer evaluations that comment very specifically on distinctive observed behaviors. Evaluations usually take the form of: "I think that is . . ." or "I believe that is. . . ."

Consider Sam as an example of a client whose goal is to lose weight. Sam reports that he lost 5 pounds last month and is feeling discouraged about how much weight he still has to lose. If I wanted to use evaluation to advance his goals, I would probably comment, "I think 5 pounds is a realistic amount to lose in a month." Since I know from reading health research that to remain healthy and predict a higher probability of maintaining the weight loss, .5 to 1 pound per week is a reasonable amount to lose, this is not only a well-researched evaluative statement, it is something that I believe will serve Sam's goals.

When professors evaluate student performance, they generally do so based on a considered opinion (or many such opinions if they have researched this) about the steps involved in mastering a particular subject matter. Then they place a value on the extent to which a given student has achieved each step in the process of mastering that content. "Excellent," "very good," "good," "fair," and "poor" and the corresponding grades are all evaluations.

Giving an evaluation also tips the balance of power in any relationship toward the evaluator. Since one of the goals of helping is to empower the client, evaluation by the helper can be risky and should be used with some caution. No matter how carefully given, evaluations will call forth clients' experiences in being "graded" on performance. Clients who feel graded on how they function in life may be justifiably defensive.

INFORMATION-GIVING BASED ON HELPER REACTIONS, EXPERIENCE, OR PERCEPTIONS

In addition to offering clients information based on helper expertise, helpers may offer information based on their own reactions, experiences, or perceptions. **Immediacy** involves offering information about a helper's reactions to events or experiences that are occurring in the helping relationship at the time they are occurring. **Self-disclosures** are also information about the helper's experiences, but they differ from immediacy in that they usually reference an experience the helper has had outside the helping relationship. **Feedback** involves returning to the client observations about behavior the client may be unaware of. Interpretations are information about the helper's perceptions of the meaning of a particular behavior, feeling, or thought. Each of these information-giving skills rests on offering information to the client based on helper reactions, experiences, or perceptions. Each skill is different from the others in key ways.

Immediacy

Immediacy is a type of information-giving and self-disclosure that involves the helper briefly commenting on her or his own immediate experiences in the interaction with the client as the experiences are occurring. To be immediate, the helper must be aware of both her or his own and the client's experience and be able to comment on each appropriately to explore the helping relationship itself as an avenue for advancing the client's goals. The purpose of immediacy is still to advance the client's goals, so although helpers may be aware of many of their own experiences during a helping session and are generally focused on and aware of the client's experiences, comments about the helper's immediate experiences are used sparingly and only when such comment will advance the client's goals. So, although I generally think of expressing my feelings as a positive addition to most relationships and may be aware of my own feelings about a client's behaviors, I would only express those feelings in a helping relationship if it served to advance the client's goals. In my other personal relationships, I decide to comment on my immediate experiences of another based on different objectives. If I already know that a relationship norm includes this type of comment or if I want to advance a particular relationship to include this type of immediacy, I may decide to express my immediate feelings about what may be going on in a relationship. There is a risk in any relationship when one person moves from discussing things outside the immediate relationship (e.g., other people or events) to discussing the immediate relationship between the two or more people involved with one another.

For many people, this type of discussion is more anxiety-provoking. Imagine two friends telling each other about how things went in their classes today and then contrast this with the same friends telling each other how things went in their relationship just now. "I really like my class in interviewing and psychotherapy techniques; we almost always have exercises to help us learn the concepts. That usually makes it easier for me to understand" is quite different than "I really like our friendship; we almost always tell each other what we think. That makes it easier for me to trust you" or "I don't like how we've been doing our relationship; it's hard for me when you only call if you have a problem." Talking about "there and then" events or people other than those immediately involved is less risky than talking about what is "right here and right now." If it feels more scary, it's because it is.

Helping relationships differ from friendships in that part of the helper's role is putting the client's goals ahead of the helper's personal wishes about the relationship. A friendship assumes a more equal give and take of personal wishes. In my friendships, I get to exercise my wishes about the relationship, as do my friends. And while I have some friends with whom I can regularly talk about how I feel about a particular behavior of theirs, I only tell clients about their immediate impact on me when it serves to advance *their* goals for helping. I always have the option of waiting and taking my exploration of feelings to my supervisor whose role is partly defined as helping me to address my needs as a helper. So, in addition to considering the risk involved in talking about immediate concerns, helpers must remember their role as one focused on the client's needs rather than their own.

Immediacy comments can be used: to bring forward a client's awareness of how they are perceived by another (e.g., the helper); to explore the helping relationship itself; and as a prelude to other helpers' opinions or perspectives. Therefore, if a client whose goal is to work on improving his relationships with others and who has been wondering how others could possibly find him disrespectful when he is late came to my office late for an appointment, a comment about any reactions I had to his real and immediate tardiness might be appropriate. Such a comment could help the client realize the impact of this type of behavior. If a safe relationship has been established, the client may enjoy this immediacy with greater security than feedback from someone not paid to put his needs first.

Some theories of helping suggest that the real and immediate relationship with the helper holds parallels to other important relationships in the client's life (e.g., object relations theories and humanistic theories). Therefore, what occurs in the real and immediate relationship between the helper and the client may have useful information for both to explore in the interest of improving other relationships. Beginning with an immediate and genuine helper reaction can be a way to pave the way for discussion of either the client's impact or the helping relationship. Other professional helping theorists (Carkhuff, 1979; Rogers, 1951, 1959) view immediacy as the pinnacle of helping. From this perspective, offering the client a genuine reaction that reflects what was present right then for the helper is the ultimate in establishing a helpful interaction.

Self-Disclosure

Related to immediacy is self-disclosure. **Self-disclosure** is also a type of information-giving that involves the helper telling about some part of her or his own life experiences that matches the client's experiences and goals as an illustration of some point that may advance the client's goals (Worthington, n.d.). When a helper discloses personal information, the focus still remains on the client. In other relationships, there is an expectation that both people will share fairly equally in revealing experiences, feelings, and ideas. This expectation of reciprocity is not the case in professional helping. In a helping relationship, the helper only shares that which is of benefit in promoting the client's goals.

Consider one of my clients who had just experienced the death of a parent. She talked about feeling strangely disconnected and like she was simply going through life on "auto pilot." She was worried that this meant that her grieving was abnormal and kept trying to "focus" herself, but without success. I had been considering whether to tell her about my own similar experiences following the death of my paternal grandmother. When she asked whether I thought she was weird, it was clear that such a disclosure would be a way to offer valuable information without passing a value judgment about her sanity. I knew she viewed me as being relatively healthy and also as a judge of mental health. With an indication that the timing was appropriate, together with my knowledge from past interactions that she was seeking help to learn how to have various feelings without harsh self-judgments, I decided that such a disclosure could advance her goal. I told her about this small piece of my own experience. I told the incident itself very briefly because the point being made was not that we were building a relationship based on our similarities. The point was to "normalize" feelings about those disconnected feelings she had been having. I quickly refocused the attention on her feelings about her disconnectedness after the brief disclosure: "I remember that it was hard to let myself feel that way without thinking I was weird; it sounds like that's been hard for you, too."

By disclosing only the part of my own story that matched her experience and quickly reflecting her feelings, I was able to use my experience as a tool to help her "normalize" and explore the difficulties she wanted help with: the challenge of gently permitting herself difficult feelings without self-judgment. In fact, I had modeled exactly what she needed to do for herself. To have said, "Oh, I've done that, too," may have felt like I was minimizing or dismissing this experience of hers. Clients often seek help when they are feeling vulnerable or less capable. It is easy for them to feel that the way a helper has dealt with something is *the* way to do so. Clients feeling that they are in competition with their helpers about how something should have been handled is often a concern. Shifting the focus back to the client as soon as possible can avert some of the competitive feel of a helper's disclosures.

Helpers judiciously decide when and how much to tell and are guided by a variety of reasons that advance the client's goals. Self-disclosures can enhance trust, reduce isolation, invite the client to disclose more, and promote viewing experiences from a different perspective (Cormier & Cormier, 1991). Self-disclosure also holds the danger of shifting the focus from the client to the helper, being irrelevant to the topic or the client's worldview, or trivializing the client's experience (Evans, Hearn, Uhlemann, & Ivey, 1993). Because the same responses are such a double-edged sword, and to maximize the possibility that a self-disclosure will be useful and minimize the possibility of negative effects, helpers should use self-disclosures sparingly and selectively, emphasizing the common issue aloud, and only after an extended relationship has been established (Doyle, 1998).

Offering Feedback

Many of the same principles are involved in offering **feedback,** whether it be from a teacher to a student, a classmate to a fellow classmate, or a helper to a client. Readers may recall from Chapter 2 that for feedback to be helpful, it should be as specific as possible and should include specific observations. In the same way that feedback can teach helpers effective helping behavior, feedback can help clients to (1) develop behaviors they do not ordinarily engage in or are not ordinarily aware of; (2) observe their own behavior and its impact; (3) improve or modify a behavior that is not effective; or (4) refine a behavior that is satisfactory, but not exceptional or consistent. Feedback, you may recall, involves making a statement of ownership of the observation by using the word "I," following that with a word indicating a form of observation, and then specifying the behavior and identifying the time frame in which the behavior occurred. The formula for effective feedback looks like this:

> *Feedback*
> "[I] + [observation word] + [specific behavior] +
> [time frame]"

Following a comment about specific behavior with a self-disclosing comment about its impact can also be useful feedback to a client. In fact, thinking of feedback as a type of self-disclosure can help facilitate recognition that some risks are involved in giving feedback. It is important to remember that whether the feedback is being given to a classmate or a client, giving information about the personal impact of a behavior still involves using statements that begin with "I" and includes an indication that the impact is not forever but has or had a temporary effect. For example, "I noticed that you arrived late today and last week. I would rather start on time," not only describes a specific client behavior, but the impact is described in terms of its immediate personal effect on the helper and suggests a direction for future meetings. The formula for effective feedback with a statement of impact is more complex, but you may recall that it looks like this:

Feedback with a Statement of Impact
"[I] + [observing word] + [specific behavior] + [I] + [felt/thought] + [specific feeling or thought] + [time frame for behavior]"

Feedback may also include suggested improvements in clients' behaviors just as it did in classmate feedback, and the specific skills for providing feedback to clients can follow a similar formula. Further, clients do not only receive feedback but often offer feedback to helpers. It is important to remember how to both give and receive feedback. Clients imitate helpers' behaviors and, in a sense, helpers become models for how to give and receive feedback graciously by their own examples.

Interpreting

On a note related to feedback, **interpreting** is another type of information-giving and self-disclosure that involves the helper offering his or her own perceptions of the meanings of the experiences, behaviors, ideas, or feelings that the client has reported. Again, advancing the client's goals is critical to keep in mind in order to use interpretations effectively. Although it is the helper's meanings associated with a particular experience, thought, or feeling that are being offered, interpretations are still intended to directly address the client's stated goals. Take as an example the client who has an incomprehensible but disturbing dream. I may hazard a guess as to what that means for her, if and only if I know my client and her background, experiences, and values pretty well. Even those professional helpers who regularly use interpretations (e.g., psychodynamic theories of helping) recommend that interpretation be based on the client's perspectives rather than on universal meanings (Hill & O'Brien, 1999a). More often, professional helpers are positioned to interpret waking behavior and only those meanings specific to the clients themselves. Universal meanings are rare.

Robert Doyle (1998) recommends using interpretations or evaluations for the purpose of integrating many different elements of the helping interactions (tests, interviews with others, client reports); for reframing or redefining the client's perspective (a client labels her- or himself as *ruminative*—the helper recasts this picture using a less harsh label, like *thoughtful,* or one that prompts a more profound examination, like *obsessive*); or to interpret reasons for a client's behavior (a client who abuses may have learned that being a man means being in control; linking these allows exploration of the possible cause and effect of his abuse). Clara Hill and Karen O'Brien (1999a) suggest that interpretations are statements that simply go beyond what the client has stated or recognized to present a new or alternate meaning, reason, or explanation for behavior, thoughts, or feelings and to invite the client to see these from a new perspective. Interpretations can also draw hypotheses about the meaning or relationships between behaviors, thoughts, and feelings (Cormier & Cormier, 1991).

Interpreting, like evaluating, can help clients expand or modify their frame of reference (Doyle, 1998). Helpers use interpreting responses when they want clients to become more aware of their behaviors, thoughts, and feelings; to gain a new or fresh perspective; to reorganize their thinking around a new concept of the difficulty; or to enhance their self-understanding. Interpretations address not what the client actually said but what they may have implied; they offer explanations. Interpretations that are close to what a client has actually said or thought, those that focus on what the client has control of, and those given with a "positive spin" or with an emphasis on the positive implications of the interpretation or the explanation are likely to be best received by the client. Moreover, studies suggest that interpretations are most effective if offered in a tentative manner so as not to overwhelm and if they offer the client the responsibility of making the value or interpretation on their own. So, statements like "These events indicate that you can . . ." tend to work better than statements like "The test results indicate that you cannot . . ." Tentative statements like "Your strengths appear to be . . ." rather than "Your strengths are . . ." are also more effective (Cormier & Cormier, 1991).

The job of interpreting does not end when the helper has delivered a clever pronouncement about relationships, causal explanations, or meanings. Following up by checking out what the client heard, what they think, and how they are reacting to the interpretation is critically important to working through the client's understanding and use of that interpretation.

Checking Out Reactions to Interpretations
"[Implicit message] + [slightly different view of issue] + [positive aspects under client control] + [words that match the client's vocabulary] + [checking out the usefulness]"

Some helping theorists believe that interpretations should only come from clients (e.g., client-centered theories). My own bias about interpretations is to believe that it is generally useful to ask the client about perceived meanings first and then if they cannot generate one, to offer my perceptions about the behaviors, thoughts, or feelings. This engenders a sense of collaboration and conveys the clear message that I believe the client to be her or his own best expert.

The timing of interpretations is also crucial to their effectiveness. Using interpretation skills too early in the helping relationship can result in intimidating the client or the helper by basing responses on insufficient information. Either way, interpretations are likely to be rejected as clients seek to protect themselves against what is in reality an intrusion into their domain—their personal experience. Clients must show some readiness to hear an interpretation before it will be useful. In fact, the most effective interpretations are those that go only slightly beyond what the clients could have formulated themselves (Brammer, Shostrom, & Abrego, 1989).

As important as timing within the helping relationship is the timing of an interpretation within a given session. Interpretations that are offered early in the session can be examined more thoroughly and those offered too late in the session give the client the feeling of a "hit and run" accident. Waiting until late in the session almost ensures that there will be insufficient time for client or helper to address the client's reactions. Some new helpers tend to work up their courage about giving an interpretation and may compromise the timing by delivering it too late in the session. A better way to approach this might be to consult with a supervisor in advance of the session in which an interpretation may be offered so that it can be offered early in the session. Other new helpers err by offering interpretations too early in the relationship. They may be unconsciously trying to demonstrate their prowess at figuring out clients or revealing their clever intuitions. Perhaps they believe that if the clients see how clever and insightful they are, the clients will have the confidence in them that they (the helpers) themselves may lack. A better approach for the uncertain helper is to remember that an empathic relationship must be established before any interpretation will be useful, and the helper should find sources of support for the normal uncertainty that accompanies new endeavors.

Basing the interpretation on the actual client message rather than helper bias or projected values is as important as timing is in the session or the relationship. Again, it is important to remember that it is the client's goals that must be advanced with interpretations. Projecting helper values or biases can result in rejection by the client and a client feeling misunderstood. It may also result in setting the helper up as the authority about the client's behaviors, thoughts, or feelings. Likewise, overusing interpretations will result in client overdependency.

Although studies have found that clients find some interpretations helpful, more interpretations more helpful, and interpretations in general to be consistently helpful (Hill & O'Brien, 1999a), interpretations must still be timed appropriately, delivered with moderate depth, focused on the client's own messages, and must be collaborative to be most useful. If helpers make it their responsibility to figure out the meaning of a particular event, experience, idea, feeling, or behavior, they may be perceived as a clever authority or they may enhance their expert power in the situation, but there is little reason to assume that clients will assume responsibility for making meaning of their own behaviors, thoughts, or feelings.

INFORMATION-GIVING BASED ON OBSERVED DISCREPANCIES: CONFRONTATION

The last skill to be addressed in this chapter is one that offers clients information through the helpers' observations of clients' discrepancies. This information-giving skill is called **confrontation.** More specifically, confrontation is a verbal skill that involves offering a client information about discrepancies, conflicts, or mixed messages observed in the client's reports, behaviors, feelings, or thoughts. The aim of a confrontation is to offer clients a supportive, if unexpected, glimpse of a discrepancy for the purposes of helping clients explore other ways of perceiving themselves or enhancing their awareness of incongruities in behaviors, thoughts, or feelings (Cormier & Cormier, 1991). Confronting inconsistencies may help clients reduce ambiguities in their experiences and understand themselves more fully (Carkhuff, 1978), experience ambivalent or conflicting feelings, admit to deeper or different feelings, or acknowledge more of their feelings, motives, and wishes (Hill & O'Brien, 1999a). Changing client perceptions or self-awareness may invite clients to make changes in the dissonant behaviors, thoughts, or feelings.

Confrontation is a helping skill that involves reflecting to a client any one of a number of discrepancies that may exist in the client's reports (Cormier & Cormier, 1991; Hill & O'Brien, 1999a). Discrepancies or inconsistencies may be found between the following reports:

- two verbal messages
- a verbal and nonverbal message
- a current report and a previous report
- a client's view and a helper's view of a particular behavior
- a client's judgments about her or his strengths or limitations, as in an inconsistency in self-perception and experience
- clients' perceptions about their "idealized" picture of themselves and what is "real" about who they are
- a client's words and actions
- two nonverbal behaviors that are or seem inconsistent

A client may make two verbal statements that are inconsistent. An example might be a client who says, "I'm not having any problem with my friend doing better at this class than I am," and also says, "I just wish that I didn't have to see my friend every day; her A, is like, in my face." Enhancing the client's awareness with a confrontation like, "I hear you saying that you're not having any problem with your friend's performance in the class, and I also hear you saying you wish you didn't have to see her and feel that grade difference in your face," may allow the client to acknowledge what she sees as unacceptable feelings about her friend or herself.

Another type of discrepancy that may be observed aloud can be between verbal and nonverbal behavior. Consider the client who says, "I'm fine with the D I got in that class" while slouching and talking very softly. "I hear you saying that you are fine with the grade, and I also see you slouching and hear you talking very quietly" is an example of a helping response that confronts this discrepancy. Exploring both pieces of information may invite the client to see that she or he is not fine when thinking about the grade.

There may be discrepancies in what a client is saying now versus what she or he said previously. For example, one client reported she came from a working-class background and later reported that she took horseback riding lessons throughout her childhood. A helping response that put the two seemingly conflicting fragments alongside each other, like "Earlier I heard you say that you came from a working-class family and now I also hear that you took riding lessons," can invite clients to resolve this inconsistent perception either by determining that what they thought of as "working class" did not tell the whole story about what her parents wanted for her or may help her see how much that meant, or she may establish that horseback riding lessons were not very expensive when she took them. Any of these resolutions to the seemingly conflicting information could have substantial benefits to the client.

There may be discrepancies between a client's views and a helper's views of a particular behavior. For example, a client who perceived himself as socially skillful reported that he could not speak when asked for his opinion at a party. Pointing out that "I heard you say that you see yourself as socially skillful and also that when you were asked for your opinion at the party you couldn't speak" helped him to explore what it was about the party or the people present that contributed to this difficulty and invited him to see a more complex picture of himself and his social skills. Of course, when pointed out, such a discrepancy could result in the client changing his perception of himself as socially skillful. Even so, it is important to note that the perception need not be eliminated, but it may require modification to include the unexpected information that the client has difficulty being spontaneous and articulate in some social situations.

There may be discrepancies in a client's judgments about her or his strengths or limitations, as in an inconsistency in self-perception and experience. For example, a client who perceives herself to be a doormat reports that her work as an administrator is going well. Knowing that administrative skills require a certain amount of asser- tiveness could lead the helper to note this discrepancy in a statement like "I've heard you refer to yourself as a doormat a number of times and I'm also hearing that your work as an administrator is going well."

The confrontation could allow the client a surprise look at her strengths. Likewise, a client who says, "It's not like I raped her, I just had sex with her when she was drunk," would probably benefit in the long run from hearing the confrontation "I've heard you say that you didn't rape her and I also know that the definition of rape includes having sex with someone who is drunk."

Confronting discrepancies between a client's perceptions about their "idealized" picture of themselves and what is "real" about who they are can invite growth. Both client-centered theories of helping and rational-emotive theories of helping believe that it is precisely the incongruence between what a client has incorporated about themselves as the ideal and their "real" selves that produces some thorny difficulties in life. So, when a client says she wants to be in a relationship and she can't, a helpful confrontation might be to point out the discrepancy saying, "You say you want to be in a relationship and you say you can't." Pointing out such a discrepancy can create some dissonance that can serve as an impetus to change unreal (i.e., irrational) beliefs.

Discrepancies can often be found between words and actions, as with my students who tell me that they want to get into graduate programs that require very good grades and then also report that they spend a lot of their time outside of class partying or sleeping off their partying. A confrontation like "I've heard you say that you want the grades you need for graduate school and I also hear your frequent reports about partying and sleeping off your partying" can invite exploration and change of either words or actions to reflect the higher priority.

Two nonverbal behaviors can be or seem inconsistent. An example of this is the client who smiles and cries at the same time. Many people believe that smiling softens the perceived unpleasantness of crying. Most often, clients are themselves uncomfortable with crying, and a supportive confrontation that involves a simple observation of this like "I notice that you are crying and smiling while you do that" usually allows for a more complete exploration of the client's reactions to her or his own crying.

Helping clients to see two or more feelings about the same person or event can encourage more emotional complexity. Take, for example, the client who is really angry at her friend's recent betrayal of her confidence and who also feels proud of recognizing and saying something about it. Reflecting both sentiments in a confrontation like "I heard you say that you are angry and I also heard your pride in seeing it for what it is and saying what you felt about it" invites the client to acknowledge complex, multidimensional feelings.

Contrary to the popular connotation of the word, *confrontations* in a helping context need not involve hostile, ugly interactions. Neither is the image of bombarding people with so much information about themselves that they can scarcely deny something (e.g., out-dated views of family interventions with alcoholics) an accurate image of confrontation. In fact, when a helper is angry at a client for some behavior, this is not the time for a confrontation. Confrontations must be founded on a strong understanding of the client, on enough interaction to have laid such a foundation, and on the client's clear sense that the information being offered is given with care and concern for the client's welfare and in the interest of advancing the client's goals. That kind of assistance is unlikely to occur when the helper is angry or frustrated at the client's behavior. Instead, when a strong relationship has been built in which the client is relatively certain of the helper's concern, she or he is more likely to hear and unravel the meaning of the discrepant observations.

There are two formulas I use in confrontations:

Confrontation
"[observation] + [discrepant observation]"

OR

"[observation] + [observation] +
[A question about the personal meaning of the discrepant observations]"

The second formula would look like this: "I have observed/ noticed/heard/seen . . . and I have also observed/noticed/heard/seen. . . . I wonder what that means for you?" A confrontation begins with a statement about the discrepancies noted. This statement should offer as clear and specific a picture of observable differences as is possible. Using the skills of observation described earlier, the helper works to separate observation from assumption and then states the observations aloud. For example, "I've heard you say that you think of yourself as pretty lazy and I've also noticed your discipline in getting all of your assignments in early and done well." In each case, a specific observation is offered to focus the client's attention and to document for the client the specific discrepancy the helper wants the client to consider. Further, the words chosen to indicate the discrepancy offer a contrast that specifically highlights the contrast itself. This can then be followed by a question like "What do you make of that?" or "How do you make sense of that?" or "What do you think that's about?" The question invites the client to focus on and explore the discrepancy and in this case modify either the view of themselves as lazy or explain how the behaviors being referred to still fit their perception of laziness. If a client is unable or unwilling to suggest a meaning for the discrepancy, often it is wisest for the helper to drop it. The seed has been planted. It can always be cultivated later. The helper could offer an interpretation, though some caution should be exercised—providing meaning is quite different than inviting a client to supply their own meaning about themselves.

In a sense, confrontations advance a client's goals by highlighting **cognitive dissonance.** For those who have not studied social psychology, cognitive dissonance occurs whenever behavior, attitudes, or feelings contain discrepancies (Festinger, 1957; Pettijohn, 1989). According to the theory, when people are aware of a discrepancy in these areas of functioning, there is a natural tendency to attempt to bring the inconsistencies into congruence either by changing the attitude, the behavior, or the emotion. The easiest change is the most likely. Bringing to clients' awareness such a discrepancy invites them to resolve the discrepancy. The helper may also be able to assist the client in determining what element could be changed most easily to advance the goal. If the client is working toward changing his self-concept to a more positive one, it would be to his benefit to change his perception of himself as lazy, rather than broadening lazy to fit his behaviors. It is not uncommon for people to adopt an image of themselves based on previous information that no longer includes some behaviors that would stand in stark contradiction. Take, for example, students who grew up with learning disabilities and are now doing well in college. It may be time to confront a new image and claim a label other than "disabled" or to view "disability" with a new lens that includes abilities. Or consider the woman who was abused by her husband who has established a network of strong, supportive people around her. She may need to reconsider the label of "victim" or even of "survivor." She

EXERCISE **7.1**

Advancing a Client's Goals through Information-Giving

In each of the following examples, identify whether the response is advice, instruction, direction, suggestion, problem-solving, evaluating, immediacy, self-disclosure, feedback, interpretation, or confrontation.

- "I think that you should go to graduate school next year instead of waiting."
- "I noticed that you said you don't get along with people very well, and you also said you've been married 20 years."
- "In my experience, I've found it helpful to begin writing projects far ahead of the deadline, so that I can take on little chunks at any given point in time."
- "When I hear people saying, "We'll see," I usually think that they really mean to say, "No," but are afraid of being harsh or of not being liked."
- "When I was first "coming out" myself, I tended to drink much more than I do now. I think it was a way to calm my anxieties. Not the best or only way, but the way I used for a while."
- "It seems like you have a couple of options; you could decide to go to the hospital or you could decide to turn over that decision to me."
- "There are several steps involved in getting into a well-respected graduate program in a field that trains people to do therapy. You need to maintain a GPA of at least 3.0 in a 4-point system. You'll need letters of recommendation from people who you've worked with very closely, who know your work very well. You'll also need to meet various requirements each program sets. The first step in accomplishing all of these objectives is to begin familiarizing yourself with the different programs and their requirements."

---

may require a new perception of herself to capture the fact of her role in designing not only a nonabusive situation, but one that does the opposite of harming her.

Clients may have any number of reactions to confrontations. They may deny the discrepancy or disagree with it, be confused by it, falsely accept it, or genuinely accept it. Denial may indicate that the

EXERCISE **7.2**

Advancing a Client's Goals through Confrontation

In a dyad, practice taking turns as the helper or the client. The client should role-play one of the client parts, while the helper practices confronting each type of discrepancy. The following are examples for you to practice:

- a client who say things are fine while crying
- a friend who says she has quit drinking while carrying a beer
- a student with a GPA of 2.0 who says she wants to go to medical school
- a woman who takes care of everyone's needs except her own
- a man who works 80 hours a week who says he places a premium on "family values"
- a client who disparages African Americans, Latinos, Asian Americans, gays, and lesbians, who says that his or her most important values come from being a Christian
- an anorexic client who says she needs to lose weight
- a red-faced client who smashes his fist on the coffee table while shouting that he's not angry

client is not ready to hear the confrontation. The client who wants to deny the confrontation can discredit the helper, devalue the importance of the topic, or seek support elsewhere to dispute the confrontation. Confusion about the confrontation may be genuine or a way to keep from acknowledging it. Sometimes clients agree just to get the helper "out of their face." I recommend that helpers quickly return to listening responses, such as reflection and paraphrasing after a confrontation, and neither defend nor repeat the confrontation. Again, the seeds have been planted; they can be cultivated at any later point.

SUMMARY

In summary, this chapter has described a number of information-giving skills that can advance a client's goals. Helping may proceed from establishing an interchangeable understanding of a client's experiences, thoughts, and feelings and may involve advice, instruction, direction, suggestion, problem-solving, or evaluation; immediacy, self-disclosure, feedback, interpretation; or confrontation. Readers have probably observed that each of the advanced skills is said to be used sparingly. This is not a misprint. By themselves, each is used only sparingly. Most of the foundation for any kind of helping still rests on establishing an empathic relationship using nonverbal skills, paraphrasing content and reflecting feelings, identifying clients' strengths and limitations from their perspective, and helping clients to establish and monitor their own goals. There are different theories of helping that guide the use and the frequency with which these advanced and other skills are used. The observant reader has probably also noticed that I have repeatedly reminded helpers that the focus remains on the client regardless of the type of information being offered by the helper. In addition, I have continually made reference to the risk of helpers disempowering clients by assuming too much responsibility for change through information-giving. Finally, the insightful reader has probably also noticed the many comments that suggest that the different skills are used with more or less frequency in different frameworks about helping. Part Two of this textbook offers views of many theories of helping and ways in which the microskills, advanced skills, and other skills unique to each theory are used in each framework to help clients achieve their goals.

EXERCISE 7.3
Putting It All Together

Audiotape yourself interviewing someone you have met with before. Demonstrate empathy through several interchanges in which you paraphrase the content and reflect feelings correctly. When appropriate, shift the conversation toward personalizing the meaning and preparing for action. Look for an opportunity to demonstrate any one of the information-giving skills. Transcribe the interview and make two copies. Read one copy of the transcript, and following each response, identify and correctly label the responses you made and rate each according to the rating system used in the text. Give the other copy to a classmate to review. Ask her or him to label and rate each of your responses. Discuss any discrepancies observed in the labeling or rating. Decide which label and rating you believe is closest. Turn in a copy of the transcript with your final labels and ratings to your professor for additional feedback.

PART TWO

Theories of Helping

8 Person-Centered Theory of Helping

CONTEXT

The person-centered theory of helping, developed and articulated by Carl Rogers, is a phenomenological, humanistic theory of helping. In any science, phenomenology is the branch that emphasizes classification and description rather than explanation (*Webster's Unabridged Dictionary*, 2001). Phenomenological psychology focuses on describing human experiences and the unique phenomenal field of individuals or everything experienced by a person at any given time. The phenomenological psychological theories include both existential theory and humanistic theory, which share a common belief that each person uniquely experiences the environment and themselves, and those unique perceptions and feelings determine a person's reality and behavior. Further, each person's experience of immediacy determines behavior and feelings. This immediate experience is sometimes referred to as the "here and now," and contrasted with the "there and then" approaches of other theories. From the person-centered perspective, humans are considered active participants in determining the course of our lives and the development of our personalities and our problems.

Many people are confused about the meaning, similarities, and differences in phenomenological, humanistic, and existential theories. A complete explanation of all of the differences and similarities between the theories is beyond the scope of this text. Some explanation of each, however, is helpful to understanding the context in which Rogers's person-centered theories evolved.

Existentialism is a nineteenth-century European philosophy applied to theories of therapy by European analysts who were critical of both the then-prominent psychoanalytic views of human behaviors as being largely determined by biology and the behaviorists who viewed behavior as determined by learning and conditioning. In the age-old debate about whether nature or nurture is more influential in determining behavior, psychoanalytic theorists clearly developed the nature side of determinism, while behaviorists developed the nurture side. Existential, humanistic, and phenomenological theories all laid claim to what has since been called the "third force" in psychological theory. In this third force, individuals themselves were thought to determine behavior through choices they made.

According to existential theory, people are always in the process of becoming; we have the capacity for awareness and the freedom and responsibility to make choices. When translated into the practice of professional helping, this philosophy calls for a helper to facilitate client recognition of her or his full range of choices and to emphasize the client's responsibility for options the client selects in her or his life. Existentialists also take the position that people face anxiety as a result of their awareness of death, freedom, isolation, and the intrinsic meaninglessness of the world. This existential anxiety and awareness prompts humans to impose meaning and subsequently to develop identity (Bugental, 1978).

Although also a branch of phenomenology that focuses on describing subjective experiences, meaning, and choice, humanistic theories suggest that humans grow, change, and develop less out of a reaction to the anxiety of facing mortality or the meaninglessness of existence and more from the "natural" potential we can realize and on which we act. We find meaning through this natural potential. When translated into therapeutic goals, then, humanistic helpers create a climate in which people may become aware of, develop, refine, and act on their potential.

Both existential and humanistic theories hold that experience is unique and can actually only be understood by the person having the experience. Therefore, each person is the best source of information about her- or himself. The process of helping requires that helpers enter the subjective world of their clients and convey understanding of the clients' perceptions and the meanings that the clients ascribe to their experiences. Both humanistic and existential theories facilitate focus on a description of client experiences rather than on explanations of how behaviors and feelings came to be.

Both theories emphasize the nature and development of the helping relationship. In existential theory, the helper serves as a model and companion in a client's search for awareness, responsibility, and meaning. In contrast, in humanistic theory, clients are empowered by their relationship with the helper to use their own choices to become more authentically themselves—to more fully realize and act on their natural potential. This process of realizing and acting on one's potential has been called **self-actualization.** The term itself was first coined by Kurt Goldstein (1959) to refer to the natural capacity of humans for healthy development and full expression.

Rogers's person-centered theory is an extension of humanistic theory and focuses on the relationship environment created by helpers and the characteristics that helpers must bring to the relationship to create such an environment. Like his own theories about self-actualization as a life-long process rather than a fixed state, Rogers's ideas as a theorist evolved as they were actualized in his writing.

His first job after receiving a doctorate in clinical psychology was working with delinquent and disadvantaged youth. This work led to Rogers's (1939) earliest work, which emphasized a nondirective approach to understanding the client and communicating that understanding. While presenting a paper at the University of Minnesota in 1940, Rogers realized that his views constituted a new contribution to the field that focused on clients' responsibility for choices, therapists' establishment of trust, and therapists' giving permission for clients to explore feelings and choices. This lecture generated Rogers's (1942) *Counseling and Psychotherapy,* a book about the nature of the helping relationship and the nondirective approach. It set the stage for the controversial client-centered approach that followed (Thorne, 1992). In *Client-Centered Therapy: Its Current Practice Implications and Theory,* Rogers (1951) developed more fully his theories of personality development, the development of problems in living, and the nature of psychotherapeutic change. His person-centered perspective began with the publication of *On Becoming a Person* (1961), which described his philosophy of life, research, and teaching and the perspectives that moved well beyond individual change to include political activism and change. *Carl Rogers on Personal Power* (1977) and *A Way of Being* (1980) continued this work by applying his approach to different cultures and political change. Rogers's theories evolved from the description of building relationships that could effect personal change to building relationships that could effect social and political change.

A VIEW OF HUMAN NATURE AND THE DEVELOPMENT OF PROBLEMS

Common to the humanistic perspective, Rogers (1987a) firmly believed that at the core of each individual was a trustworthy and positive being capable of living an effective and productive life, making constructive changes, and self-understanding. Just as a seedling given appropriate conditions will automatically grow into a plant, humans left to their own natural capacity for actualizing potential will grow in a positive direction and move toward psychological health. This inherently positive view of what is natural to humans has implications for the helping practice. According to this perspective, the role of the helper is not that of expert authority who doles out advice to be followed by clients. Rather, this perspective focuses on helpers creating an environment in which barriers to self-actualization are removed so that a client's own expertise at problem-solving and encountering obstacles can be successfully realized.

If humans come into the world hard-wired, so to speak, with the capacity for realizing and then acting on their own presumed positive potential, how do problems develop? According to Rogers, natural self-actualization is thwarted by an equally natural human desire to be liked by and regarded positively by others. As humans develop awareness of themselves and others, we become more aware of others' regard for us, which then directly affects our regard for ourselves. When others set criteria for what is valuable in us, we begin to set similar criteria for what we perceive to be valuable in ourselves. As we evaluate our own experiences and self based on the beliefs and values of others, we often limit the fullest expression of our potential. These **conditions of worth,** imposed first by others and then incorporated into self-perception, then lead to an incongruence between our real self (the fullest expression of who we could become) and our ideal self (the self we develop to please or accommodate others). This incongruence leads to the development of distortions that may range from defenses against anxiety (e.g., rationalization, fantasy, projection, paranoid thinking) to psychosis (Holdstock & Rogers, 1977). The antidote to conditions of worth and incongruence that are at the root of psychological problems is **congruence** and unconditional positive regard from someone. Concepts of how problems develop have implications for the helping process.

THE HELPING PROCESS

Goals

The goals of person-centered helping are not determined by the helper, but by the client. However, in general, through establishing a therapeutic or helpful atmosphere, clients begin to move away from accommodating the expectations of others and toward being the fully functioning person they have the potential to be. According to Rogers (1961, 1969), a fully functioning person is one who is able to be open to new experiences, trusts in her- or himself and others enough to fashion fully congruent relationships, evaluates her- or himself realistically, and is able to assume personal and social responsibilities. Rogers saw that this, too, created expectations as an ideal and recognized that this was not actually attainable. His concept of the fully functioning individual included the idea of being open to continued growth toward this potential. As clients continue to grow, they become less defensive with others, more realistic in their perceptions, and better at problem-solving (Rogers, 1969).

These goals have a lofty, idealized ring to them, and they are goals often voiced by many helpers. Encouraging clients to listen to themselves and follow their own direction, however, takes strength of conviction in the basic premise of humanistic philosophy and no small measure of trust that clients will in fact seek and find their own best solutions to a problem. Further, it is not the situations clients choose to change or decisions they make that helpers agree with that tests this conviction. Rather, decisions that appear maladaptive to the outside observer are perhaps those most difficult for helpers to endorse.

I remember vividly my first encounter with a woman who I knew would be abused if she returned home. I struggled inside myself about whether it was consistent with my own Rogerian training and beliefs to use my skills as a therapist to persuade her not to go home. Regardless of how I proceeded, her well-being was at stake. I could certainly discuss my concerns genuinely, but if I persuaded, influenced, or manipulated her into not returning home, I would be disrespecting her power to choose her own path and would instead convey a clear message that I did not believe her to be a capable person. For a therapist to convey such messages would result in at best dependency and at worst client debilitation. If she chose to return home, she would be harmed by her husband. I decided to respect her decision to go home and quietly sobbed later.

The impact of a genuine commitment to client self-determination can be painful. Allowing, even facilitating, someone's own choices also means allowing her or him to experience the natural consequences of those choices. In this case, for me it meant living with the knowledge that someone could be hurt, or worse, as a result of the choices she and I both made. This extreme example provides a vivid illustration of the way in which the goals of helping from a person-centered perspective demand a different role for the helper.

The Helper's Role

The role of the helper according to a person-centered perspective is not anchored in *doing*, but in *being*. According to Rogers, the personal characteristics and attitudes that a helper brings to helping relationships facilitate the development of a fully functioning person, rather than the helper's knowledge of therapeutic techniques. In a sense, then, helpers use themselves and their ability to develop and maintain a genuine relationship as instruments of change. By creating a climate in which congruent and genuine interaction takes place and a relationship that conveys unconditional positive regard for clients, the helper creates the necessary and sufficient conditions in which clients can explore themselves and their feelings and behaviors, see new possibilities, and create their own changes based on their own values. According to Rogers (1961), this is the only type of relationship in which change can occur. The specific characteristics of this relationship were outlined by Rogers (1957, 1959, 1987a) in six points:

1. The two people involved in a helping relationship must be in psychological contact with one another. This places responsibility on the helper for creating an atmosphere in which a relationship of mutual respect and trust can develop; an atmosphere in which a client can explore feelings, attitudes, and prescriptions, and can focus on the present; and an atmosphere in which what the client says can be accepted without value judgment.

2. The client must be experiencing anxiety or discomfort from the incongruence or discrepancy between her or his real and ideal self. Incongruence motivates change. The helper facilitates client awareness of incongruence.

3. Helpers must be genuinely and congruently themselves in the relationship. Rather than disclosing everything to a client, this principle indicates that the therapist is aware of her or his own feelings and makes them available where appropriate to further the relationship.

4. The helper accepts and appreciates the client as she or he is. No judgments are made about the client's worth as a person. This does not imply that helpers must like everything a client says or does, rather that helpers afford clients respect as human beings without imposing conditions on the client's value.

5. The helper empathically enters the client's world without being influenced by her or his own values and communicates that to the client. The process of actively listening to and reflecting back to the client that the helper has understood the client's experience from the client's standpoint, even without full understanding, is an intention that fosters discussion and self-awareness. (This 1975 definition by Rogers of empathy is different from that of other theorists.)

6. Empathy and unconditional regard are perceived by the client. It is not enough for the helper to convey these—the client must perceive that she or he is being understood and accepted.

The focus of person-centered helping is not on helping clients solve a problem, but on helping clients to grow and develop a better understanding of themselves such that they may actualize themselves more fully and deal more effectively with the problems and issues facing them. Congruence or genuineness, unconditional positive regard or acceptance, and accurate empathic understanding are the three personal characteristics of the helper that form the central part of any helping relationship according to this approach.

Assessment

Assessment often precedes therapy or counseling. Many agencies offering professional helping services conduct an intake process that involves a variety of assessment procedures, such as psychological testing, diagnostic interviewing, and identifying client strengths and limitations. Person-centered approaches may appear on face value to eschew assessment. In fact, Rogers objected to testing in his early writings, although later, he wrote that he thought it could be helpful, particularly if a client requested it.

Perhaps what is most important to note is that from a person-centered perspective, it is a client's assessment of her- or himself that is more critical than the therapist's assessment or an external measurement of some specific characteristic. At this point in history, when measuring the effectiveness of short-term therapies seems to be gaining in importance, it is difficult to imagine professional helping without some external measurement. While incorporating some assessment may not be something a helper can opt out of, the spirit of the person-centered approach would suggest that involving the client in a collaborative assessment process is critically important.

Techniques and Process

Although some glibly suggest that there are no techniques in the person-centered approach, I would argue that the major techniques of a person-centered approach are those that have since been named the *microskills of helping.* Students who have already read and begun to practice the microskills discussed in Part One of this text may be pleased to note that the person-centered approach uses primarily these techniques. According to a person-centered approach to helping, helpers must demonstrate specific skills in the relationship in order to convey genuine, nonjudgmental understanding and a commitment to respecting the client's capacity for self-direction. They include nonverbal attending and following and minimal verbal responses (connoting acceptance); reflection of content (conveying an understanding of the client's experience); reflection of feeling (conveying both genuineness and empathic understanding of a client's affective experience); clarification (which communicates psychological connection and allows the client to explore and develop her or his experience without judgment); and confrontation and interpretation (which facilitate self-awareness without judgment).

Although in his earliest writing Rogers advocated more paraphrasing and clarifying, his later work suggested self-disclosure on the part of the helper and some interpretation of feelings. Still later, Rogers's position shifted to allow for more congruent, immediate, and active sharing on the part of the helper. Early Rogerian helpers appear different from their more contemporary counterparts, who are more likely to offer feedback, questions, and interpretations in the natural course of psychological contact and genuine interaction with clients.

The process of helping involves the techniques outlined earlier and appears to follow seven phases (Doyle, 1998):

1. The experience of being cared for and the sense of freedom to express anything on one's mind.
2. A slow unfolding and airing of one's attitudes and perceptions and a sort of cathartic release of feelings.
3. Gradual movement toward becoming less defensive about feelings.
4. Awareness of incongruities and factors related to those incongruities.
5. A more accurate perception of self, problems, and relationships.
6. An increase in strength to deal with problems and an enhanced ability to make decisions.
7. A gradual but definite sense of an integrated ideal and real self; increased facility for self-direction, self-confidence, and positive insight.

This process is not presumed to be smooth or linear. For many clients, it may be a path with ups, downs, and some rough and painful spots. An effective person-centered helper guides the client through this self-actualizing process.

RESEARCH

Rogers (1942) clearly opened the helping field to *outcome research*. Believing that the effectiveness of therapies should be measured, he recorded his sessions and subjected the transcripts to critical examination in teaching and research activities. He challenged clinical research to expand its horizons sufficiently to allow for different mechanisms for assessing effectiveness. Research about the effectiveness of the person-centered theory of therapy has primarily focused on the conditions that Rogers believed were necessary and sufficient for change (e.g., Beutler, Crago, & Arezmendi, 1986; Truax & Carkhuff, 1971;

Truax & Mitchell, 1971) and for comparing person-centered therapies to other therapies.

A relatively recent **meta-analysis** of Rogerian therapies found positive changes between pre-treatment and post-treatment and more powerful effect sizes than a waiting list or a no-treatment control group (Greenberg, Elliot, & Lietaer, 1994). However, when compared to cognitive or behavioral therapies, there were slightly stronger effects favoring these therapies. This research seems to suggest that person-centered approaches are more effective than no treatment, but may be less effective than cognitive or behavioral approaches. However, comparing a therapy based on "being" to ones based on "doing" poses some problems. Although continued research is needed to draw conclusions about the effectiveness of person-centered therapies, significant challenges remain in operationalizing the core conditions and measuring the effectiveness of being rather than doing.

CRITIQUING

Person-centered approaches to helping have been around a long time now and have seen many iterations. From Rogers's own evolution, to his students' interpretations (e.g., Carkhuff, 1969, 1977, 1978, 1987), to partial adaptations like Eugene Gendlin's (1981) focusing approach or Ann Cornell's (1993) modifications of Gendlin's approach, to the introduction of the concept of the microskills of helping (Ivey, 1994; Ivey, Ivey, & Simek-Morgan, 1997), to Clara Hill and Karen O'Brien's recent *Helping Skills* published by the American Psychological Association (1999a), Barbara Okun's *Effective Helping* (2002), and even this textbook, person-centered theories of helping have influenced many professional helpers. Rogers himself has been influential in helping individuals, couples, and groups (Rogers, 1942, 1970, & 1970, respectively). In his later years, Rogers made a point of applying his principles of establishing genuine, empathic, and respectful relationships to social conflicts around the world like those in Northern Ireland and South Africa (Rogers, 1970). His principles (1987c) are still being used by the Carl Rogers Institute for Peace in La Jolla, California (Saley & Holdstock, 1993). His books have been translated into twelve languages and are actively read in thirty different countries. The longevity and far-reaching impact of his theories is a testimony to the power of Rogers's ideas.

Perhaps more than any other theory of helping, Rogers's ideas have been incorporated into professional training about the nature and skills of professional helping relationships. His focus on what constitutes a relationship in which change can occur has been enormously influential. Virtually every theory of helping discussed in this text relies on a foundation built from the listening skills first articulated by Rogers.

Despite their longevity and pervasive influence, Rogers's theories have lost popularity in recent years among students of professional helping (Cain, 1988; Combs, 1988). Students complain that they are too simple, that they are limited to attending and reflecting, that they lead to undirected rambling, that they emphasize the character rather than the problem-solving skills of the helper. Also, individuals may not necessarily have an actualizing potential and hence cannot trust their own directions or find their own answers, and helpers should not abdicate responsibility and should advise and direct clients.

Obviously, some complaints reflect misunderstanding of Rogers's work. Some complaints may also be born of a generation of professional helpers raised in an age of rapid solutions. The influence of an insurance industry that demands brief, more tangible behavioral changes as goals cannot be underestimated in its intolerance for the length and intangibility of helping based on being. Other criticisms leveled against the person-centered approach include its apparent emphasis on Western European and Anglo-American values despite its worldwide popularity. A shift in both the zeitgeist and ethical standards for helping has recently demanded that theories of helping respond to the needs of American ethnic minority clients, some of whom expect more direction from helpers. These needs appear, at least on the surface, to be inconsistent with Rogers's nondirective approach.

Philosophically, there are criticisms of Rogers's person-centered approach as well. Humanism assumes a kind of responsibility for one's own choices that further assumes a priori that choices exist for all humans. As those of subordinate status, whether in Africa, Bosnia, or the United States, can attest, not all people enjoy the same freedom to choose a self-directed path that those of power and privilege enjoy. In this way, Rogers's theories are limited by his own perceptions of choice as a white, middle-class, well-educated man. Even his core conditions are difficult to translate across ethnic and gender differences. Genuineness may look different in one whose status demands circumspection, and movement away from the expectations of others may not constitute truth to self where self is defined in relationship with others. For person-centered theories to speak to helping all people, its implicit ethnic, gender, and class biases must be addressed.

Even noting its limitations, the person-centered approach to helping has been enormously influential in training professional helpers to create and maintain helping relationships that foster change, growth, and development. Rogers never intended that his own theories would constitute a static fixture. He hoped that they might constitute a process that would facilitate further theoretical development. Any facilitation is a process that, by its definition, continues to effect change long after the actual precipitant. Rogers's theories of helping can be said to have facilitated significant changes in the discipline of professional helping.

CHAPTER

9   Behavioral
Theories
of Helping

CONTEXT

Behavioral theories of helping cannot be attributed to any one theorist. Behavioral theories of helping are based on principles taken from the psychology of learning and conditioning, and they focus on how a person behaves. Behavioral theories study how human behavior is developed, acquired, changed, and even eliminated. The first behavioral theories focused exclusively on observable behaviors, like verbal and motor behaviors, although subsequent adaptations of behavioral theories have also focused on internal, covert behaviors involved in learning. An important difference between overt, observable behavior and covert behavior is that covert behaviors must be measured indirectly, perhaps through self-report or with specialized equipment (Sarafino, 1996).

During the first half of the twentieth century, dominant explanations suggested that behavior was the result of internal "forces," such as biology, heredity, drives, motives, conflicts, and traits. Psychologists such as John Watson (1913, 1930) and B. F. Skinner (1938, 1948, 1953, 1954) began to develop a different perspective based in part on Lockian philosophy. John Locke (1632–1704) had suggested that children entered the world as blank slates on which "experience" wrote. Watson and Skinner began systematic examinations of the ways in which behaviors could be learned. Their position was that nearly all behavior was learned and, rejecting the philosophical approach, they drew on scientific methods to demonstrate these principles.

In 1927, a Nobel prize–winning Russian physiologist named Ivan Pavlov was studying the role that salivation played in digestive processes in dogs when he observed that dogs salivated before food was actually in their mouths. He concluded that the association between the sight of food or the approaching lab technician and salivation must have been learned. Moreover, he suggested that the response had been learned through its association with the automatic reflex of salivating as a reaction to food (**classical conditioning,** also called **respondent conditioning**). Pavlov's now famous discoveries with dogs salivating involved observations that although salivation is a natural response to the presentation of food, other events paired with the presentation of food could also elicit salivation.

Although dogs and salivation do not sound much like professional helping, the discovery led to the systematic exploration of respondent conditioning principles and to behavioral helping theories. Humans also learn to respond through association. In the early 1940s, Joseph Wolpe began applying Pavlov's principles to models for solving human problems thought to have developed through such conditioning.

In addition to learning through association with reflexes, people also learn from the consequences that follow a behavior. The process of learning through consequences is called **operant conditioning** (also called **instrumental conditioning**). B. F. Skinner is credited with developing and refining the principles that define and distinguish behaviors that operate on the environment and produce consequences. Skinner's work has become the foundation for two other types of helping practice: applied behavior analysis and behavior modification. Skinner (1938, 1953) established the basic techniques and terminology used in the study of human operant behavior. He distinguished between two types of behavioral consequence: reinforcement and punishment. In reinforcement, a consequence causes an increase in the performance of a behavior, whereas in punishment, a consequence causes a decrease in the incidence of the behavior. Although reinforcement is popularly thought to involve consequences that a person may find pleasant, positive, or rewarding, and punishment is thought to involve consequences that one finds negative or aversive, these reactions are not what define a consequence as reinforcing or punishing. It is the impact on behaviors that defines reinforcement or punishment.

The best way to define whether something is reinforcing or punishing is to observe its effect. If something increases a behavior, it is, by definition, reinforcing. If something decreases the behavior, it is by definition punishing. Since Skinner's work, others have discovered that behavior is not only influenced by consequences, but by what precedes the behavior, or its antecedents. An important type of learning also takes place as people find and learn cues that precede certain consequences. Although instructors and texts often treat respondent and operant conditioning as though they were two separate processes, in real life, the two types of conditioning occur together.

Albert Bandura's (1962, 1969, 1975, 1977; Bandura & Walters, 1963) now classic experiments illustrated yet another type of human learning. In Bandura's studies, children watched one of three films showing an adult perform an aggressive act, such as hitting a Bobo clown doll with a mallet. In one of the films, the adults were shown being punished; in another, they received a reward; in still another, there were no consequences. The children were then taken to a room with a Bobo doll and told they could play with the toys in any way that they wished. They tended to copy the adult's behavior in the film version they saw, but the children who had observed the adult being punished behaved less aggressively than the other children. These experiments certainly have implications for the imitation of aggression through observing media violence, but they also form part of the foundation for understanding that modeling, imitation, and vicarious and social learning are effective ways to acquire and change a vast array of behaviors ranging from simple responses (such as shaking a tambourine—Griffin, Wolery, & Schuster, 1992) to complex social behaviors (such as drinking—Caudill & Lipscomb, 1980; or fear—Venn & Short, 1973).

That learning could take place through observation also became part of a shift in attention toward less observable and less tangible, and more complex and more pervasive social learning models. Numerous examinations of the cognitive processes (i.e., mental activity such as thinking and reasoning) that could precede or follow behavior showed that plans, expectations, beliefs, and rules could also constitute covert antecedents to behavior (Sarafino, 1996). The study of mental representations that precede behavior led to the development of cognitive-behavioral theories of helping discussed in Chapter 10.

The 1950s, 1960s, and 1970s saw the emergence of applications of learning and conditioning principles to professional helping practices and changing people's behavior. Joseph Wolpe (1958, 1973) developed respondent conditioning and counterconditioning techniques that were highly effective in reducing fears and anxieties. Applied behavioral analysis focused on ways to apply the principles to educational settings and social problems like child rearing, crime, and mental illness (Skinner, 1938, 1948, 1953, 1954). Techniques for applying the principles to therapy gave birth to behavior therapies (Lazarus, 1971; O'Leary & Wilson, 1975; Rimm & Masters, 1974).

Behavioral theories focus on behavior, and professionals who apply these theories to helping place a strong emphasis on: defining status and progress in terms of behavior; being able to measure the behavior in some way; and, whenever possible, assessing covert behaviors in terms of overt action. The process of helping from a behavioral perspective involves changing aspects of the person's environment, specifically, changing the antecedents and consequences of a behavior to effect changes in behavior. Changing behavior begins with an understanding of the behavioral perspective about human nature and the development of both useful and problematic behaviors.

A VIEW OF HUMAN NATURE AND THE DEVELOPMENT OF PROBLEMS

Early philosophers like John Locke argued that human beings come into the world as *tabula rasa* (blank slates) to be written on by their environments and experiences, while later behavioral theorists proposed that the mechanisms of conditioning and learning began with innate reflexes. As often happens in theory development, behavioral theory developed in part in opposition to earlier theoretical emphases on "natural" instincts, such as drives, inborn potential, feelings, motives, and conflicts. An obvious, although often eclipsed, assumption about human nature and development made by behavioral theorists is that humans are naturally capable of being conditioned and of learning from experience. As the earliest experimentation demonstrated, other animal species and humans alike enter the world with natural reflexes and at least rudimentary biological motives that facilitate learning and conditioning processes. Nonetheless, behavioral theorists place primary emphasis on behaviors that can be observed and measured, and on the conditions that precede behavior, occur during the behavior, and follow a behavior. Many studies focused on those events that served to elicit and maintain behavior. Behavior, whether it is problematic or useful, is governed by the same principles of learning and conditioning. Humans can learn behaviors in many different, though related, ways.

When a stimulus is capable of naturally producing a certain response, another stimulus may be associated with it in time (called *temporal association*) or in location (called *spatial association*), and eventually, the second stimulus will elicit virtually the same response. This process has been called **classical conditioning.** The stimulus (such as food) capable of producing a response that had not been conditioned is called an **unconditioned stimulus (US)** and the response (such as salivation) that occurs to such a stimulus is called an **unconditioned response (UR).** The stimulus (such as a bell) that gets paired with another response that has been conditioned is called the **conditioned stimulus (CS)** and the response (such as salivation) to that newly conditioned stimulus is now called a **conditioned response (CR).** So, salivation can be either an unconditioned or a conditioned response, depending on the circumstances that elicited that response.

Of course, both animals and humans have many more reflexes than the one to salivate upon the presentation of food. We blink in response to objects approaching our eyes; we suck in response to something approaching our cheek; we startle in response to loud noises and sudden, unexpected events. By now, many students have heard stories of experiments in a process called **stimulus generalization.** A sudden loud noise was paired with the presentation of a white rabbit, conditioning a young boy to fear the previously loved white rabbit. Moreover, his fears began to extend to those things resembling the white rabbit, such as his favorite uncle's white beard.

Most students of helping theories are pretty unenthusiastic about the Pavlovian experiments until they realize the implications these basic principles of conditioning have for the development of problems among clients. Consider the following scenario extrapolated from my own clinical practice.

A woman is sitting at home one night, reading a book in her living room, when she sees the locked doorknob turn. Immediately, the door crashes in and a stranger enters her home, grabs her from her chair, throws her to the ground, and rapes her.

The principles of conditioning make it easier to understand how the woman came to experience symptoms of what psychologists call **posttraumatic stress disorder (PTSD).** In PTSD, victims of life-threatening circumstances or situations that threaten grave harm come to respond to the stimuli associated temporally and spatially with the event in much the same way that they responded to the initial traumatic event. They may develop startle responses to any or all of the stimuli present during the trauma. They are not only fearful of the event itself, as anyone would be, but often, they fear anything associated with the event. They want to avoid even benign things that resemble the horrible event.

To someone with an understanding of classical conditioning principles, it would be no surprise to find that the woman in this example might fear sitting home alone, reading, doorknobs turning, or men. It is even possible that she may fear those things less obvious to an outside observer of the event, like the carpeting she felt under her feet just before she hit the ground or the feeling of relaxing just before the entire event occurred. Any or all of these stimuli are now capable of eliciting the same fearful response because of their association with the natural fear response to an unexpected event, a loud noise, or bodily harm. A helper who understands how these associated stimuli could become problems is in a better position to provide helpful countermeasures. Helpers who do not understand these principles may attribute the woman's behaviors to her own idiosyncracies or some personal pathology.

According to behavioral theories of helping, behaviors, whether useful or problematic, are not only learned through association with natural reflexes. Humans and animals also acquire behaviors as a result of the consequences of the behavior. Behaviors may be followed by events or objects that either increase or decrease the likelihood that the behavior will be repeated. If a behavior is followed temporally by something that serves to increase the likelihood of that same behavior, we say that the behavior has been reinforced. A **reinforcer** can be any object or event that serves to increase the likelihood of the behavior being repeated. So an event or object is not defined as a reinforcer based on a person's perceptions of it as rewarding, but rather on the effect it has. Consider a simple example of a problem behavior. If your little brother takes a cookie without asking and your mother yells at him and he turns around and takes another cookie, one would have to conclude that the yelling served as a reinforcer. Reinforcers facilitate the development of behaviors. If I think that candy is great and so decide to give it to my niece after she carries out the trash and the next trash day she doesn't carry it out, no matter how great I think candy is, candy is not a reinforcer for her for trash-carrying-out behavior.

When a person is initially acquiring behaviors, reinforcers must be given with perfect consistency (called **continuous reinforcement**), or when the reinforcer is taken away, the behavior will likely disappear (called **extinction**). Once a behavior is firmly established, reinforcers can be given at varying intervals. This is called **intermittent reinforcement,** and behavior maintained by intermittent reinforcement is extremely resistant to elimination. Most human behavior, useful or problematic, is actually maintained through intermittent reinforcement.

Behaviors may also be followed by events, objects, or responses that decrease the likelihood that the behavior will be repeated. If it has that result, the event, object, or response is called **punishment.** No matter how unpleasant the perception of an event or object is, if it doesn't reduce the likelihood of the response, it cannot be called a punishment. Although many people would see incarceration as a very unpleasant experience, if it does not reduce the likelihood of a particular crime, it cannot be considered punishment from a behavioral perspective. Part of the difficulty in using punishment as a mechanism for eliminating certain behaviors is that research has established that to have the desired effect of reducing the likelihood of the behavior, the event, object, or response must almost immediately follow the behavior and must be of a certain strength.

Some behaviors are learned through avoiding unpleasant or aversive situations, events, or objects. Take, as an example, parking behavior. Putting coins into a meter is rarely followed by objects, events, or responses that increase this behavior. I can't remember the last time someone applauded me for feeding a parking meter. It is even rare for a meter enforcement officer to immediately give someone a ticket who stays too long at the meter. Nonetheless, most people put money into parking meters regularly after parking to avoid getting a parking ticket. This is a simple but good example of what is called **avoidance learning,** which is maintained by intermittent punishment.

Humans also acquire new useful or problem behaviors through a process called **shaping.** Shaping involves establishing the desired behavior (called a **target behavior**) by finding something that operates as a reinforcer for the person, and offering the reinforcer following behaviors that could be thought of as being close to the target behavior. This is called **approximating** the target behavior. It is even possible to string together a number of behaviors that more and more closely resemble the target behavior, to offer reinforcements for each, and to raise the criteria for getting the reinforcement over time. The behaviors in such a string are called **successive approximations** and the process of stringing together is called a **chain.** Behavioral theories suggest that humans can acquire previously nonexistent behaviors through such a process.

Humans and other animals also learn useful behaviors and problem behaviors vicariously. **Vicarious learning** occurs when new behaviors are acquired by observing the behavior of others and the outcomes their actions produce. While seemingly simple, Bandura's series of experiments demonstrated the power of observational learning. People tend to imitate models—other people—and are influenced by the consequences that follow behavior other than their own. Likewise, undesirable behaviors can be modified by observing different models—other people or different outcomes. This has important implications for helpers, who may serve as models themselves or may provide models rather than having to rely on immediate or continuous reinforcement to help a client develop a particular behavior.

Finally, complex social and cultural behaviors, whether useful or problematic, can be acquired through processes in which other people, programs, or institutions, called social or cultural agents, combine all of these mechanisms of learning and conditioning to impart training. This process is called **socialization** or **acculturation.** Consider for a moment how humans in the United States generally learn to wear clothing when going outside. This is one example of a complex social behavior. Parents may instruct young children to wear clothing, but as anyone who has raised children knows, instruction may not be enough. Wearing clothing is not a natural, reflexive behavior for children. Sometimes children may wear clothes to avoid parents yelling at them, sometimes because they hear praise from parents for wearing clothes. Humans may wear clothes because we see other humans wearing clothes. Sometimes adults wear clothes to avoid getting arrested. Going naked outdoors in the United States has also been modified by social institutions, like laws, and by implementing social consequences, like fines and jail time.

To sum up, according to behavioral theories of helping, humans learn various useful or problematic behaviors through direct instruction, classical or respondent conditioning, operant or instrumental conditioning, modeling and imitation, and social learning. It follows, then, that undesirable behaviors can be eliminated by breaking the association with stimuli associated with the behavior, by taking away those stimuli that are acting as reinforcers, by introducing stimuli that act as punishment, by changing consequences for models or changing models for an imitated behavior, and by changing social agents, institutions, or programs. As with any helping intervention or prevention strategy, behavioral theories about helping proceed directly from the assumptions about human nature and development on which they are based. In the case of behavioral theories of helping, it is the principles of learning and conditioning derived from psychological experimentation that have important implications for the process of helping.

THE HELPING PROCESS

Goals

According to behavioral theories, the goal of helping is to assist clients in acquiring new behaviors, changing or modifying existing behaviors, or eliminating undesirable or maladaptive behaviors. Targeted behaviors can be specified by the client, by the helper, by someone else in the client's life, or in a collaboration between any or all of these people. Once targeted, behaviors are carefully observed and defined. Helping from a behavioral perspective can involve modifying overt behavior, but behavioral approaches have also been used to modify some of the subtle, unseen physiological changes that often accompany behavior. Behaviorally-oriented helping can be used to change, modify, or eliminate simple behaviors or complex constellations of behavior. The focus of behavioral helping approaches is on current problem behaviors. While past experiences are recognized as precipitating the current behaviors, except insofar as information may be useful in designing a process to change a current behavior, no particular emphasis is placed on talking about the problem or developing insight about the origins of the problem behavior. The emphasis of behavioral helping is on identifying behaviors that require acquisition, modification, or elimination.

The Helper's Role

As specific behavior is the focus of helping and behaviors are thought to be acquired or learned, the role of the helper from a behavioral perspective is that of instructor, reconditioner, coach, consultant, and researcher. Through careful interviewing, the behavioral helper listens, paraphrases, and asks questions. The helper assesses the associations that the client may have made in acquiring the problem behavior. The helper explores contingencies that are likely to maintain the behavior, models for the problem behavior, and social institutions that may promote or act as diffuse reinforcements. The helper then instructs the client and consults with anyone else relevant to changing the behavior in the principles of modifying the association, contingencies, or models.

The specific modifications that must be made to effect change vary in each situation and for each person. Because of this, although learning and conditioning techniques are based on experimental research demonstrating their effectiveness, there are many techniques to draw from, and plans of action can be customized for each client and each behavioral problem.

Assessment

The behaviorally-oriented helping process begins with gathering as much information as possible about the circumstances that maintain the behavior or multiple behaviors. This careful and detailed assessment focuses client attention on operationally defining the target behavior, and on identifying the antecedents and the consequences. Assessment facilitates effective and timely change.

One assessment tool is called a **behavioral interview** (Busse & Beaver, 2000). In a behavioral interview, the helper establishes a relationship with the client with the goal of understanding the client's problem behaviors. Questions are answered about the antecedents and consequences of the behavior, and both helper and client map a plan of action. Other people who are relevant to the client's problem behaviors may also participate in the behavioral interview. The interview questions are focused on the target behavior, but also address the circumstances of the behavior and the specific associations, reinforcers, and models that maintain the behavior. The interview gives the helper valuable information for designing appropriate change mechanisms with the client.

Problem behaviors may also be assessed by **behavioral self-report** or **rating scales.** The Beck Depression Inventory (BDI) (Beck, Steer, & Brown, 1996) assesses behavioral, affective, and cognitive changes associated with depression. The Social Skills Rating System (SSRS) (Elliott, Busse, & Gresham, 1993) is a self-report measure of social behavior. The Adolescent Behavior Checklist (ABC) (Adams, Kelley, & McCarthy, 1997) assigns frequency ratings about how often a social behavior occurs to gather information about adolescent social skills. Each of these scales uses behavioral ratings to assess the nature, frequency, duration, and magnitude of problem behaviors.

Sometimes clients and others close to the client, such as parents, peers, or teachers, complete checklists of behaviors or rate various circumstances to facilitate the process of designing an effective plan. When others in addition to the client complete assessment tools, close agreement between raters about the observations is important. This is called **inter-rater reliability.** Using others to help assess behaviors is consistent with the theoretical foundation since the emphasis in behavioral helping is on observable behaviors.

While it is possible for helpers to ask questions of the teachers or other students, sometimes a picture is worth many words in giving an accurate description of the circumstances surrounding a behavior. **Naturalistic observation** involves recording the frequency, duration, and strength of target behaviors in the setting in which they usually occur. For example, a child experiencing difficulties in school may be observed in the classroom to get a clear idea of the specific environmental contingencies that may be maintaining her or his behavior. Simulated settings may be used to create environments that are analogous to the situation in which the behavior occurs.

A detailed analysis of the antecedents (A), behaviors (B), and consequences (C), called a **functional behavior analysis,** is sometimes conducted to inform the helper of the context of the behavior and to give a clearer indication of the function the behavior may serve for the client (Kazdin, 1994b; Sarafino, 1996; Schloss & Smith, 1994).

Finally, physiological measures may help to assess target behaviors. For example, galvanic skin response, muscle tension, heart rate, and respiration rates can offer clues about levels of anxiety. Physiological measurements are the basis for biofeedback mechanisms that help clients to both monitor and change specific problems, such as migraine headaches, as well as overall stress.

Helpers generally choose assessment techniques based on their own training, the availability of the method, or because it best fits a plan or technique commonly used in addressing the behavior the client is seeking to change.

Techniques and Process

The process of helping from a behavioral perspective is an active, collaborative, and instructive model in which the helper and client focus on a specific plan for the client to acquire, reduce or eliminate, or modify specific behaviors. Helping begins with careful assessment of how a behavior has been learned or conditioned and what circumstances are serving to maintain the behavior. This assessment is followed by techniques that help clients to acquire new behaviors, modify existing behaviors, or eliminate problem behaviors. Behaviorists' emphasis on techniques as process has been criticized as overlooking the relationship context of helping and the clients' experience of helping. While later behavioral theories have prompted helpers to attend to the context in which the techniques take place, many behavioral helpers would argue that instructing clients about effective techniques for behavior change is still the fundamental helping process.

Behavioral helpers have access to a vast array of techniques supported by well-established methods for testing the techniques' effectiveness. One component of behavioral techniques—punishment—will be explained, but not emphasized, for three reasons. First, it is difficult to apply punishment both effectively and ethically to modify behavior. Second, well-researched methods for changing behavior exist that do not include the use of punishment. Third, well-documented ethical controversies surround the use of physically aversive stimuli (Ammerman & Herson, 1993; Kazdin, 1984; K. L. Miller, 1975; Sarafino, 1996; Whaley & Mallot, 1971). Edward Sarafino (1996) recommends the use of punishment only as a last resort after other methods of behavior modification have been tried and failed or if the targeted behavior is a dangerous one, and then only when the types of punishers are acceptable by legal and ethical standards.

Punishment is a consequence that suppresses the behavior on which it is contingent, decreasing its frequency, duration, or magnitude. **Positive punishment** involves adding an aversive stimulus or condition as a consequence of behavior. **Negative punishment** involves taking away something the person already has. Several factors affect the effectiveness of punishers. Punishment techniques achieve rapid results in partially or completely suppressing undesirable behavior, a plus when the behavior is embarrassing or dangerous. On the other hand, punishment has been found to produce negative emotional reactions, escape from the aversive stimuli or the helping situation, and sometimes aggressive behavior (Azrin & Holz, 1966; Hutchinson, 1977; Mayhew & Harris, 1978). To be used effectively, punishment must be administered immediately following the problem behavior, must be intense in its magnitude, and must be accompanied by instruction and reinforcement of alternative responses.

Other strategies are considered generally more effective than punishment to decrease the incidence of problem behaviors. Techniques are chosen based on the behavioral goal and the environmental forces that have preceded, shaped, elicited, and followed the targeted behaviors. Behavioral problems are considered simple or complex because of the stimuli that maintain them or the number of different actions that comprise them, not because of the impact of the problem on the client.

For relatively simple behavioral problems, managing the contingencies of the behavior may be most effective. **Contingency management** involves a careful assessment of the antecedents, behaviors, and consequences of the problem behavior. Operant learning principles are then applied to shape (if the target is a new behavior to be acquired), reinforce (if the target is ensuring a stable response rate), or extinguish (if the target is reducing or eliminating the problem behavior).

Managing the antecedents, the behaviors themselves, or the consequences can be effective in changing target behaviors. For example, differentially reinforcing, systematically reinforcing the performance of an alternative response, reversing a habit, self-monitoring instructions, and extinction of the reinforcements are effective in reducing problem behaviors.

If the target behaviors are ones that have been classically conditioned, counterconditioning measures are generally considered most
effective in helping clients to change. Counterconditioning measures
include **systematic desensitization, imaginal flooding,** and *in
vivo* **desensitization.**

In systematic desensitization, the association between a response
and a stimulus is broken through gradual introduction of the associated stimuli in a circumstance in which the response cannot occur
(Wolpe, 1958, 1973, 1990). A client who is afraid of driving might be
a good candidate for systematic desensitization. A behavioral helper
would begin an assessment by asking about the things associated,
either by time or location, with driving that the client fears. (Most
desensitization plans include a focus on either time or location.) After
helping the client to identify all of the associated features of her or his
fear of driving, the helper would work with the client to lay out the
associated features in increments of either time or space and assign
measures of discomfort. These measures of discomfort are called
subjective units of disturbance (**SUDS**). The associated features
are then arranged in order of discomfort, called a hierarchy of the
stimuli.

Before proceeding, the helper teaches the client deep-muscle
relaxation strategies. Relaxation has been found to be incompatible
with anxiety and fear (Wolpe, 1958, 1973, 1990). In other words, feeling fear or anxiety simultaneously with relaxation is virtually impossible. Therefore, if paired with relaxation, stimuli that were previously
associated with fear or anxiety responses will lose that connection.

The type of relaxation used in **counterconditioning** helping
processes is called **deep-muscle relaxation** because it involves the
progressive relaxation of various muscle groups. Helpers using deep-
muscle relaxation techniques first teach clients to be aware of tension
in the various muscle groups and then to recognize the differences
between tense and relaxed muscles. The helper then focuses the client
on relaxation alone. The process of instructing a client about relaxation
may be done in the helper's office, with tapes that the client uses at
home, or a combination of the two.

Once the client has learned to relax muscles deeply at will, the
next part of the systematic desensitization plan begins. Beginning at
the very lowest rating of discomfort, the helper guides the client to
imagine the associated features. In the example of a client who is afraid
to drive, this might mean picturing wanting to go to the grocery store,

finding the car keys, opening the garage door, and so on. If the client feels discomfort, the guided imagining stops, and together the helper and client try to arrive at a less uncomfortable step. Between the step of wanting to go to the grocery store and the "finding the car keys" step, the helper and client may insert images of checking the pantry shelves for the car keys or making a shopping list. Each stimulus in the hierarchy is introduced incrementally until the client can imagine the most fearful of the stimuli while still remaining relaxed.

In vivo desensitization involves a similar process to systematic desensitization except that fearful or anxiety-provoking stimuli are introduced in reality rather than being imagined. On the other hand, in a behavior modification process called *imaginal flooding*, helpers guide clients to imagine increasingly more frightening or anxiety-provoking images based on their interview information. In fact, clients are asked to imagine the most frightening circumstance related to their problem behavior they can think of. Based on the same principles of counterconditioning as systematic desensitization, imaginal flooding exposes clients to all of the stimuli that have been established to be frightening or anxiety-provoking in a very short time frame—even in just one meeting. Repeated exposure to the imagined stimuli in the absence of real threat is thought to desensitize clients to the fearful stimuli.

Behavioral helpers can also use principles of **modeling** to assist a client in making changes. Helpers may model new behaviors themselves or may help the client find other appropriate models for a new behavior. Modeling may be overt or covert. The client may also serve as her or his own model.

One way that helpers serve as models is through demonstration to reduce anxiety (Spiegler & Guevremont, 1998). Take an example of a client who is facing a first job interview. A helper may offer to demonstrate an interview situation with a client through a role-play of the interview. Clients may be motivated to imitate behaviors they see as each takes on the role of interviewer and job candidate while they practice the job interview. Initially, the helper models appropriate job interviewing behaviors, while the client observes and then comments. Then the client imitates the model while the helper observes and comments. This can continue until the client has a clearer sense of how to behave in an interview and the anxiety is reduced.

Modeling and rehearsal are not only useful in developing new behaviors, but in modifying old ones. When I worked for the Domestic

Abuse Project in Minneapolis, abusive men received instructions about how to resolve conflicts in a nonviolent fashion. Professional helpers and other group participants served as models who resolved conflicts without abuse while the men observed, commented, and then took turns rehearsing nonviolent approaches to resolving conflicts.

Assertiveness training is based on modeling, rehearsal, and operant behavioral approaches. Clients are taught to express feelings and thoughts in a direct, honest, and socially appropriate manner that respects the directness, honesty, and appropriateness in others (Jakubowski, 1977). Assertive, nonassertive, and aggressive behaviors are assessed using interviews, role-plays, and questionnaires designed to help clients discriminate between the behaviors. A series of modeling and rehearsal exercises involves helper feedback and facilitates shaping successive approximations to assertive behaviors. In other words, helpers model assertive responses and offer feedback while clients practice getting more and more assertive in their own responses. Sometimes desensitization may be used in combination with these techniques to gradually expose clients to situations in which they experience themselves asserting their thoughts and feelings. In the absence of her or his worst fears, a client's discomfort when behaving assertively is reduced or eliminated.

RESEARCH

Outcome research demonstrating the effectiveness of behavioral helping strategies is abundant. Because behavioral theories of helping were derived from scientific methods in psychology, behavioral helping techniques have been subjected to the same testing, validation, and rigorous experimental processes used in investigating any scientific question. They have been validated under controlled conditions that establish the reliability and validity of the methods. Those who advocate the use of behavioral techniques are often specifically trained in research designs that can demonstrate exactly how, how often, and under what circumstances each technique works or does not work.

Behavioral strategies have been found to be effective in helping both children and adult clients address many mental health problems. Behavioral interventions have proven effective for both simple (e.g., off-task behavior) and complex (e.g., ADHD) classroom behaviors

(Schloss & Smith, 1994). More complex mental health problems have also been successfully addressed using behavioral strategies. These problems include depression (Frame & Cooper, 1993; Hoberman & Clarke, 1993), obsessive-compulsive disorders (Pinto & Francis, 1993), posttraumatic stress (Caddell & Drabman, 1993; Foy, Resnick, & Lipovsky, 1993), and a variety of phobias (O'Leary & Wilson, 1975; Sharf, 1996; Wolpe, 1958, 1973, 1990). Behavioral helping strategies have even been shown to be effective in helping clients with complex psychological distresses resulting from borderline personality disorder (Linehan, 1993a, 1993b), antisocial personality disorder (Doren, 1993), and pervasive disorders like autism (Luiselli, 1993), schizophrenia (Morrison & Sayers, 1993), and mental retardation (Scherzinger, Keogh, & Whitman, 1993).

The same behavioral strategies used to address classroom and mental health problems have been extended to help change social behaviors. These include littering (Osborne & Powers, 1980), gasoline conservation (Foxx & Hake, 1977), recycling (Geller, Chafee, & Ingram, 1975), and racial stereotyping (McMurtry & Williams, 1972). Medical settings have adopted behavioral techniques to help clients adhere to medical regimens (Gillum & Barsky, 1974). Other medical programs, such as weight control (Johnson & Boggess, 1993), smoking cessation, and the reduction of alcohol consumption (Kazdin, 1994b), utilize behavioral strategies. In short, the extent to which behavioral programs may be designed to help clients acquire, change, or eliminate behavior is only limited by the creativity and ethics of the behavioral helper.

CRITIQUING

Behavioral helping has been seen alternately as a panacea for all mental health and social problems and as an inhumane and superficial blight on the face of helping theory. Behavioral helping techniques have been widely researched but also widely criticized for research conducted with very small samples that may not be generalized to other client problems. (Often, one client serves as her or his own control group and changes made are reported in a study of one client.) Even though collections of these small sample studies have been meta-analyzed to show the overall effectiveness of behavioral helping (e.g., Kazdin, 1985a), some critics suggest that the minute behavioral focus may mean that the techniques bear little resemblance to more complex problems clients bring to helping professionals. Critics suggest that if behavioral techniques do not actually address the complex behaviors found in real clinical settings, then underlying problems may not be adequately addressed by these methods.

Other critics see behavioral techniques as inhumane. Their rationale claims that behavioral techniques do not focus on the clients' experience of themselves, the helper, or the helping experience, and therefore the techniques treat only the problem behavior and not the whole person. The mechanical, systematic, empirical model of behavioral helping is seen as a universal, cookie-cutter approach to individual and unique problems, which offends the sensibilities of some who advocate individualistic approaches to helping.

Still other critics have voiced concerns about the ethics of who decides what behaviors are maladaptive and whether adaptation to an unfair social system can be considered an ethical goal. Too often the individual environment is modified, rather than the larger social environment, even when it is the latter that is the problem.

Despite criticisms, there can be no dispute that behavioral helping techniques are effective in treating many problems for which people seek help. Based on principles of learning and conditioning that were developed, refined, and validated in controlled laboratory settings and were also shown to be effective with myriad human problems, these theories have been influential in moving helping practice from art to science. The promise of individualized, short-term, proven effectiveness for change is no small thing in an age of accountability and managed mental health care. Because behavioral strategies do not rely on subjective experience or elusive traits, helpers can focus on clients' problem behaviors and strengths. The effectiveness of behavioral techniques is no longer in question. The issues that remain involve how to integrate behavioral techniques into ethical, legal, personal, and professional value systems and theoretical frameworks and how to address both individual problems and systemic social problems.

10 Cognitive-Behavioral Theories of Helping

CONTEXT

Cognitive-behavioral theories of helping are not one approach, but a category that includes several theories of helping. These theories share a common emphasis on the role of mental processes (i.e., cognition) in behavior and feelings. The category includes: rational-emotive behavior theory (Ellis, 1962, 1994; Ellis & Grieger, 1977, 1986; Ellis & Harper, 1977; Ellis & Whitely, 1979; Maultsby, 1984), cognitive theory (Beck, 1963, 1967, 1976; Beck, Rush, Schaw, & Emery, 1979), and cognitive-behavior modification theory (Meichenbaum, 1977, 1985, 1986, 1996). Cognitive-behavioral theories have been derived from professional helping practice. All share an emphasis on collaborative relationships between helper and client; a belief that client difficulties are largely the result of difficulties in cognitive processes; an emphasis on changing cognition as a way to change behavior and feeling; and a time-limited, educational approach to circumscribed problems.

Rational-emotive behavior therapy (REBT) was developed and articulated beginning in the mid-1950s by Albert Ellis, a clinical psychologist. As Ellis's emphasis evolved from investigating the impact of rational and irrational thought on behavior to include the interactive cause-and-effect relationship between behaviors, thoughts, and feelings, the name of this approach changed from rational therapy to rational-emotive therapy (RET), and finally to rational-emotive behavior therapy (REBT). Aaron Beck, a practicing psychiatrist and psychoanalyst, developed **cognitive therapy (CT)** in the 1970s (Beck, Rush, Shaw, & Emery, 1979). CT is a type of helping focused on correcting systematic errors in client reasoning and thinking that are believed to be underlying such psychological problems as depression. Donald Meichenbaum, a clinical psychologist, developed **cognitive-behavior modification (CBM)** principles based on the idea that covert processes of thinking and internal dialogue can be directly observed and modified just like overt behaviors (Meichenbaum, 1977). Modification techniques include association, operant conditioning, modeling, and rehearsal.

A VIEW OF HUMAN NATURE AND THE DEVELOPMENT OF PROBLEMS

Cognitive-behavioral theories of helping integrate learning and conditioning principles of behaviorism with an emphasis on human information processing (thinking, reasoning, planning, expectations, beliefs). Like behavioral theories, cognitive-behavioral theories share the belief that humans have an innate potential for learning and being conditioned by environmental influences. Unlike strict or radical behaviorists, cognitive behaviorists also posit that between external stimulus and response is a person with internal stimuli of her or his own. More than passive recipients of external forces that shape, reinforce, and model behaviors, humans are seen as employing internal processes like interpreting, anticipating, and making decisions about life events. Because of this, cognitive-behavioral theories of helping incorporate a philosophical belief in individual responsibility for constructing meaning. Behavior is still viewed as being learned through association, reinforcement, and modeling, but humans also process information about those associations, reinforcers, and observed models and make decisions about their behaviors.

Like humanistic and existential theories, cognitive-behavioral theories assume that humans are active participants in creating reality through perceptions and meanings ascribed to experience. Cognitive-behavioral theories of helping believe that humans are born with a potential for processing information about experiences and the environment. How information is processed affects behavior and feeling. Humans, then, are active participants in creating behavior, personality, and problems.

Internal activities like information processing and meaning-making cannot be directly observed. It is language that provides clues to these internal cognitive processes, and language not only reflects, but also shapes knowledge, logic, plans, ideas, expectations, beliefs, and problems (Whorf, 1956). According to cognitive-behavioral approaches to helping, behavior and feelings can be shaped, reinforced, and modified by shaping, reinforcing, and modifying someone's thinking.

Cognition can serve as an antecedent to behavior, can constitute the behavior itself, or can follow as a consequence of behavior. Beliefs and expectations about ourselves, about others, and about the ways in which the world is structured can signal behaviors. Humans can imagine solutions to problems and even rehearse solutions in advance of facing a situation or problem. Cognition can also serve as a reinforcement for behavior—a reinforcement that is immediately and easily available when modifying behavior. Humans can imagine feelings or events, and the images themselves can increase the probability that a behavior will be repeated. Imagining a negative outcome can result in human avoidance learning. Thoughts can serve as punishment or aversive stimuli as reprimands, and admonishments that were once external are internalized through modeling. Cognition is in essence an internal dialogue that can be learned, conditioned, and modified or changed.

While many believe that events cause feelings and behavior, and that problematic events cause problematic feelings and behaviors, Ellis disputes this equation in what he calls the "**ABC model**" of behavior. Ellis's model can be displayed as follows:

A (activating event) $\rightarrow$ B (belief) $\rightarrow$ C (consequence)

Rather than events causing feelings or behaviors, Ellis argues that it is beliefs that lead to such consequences. Applied to a common-life experience like a less-than-perfect exam score, this model would suggest that rather than the test grade's causing you to feel badly, it is your beliefs about the score that lead to your feelings.

Similarly, Beck holds that understanding the nature of an emotion or emotional problem requires a focus on the cognitive content of an individual's reactions to events. He suggests that people have personalized ideas that are triggered by specific stimuli and that these ideas then lead to emotional responses. Beck called these ideas **auto-**

matic thoughts. He contends that emotional difficulties are the product of automatic thoughts marked by characteristic logical errors that lead to **cognitive distortions.** Change is effected through guided discovery, which consists of examining automatic thoughts, testing evidence for and against them, and then restructuring the distorted thinking.

Meichenbaum focuses on client awareness of behaviors, thoughts, and feelings and impact on others as a prerequisite to change. In cognitive-behavior modification theory, change is the result of teaching clients to modify their internal dialogue or self-talk. His emphasis is on development of practical problem-solving skills, coping skills, and stress-inoculating skills.

The three approaches share much in common philosophically and differ primarily in their recommended helping processes. Whereas Ellis's approach is one of persuading a client that her or his beliefs are irrational, Beck's approach is to encourage clients to gather evidence for and against continuing particular beliefs. Meichenbaum teaches a self-instructional form of cognitive restructuring.

THE HELPING PROCESS

Goals

The goal of cognitive-behavioral helping is to assist clients in identifying, challenging, and changing cognitions that are negatively affecting their behavior or feelings. The specific goal of REBT is to minimize emotional disturbance and self-defeating behaviors by acquiring a more rational philosophy of life. REBT aims at changing philosophical values that result in problems. Even more specifically, REBT helpers work with clients on self-interest, social interest, tolerance, flexibility, acceptance of uncertainty, commitment, scientific thinking, self-acceptance, risk-taking, higher tolerance of frustration, and taking responsibility for disturbances (Ellis, 1979, 1991; Ellis & Bernard, 1986; Ellis & Dryden, 1987).

The goal of CT is to modify or eliminate automatic and dysfunctional thoughts so as to change behavior or feelings. Distortions in thinking are heard, understood, and challenged, and the helper encourages more adaptive thinking to replace the distortions. The goal of CBM self-instructional training is to teach clients a way to teach themselves how to deal effectively with various situations (Meichenbaum, 1974). Stress-inoculation, also developed by Donald Meichen-baum (1985, 1996), is designed to give individuals an opportunity to cope with mild stressors as a way to "inoculate" them to tolerating stronger fears or more aversive stressors.

The Helper's Role

The role of the helper in any cognitive-behavioral perspective may be that of consultant, trainer, educator, or collaborator and differs depending on the specific theory from which the helper draws. The rational-emotive behavior therapy helper emphasizes the educational and persuasive nature of the helping relationship. A helper is alternately a sort of logician challenging self-defeating ideas; an encourager helping clients to discover irrational beliefs that motivate disturbed behavior; a persuader demonstrating through logic, humor, and absurdity the illogical nature of client thinking; an instructor teaching a logical approach to assessing illogical deductions that foster self-destructive behaviors and feelings; and, at times, even a director assigning clients the task of countering their own "propaganda," challenging their irrational beliefs, and substituting them with rational beliefs and a more rational philosophy of life.

The cognitive therapy helper teaches the client to identify, observe, and monitor distorted and dysfunctional cognition through a process of empirical evaluation. Collaborating with the helper, clients evaluate the evidence supporting their thoughts and then test the reality of their thinking. CT uses a Socratic method of asking questions to guide a client's discovery of the connection between behaviors, thoughts, and feelings; to explore the evidence for specific thoughts; and to test alternative interpretations.

The cognitive-behavior modification helper works collaboratively with clients to become more aware of their self-talk, trains them to change this internal dialogue, and then teaches them more effective skills to practice. As the client practices new self-talk, she or he is expected to observe and assess the outcome.

Assessment

In the same way that behavioral helpers must assess the antecedents, behaviors, and consequences of behaviors in order to facilitate change, assessing the thought processes that precede, occur during, and follow any given behavior or feeling is critical to cognitive-behavioral help-ing. Whether the helper calls the focus irrational beliefs, automatic thoughts, or self-talk, the first step in a cognitive-behavioral change process is an assessment that consists of identifying the internal statements clients make about themselves, others, and situations and the consequences of such statements.

In REBT, the helper interviews a client to establish which state-ments may be operating to create difficulties. The helper is alert to commonly internalized irrational beliefs that lead to self-defeating behavior and feelings. Some common beliefs are:

> "I must have love or approval from all the significant people in my life."
>
> "I must perform important tasks competently and perfectly well."
>
> "Because I really want people to treat me fairly and considerately, they absolutely must do so."
>
> "If I don't get what I want, it's terrible, and I can't stand it."
>
> "It's easier to avoid facing life's difficulties and responsibilities than to undertake more rewarding forms of self-discipline."

In cognitive therapy, **dysfunctional thoughts** are identified that include automatic thoughts, cognitive distortions, and cognitive schema. These may be identified using an interview in which inquiries are made about the client's thinking. They may also be assessed by the client by keeping track of her or his thoughts in a **Daily Thought Record (DTR).** The types of automatic and dysfunctional thoughts that Beck suggests helpers look for in clients experiencing problems include:

- **arbitrary inferences,** which are conclusions without supporting and relevant evidence. This includes **catastrophizing,** or think-ing of the worst possible scenario or outcomes in a given situation.
- **selective abstraction,** which consists of forming conclusions based on an isolated detail of an event and ignoring other infor-mation or missing the significance of the total context.
- **overgeneralization** or holding extreme beliefs on the basis of a single incident, and then applying these to dissimilar events.
- **magnification** or **minimization,** which consists of perceiving an event in a more heightened or lesser light than it deserves.

- **personalization,** which is a tendency for people to relate external events to themselves.
- **labeling** or **mislabeling,** which means allowing imperfections or mistakes made in the past to define one's self.
- **polarized thinking,** in which clients interpret events in an all or nothing fashion or categorize experiences into either/or extremes.

Beck also uses written activities and satisfaction schedules to assist clients in recording their daily activities and level of satisfaction.

Meichenbaum's CBM emphasis, like Beck's CT, engages clients in a collaborative examination of the cognitive content and its connection to their difficulties. At the point of assessment, the CBM helper is teaching clients to listen to themselves or to be aware of their thoughts, feelings, actions, physiological reactions, and ways of interacting with others.

Techniques and Process

Cognitive-behavioral techniques fall into two categories. Both Ellis's rational-emotive therapy and Beck's cognitive therapy use methods called **cognitive restructuring.** Meichenbaum uses a cognitive skills training approach, which includes training in areas such as stress-inoculation (Meichenbaum, 1985), coping skills (Meichenbaum, 1985, 1986), and problem-solving (D'Zurilla & Goldfried, 1971; Goldfried & Davison, 1994).

Cognitive restructuring begins with identifying the activating events and the self-talk that follows the events. After the consequences of different self-talk are identified, the REBT helper begins to dispute the irrational beliefs the clients make about themselves, others, and the activating event. Albert Ellis and Michael Bernard (1986) describe three components to this disputing process—detecting, debating, and discriminating—that should be modeled by REBT helpers. According to this approach, doing so will help clients learn to detect their own irrational beliefs, particularly the "shoulds," "musts," "awfulizing," and "self-downing." Helpers argue clients out of their irrational beliefs with the understanding that clients will eventually learn to argue themselves out of the beliefs. Finally, helpers make discriminations between irrational and rational beliefs until clients learn to make these distinctions themselves.

This process is thought to lead eventually to new beliefs or life philosophies which result in new feelings and behaviors. Philosophical restructuring involves acknowledging that the client is largely responsible for creating her or his own difficulties; recognizing that the client has the ability to change the difficulties that stem largely from irrational beliefs; gaining a clear perception of the irrational beliefs; seeing the value in disputing those beliefs; working hard to counteract those beliefs to change dysfunctional behaviors and feelings; and practicing these skills for the rest of the client's life.

Picture again the student who fails an exam in school. A rational-emotive helper would point out that it is not the event—the exam—that causes any particular behavior or feeling, but rather the irrational things the student is telling her- or himself about that event that will result in the behavior or feeling. The helper may begin by examining the internal statements being made after the event about self, other, or the event. If a student thinks, "I am stupid" (called **self-downing** in REBT), the student will likely feel inadequate or worthless. Such feelings will be consistent with giving up or not wanting to work very hard. After all, nothing can be accomplished by working if one is stupid. If on the other hand the student thinks, "I am competent enough, though this exam sure didn't show it," the student may be better able to feel hopeful about subsequent exams and apply her- or himself to the process of studying. Instead of thinking, "I might as well give up," the student may think, "I'd better study harder next time." Each statement can obviously lead to different feelings and behaviors.

The REBT helper would also examine the irrational expectations clients have about life events. If a client has the expectation that she or he should always do well and always demonstrate competence, and then fails at something or makes a mistake, the stage may be set for thinking of her- or himself as incompetent. Returning to the student who failed an exam, if the student is used to thinking, "I always do well," the failed exam may lead to self-recriminations. If the student is used to thinking, "I generally do very well, and I'm generally competent, though sometimes I'm not," and then confronts a failure, the student is much more likely to interpret the failure as "just one of those times when I didn't do well or wasn't as competent." The latter leaves room for the possibility that other times could be different, leaving the student with a more hopeful feeling and more effortful behavior.

Ellis recommends the use of more emotively oriented techniques like imagery, role-playing, shame-attacking exercises, and forceful self-statement and self-dialogue. He also recommends the use of activity homework, reinforcements, and penalties.

In Beck's cognitive therapy, the professional helper works together with the client to test out his or her thinking. This process is referred to as **collaborative empiricism.** After inquiring or reading the DTR, cognitive helpers use **guided discovery** to escort clients through the process of discovering fallacies in their thinking. Guided discovery consists of three main components: role-playing, the three-question method, and testing beliefs. In role-playing, the client or the helper enacts a situation to illustrate a problem or a solution. In the three-question method, the helper first questions a client's evidence for a particular belief she or he holds, then offers at least one alternative interpretation for the belief, and finally challenges whether the belief is actually true by giving evidence of contradictions in the belief or automatic thought. In testing beliefs, the helper challenges the client's statements.

Meichenbaum, like Beck, also uses an educational model that stresses a working alliance between helper and client. Didactic presentation, Socratic questions, and guided self-discovery support a three-phase process of change. In the first phase, clients are taught to observe their own behaviors, feelings, interactions, and internal dialogue and to reconceptualize their problems as the result of their own self-talk. In the second phase, clients who have begun to recognize opportunities for behavior change see that the chain begins with self-statements that are incompatible with their previous behavior. In the third phase, clients learn more effective coping skills and practice them in real-life situations.

RESEARCH

Both the concepts underlying cognitive-behavioral theories of helping and the effectiveness of the helping techniques have been widely researched. A large number of meta-analytic studies have demonstrated the usefulness of REBT-helping when compared to psychodynamic and humanistic treatments and to control groups (DiGiuseppe & Miller, 1977; Lyons & Woods, 1991; McGovern & Silverman, 1984; Silverman, McCarthy, & McGovern, 1992). Studies have not been as clear in distinguishing the effectiveness of REBT from other cognitive and behavioral techniques. In addition, studies have found CT at least equal to pharmacologic therapies in effectiveness (Elkin, 1994; Robinson, Berman, & Neimeyer, 1990) and perhaps superior in some respects for the treatment of depression (Dobson, 1989; Elkin, 1994). Cognitive-behavioral therapies have also been successful in reducing anxiety (Hollon & Beck, 1994), although studies differentiating behavior therapies from cognitive therapies have been less conclusive (Butler, Fennell, Robson, & Gelder, 1991; Chambless & Gillis, 1993; Durham & Turvey; 1987). Although efficacy has been demonstrated in general, additional research has been recommended to establish differences in effectiveness of the various types of cognitive-behavioral helping and whether cognitive-behavioral techniques are more beneficial than behavioral strategies when addressing the same problem.

In addition to comparative outcome studies, other research has examined concepts within REBT and CT, such as the connection between irrational beliefs and suicide (Woods, Silverman, & Bentilini, 1991), hassles or problems in daily living (Harran & Ziegler, 1991), and general physiological arousal (Master & Miller, 1991). Other studies have established a connection between negative thinking and depressed feeling and behavior (Haaga, Dyck, & Ernst, 1991).

CRITIQUING

Many theorists emphasize building a collaborative relationship in which clients empirically test their own behaviors, thoughts, and feelings. Although Ellis, Beck, and Meichenbaum all speak to collaboration and empiricism, many critics argue that their models are built more on persuasion. Certainly the outcome research demonstrating effectiveness is not disputed, but the change mechanism at work may demonstrate the power of persuasion, rather than the effectiveness of collaboration and rational, empirical experimentation with new ideas by the client. Further, some have questioned whether direct teaching, persuasion, or confrontation is the best approach to changing internal dialogue.

As someone whose career has revolved around helping victims of abuse, I have wondered whether confrontive, persuasive, or directive approaches may be harmful to clients who have been abused. A client who has learned through painful experience to comply with someone in power may simply accommodate a strong authority. Changes accomplished for these reasons may not serve clients when they face situations on their own. Helpers who subscribe to sociocultural theories of helping have also wondered whether approaches that identify the helper as the one capable of defining what is rational or irrational may promote misuse of the helper's power and disempower clients. The criticisms need not eliminate cognitive-behavioral approaches to helping. Rather, they require cautious and intentional choices by helpers.

Cognitive-behavioral theories focus on the present rather than the past, and on the immediate rather than the unconscious. This focus assumes that the client's behavior is being influenced by what is in his or her immediate awareness and may overlook behavioral influences of which the client is not aware. Critics point to the danger of ignoring underlying causes and neglecting the reflection of clients' feelings. Along this same line of thinking, some critics question the Western, male emphasis on rational thought. One negative view of cognitive-behavioral helping therapies sees them as trivializing client emotional experience and relegating emotional experience to one that requires control or change through superior rational thought. Some critics also consider this "power of positive thinking" superficial and simplistic.

Despite criticisms, cognitive-behavioral approaches are among the fastest growing and most heavily researched of the theories of helping. In the age of short-term, problem-focused mental health insurance programs, cognitive-behavioral approaches to helping will undoubtedly fare well. Further, cognitive-behavioral self-help techniques adapt well to mass media presentation and may even facilitate the prevention of some problems.

CHAPTER

11 Psychodynamic Theories of Helping

CONTEXT

Psyche was an immortalized nymph from Greek mythology who personified the soul. *Psycho-*, taken from the word *psyche*, is a prefix used to indicate soul, mind, or mental activity when combined with other terms. The word *dynamic* is taken from *dynamis*, indicating power or strength; pertaining to energy or power in motion; involving or causing energy, motion, action, or change. The psychodynamic theories of helping are a group of theories that emphasize viewing people as energy systems. Health is viewed as the availability of energy, and problems are the result of investing energy in static or fixed maladaptive protective mechanisms, rather than dynamic adaptation to the environment. The release of energy is seen as the solution to such difficulties.

Psychodynamic is actually an umbrella term for theories of helping that include Freud's drive theories, ego psychology theories, interpersonal theories, object relations theories, self theories, and self-in-relations theory—a relative newcomer. Each of the theories included in psychodynamic theories has slightly different views of human nature, the nature of health, problems, and solutions. Each will be considered in turn.

This chapter is structured so that each theory under this umbrella term can be considered separately for its views of human nature and the development of problems. As they actually share many of the same goals, process considerations, and techniques, these components will be considered together and any differences highlighted. The chapter begins with Freud and then proceeds to tell the story of the various shifts in thinking that accompanied those who followed in his theoretical footsteps.

A VIEW OF HUMAN NATURE AND THE DEVELOPMENT OF PROBLEMS

Freud's Drive Theories

It would be a rare professional helper or helping theorist whose thinking has not been influenced by Sigmund Freud's drive theories of helping. Indeed, Freud's work has had a ubiquitous influence in daily life and although his work has been heavily criticized, it has provided both seminal and reactive influence on many theories of personality and professional helping. Freud's assumptions that early experiences affected later development and personality still prevail. He pioneered the view that behavior could be motivated both by experiences of which people are aware (conscious) as well as experiences of which people are not aware (unconscious). He focused on differences in personal development based on the biology of sex. He taught the world that sex and gender were influential phenomena in an individual's development.

Freud's theory of human nature is referred to as **deterministic.** He viewed human behavior as determined by biological drive states and instincts. Freud assumed that human beings came into the world with a biological self, instincts, and basic biological drives; that behavior and personality were determined by instincts and drives; and that each developed through a series of intrapsychic conflicts between competing drives and instincts. His view of human nature is one in which individual biological drives are tempered by social expectation and both are mediated by an evolving rational self. Human nature is thus perceived as something that must be modified by social expectation and rationality in order to become acceptable.

Each person, in Freud's perspective, is born with two basic instincts from which major sources of motivation derive. The life force instinct, called **Eros,** houses the sexual/reproductive motives, called the **libido.** The death force, called **Thanatos,** was considered the seat of aggressive motivation. Not only are these forces at odds within each person, but other conflicts, too, determine individual personality structure and functioning. Conflicts may be **conscious** (something a person is aware of) or **unconscious** (outside a person's awareness).

Conflict and the resulting distribution of energy are presumed to give rise to three personality structures. The **id** is the structure of personality present at birth and includes instinctual urges that demand tension-discharge as quickly as possible without regard to values, ethics, logic, or concern for others. More than simply the source of impulses and desires, though, the id is also considered the source of fantasy, creative and imaginative thought, and endeavor. The **super-ego** is the personality structure that develops through a series of conflicts and stages during which individuals identify with the same-sex parent. Through this identification, individuals incorporate the ideals and values of a society. If the id is the "I want what I want when I want it" part of individuals, then the superego is the "you can have what we've got if it's appropriate" structure, and conflicts appear inevitable between individual and social desires. According to Freud, the **ego** develops primarily to mediate conflicts between the id and superego. It is assumed to have executive authority and the capability of organizing, and it accesses perceptions, learning, memory, and rational thought. The ego institutes controls to delay gratification until a suitable object is found. In a sense then, the ego is the "you can have what we've got when we find it" part of the personality.

According to Freud, the structure of individual personalities develops through stages during which energy (libido) is focused on and released through specific biological functions. The earliest is the *oral stage* when, for the first year or so of life, infants are focused on their mouths as a source of need gratification. Infants whose oral needs are relatively well satisfied develop a positive view of their ability to depend on others for their care. However, energy may also become **fixated** at this stage if oral needs are either under- or overgratified. Oral needs that are undergratified may result in individuals seeking comfort through oral dependencies like eating, smoking, or drinking. If oral needs are overgratified, individuals may come to depend on others to the exclusion of functioning on their own.

At the second or third year, children focus on bowel functioning as a source of gratification. Not only do children get pleasure from stimulation of the anal erogenous zone and even their own feces, but they struggle with parents to experience control of retention and elimination and struggle for mastery of their own bodily functions. During this stage, called the *anal stage*, children are met with restrictions. For some children, this is the first time they have encountered constraints. The ways in which such restrictions are placed on gratification have implications for later development. Children whose anal needs are over- or undergratified concentrate a certain amount of energy on this stage and may become stubborn, rebellious, controlling, or explosive.

During the next few years, children receive gratification from a focus on their genitals. Freud's belief about this period, called the *phallic stage*, was that it laid the foundation for both morality and adult sexual relationships. This period of development contains some of Freud's most controversial and widely criticized assumptions about human nature and development. According to his theory, children at this stage develop intense, erotic desires for the parent of the opposite sex and competitive feelings toward the same-sex parent. For a boy, this energy directed at his mother (called the **Oedipal complex**) is accompanied by a fear of being castrated for his desires by his father, and identification with the father is thought to avert the extremely threatening rivalry. He then incorporates his father's values and sense of morality—in short, he develops a superego. He can "have" his mother through fantasy.

Girls lack penises and cannot experience the intense castration anxiety associated with their desire as do boys, so girls go through a different process (called the **Electra complex**). Desiring their fathers and realizing genital differences, girls were thought to experience penis envy and to identify with mothers in order to be able to please and appease the powerful father and share in his phallus symbolically by being able to offer him a child. Freud believed that without the fear of castration as an impetus, girls must necessarily be morally inferior to boys.

The *latency period*, from around 6 to 12 years of age, is when children apparently lose interest in sexual fantasy and genital stimulation and focus energy on peer socializing and the world beyond their parents. During this time, according to Freud, they develop protections against different types of anxiety called *ego defenses* or *defense mechanisms*. Freud identified a number of defense mechanisms (see Figure 11.1).

Defense mechanisms serve to protect the ego by distorting the reality of various anxiety-provoking stimuli or responses. According to Freud, problems in personality develop from static energy left at a given stage of development and over- or underutilization of these

FIGURE 11.1   Freud's Ego Defense Mechanisms

Defense Mechanism	Definition
Denial	Refusal to acknowledge anxiety-provoking stimuli
Repression	Motivated forgetting of anxiety-provoking stimuli
Projection	Disavowed ownership of the anxiety-provoking stimuli and simultaneous assignment of ownership to another
Introjection	Incorporation of the values, beliefs, ideas, or feelings of another to avert anxiety
Rationalization	Explaining or justifying a response to anxiety-provoking stimuli
Intellectualization	Pursuit of intellectual understanding of anxiety-provoking stimuli or responses
Sublimation	Investing energy in more acceptable impulses to avoid anxiety
Reaction Formation	Developing a response almost opposite to the original reaction in order to avert anxiety associated with the original reaction

devices designed to protect the ego. While protective, ego defenses also divert energy away from constructive activity and distort reality. If overutilized, more energy is invested in the defense and less is available to negotiate the demands of everyday life. If underutilized, anxiety threatens the integrity of the ego, resulting in less rational thought or behavior.

The final psychosexual stage, called the *genital stage,* develops at puberty. During the genital stage, energy is focused on others rather than on oneself, and individuals begin to develop heterosexual relationships. Freud assumed that human development proceeded necessarily to heterosexuality and was completed by early adolescence.

Ego Psychology Theories

A number of Freud's followers who generally agreed with his theories about drives and instincts focused more attention on the functioning of the ego and its protective mechanisms or defenses. This group, called ego psychologists, includes Heinz Hartmann (1958, 1964), Anna Freud (1936, 1965), and Erik Erikson (1950, 1968, 1982).

Heinz Hartmann's theory elaborated on the function of the ego. He sought to preserve the drive model, but to modify the perception of the ego as an agent in service of the superego, which derived its energy from the id (Meissner, 1988). His idea was that the ego not only mediated conflicts between id and superego, but could operate without being at odds with either. According to Hartmann, in addition to their role in conflict resolution, behaviors Freud saw only as mechanisms of defense could be better understood as serving an adaptive function. That is, they help individuals adapt to environmental demands.

Examining the behavior of someone coping with cancer will highlight the difference between Freud and Hartmann's theories of the function of the ego. In Freud's original model, someone who faces the real threat of cancer by researching all that has been written about the particular type of cancer she or he faces could be said to be intellectualizing to avert anxieties—one of Freud's ego defense mechanisms. Hartmann, however, examined how these same conscious coping functions of the ego (e.g., perceptions, thought, and memory) help the individual adjust to the realities of life with cancer. Problems, according to Hartmann, develop not as a result of the fixation of libidinal energy at an early stage of development, but in adaptation to real environmental demands. Problems result in the diminution or absence of appropriate ego functions. In other words, the nature of the real environment could be such that problems developed as a more satisfying solution than would the "normal" one.

Anna Freud's work with children was the impetus for her concept of the gradual development of various behaviors, called **developmental lines.** Two examples of developmental lines are the movement from dependency to self-mastery and the movement from an egocentric focus to an other-focus. As her theories emphasized the gradual development of ego, her approach to therapy emphasized the ego and its defenses (Greenberg & Mitchell, 1983; Sharf, 1996). Agreeing with Hartmann, she placed more significance on real threats from the external world creating a need for ego defense.

Erik Erikson, a student of Anna Freud, contributed a model of development that continued throughout the lifespan and demonstrated the social implications and challenges of each stage of development, as shown in Figure 11.2.

In summary, the ego psychology theories moved away from Freud's emphasis on biological drives as primary forces motivating

FIGURE 11.2   Erikson's Stages of Development

Age/Stage (Freud's Stage)	Task or Challenge
Infancy/ Basic Trust vs. Mistrust (Oral)	Rather than emphasizing biological drives being satisfied, the task at this stage of development was presumed to focus on development of trust or mistrust that the primary caregiver would provide for basic needs. Unsuccessful resolution could result in fixation of valuable life energy in mistrusting others.
Early Childhood/ Autonomy vs. Shame and Doubt (Anal)	The ability to successfully master independent (bowel and bladder) control and parents' responses to such control are the challenges of this life stage that shape the later development of a sense of autonomy or feelings of shame and self-doubt.
Preschool Age/ Initiative vs. Guilt (Phallic)	Overcoming the rivalry for the opposite-sex parent and anger toward the same-sex parent is the challenge of this life stage that directs energy toward initiating competencies. Disallowed participation can result in later guilt for independent motivation.
School Age/ Industry vs. Inferiority (Latency)	Developing basic skills for cognitive undertakings is the challenge of this life stage. Without such development, a sense of inadequacy or inferiority can result.
Adolescence/ Identity vs. Role Confusion (Genital)	Developing confidence that others picture us as we see ourselves is the challenge in this key stage of life. Career, educational, and life goals are set, or a sense of confusion can result.
Young Adulthood/ Intimacy vs. Isolation (Genital)	Social and work relationships as well as an intimate relationship with a significant other develop during this life stage. Without these, a sense of isolation results.
Middle Age/ Generativity vs. Stagnation (Genital)	The challenge of this life stage is to move beyond intimacy to take on responsibilities for facilitating the development of others. Apathy can result from an unfulfilled sense of productivity or contribution.
Later Life/ Integrity vs. Despair (Genital)	As individuals reflect on life accomplishments, the challenge is to come to terms with what they have contributed and pass this along to others or face the resulting despair.

development. The role of the ego was not simply the reactive role that Freud described—one that drew energy from base instinct and impulse and served socializing aims. Ego psychology theorists view problems as the result of fixated or static energy that once served an adaptive function but may no longer be necessary.

A Social-Psychological Perspective

Karen Horney was perhaps the first of the psychodynamic theorists to introduce the concept that the environment, especially as it involves social and political forces, accounts for much development. Like Freud, she believed that early childhood experiences were important in shaping individuals. Unlike Freud, she posited that it was social influences, including the social position of children (subordinate and helpless) that accounted for human development. Humans come into the world requiring care and this initial dependency also fosters resentment and hostility. Because of the unacceptability of resentment and hostility, particularly from children, basic anxiety develops. According to Horney's approach to helping, in order to protect against this basic anxiety, people select one of three characteristic ways of being in the world: (1) moving away from people by detaching; (2) moving toward people through love; (3) moving against people through aggression. These characteristic ways of protecting against basic anxiety result in characteristic problems (1937, 1967).

Interpersonal Theories

Interpersonal theorists like Harry Stack Sullivan furthered an emphasis on relationships by introducing the idea that personality consists of a relatively enduring pattern of recurring interpersonal relationships and that individuals cannot be studied apart from those relationships (Sullivan, 1953). Early relationships are thought to be crucial in initiating patterns that are reflected in later developmental stages. According to interpersonal theories of helping, relationships could be conceptualized as a series of concentric circles. The innermost circle is the relationship with the "mothering one." After learning to speak, the circle is expanded to include other children. This is then expanded to include same-gender friendships during pre-adolescence and heterosexual relationships during early adolescence. With later adolescence, vocational and educational relationships develop, followed by satisfying sexual relationships in adulthood. Problems are the result of maladaptive patterns of behaving developed in the context of any of these relationship spheres (Burton, 1972).

Object Relations Theories

Free of biological emphasis and more purely psychological, object relations theories suggest that people's basic motive is to relate with other people. Like the ego psychology theorists, object relations theorists deemphasize the id and drive states and focus on the ego. Like the interpersonal theories, they emphasize relationships. "Object" in object relations theories refers to the target of a need or that which will satisfy a need (Cashdan, 1988; St. Clair, 1996). According to these theories, the libido is object-seeking and highly directed toward other persons. Relationships are presumed to develop to satisfy needs. Objects may be people and may be real or imagined. They may be internal images or external relationships. Each theory emphasizes critical and significant relationships, called the *objects* of aggressive and erotic impulses.

According to object relations theories, initial relationships are the single most important factor in development and constitute a sort of template on which later relationships are patterned (Cashdan, 1988; St. Clair, 1996). Further, they constitute the early formation and differentiation of psychological structures that comprise inner images of self and others. Human dependency results in lack of differentiation from or fusion with caregivers. Development involves movement toward independence and autonomy by means of a supportive relationship. Rather than focusing on biological erogenous zones, object relations theories concentrate on early life development of relationships. Problems, then, are the result of developmental arrests in relationship experiences, rather than intrapsychic conflicts.

Object relations approaches to helping began in the early 1900s in Britain with the work of Melanie Klein (Cashdan, 1988; St. Clair, 1996). Klein studied young children to further her understanding of drive theory and its implications for relationships. She viewed instincts as seeking and becoming bound to people as objects through fantasy. One of her students, W. R. D. Fairbairn, suggested that it was not the primitive id whose fantasies are bound to people, but the ego. He suggested that there is a drive to relate and the object of this drive is always a person. His theories reaffirmed that it is a real relationship that humans seek. In a sense, this concept completed the transition from Freud's drive structure. It became a relational structure model that focused on the development of a core conflict—relational dependence at an early age—rather than emphasizing instinctual drives. Infants grow from utter dependence to become mature, separate, differentiated objects in their own right.

In the 1950s, Donald Winnicott agreed that the infant was psychically merged with the mother and that this was a function of a baby's need for care as well as the required maternal preoccupation with putting babies first. He emphasized the relationship with the mother and the conditions of the environment that shape development. He coined the term **good enough mothering** to capture the idea that mothers do not need to be perfect. Instead mothers need to supply an adequate nurturing environment to facilitate maturation. Others could also provide this **holding environment** in which children could develop a sense of self with adequate nurturing (St. Clair, 1996). According to Winnicott, humans instinctually move from total gratification and the primacy of self needs, to tolerance of separation and independence, and finally to the social and interactive context of the environment. Movement is made by internalizing support and comfort, developing objects to relate to, and becoming independent and autonomous.

Moving from one stage of development to another is often facilitated by using a **transitional object** (Sharf, 1996; St. Clair, 1996). A transitional object is a familiar item that offers consolation and reassurance. People embrace these objects when life feels unsettled or risky. A favorite soft blanket or stuffed animal are common transitional objects carried into early separating experiences like heading off for preschool or kindergarten. Some adults are brave enough to tell about transitional objects they still carry, such as an old cherished teddy bear, or new adult versions that serve the same function, such as a coffee mug transported from job to job.

In the 1960s, Margaret Mahler (Cashdan, 1988; Mahler, 1968; Sharf, 1996; St. Clair, 1996) emphasized the **psychological birth** of individuals in her model of object relations development. Mahler's model, like Winnicott's, emphasized movement through a series of developmental stages from an undifferentiated to a separate individual. During the first few weeks of life, one cannot differentiate between the infant's own attempts to reduce tension by eating and the mother's attempts to reduce tension by feeding the infant. The final developmental stage is that of a stable identity separate from an also stable concept of mother and others. Problems are framed as a distortion in relationships or fixation of energy at an early stage in this process of separation and individuation. Professional helpers who use this model of psychological development find it useful to conceptualize various tasks during the lifespan as evidence of continuing separation crises.

Self Theories

Hans Kohut developed the **self theories** from his clinical work with narcissistic men in which he observed similarities between normal and abnormal narcissism (Kohut, 1971, 1977, 1984; Sharf, 1996; St. Clair, 1996). Kohut believes that self develops as an infant seeks and cues surrounding caregivers to gratify her or his needs. Self theories emphasize the role of the environment in relation to the primary caregivers in the development of a self.

Kohut considers the development and maintenance of a self to be the central and motivating core of the individual. Kohut expects that children will develop a sense of self when provided with adequate mirroring and idealization from the environment. This perspective puts instinctual development into both a social and an interactive context. The result is a focus on the seminal role of parenting in the development of a self, and parenting failures are emphasized when problems develop. Specifically, self theory views psychological limitations in empathy as causing parenting failures.

In order to develop a self, an infant needs mirroring, challenge, and a balance of the two. Like Freud, Kohut focused on the intrapsychic experience of the individual; like other neo-Freudian and interpersonal theorists, Kohut emphasized environmental factors, specifically parental empathy in shaping experience, identity, and problems.

Self-in-Relations Theories

Self-in-relations are relational theories of development and helping that were developed by a group of professional helpers and theorists at the Stone Center for the Development of Women in Wellesley, Massachusetts, including Judith Jordan, Alexandra Kaplan, Jean Baker Miller, Irene Stiver, and Janet Surrey (1991). Emerging from their clinical observations and group theorizing about the development of young women, the self-in-relations theories suggest that women first define themselves in the context of a relationship. As the complexity of their relationships grow, so does the complexity of their self-definition.

A fully functioning self is not viewed in the terms of traditional object relations theories as an independent, autonomous construction, but as an interconnected one. Self-in-relations theories hold that people are first and foremost relationally oriented; they depart from other relational theories to posit that people grow, change, develop, and define themselves in the context of these relationships rather than apart from them. As such, the concept of self cannot itself be neatly distinguished from these relationships, hence the hyphenated label— self-in-relations.

Like object relations theories, self-in-relations theories hold that first relationships are important to development and that the mother-daughter relationship is an especially powerful template by which young women develop. Like self theories, self-in-relations theories emphasize the central role that empathy plays in human development, particularly for women. Empathy is defined as the capacity to share in and comprehend the momentary psychological state of another and involves affective arousal and cognitive structuring. Flexibility rather than impermeability of ego boundaries is essential to the process of empathy. Empathy relies on a high level of psychological development and ego strength as it calls on an individual to have a well-differentiated sense of self and sensitivity to differences in others.

Unlike self theories, self-in-relations theories hold that self is an internal representation of oneself in relation to others. The concept of being-in-relation is the pivotal construct of this theory which posits that self and a sense of self is neither developed nor maintained in isolation from others. Self is thought to develop in a context of mutual empathy, and, unlike object relations theories, people do not necessarily move from utter dependence and self-absorption toward independence and autonomy. Rather, humans are thought to move toward increasingly complex interactions, mutual empathy, and definitions in context. Through the initial and each subsequent relationship, a template is created in which one develops a sense of one's capacity for and pleasure in identifying with another; connectedness; and a complex awareness of needs and realities of other and self. From the perspective of self-in-relations theories, problems are the result of inadequate, disrupted, or flawed connections or from disconnections, difficulties in relinquishing one internalized image to make way for new relational images, and difficulties in self-nurturing.

THE HELPING PROCESS

Goals

The goal of helping from psychodynamic perspectives is to create significant changes in personality structure and behavior. By making the unconscious conscious through insight, fixated energy is released, thereby allowing maladaptive habits to be changed and new behavioral choices to be made.

Each psychodynamic theory expresses the goals of helping a little differently. From a drive perspective, helping involves an emphasis on increasing awareness of sexual and aggressive drives and resolving early conflicts in dependency, control, moral values, and relationships. Helping from an ego psychology perspective involves more emphasis on strengthening the ego and its defenses for alternative adaptive responses to real life situations (Rockland, 1989). From an object relations perspective, helping is focused on creating a new relationship template from which alternative interpretations can be made and new relationship options entertained or enacted. From a self-psychology perspective, helping involves examining idealized views of parents and the impact of self-absorption that create difficulties in interpersonal relationships. From a self-in-relations perspective a new template for mutual empathy, a balance of autonomy and connection, and alternative definitions of self-in-relationships are the goals of helping.

The Helper's Role

The helper's role differs somewhat when viewed through the lens of each of the psychodynamic subtypes. The common thread of most psychodynamic traditions is that the helper presents the client with an ambiguous situation or relationship onto which the client can project feelings, needs, thoughts, past conflicts, relationship templates, and other issues. The helper then interprets the themes present in the client's responses. As in other theoretical schools, helper-client relationships are developed through the use of all of the microskills; however, psychodynamic helpers rely more often on interpretation to advance clients' goals. Helpers interpret what they hear and listen carefully for clues about a client's early conflicts or ungratified needs, ways in which clients have used defenses to survive, critical or difficult relationships, inadequate parenting, and disconnections. Psychodynamic helpers usually interpret material of which the client is not conscious as a way to facilitate client awareness or insight, considered key to advancing client change. The focus of psychodynamic helpers' interpretations differs depending on their perspective. For example, object relations–oriented helpers focus their interpretations more on the relationship as a means of understanding client relational functioning; drive-oriented helpers emphasize early, unresolved conflicts in their interpretations; and ego psychology–oriented helpers focus more of their interpretations on early, and no longer effective, defenses developed by the client. Regardless of the specific focus of interpretations, the role of the psychodynamic helper can be generally characterized as that of observer and interpreter.

Assessment

Psychodynamic helpers most often assess client functioning indirectly or by inference. If a behaviorally-oriented helper wants to see the conditions that support or maintain student behavior in class, the helper is likely to go to the classroom her- or himself or ask a teacher to observe and record classroom behavior and its antecedents and consequences directly. On the other hand, a psychodynamic helper might administer a test to a student or observe client interactions in the helping relationship and then infer classroom (or other) behavior from these observations. The inferences would be used to offer interpretations to the client.

The assessment tools most frequently associated with psychodynamic helping traditions are called **projective techniques.** A projective technique is any device in which an ambiguous stimulus is presented to a client, who then responds, revealing something about her- or himself and her or his characteristic functioning. In projective techniques, clients are presented with ambiguous or unstructured stimuli and invited to impose a structure or meaning. The theory behind projective techniques suggests that by imposing structure or meaning, the client reveals something of her- or himself and how she or he may structure other life experiences—life being considered an ambiguous experience. Examples of projective techniques include interpretive tests and sentence stems, but also include the helping relationship itself, dreams, slips of the tongue, and free associations. In any ambiguous situation clients can project something about themselves. Because the stimuli are ambiguous, clients have a nearly infinite range of responses, and helpers make interpretations along many different dimensions of functioning, such as ego defenses and needs.

William Shakespeare (1564–1616) made some of the earliest written references to projective techniques when referring to people's interpretations of clouds, while Sir Francis Galton (1879) suggested word-association as a method of projective assessment, and others experimented with pictures as projective devices (e.g., Binet & Henri, 1896). However, it is clearly Hermann Rorschach's (1921) use of inkblots as a method of diagnostic assessment that systematized the use of projective techniques in professional helping. When the **Rorschach test** is used as an assessment technique, psychodynamic helpers generally present each of ten inkblot cards in a specific sequence and ask clients to tell what they see. The helpers then record verbatim what a client said and how long it took for the client to respond, how long the client spent with each card, the position of the card when the client responded, how many responses were made, and the character and content of each response. Any other spontaneous utterance made by the client is recorded as well. Scoring schemes vary (e.g., Exner, 1974, 1993; Schafer, 1954), but most employ three major components: (1) location of the area of the card to which the client responded; (2) content or nature of what the client saw, such as animal, person, rock, and so on; and (3) determinants or those aspects of the card that prompted the client's response, such as the shading, color, texture, and so on.

In 1935, C. D. Morgan and Henry Murray introduced the **Thematic Apperception Test (TAT).** The TAT comprises 31 ambiguous pictures. The helper shows several pictures to the client, one at a time, and asks the client to create a story about each picture. Clients are asked specifically to describe what the situation is in the picture, what events led up to the situation portrayed in the picture, what the outcome will be, and what each of the characters in the picture is thinking or feeling. Systems for scoring and interpreting the TAT are influenced by the theory to which the helper using it subscribes (Todd & Bohart, 1999).

Sentence completion blanks are relatively simple methods of projective assessment. In tools like the *Incomplete Sentences Blank (ISB)* or the *Rotter Incomplete Sentences Blank,* a number of sentence stems are provided, such as "I like . . ." or "What annoys me . . . ," for clients to complete. Different scoring schemes have been developed for a number of variables describing clients' adjustment. Compared to the Rorschach or TAT, sentence completion assessment is more direct, can be more objectively and reliably scored, and requires less extensive training to administer (Trull & Phares, 2001).

In the psychodynamic tradition, assessment is used throughout the helping process. The psychodynamic helper uses assessment techniques to facilitate client awareness of what is unconscious in order to free up fixated energy. This happens through a number of interpretative techniques and several variations on the process of helping.

Techniques and Process

The drive-oriented (Freudian) helper seeks to establish basic trust with the client and then encourage a regressive **transference neurosis.** A transference neurosis is a relationship that consists of a client attributing to the helper those qualities or characteristics of a significant person, generally a primary caregiver, and then transferring to the helper early drive gratification difficulties (Meissner, 1988). The client relates to the helper as she or he would to that person, and, through the helper's interpretations of the client's defenses (Kapelovitz, 1987), the client gains an understanding of these defenses and discharges the energy associated with feelings from that previous experience.

The helper, drawing from an ego psychology perspective, would take a slightly different approach. Also encouraging a transference relationship, the helper would interpret ego defenses as an adaptive way of dealing with early conflicts and the transference as another adaptive way for the ego to seek strength (Greenberg & Mitchell, 1983). Analysis would focus on and modify the judging function of the ego to facilitate the adaptive process by providing a framework for reworking transference distortions. So, while the ego psychologist would see the same conflicts, ego functioning would be assessed for its adaptive value. The helper would focus on real behavior, real conflicts in real relationships, and social reality as indicators of an adaptive dynamic in service of survival. Interpretations would focus on increasing ego functioning to examine the purpose that those mechanisms served and how the very ways in which a client may have protected her- or himself earlier may now compromise ego functioning.

Object relations–oriented helpers also expect clients to regress to previous states of relational difficulties in order to resolve associated relational issues. Unlike drive and ego psychologists, in object relations helping, it is the helping relationship itself that provides a corrective relationship experience, proceeds at the client's own pace, and enables clients to perceive alternative ways of viewing experiences and relating to others. Object relations helpers view problems as the result of distortions in early relationships or fixated energy at stages along the path toward separation and individuation. Helping from this perspective focuses on restoring the capacity to make full and direct contact with others (Cashdan, 1988; St. Clair, 1996). The helper's relationship with the client becomes a new template for how someone can look at things as good, bad, or in-between, and still maintain a feeling of connection. Clients can slowly give up unnecessary defenses and compensatory adaptations and retrace missed developmental steps. Through this, clients also acquire a greater capacity for self-esteem regulation and relational mutuality, indicating a move toward self and object constancy.

Helpers operating from a self-psychology perspective create a relationship that emphasizes either mirroring or idealizing. Both constitute a revival of key developmental phases in childhood. Clients would be expected to mobilize their grandiose selves in a mirroring transference, trying to hold on to a part of their primary narcissism by concentrating perfection on a grandiose self. An idealizing transference mobilizes the parent image and the clients striving to stay merged with the parent. The process involves a sort of controlled regression to allow for a client to re-experience adequate parenting and successful early narcissism and omnipotence. The helper focuses on providing accurate and empathic understanding, without gratifying a client's narcissistic needs. The helper neither agrees nor disagrees with them, but rather works to keep concerns viable long enough to analyze and interpret them. The narcissistic needs are then allowed to be gradually and spontaneously transformed into normal self-assertiveness and devotion to ideals (Baker & Baker, 1987; Eagle, 1984; Kohut, 1966, 1971, 1977, 1984).

The helping process in self-in-relations theories has not been as fully explored as the development of the connected self and problems that arise from disconnection (Jordan et al., 1991; J. B. Miller, 1986).

Like other psychodynamic theories, the self-in-relations perspective, too, emphasizes the helping relationship as a mechanism for change. Helpers establish a mutual empathy with clients, examine identity in the context of the current helping relationship as well as previous relationships, and encourage a balance of autonomy and connection in the lives of clients.

A number of techniques have been developed to help clients become aware of unconscious material. Clients may be asked to **free associate** or relate anything and everything of which they are aware. This may include bodily sensations, feelings, fantasies, thoughts, memories, or recent events. The helper then listens for meanings, themes, disruptions, slips of the tongue, or omissions and interprets each. Psychodynamic helpers convey empathy and neutrality so as not to interfere with the client's own material or the development of the transference relationship.

Resistance to the helping process may also be examined and interpreted for its value in understanding the transference relationship. **Resistance** can be described as a client-imposed barrier to being helped. It can take many forms, such as being late for appointments, forgetting appointments, losing interest in helping, or the inability to remember or free associate. Outside of the helping session, resistance may take the form of acting out other problems, such as drinking excessively or having an extramarital affair. Listening carefully for resistance to the helping process and interpreting that resistance is a particularly important technique used to enhance awareness.

Helpers interpret dreams not only for their **manifest content** (what the client actually perceived during a dream), but also for **latent content** (the symbolic and unconscious motives represented in the dream material). The transference relationship is interpreted to help clients unearth relational difficulties.

Helpers with a psychodynamic perspective also interpret their own **countertransference.** Countertransference in its broadest sense includes both conscious and unconscious feelings of the helper toward her or his client. To interpret countertransference, helpers try to understand their own feelings, their client's feelings, and the interaction between the two. Psychodynamic theorists encourage helpers to attend to their reactions and interpret them in light of their perspectives about the origins of the client's problems, rather than acting on them. So, if I am angry at the excessive self-absorption of a narcissistic client, I will check in with myself instead of directly venting my anger at their self-absorption. I would note my feelings and ask myself whether this is the way that the client's parents may have reacted to normal childlike needs for self-importance, whether others may perceive the client's self-absorption in a similar way, and whether the client may have missed opportunities for mutuality in previous relationships. These concerns are sometimes stated aloud, if they are deemed appropriate and hold the possibility of benefiting the client. In this way countertransference can promote further consideration by the clients so as to gain an enhanced understanding of themselves.

Although somewhat different in terms of their focus, all psychodynamic helpers liberally use interpretation as a tool to help a client understand his or her experiences. Helpers may interpret free associations, dreams, slips of the tongue, transference, countertransference, unconscious defenses, and early childhood experiences and may focus on ungratified needs, adaptive ways in which clients used defenses to survive, critical or difficult relationships, inadequate parenting, or disconnections, depending on their perspective. Helpers who use a psychodynamic orientation still carefully attend to the timing and process of each interpretation in order to facilitate client awareness.

RESEARCH

Because psychodynamic helping processes are lengthy, complex, and based on concepts difficult to define and measure, investigators have found it difficult to design research processes to test their efficacy. Freud himself initially believed that research was unnecessary and that clinical observations were sufficient to test effectiveness. Relying solely on clinical observations to establish effectiveness is considered inadequate by today's standards, which emphasize accountability. On the other hand, psychodynamic concepts rely on context for meaning, so laboratory testing may not reflect them as accurately as the clinical setting. Despite the difficulties associated with researching psychodynamic theories of helping, some investigators have taken up the challenge. The research falls into three categories: (1) studies that attempt to establish the mechanisms of change in psychodynamic helping models, (2) outcome studies comparing the effectiveness of psychodynamic helping to wait lists and to other helping models, and (3) studies of the various concepts of the theories.

Early studies conducted by psychoanalytic therapists appeared to demonstrate that psychoanalysis was effective across diagnostic categories and cultural differences (e.g., Knight, 1941), and subsequent surveys showed similarly positive results (e.g., Bachrach, Galatzer-Levy, Skolnikoff, & Waldron, 1991; Fonagy & Target, 1996). Survey research of this type has been criticized for its potential for bias. Clients who invest considerable time and money into psychodynamic therapy may be inclined to view it positively. More recently, studies investigating the effectiveness of psychodynamic helping have been designed to compare psychodynamic helping to no-treatment conditions and to cognitive and behavioral approaches. These studies have consistently found helping based on a psychodynamic perspective to be more effective than no treatment, but slightly to considerably inferior when compared to cognitive and behavioral approaches (Anderson & Lambert, 1995; Crits-Christoph, 1992; Grawe, Donati, & Bernauer 1998; Henry & Strupp, 1991; Shapiro & Shapiro, 1982; Sloane, Staples, Cristol, Yorkston, & Whipple, 1975; Smith & Glass, 1977; Smith, Glass, & Miller, 1980; Svartberg & Stiles, 1991). These studies were predominantly developed by cognitive and behavioral researchers, so again the question of bias must be raised. Nonetheless, in the absence of other more positive research, psychodynamic theories of helping may be relegated to the position of influential theory, but less effective treatment than successor theories.

Extensive studies have assessed changes taking place in psychoanalytic therapy and analysis for those client and helper factors that account for changes in each type of helping. One study followed 42 clients for 30 years under the auspices of the Menninger Clinic (Wallerstein, 1986; Wallerstein & Weinshel, 1989), and another study examined predicted success (Luborsky, Crits-Christoph, Mintz, & Auberach, 1988). The findings of these studies have lent some insights into the types of clients who fared better with psychoanalytic therapy and psychoanalysis and the types of helper behaviors that contributed to that success. Douglas Wallerstein (1986) suggested that many clients changed due to the "transference cure" or a wish to please the therapist. Luborsky et al. (1988) found that when helpers were more interested, energetic, and involved, sessions proceeded better than when they were inactive, impatient, or hostile. Clients who felt understood by the helper reported understanding themselves better and experiencing fewer conflicts.

Researchers have also focused efforts on creating assessment tools to measure improvements in social relationships, maladaptive patterns of behavior, and changes in cognition (e.g., Horvath and Greenberg's Working Alliance Inventory, 1989). Still other researchers have attempted to find support for the concepts in psychodynamic theories of helping with some success (see Hjelle & Ziegler, 1992, and Davis & Schwartz, 1987, for discussions about repression). Research on attachment relates some attachment styles in childhood (e.g., Ainsworth, 1982) and some stages of separation and individuation (Bretherton, 1987) to later behaviors.

CRITIQUING

The constructs of psychodynamic theories of helping have been criticized for being difficult to understand and convoluted. At least one archival researcher has demonstrated that Freud himself may have changed his theory about female sexual development in response to political pressures about his earliest clinical observations regarding widespread incest (Masson, 1984). Others have criticized psychodynamic constructs for lacking face validity, although research has shown limited support for some of these constructs. The most lengthy and therefore most costly of all of the helping approaches, psychodynamic helping is not particularly well supported by research to date and is hard to justify during a time when insurance resources are scarce.

Other researchers have shown that psychodynamic theories of helping reflect significant gender and ethnic bias (e.g., Brodsky & Hare-Mustin, 1980; Hare-Mustin, 1984). The theories are patriarchal and Eurocentric in both form and structure (Prochaska & Norcross, 1999). The concepts of female penis envy and moral inferiority have enraged feminist theorists, while the notion that psychological health involves rationality and movement toward autonomy appears to be not only androcentric, but Eurocentric (Ivey, Ivey, & Simek-Morgan, 1997). The emphasis on mother as caregiver certainly presents a biased view of parental impact on development. The idea that "biology is destiny" legitimizes the subordinate status of women and North American ethnic minorities. In fact, the absence or limited acknowledgment of systemic or cultural forces in development and helping is a major criticism of these approaches to helping.

Nonetheless, psychodynamic theories of helping have been enormously influential in shaping many other theories of helping and have directly and indirectly influenced many professional helpers. Psychodynamic theories have played a significant pioneering role in the development of critical helping concepts. Psychodynamic theorists have been instrumental in suggesting that both forces we are aware of and those we are not are influential in the development of identities and problems; in encouraging structural changes in personality; in highlighting the impact of insight as a change mechanism; in introducing the relationship between helper and client as an important source of material for understanding; in recognizing the impact of sex and gender in development; and in acknowledging the impact of early childhood experiences and parenting influences. These are only a few of the acknowledgments due to the psychodynamic theories of helping.

12 Family Systems Theories of Helping

A **system** is a set or consistent arrangement of things so related or connected as to form unity or to operate as a whole. In biology, the use of the term *system* refers to a number of organs that act together to perform a main bodily function (e.g., the digestive, circulatory, and nervous systems). In chemistry, a system indicates substances that together approach equilibrium or a state of balance between opposing forces. In chemistry, the point in certain chemical reactions at which the products of two reactions consume each other at the same rate yielding no change in their net concentration is called *equilibrium*.

CONTEXT

Although some date the actual beginning much earlier, systems theories emerged with vigor in several disciplines in the 1950s and 1960s. General systems theories in biology advocated studying organisms as a whole rather than reducing the organism to its smallest elements (von Bertalanffy, 1968). Cybernetics applied complex computing mechanisms to the study of the human nervous system and the methods of communication and control it utilizes. Together with some basic mathematic principles, systems theories also influenced and became the foundation for family systems theories of helping.

Family systems perspectives posit that individuals cannot be understood without assessing the system in which they are embedded. Families cannot be understood except within the context of the neighborhood, community, or social system in which they function.

If any part of a system changes, the whole system changes. Otherwise, systems maintain a steady state called **homeostasis.** Again borrowed from biology, homeostasis refers to mechanisms within the neuroendocrine system that are activated to regulate functions like blood pressure and temperature if physical changes start to exceed normal limits. These mechanisms operate on feedback. In family systems helping models, feedback also serves to regulate systemic functioning. *Positive feedback* is information that amplifies a need and results in change, and *negative feedback* is information that results in balance or limited deviation from the status quo.

Families are assumed to also possess regulatory feedback mechanisms that maintain an acceptable balance. Information is in a sense the energy of human systems, communication the mechanism by which energy is moved from one part of the system to another, and feedback the mechanism by which change is precipitated. Systems may be understood in terms of their communication, their structure, their impact over time, or their ability to solve problems.

A number of approaches to family systems theories of helping have been developed. The four major perspectives presented here are the communication, structural, intergenerational, and strategic and solution-focused approaches. Family systems theories focus more on the development of problems and how problems may be changed than on human development. All contain valuable information about human development in the context of understanding the nature of problems.

A VIEW OF HUMAN NATURE
AND THE DEVELOPMENT OF PROBLEMS

Just as cells are small units within human beings that together make up organs, which together make up systems that determine bodily responses, the family systems perspectives presume that human beings are one unit of a family. Humans who are connected or related can make up **subsystems** and systems that function as a whole greater than the sum of the parts. In addition, families function together to make up a community or society.

Systems and subsystems are organized to create boundaries or limits around themselves. In biology, cell membranes or skin constitutes a boundary between one cell or another, one human or another. In family systems, the term **boundaries** usually refers to the rules that limit types of interactions or relationships one may engage in. For example, monogamy is a rule that binds two persons into a sexually exclusive relationship. Given the terms of many heterosexual marriages, having an affair is thought of as "out of bounds" or going beyond the boundaries of the relationship. Boundaries, in any system, whether chemical, biological, or relational, may be clear or unclear, permeable or fixed. Boundaries can serve to protect a system or to exclude outside forces. The same boundaries that may protect may also serve to keep what is inside hidden from view or intervention. Boundaries that prevent outside intervention may also obstruct protection if what is occurring inside a family is damaging.

Clear boundaries ensure that the system will be protected from intrusion by forces outside the system. At the same time, they are obvious enough to be visible, perhaps even transparent. Unclear boundaries result in less visibility. They may be present, but unable to be seen. Therefore, unclear boundaries may be violated without intention.

Fixed boundaries remain in place, regardless of changes inside or outside the system. Boundaries may also rigidify in such a way as to prevent the kind of elasticity often required to accommodate changes inside or outside the system.

Systems in which boundaries, communications, and differentiations are clear and fixed are assumed to function in the best interest of all of their component parts or subsystems. So also is a family system with clear boundaries, communication, and differentiation between its members thought of as functional. Dysfunction is assumed to be the result of either structural or functional difficulties manifest in unclear, too rigid, or too permeable boundaries, faulty communication, or inadequately differentiated structures within the system. Dysfunctional systems result in problems for individuals within the system, but may serve to hold the system intact. So, although individuals manifest problems, systems theories of helping suggest that individual problems serve a function for the family and are best understood as an expression of dysfunction within the system. These assumptions about the development of problems are quite different from theories of helping that focus on individual processes that determine behavior and problems.

Communications

According to some family systems theories, family functioning is best understood through the communication patterns in the family (Satir, 1967, 1972, 1983, 1988). Faulty communication within a system can both result in and signal problems. Some of the first problematic communication patterns to be investigated were those that occurred in families with a schizophrenic member. Bateson, Jackson, Haley, and Weakland (1956) outlined a phenomena called **double-bind communication** found in such families. In a double-bind message, the communication is not only unclear, but sent in such a way that the receiver cannot respond in any way without risk and cannot refuse the message. In the game of chess, the player who is in checkmate must make a move, but cannot move in any direction without risk. This emotional or relational "checkmate" was thought to constitute the beginnings of schizophrenia (often referred to as "schizophrenogenic").

Virginia Satir (1983) outlined four defensive patterns of communication in families that both signaled and resulted in problems: blaming, placating, computing, and distracting. Each is associated with verbal and nonverbal messages that are incongruent. Each is used to get around the threat of rejection and to hide perceived weaknesses. Each results in faulty communication in a system.

The **placater's** nonverbal behavior says, "I am helpless," the placater's words say, "Whatever you want is fine," and, inside, the placater is feeling worthless. The placater talks in an ingratiating way—pleasing, accommodating others, sacrificing self to gain the approval of another. Placaters strive to be too many things to too many people and a strong sense of self suffers in the balance. In a technique she called family sculpting, Satir (1983, 1988) often directed people to get into the physical position that depicts each position. For now, readers may find it useful to picture getting down on one knee, wobbling a bit, putting one hand out in a begging fashion, and straining head and neck. The placater's voice grows weak from the physical position, and communication is consistent with a belief of worthlessness.

The **blamer** is considered a complementary position to the placater (Satir, 1983, 1988). The blamer's words say, "You never do anything right," the body posture and message is "finger pointing," sentences start with "you," and inside, according to Satir, the blamer is feeling lonely and unsuccessful. By sacrificing others to maintain their self-worth, blamers fashion isolation from their wish to avoid responsibility.

Computers is the term Satir uses to refer to people who choose ultrareasonable words, a rigid, motionless, contained posture, dead-pan expression, and lackluster voice to indicate that their emotions are tightly checked against the threat of vulnerability. **Distractors** are those people who interject irrelevant words, have body postures that are off balance from moving in so many different directions simultaneously, and, as a result of avoiding a clear position, feel like no one knows or likes them, that there is no place for them.

For communication systems theories, it is patterns of communication that signal decreased self-worth and the use of these crippling patterns results in a continuing spiral of low self-esteem. The problematic patterns must be addressed to enhance individuals.

Structure

Salvador Minuchin (1974) emphasized examining the structure of relationships within a system to understand problems. Minuchin identified subsystems that make up the organization of the family system and believed that problems in family structures both reflected and shaped individual problems. Relational structures and subsystems are marked by boundaries that define who participates in the subsystem, and when and how. For example, there is a parental subsystem and a sibling subsystem and the boundaries of each function to define who participates in the interactions. Parental boundaries are closed to only the spouses to protect their privacy as a couple. Sibling subsystems exclude parental involvement to afford siblings a way to plan how to negotiate with parents.

Within family subsystems, different alignments, coalitions, and boundary configurations affect the subsystem and overall family structure. **Alignments** are ways members join with others and oppose each other, while **coalitions** are connections born of opposition against another. Two types of family structures with respect to boundaries are thought to result in problems: the disengaged family and the enmeshed family. In the **disengaged family,** the boundaries are so rigid that there is little or no contact between family members. Family members operate in isolation and each neglects the others' needs. Antisocial behavior may develop from this type of family as children are left to fend for themselves without adequate resources to do so. In the **enmeshed family,** on the other hand, boundaries are so diffuse or permeable that each is affected by and may be overinvolved in the business of the other. For example, if boundaries are permeable between nuclear families, extended family members may feel free to pass judgment about child-raising practices. Permeable boundaries between parents and children are thought to promote incest. In an enmeshed family, inadequately differentiated roles of parents and spouses or children are at the root of dysfunction. According to Minuchin, family structures should be hierarchical. As one subsystem, the parents should have more power over the child subsystem, and problems can also result from a level or flat structure in which children either make or share in rule-making for the system.

When the rules become inoperative, the boundaries too rigid or too impermeable, if the family doesn't function in a hierarchy with parents having more responsibility than children and older children more responsibility than younger children, or when alignments or coalitions disrupt function, the structure is said to be dysfunctional. Examining individual symptoms and interactions offers keys to establishing the structural problems in the family system.

Functioning over Time

Murray Bowen (1961, 1972a, 1972b, 1976a, 1976b, 1991) extended the concept of family structures beyond the immediate nuclear family to include the functioning of previous generations. His position is that humans grow, change, and develop toward differentiation of self in intergenerational family contexts. Distinguishing intellectual processes from feelings and keeping emotions under rational control, while objectively experiencing the intensity of family life, represents, for Bowen, clear **self-differentiation.** Problems arise when individuals are unable to adequately differentiate themselves from their families of origin or when rational thought is swamped by feeling. Both are referred to as **fusion.**

Fusion leads to a sort of "emotional oneness" that in one sense protects against a perceived threat and in another results in a family or couple so stuck together one cannot change or adapt without dragging the other along. When a couple or family is fused, each feels so vulnerable alone that Bowen believes they seek **triangulation,** or involvement from a third party, to bolster their position. An insecure partner may seek children, neighbors, parents, or another lover to support them.

Triangles make for very stable geometric designs and family structures. Triangulation makes differentiation difficult, as each side in the triangle jockeys for a comfortable position. A common example of triangulation in families is a mother and child with a passive or withdrawn father cast as outsider. Mother and child interact leaving father out. When father tries to bond with mother, the child is left out. When father makes any attempt to create a bond with the child, the mother is left out. Each person may react to the isolation by being upset and may resolve the upset by differentiating self further, or what Bowen calls **emotional cutoff.** Emotional cutoffs are also a way to cope with unresolved triangulated attachments with parents. The patterns may include running away, denial, or compartmentalizing the problems if living close to each other. Whether the effects of triangulation are cured geographically or psychologically, the person who does not resolve the parent triangulation, according to this system perspective, both wants intimacy and fights it.

Triangles not only occur within a nuclear family, but can occur across generations when parents project their own anxieties or inability to differentiate onto children in an attempt to regain their own homeostasis. The family triangled as such needs the child for stability and thus makes it more difficult for the child to differentiate, and so it may go for generations. This is called a multigenerational transmission of the problem and results in decreasing levels of differentiation as children of inadequately differentiated parents choose partners of similar differentiation and beget children of even less differentiation. Problems, from Bowen's perspective, are the result of inadequate differentiation of self from the family emotional system and triangles that interfere with differentiation. Examining the patterns of triangulation that resulted in failed differentiation across generations is the focus of intergenerational family theories.

Problem-Solving

Jay Haley (1963, 1971a, 1971b, 1976, 1984) and Steven de Shazer (1985, 1986, 1988) represent a fundamental and more recent shift in thinking about family helping. Rather than focusing on problems, their approaches focus on solutions to family problems. Haley and de Shazer are examples of strategic and solution-focused approaches (respectively) to family helping. Both share in a belief that the emphasis of helping should be on strategies to solve problems families present, though they differ in some key approaches to solving such problems. The assumption of de Shazer's solution-focused helping is similar to humanistic theories of helping in that he believes that solutions to problems are inevitable if clients are reminded to attend to their own previously successful solutions. Haley shares with Satir a focus on observing communication and interactions among family members, though he pays particular attention to the structure of power within the family, the ways in which parents handle their power, and the power of the helper in designing solutions. De Shazer emphasizes helping clients notice what they are doing right in the belief that clients already know how to solve their problems; they are just not paying attention to ways to make things better. He rejects the traditional notion of client resistance and instead focuses on complimenting clients on what they are doing to try to solve the problems they face and reminding them of what they have done that worked in the past to solve such problems.

THE HELPING PROCESS

Goals

The goals of any systemic theory of helping is to enhance the system so as to better serve the individuals within it. Family systems theories of helping, while somewhat distinct in specific objectives, agree that it is the family that is the focus of helping. According to family systems perspectives, individual behavior and problems are best understood in the family context in which they developed. So the family provides the context for understanding how individuals function in relation to others, how individuals behave and what problems they develop. Systemic helpers do not deny the importance of the individual. Indeed, most believe that it is the individual who carries symptoms for an entire family, perhaps even generations of families. Rather, family systems helpers believe that just as family systems are powerful influences on behavior and the development of problems, families can be powerful agents of change if rallied to correct the problems experienced by individual members.

The primary goal of helping from a systemic perspective, then, is to change the system to effect change in each of the individuals within the system. The challenge for helping, from a systems perspective, is that any system has a tendency to seek homeostatic balance and there will be at least as much power operating against a positive, direct change as in favor of it. In chemistry, a catalyst is a substance that either speeds up or slows down a chemical reaction, and in medicine, it is the counteracting agent employed to arrest problematic processes within a system. Whether a catalyst for changes in communication, structures, strategies or solutions, the family systems helper can be thought of as a catalyst for change in the family system, speeding up or slowing down necessary changes and employed to arrest problematic processes within the system.

The Helper's Role

Though family systems perspectives generally consider helpers to be catalysts for change in families, each of the different family systems perspectives conceptualizes the role of the helper in a somewhat different way. Those whose emphasis is on communication patterns (e.g., Satir) view the helper as one who observes the pattern of communication, structures interactive situations so that members can see or experience those patterns of communication themselves, teaches new communication skills, and then guides rehearsals of new behavioral and communications patterns.

Influenced by Carl Rogers, Virginia Satir believed that since it is helpers who facilitate the process, who the helpers are, rather than the specific strategies they employ, may be more important. Family members are assumed to have the potential to move toward growth with sufficient nurturance, support, safety, and validation from the helper (Satir & Bitter, 1991). The helper is essentially a resource person who is in a unique position to observe the family communication utilizing a wide-angle lens to see each member's viewpoint and offer positive feedback to amplify needs. Helpers facilitate a process that models effective communication to enhance the likelihood that each family member, once validated and supported, will elect a change that facilitates growth for the system and self-actualization.

Those who focus on family structure (e.g., Minuchin) not only make observations but join the family in a position of leadership, map their observations of the structure, and then intervene to transform the structure of their relationships. Change will necessarily occur, according to structural helping theory, through modification of transactional patterns and family organization. The helper's role changes from initially joining the family, to directing situations in which families enact their relational styles, then sitting back and commenting on or casting a new light or a different interpretation on a problem with support and challenge to help a family relearn homeostatic balance without stereotyped patterns of relating to one another.

Bowen, whose emphasis is on multigenerational transmission of problems in differentiation, sees himself as an objective researcher who helps family members assess and understand their relational styles. Bowenian helpers might be thought of as functioning as teachers, coaches, and neutral observers. They teach about triangulation and then expect clients to go back to their families of origin either literally or figuratively and extricate themselves from the patterns. They coach the client about alternatives and how to view their situations neutrally. The helper must be aware enough of themselves and their own families of origin not to distort either their own or a client's personal history and to model alternative ways to perceive situations. The intergenerationally focused helper is more concerned with managing her or his own neutrality than with technique.

Strategic helpers like Jay Haley perceive the role of the family systems helper to be the primary designer of family solutions. To the extent that symptoms are seen as metaphors for ways of feeling or behaving within the family, strategic helpers look for the message being communicated as a metaphor of the symptom. Although strategic helpers ask family members for their perspectives about the problems they face, it is the helper who decides on the helping goals and designs a solution. Solution-focused helping, by contrast, shares with humanistic theories of helping the belief that clients can and will solve their own problems if they strengthen and enhance positive functioning. The helper's primary role is one of pointing out past solutions and successes.

Assessment

Few specific psychological tests are advocated by family systems helpers. Rather, family systems helpers generally make observations about patterns of communication, structure, and interactions within a given family to assess the nature of problems. Several examples may help to illustrate this. A family systems helper drawing on Satir's communication model would listen carefully to descriptions of and examples of communication patterns before asking family members to assume an illustrative physical position. Bowenian family systems helpers are likely to teach family members to create **genograms** and may create one for themselves to use in assessing family patterns across generations. Minuchin and other structural family systems helpers assess the structure of relationships depicting the types of coalitions, alignments, and boundaries being observed while interacting with the families. Haley and de Shazer would each emphasize helpers' observations of solutions to problems. Each of these helper assessments serves to assist clients and helpers in establishing the roots of individual and systemic difficulties or solutions to problems.

Techniques and Process

Family systems perspectives view helping as a process of positive feedback. The perspectives may differ in the content of the feedback. Information may be offered about client communication patterns, the structure of relationships, or strategies for solving problems. Each perspective may advocate different techniques for conveying feedback. Information may be offered through helper interpretation, didactic instruction, or exercises designed to raise awareness. In family systems helping, feedback is presumed to amplify the need for a change in the system.

With an emphasis on communication patterns and a belief in the potential for self-actualization and growth, family systems helpers who follow Satir's approach focus on the relationship that develops between the helper and the clients. Satir (1967, 1983) recommends that helpers model emotional honesty, congruence, and understanding of the system and communication patterns. They create a setting in which clients can risk examining their communication styles, a setting that helps families build self-esteem, identify assets, and decrease threats by setting boundaries and reducing defensive communication. This shows that the hidden and forbidden are acceptable to explore, restores client accountability, delineates roles and functions, points out discrepancies in communication, and identifies nonverbal communication.

Two of Satir's unique techniques are **family sculpting** and **parts parties.** Family sculpting consists of asking family members to physically position themselves according to the helper's observations of their communication styles. A sort of assessment strategy, this also raises each members awareness of their own and others interpersonal boundaries and communication. Parts parties involve reclaiming parts of self that have been disowned, denied, or distorted. Clients create short enactments of different parts of themselves by giving each a name (e.g., a name of a famous person personifying a trait) and then interacting with others who have also named a particular part.

Minuchin employs methods that allow active, directive, well-thought-out manipulations of the system and change in the inappropriate structures. He recommends that helpers do most of the work. The helper must:

Join a family by engaging its members and subsystems and speaking their language;

Map the "psychopolitical" structure identifying boundaries and transactional styles;

Accommodate their styles of interacting and their family hierarchies;

Track sequences in their interactions;

Ask them to act out conflict situations in order to intensify relational styles and to get a clearer picture of how they structure interactions to solve problems;

Cast new light on or provide alternative interpretations of problem situations to allow family members to see a problem from various angles and relieve the individual burden of the "identified" patient;

Restructure family boundaries by breaking up the usual patterns (blocking, softening rigidity, and supporting permeable boundaries); and

Issue directives to clients to help them liberate themselves from a destructive structure.

Bowen's most well-known technique is his drawing the intergenerational influences on any given individual. Called making a **genogram,** this relatively simple process is designed to allow clients to see the multiple contexts from which problems developed. The helper questions and uses cognitive processes to guide client differentiation through returning to their family of origin and detriangulation. Based on the assumption that change in any part of the system will ripple into changes in other parts, the intergenerational helper need not work with the entire system in her or his office to be effective. Asking one client to begin to think more objectively about her or his family of origin by developing her or his own genograms, by returning to the family, and by responding rationally rather than emotionally to the usual family connections holds the promise of inviting different responses from others. Like a coach, the intergenerational helper also checks on progress in these assignments.

Haley and de Shazer both emphasize strategies that alleviate the problem or symptom. Strategic family helpers design tasks for families to engage in and then help the family to complete the task (Haley, 1976, 1984). The tasks are generally of two types: straightforward and paradoxical. A straightforward task is one that is a relatively simple assignment, clearly explained, and easy to accomplish. The helper is the expert who establishes what has been tried and then uses her or his expert power to gain family compliance with the assignment. Tasks are customized to the unique situation. **Paradoxical tasks** are those that ask a family to continue doing what they have sought help for in such a way that, paradoxically, they produce positive change. Both straightforward and paradoxical tasks require much experience and general guidelines are insufficient for designing the tasks (Sharf, 1996). Paradoxical tasks are reserved for families who resist straightforward tasks.

Unlike Haley, de Shazer rejects the traditional concept of client resistance to change (1985). Instead, he recommends focusing helping attention on ways that families are already trying to solve the problems they face. He advocates the use of techniques like asking clients to focus on what has been effective in the past in solving problems. Instead of emphasizing the development of problems as many family systems helping theories suggest, he uses techniques like asking clients to imagine future concrete behavioral differences that can be used as indications of change for the better. It is the clients who then find creative ways to bring these changes about (Todd & Bohart, 1999). Clients in solution-focused helping relationships may be told to pay attention to what they did when something was going well. This technique is thought to both convey the message that the client can change and it focuses attention on solution and success, rather than problems and failures (de Shazer, 1985).

RESEARCH

A number of investigators have studied the interaction of families through observation and assessment instruments developed precisely for this purpose. Douglas Olson (1986, 1990, 1993, 1996, 1997, 2000) created a **circumplex model** categorizing four levels of adaptability (chaotic, flexible, structured, and rigid) and four levels of cohesion (disengaged, separated, connected, and enmeshed) to study how families address stresses and crises. High functioning families tended to score in the midrange on the two dimensions. Robert Beavers and associates (Hampson, Hulgus, & Beavers, 1991; Lewis, Beavers, Gossett, & Phillips, 1976) studied healthy families as they went about tasks and sought to measure health by differentiating families that view satisfactory relationships as coming from outside the family to those who believe satisfactory relationships come from inside the family. Though they contrasted their work with Olson's Family Adaptability and Cohesion Scale (FACES), both have become important as criteria for measuring effectiveness of family systems helping.

A number of studies have found family systems helping to be at least as effective as other types of helping (e.g., Bednar, Burlingame, & Masters, 1988; Hazelrigg, Cooper, & Borduin, 1987; Henggeler, Borduin, & Mann, 1993). Most, however, do not define what they are measuring very well and may not really be testing the effectiveness of family systems approaches. Given that family systems approaches are also being integrated with many other helping models (Sharf, 1996), it is likely that differentiating one approach from another will be the emphasis in coming studies.

Most of the communications helping models have not been subjected to rigorous systematic research about the outcome effectiveness. Although Satir reported helping more than five thousand families and thought the strategies were generally helpful, she indicated she had done no formal outcome research. The few direct evaluations have yielded nonsignificant effect sizes (Shadish, Montegomery, Wilson, Wilson, Bright, & Okwumakua, 1993).

Surprisingly few controlled studies have been conducted on structural helping (Gurman, Kiniskern, & Pinsof 1986; Shadish et al., 1993). The well-controlled studies have indicated that structural helping is definitely superior to no treatment at all for drug abusers, but it remains largely untested with other problems. There have been no controlled outcome studies of intergenerational helping methods.

Being relatively new and largely untested, family systems helping models still need research support for their claims.

CRITIQUING

Family systems approaches have been criticized by psychodynamic theorists for their emphases on the system at the expense of understanding individual dynamics and by behavioral theorists for not specifying the mechanisms for either individual or systemic change in operational terms. They have been criticized by humanists for not validating individual choices as a determinant of behavior or problems (Prochaska & Norcross, 1999). While valuing the relational approach of family systems theories of helping, feminist theorists have also criticized the emphasis on and reinforcement of hierarchical family structures and the primacy of rationality to the exclusion of affective experience. Multicultural theories of helping suggest that family systems approaches do not traditionally take into account differences in ethnicity or families of color that may include such basic departures as the definitions of what constitutes a family. A single normative standard for what constitutes a healthy family also flies in the face of the postmodern perspective that is at the heart of both multicultural and feminist theories. So also does limiting the focus of investigation and help to families rather than larger social and cultural contexts thought to be influential. Integrationists view systems theories of helping to be of use as long as they do not try to construe every problem as systemic (Prochaska & Norcross, 1999). Challenges notwithstanding, the family systems helping models have not only broadened professional helpers' repertoire of strategies, but they have broadened our perspectives to include views of immediate contextual influences on behavior, problems, and solutions.

CHAPTER

13

Sociocultural Theories of Helping: Feminist Theories

CONTEXT

As with many of the helping theories, sociocultural theories are not one approach, but many; they cannot be attributed to one theorist, but result from the efforts of many. As the word *sociocultural* suggests, these encompass a number of theories of helping that share a common focus on the social and cultural influences that shape and maintain human behavior and problems that human beings encounter. More than other theories of helping, sociocultural theories examine not only psychological factors that may lead to individual behavior, identity, and problems, but also social and cultural influences like ethnicity, culture, race, class, gender, orientation, ability, and religion. Feminist and multicultural theories of helping are two examples of sociocultural theories of helping that recognize the importance of differences in social and cultural backgrounds in the ways that people develop and change.

The first formalized theories of human behavior, problems, and helping were focused on biology or the "nature" side of the nature–nurture debate in psychology. Early psychodynamic theories held that the primary forces determining personality and problems are biological. Also deterministic, the behavioral theories took a strong stand on the "nurture" side of the debate, suggesting that it is environment that determines behavior and human problems. Humanistic perspectives proposed a third force, human choices and decisions, that determine

219

behavior, problems, and solutions. If phenomenological theories like existentialism and humanism are often called the "third force" theories because of their emphasis on the individual's own decisions, sociocultural theories can be thought of as focusing on a "fourth force" determining behavior, identity, and problems. Including feminist theories and multicultural theories, these theories emphasize the impact of social and cultural forces, specifically status and power differences, oppression, social norms, and role expectations in the development of behavior, identity, health, problems, and solutions.

Although there has been much "cross-pollination" of ideas between feminist and multicultural theories of helping, they differ in their focus. Feminist theories specifically examine role expectations and status and power differences related to gender, while multicultural theories look more specifically at the role of race/ethnicity/culture and, to some extent, class status in shaping individuals and problems. This chapter examines feminist sociocultural theories and includes some of the foundations that have also influenced multicultural theories.

Feminist theories of helping represent a synthesis (or blend) of feminist theories with helping theories. Feminist theories of helping are theories based on integrating the psychology of women, the psychology of power and powerlessness, and the psychology of dominance and subordination particularly as these are reflected in the socialization of gender roles (Poorman, 1992). While feminist theory is a relatively well-defined philosophy, feminist theories of helping are relatively new, not always sharply delineated nor fully articulated.

Feminism and Feminist Helping Theories

While a thorough understanding of complex feminist philosophies is beyond the scope of this book, it is important to understand how this philosophy and helping theory came together to form feminist helping theory. **Feminism** is a belief that women and men are of equal value and that women should have political, economic, and social power equal to men. Contrary to some opinions, feminism does not seek to devalue men. The mandates of feminist theory include recognizing that women have been historically undervalued and have not had access to the power to change these circumstances; valuing women and women's experiences and attributes; and empowering women. The psychology of women is a critical component in acknowledging and understanding women, which is prerequisite to valuing women. Acknowledging and understanding the dynamics of power is critical to empowering clients. Unequal power has not only affected individuals, but has been built into social institutions (or become institutionalized). Individual change, though necessary, cannot alone effect equality. Consciousness-raising facilitates this knowledge, and action is required.

Feminist theories about helping evolved specifically to acknowledge, understand, and empower women, individually and collectively. In their infancy, feminist theories of helping were considered an adjunct, rather than a stand-alone, theory of helping. In other words, theories were meant to support rather than to supplant traditional theories of helping (Rawlings & Carter, 1977). Many professional helpers continue to see feminist theories of helping in this way. Feminist helping theorists have come from diverse backgrounds, and training and feminist theories of helping have evolved both in reaction to criticisms of traditional theories of helping and in conjunction with those theories. Sometimes traditional theories have provided the seeds for feminist helping ideas; sometimes they have provided the impetus to challenge previous ideas and to strike out in new directions. Still, traditional theories of helping are reflected in, shaped by, deconstructed, and reconstructed by feminist theories.

Some feminist helping theorists advocate feminist psychoanalytic theories (e.g., Chodorow, 1978, 1989; Mitchell, 1974), some endorse feminist self-psychology theories (e.g., Gardiner, 1987; Hertzberg, 1990; Wolfman, 1983), and others favor feminist object relations theories (e.g., Eichenbaum & Orbach, 1983). There are feminist humanistic theories of helping (e.g., Lerman, 1992), feminist phenomenological theories of helping (Boukydis, 1981; Hill, 1990; Mill & Ballou, 1998), and feminist cognitive-behavioral theories of helping (e.g., Blechman, 1980). Some believe that espousing feminism as a philosophical or political stance is in and of itself therapeutic (e.g., Wyckoff, 1977). Some believe that a feminist philosophy of helping exists (e.g., Sturdivant, 1980). More recently, some have suggested that although feminist theories of helping are diverse and still evolving, they also have distinctive common elements that are giving birth to more theoretically coherent (Brown, 1990), more philosophically comprehensive (Sturdivant, 1980), more ethically unified (Lerman, 1987), and more consonant feminist theories of personality development and helping (Brown, 1990; Lerman, 1987; Moradi, Fischer, Hill, Jome, & Blum, 2000; Poorman, 1993).

While some (e.g., Lerman, 1987) argue that psychoanalytic theories, no matter how they are modified, cannot be feminist, I take a more moderate position. Freudian and feminist helpers share recognition of the impact of early experience, unconscious, preconscious, and conscious motivation, a certain amount of biological motivation for action, and the crucial importance of gender in the development of women. Further, Karen Horney's understanding of the implications of social context on psychological development resembles the feminist helping theory that "the personal is political." Self-in-relations theories share with object relations theories, self theories, and feminist theories a belief that women's earliest relationship with their mothers brings female socialization to empathy and mutuality and create each other as beings-in-relationship. Still, recognizing points of agreement does not preclude criticism. Even though recent theories expand to include self in an interpersonal context, traditional analytic theory still looks to intrapsychic determinants of personality and pathology and gives inadequate emphasis to the importance of the larger (macro) environmental context.

Feminist theories of personality and helping share with phenomenological theories respect for the primacy of the individual's subjective experience of being in the world (M. Hill, 1986, 1990; Hill & Ballou, 1998). Feminist helping theorists share in the Rogerian idea that it is environmental conditions of worth that prevent self-actualization and create splits in the self. Feminist helping theorists would agree with the crucial importance of genuineness and empathy in relationships in general and in helping relationships in particular. The Maslowian idea that survival and safety are a foundation in full development certainly has implications for women and other oppressed groups. Nonetheless, feminist criticisms of the humanistic approach are precisely that it imposes too much significance on the universality of the human experience of choice. When a culture does not allow all of its members the same privilege to choose, the context itself inhibits free and independent imposition of meaning and values. Choices are clearly shaped, reinforced, punished, extinguished, and maintained by environmental contingencies.

While behavioral and cognitive-behavioral theories hold promise for feminist helping in their emphases on changing environmental contingencies and faulty thinking, some dangers have been recognized as well (Chesler, 1972; Rossi, 1964; Williams, 1977). Individual behavioral strategies do not change the environmental conditions that damage and distress women, indeed they may convince a woman that there is something wrong with her. While it is true that the technology of behavior or thought modification is neutral, it is equally true that it may be used to oppress or to enhance. Feminist helping theories charge behaviorism with the challenge of moving away from a technological fix of specific individuals and toward systemic change. The technology is useful; it must be embedded in a relationship with a real person whose ethical values clearly reflect feminist theory to qualify as feminist helping.

In some respects, the defining process of feminist helping theory is itself not unlike the struggles of women. Still in the process of self-definition after centuries of definition by, and in relation to, males, feminist helping theories now stand alone and also in relation to theories of helping that emphasize other forces in the development of behavior, identity, and problems (Poorman, 1993).

A VIEW OF HUMAN NATURE AND THE DEVELOPMENT OF PROBLEMS

According to sociocultural theories of helping, humans are the product of social and cultural influences. Human growth and development, then, are conceptualized in the social and cultural contexts in which they take place. Ethnicity, race, class, gender, orientation, ability, and religion all constitute elements of social and cultural contexts in which growth and development occur. Feminist theories of helping explore the political, social, economic, and interpersonal contexts in which women grow, change, and develop; multicultural theories examine the contexts in which people of color grow, change, and develop. Each context is influenced by a system of domination and subordination that distributes power unequally between men and women, between white people and people of color. Understanding this system by which power is distributed is crucial to understanding feminist and multicultural views of human nature and development. This understanding begins with an examination of a hierarchy or an arrangement of people, things, ideas, and so on in order of rank, grade, class, or value.

In the United States, power and resources are not distributed equally among people, but arranged in a **hierarchy** and allotted in order of status or perceived status (Gelles & Levine, 1995). Some people have more power; some have less. **Status** has historically been determined by wealth, education, and property ownership, and those who could not own property, attend school, or amass wealth attained a lesser status. Not only could women and people of color not *own* property, they were considered to *be* the property of landowners (Rothenberg, 1998). Denied education, property, wealth, and the franchise to vote, little could be changed on their own accord. The word *power* comes from French and Latin roots indicating "an ability to act," and women and people of color have been historically denied various abilities to act. Power came to denote dominion over another.

When social, political, economic, or interpersonal systems are based on a stratified distribution of power, two processes emerge: domination and subordination. People who are ascribed more power are socialized to dominate and those ascribed less power are socialized to be subordinate. Jean Baker Miller's early work (1986, originally published in 1976) has become influential in understanding the dynamics of power and powerlessness, domination and subordination.

People are defined by their relative status, power, and subsequent access to resources. Once a person or group is defined as dominant, other groups are subordinated, assigned a position of lesser value, and then treated consistently with this attribution. Preferred functions and resources tend to be assigned to those who dominate and may even be closed to subordinates. Less valued functions (such as serving the needs of dominants), on the other hand, are assigned to subordinates. This may even be reinforced with statements that subordinates are unable to perform the preferred roles due to innate defects. Subordinates are encouraged to develop characteristics that please dominants, and there can be little room to acknowledge other characteristics. Dominants determine and create institutions to support their norms, mores, and values. To be "normal" is to adhere to and continue in a pattern that is consistent with the worldview held by those in a dominant position. Culture, philosophy, morality, social theory, and even science become institutions of, by, and for the dominant group. Once established, mobility within such a hierarchy is achieved with difficulty. Once diminished, subordinated groups not only feel powerless, but are powerless. Dominant groups resist relinquishing position. To gain or maintain a position of dominance, one must subordinate others. Feminist theories of helping seek an understanding of the impact of this unequal distribution of power among men and women by examining the development of characteristic behaviors, roles, and problems among those who dominate and those who are subordinated (Jordan et al., 1991; J. B. Miller, 1986).

Domination

Gaining and maintaining dominance demands that one establish and maintain a position of superiority. This can be effected in a number of ways. Competing with others; winning, or at least not losing; actively subordinating or minimizing others; trivializing the needs, feelings, reactions, wishes, preferences, and choices of others who are of subordinate status; demanding obeisance; maintaining the primacy of autonomy for dominants while squelching independent or autonomous functioning for subordinates; and associating dependency with vulnerability or powerlessness all serve to create distance and maintain superiority.

Because dominants are in a position to make or control decisions, rules and injunctions may be used to reinforce a superior position. Conflict, perceived by those in a position of dominance to be a threat to superiority, may be eliminated by invoking science, tradition, or rule. Violence quells conflicts and reinstates dominance.

While dominants may establish and maintain power over others and control of vital resources, there are losses in interpersonal relationships and problem-solving capacity. If someone must win, never show weakness or vulnerability, or maintain strict autonomy, the capacity for connection, nurturing, and assuming responsibility for the well-being of others will be restricted. Together with a restricted capacity for empathy and vulnerability, intimacy is obviously compromised for the dominant. Since it is intimacy that may counteract stereotyped expectations, these may remain intact. Limited intimacy also curtails accurate feedback about self. Tolerance for divergent views and conflict enhances problem-solving and conflict-resolution skills. Together, these characteristic difficulties highlight a position that allows little awareness of self, position, privileges, or the costs associated with such a position. Finally, violent behavior may be seen by dominants as a viable strategy for resolving conflict when other skills are limited and when one can engage in violence with impunity.

Subordination

Those in subordinate positions learn early that survival is based on an ability to establish and maintain connections. With economic, interpersonal, or political survival in the hands of the dominant, subordinates learn to depend on dominants and others for resources. Securing resources involves learning to accommodate. Accommodation develops skills at compromise, change, flexibility, and divergent thinking, but also results in subordinates losing sight of themselves. Indeed, often the needs, feelings, and ideas of the subordinate can become blurred with the dominant's. Autonomous functioning may also be associated with hardship, ostracism, isolation, abuse, and even death. The awareness of such threats may demand that conflicts be obliterated by accommodation, compromise, indirect defiance, and even imitation.

Once a system of dominance and subordination is established, it cannot be changed simply by changing the positions of the individual players. Each position shapes behaviors consistent with the position. So, if women, gays, lesbians, people of color, the poor, or disabled people traded places with straight, white, able, wealthy men, it is likely they would become the dominants and develop characteristics that serve that position.

Of critical importance is recognizing that women and subordinated others have also developed valuable strengths either as a result of or despite subordination. This is not to say that I recommend subordination as an avenue for growth and development, only that subordination may come with seeds valuable for growth. Subordinates are thought to develop skills in cooperating, nurturing, and empathy. Subordinates develop the capacity for change and divergent thinking associated with creative problem-solving. Subordinates are skilled at participation in the development of others and at understanding weakness and vulnerability prerequisites for intimacy. Subordinates are socialized to value the primacy of relationships, but primarily relationships with dominants. While many of these skills may be externally directed or directed toward the growth and development of others in general and dominants in particular, they may also be redirected to enhance self-growth (an idea underlying feminist helping). Both the subordination of women and the dominance ascribed to men have implications for the development of behaviors, personality, problems, and the helping process.

From the perspective of feminist helping, individual behaviors and personality constellations are thought to be the direct result of cultural expectations, social context, and individual dynamics influenced by biology, childhood experiences, relationships, decisions, and environmental contingencies. Environmental exigencies are most certainly transmitted in the context of significant (family, spouses, partners, peers, friends), as well as casual relationships. They are also transmitted through media, institutions, laws, folkways, mores, and traditions.

The model Susan Sturdivant (1980) uses to describe personality development is an interactional one in which social structure, culture, and individual are assumed to be interrelated, with roles being the mediating link between society and the individual. She posits that emotional, cognitive, and social levels interact to produce personality and behavior. Kay Deaux and Brenda Major's (1987) now famous article on gender stereotyping proposed a similarly complex interactional model for understanding how both men and women come to be stereotyped and to participate in the stereotyping. Jean Baker Miller and her associates (Jordan et al., 1991) envision a model utilizing a construct of self-in-relation. I suggest a model that focuses on development of self-in-context to address the complexity of both intimate relationships and the influence of the larger, macro-context in which growth and development occur (Poorman, 1993).

Feminist helping theories utilize an environmental model of pathology and an androgynous model of mental health. This means that feminist helping theories posit that problems and distress are the logical, though dysfunctional, results of female sex-role socialization (Baruch & Barnett, 1975; Bem, 1975; Bernard, 1976a, 1976b; Block, 1973; David, 1975a, 1975b; Gove & Tudor, 1973; Gump, 1972; Maccoby, 1966; Maracek, 1976; Rose, 1975; Rossi, 1972) and specifically the socialization of women to subordinate group status (Hacker, 1976; Polk, 1974). Feminist theories of helping hold that individuals incorporate the expectancies of their respective environments and thereby carry the problems of the environments. Until female socialization can be factored out of the equation, it will be difficult to know what is intrapsychic and what is extrapsychic.

THE HELPING PROCESS

Goals

If the source of problems is social, cultural, and political inequity, the goal of feminist helping is to facilitate change (equity) rather than adjustment to the context that produced the problem. The feminist helper facilitates a variety of changes in individual clients and directly and indirectly in the contexts that produce problems for women. Goals of helping include: a critical examination of power (Rosewater & Walker, 1985); challenges to sex-role socialization (Sturdivant, 1980); externalization of sex-role socialization that has been internalized (Gilbert, 1980); client redefinition of self (Jordan et al., 1991; Jordan, Surrey, & Kaplan, 1985, 1990); and enhancement of an individual clients' critical awareness of the social and cultural context and its impact on current behavior, personality, and problems. An implicit goal of feminist helping is to help women identify and cease cooperating in their own oppression or subordination. Finally, the feminist helper facilitates recognition and actualization of strengths, even when those strengths may have been born of a subordinated status. The helper assists clients in examining, challenging, and changing dominant and subordinate roles in a variety of contexts, including the helping relationship context. This involves not only changing negative and inaccurate ascriptions (e.g., the belief that women are less capable of mathematical reasoning than men), but also reclaiming accurate but devalued characteristics (e.g., the well-researched finding that women are more relationally oriented than men).

While feminist helping may recognize many of the same goals that other traditional helping theories recognize, these will also look very different as a function of a feminist framework. For example, while most helping theories view symptom removal as desirable, feminist helping theory criticizes that simple symptom removal may contribute to the perspective that it is an individual and not her or his context that shaped and maintained the symptom in the first place. Further, feminist helping theory suggests that facilitating client recognition of the functional value of pain, anger, and the utility of conflict facilitates a more "real" change. Other examples of goals such as enhancement of self-esteem, improvement of inequality of interpersonal relationships, and enhanced role performance, also espoused by other helping theories, are influenced by feminist theories perspective.

For example, although humanists and feminists share a belief in the importance of meanings an individual may ascribe to her or his experience and both would expect that the client is most expert in her or his own behavior, feminist theories of helping would look beyond the strictly personal meanings ascribed by an individual that humanism and cognitive-behavior perspectives would examine for points of change.

In addition to the goals shared nominally with other helping models, sociocultural helping theories promote an awareness of political, social, cultural, and economic influences and prompt individuals to social action against oppression. Also called *conscientização* by Paulo Freire (1972), this may take many forms in the helping process.

The Helper's Role

The feminist helper must be knowledgeable about the psychology and experience of women to facilitate client understanding of the difference between fact and fiction, research and stereotype. Further, the helper must be willing and able to develop a relationship that models an egalitarian distribution of power and feminist values. Each involves a different type of training and preparation. Knowledge about the psychology of women can be gained through courses. Learning the microskills of helping certainly begins to build a strong relationship foundation. Applying the microskills in such a way as to model egalitarianism involves a careful examination of the dynamics of empowering clients.

Feminist helping theorists have described essential helper characteristics, such as empathy, genuineness, warmth and compassion, working toward her own optimal functioning, awareness of her own values, and the willingness to make values explicit (Sturdivant, 1980). Feminist helping theory describes the helper's role as one of facilitator and agent of resocialization (Sturdivant, 1980). Feminist helpers make self-disclosures relevant to client issues and demystify the helping process in order to eliminate the unnecessary distance or arbitrarily unequal elements of helping. As the goal of feminist helping is to create with the client an egalitarian relationship, the role of the feminist helper is that of collaborator, facilitator, coach, guide, mentor, and model, rather than director.

That there is a psychology of women (J. B. Miller, 1986; Rohrbaugh-Bunker, 1979; Stock, Graubert, & Birns, 1982) is by now indisputable. Further, the idea that ideology, social structure, and behavior are inextricably interwoven (Gilbert, 1980) is considered unequivocal in feminist theorizing. The two most salient values advocated in feminist helping theories are (1) that the personal is political (Bloom, Eichenbaum, & Orbach, 1982; Brodsky & Hare-Mustin, 1980; Chambless & Wenk, 1982; Gilbert, 1980; Hare-Mustin, 1984; Lerman, 1985, 1986, 1987; J. B. Miller, 1986; Mowbray, Lanir, & Hulce, 1985; Rawlings & Carter, 1977), and (2) that women should have equal access to all forms of power: political, economical, interpersonal, social, and in helping (Brodsky & Hare-Mustin, 1980; Gilbert, 1980; Stock, Graubert, & Birns, 1982; Israel, 1984; Lerman, 1985, 1986, 1987; Lerman & Porter, 1990; J. B. Miller, 1986; Rawlings & Carter, 1977; Rosewater & Walker, 1985).

Corollary to the two basic values held by feminist helpers are other principles: (3) those qualities characteristically ascribed to women are of value, (4) inferior status is due to inequity in the present distribution of power, (5) the primary source of problems is social, (6) while problems are social, each person is held accountable for her or his own thoughts, feelings, behavior, and goals, (7) **androgyny** is mentally healthy, and (8) both men and women are victims of the current system, though men benefit from its privileges and may be reluctant to give it up (Rawlings & Carter, 1977).

Assessment

Feminist helpers were initially cautioned to avoid psychodiagnostic testing (Rawlings & Carter, 1977). This was grounded in concerns about (1) the amply researched sexist bias of such tools, (2) the underlying assumption that problems are external to the person presenting for helping, (3) the tools themselves were often identified with theoretical frameworks inconsistent with feminist theory, and (4) testing was thought to promote the mystification of helping and powerfulness of the helper, while diminishing the client's power of self-definition.

For the most part, feminist helpers still avoid psychological testing unless specifically requested by the client, and limitations of the test known by the helper are made explicit to the client before proceeding. However, forensic psychologists like Lynn Bravo Rosewater (1982, 1985, 1986, 1987, 1990) and those involved in frequent forensic interface (e.g., Lenore Walker, 1979, 1980, 1986, 1989, 1990) have begun a reexamination of some testing instruments such as the Minnesota Multiphasic Personality Inventory (MMPI). For example, in her now famous work on MMPI testing with battered women who killed their male partners, Rosewater (1982, 1985) finds that there are characteristic profiles among abused women in general and those who kill their male partners in particular. It may be extrapolated that oppressed persons may also exhibit predictable profiles (Rosewater, 1990). Seminal work on the use of the MMPI with African Americans, Latinos, Asians, and Native Americans certainly suggests cultural differences (Colligan & Offord, 1985; Pollack & Shore, 1980; D. W. Sue, 1977a, 1977b; Velasquez, 1984). I recently used the Fundamental Interpersonal Relationship Orientation-Behavior test (FIRO-B) (Poorman & Seelau, 2001) to help to better understand the interpersonal characteristics of lesbians who abuse and those who are abused. It is a self-report mechanism in which clients describe their usual ways of being in relationships.

Psychoanalytic feminist helpers would certainly consider feminist modifications of projective methods like the Rorschach and the Thematic Apperception Test to be useful and of no contradiction. Many feminist helpers, however, would question the very basis of psychoanalytic feminism and certainly the theory underlying testing that utilizes psychoanalytic theory as its basis. At this point, objective behavioral assessment (Blechman, 1980), neuropsychological testing, and other tests under certain circumstances (Rosewater, 1982, 1985; Walker, 1985) would be considered useful by many feminist helpers. The use of some tests, such as intelligence and vocational tests, continues to be debated because of the norms upon which they are standardized and the historic and frequent misuse of the tests. Helpers who subscribe to contemporary feminist theories of helping utilize assessment tools only with a clear understanding of the risks and benefits of each test. In general, assessments from a feminist helping perspective probably involve more collaborative examination of functional limitations and strengths of clients.

Techniques and Process

The techniques and process of any helping theory are influenced by underlying assumptions and values; assumptions and values that sometimes themselves have included oppressive assumptions. Feminist helping theories have made a point of not only examining the underlying values and assumptions of other helping theories, but also of clearly formulating a set of ethical guidelines for the practice of feminist helping (Lerman & Porter, 1990). When first formulated, some of the guidelines for feminist helping went well beyond standards set by professional helping organizations in several dimensions of helping practice. Today, many of these same ideas have become incorporated into the ethical standards held by most other helping professionals. Because of the importance these ethical values hold in explaining the process of feminist helping and also because of their significant differences, especially related to power, egalitarian relationships, and social action, the ethical values of feminist helping are addressed in this section.

Feminist helpers are expected to uncover and respect cultural and experiential differences; to evaluate ongoing interactions with clients for any evidence of helper biases or discriminatory attitudes and practice; and to accept responsibility for taking appropriate action to confront and change any interfering or oppressing biases. Feminist helpers incorporate an understanding of cultural diversities and oppression into the helping process by increasing accessibility to and for a wide range of clients through flexible delivery of services; assisting clients in accessing other services; continuously working to raise their own awareness of the meaning and impact of their own ethnic and cultural background, gender, class, and sexual orientation; and actively attempting to become knowledgeable about alternatives from sources other than their clients. These standards are now also expected of virtually all helping professionals (e.g., APA Office of Ethnic Minority Affairs, 1993).

Feminist helpers are also expected to acknowledge the inherent power difference between client and helper and to model the effective use of personal power. In using the power differential to the benefit of the client, feminist helpers do not take control of the power that rightfully belongs to the client. Rather, feminist helpers fashion egalitarian relationships, openly discuss power, and use their personal power to effect social change. Feminist helpers are also ethically bound to disclose information to clients that facilitates the helping process and are responsible for using self-disclosure with purpose and discretion in the interests of clients. Feminist helpers negotiate and renegotiate formal and informal contracts with clients in an ongoing, mutual process and educate clients regarding their rights as consumers of helping services, including procedures for resolving differences and filing grievances.

Further, feminist helpers are expected to recognize the complexity and conflicting priorities inherent in multiple or overlapping relationships, also called *dual-role relationships* (American Psychological Association, 1992). Feminist helpers accept responsibility for monitoring such relationships to prevent potential abuse of or harm to clients. Since feminist helpers are expected to be actively involved in their communities, they are also expected to be especially sensitive about confidentiality. Recognizing that client concerns and general well-being are primary, feminist helpers self-monitor both public and private statements and comments.

Many helping professionals have now struggled with how and where to draw limits around dual-role relationships that involve sexual intimacies with clients, although when feminist helping practice ethics were first introduced in 1990, their clear prohibition against engaging "in sexual intimacies or any overtly or covertly sexualized behavior with a client or former client" was a radical statement. The guideline for feminist helpers remains more definitive than the standards set in many professional helping guidelines. This value reflects an understanding of the power dynamics of a helping relationship. Understanding the power dynamics of a helping relationship means understanding that sexual activities between someone in a dominant position and someone in a subordinate position always risk exploitation and even the concept of consenting sexual activity between former clients and helpers is suspect.

As is true of other helping professionals, feminist helpers are expected to work only with those issues and clients within their realm of competencies; to recognizes personal and professional needs and limitations; and to utilize ongoing self-evaluation, peer support, consultation, supervision, continuing education, and/or personal helping to evaluate, maintain, and improve the helper's work with clients' competencies and emotional well-being. Feminist helpers are expected to continually evaluate their training, theoretical background, and current research to include developments in feminist knowledge, to integrate feminism into psychological theory, and to receive ongoing training. Feminist helpers are also expected to engage in self-care activities in an ongoing manner, acknowledging their own vulnerabilities and seeking care outside of the helping relationship. In this way, the feminist helper also models the ability and willingness to self-nurture in appropriate and self-empowering ways.

Finally, feminist helpers are expected to engage in social change activities, actively questioning other therapeutic practices in their community that appear abusive to clients or helpers and, when possible, intervening as early as appropriate or feasible and assisting clients in intervening when it is facilitative to their growth. Feminist helpers are expected to seek multiple avenues for effecting change, including public education and advocacy within professional organizations, lobbying for legislative action, and other appropriate activities.

In summary, in the process of feminist helping, helpers are expected to work to establish and maintain egalitarian intimacy with diverse clients, to encourage dialogue and exploration of power differences in the helping relationship, and to practice competent feminist helping. However, in their recognition that social and cultural influences are at the root of client problems, sociocultural theories of helping recognize that help goes beyond a helper's office walls or even individual helping relationships. Helpers who subscribe to sociocultural helping theories also use personal power to empower individual clients by effecting social change.

Addressing Power in the Helping Process.   Power inequities that exist in women's lives must not be reenacted in the helping relationship. The model of a client-helper relationship that is equally respectful of each person embodies this basic principle of feminist helping and has been the source of much reflective struggle in the development of feminist helping ethics and practice. Feminists have progressed from denying power differences inherent in the helping relationship (Carter & Rawlings, 1977; J. B. Miller, 1976) to acknowledging that we must deal with power responsibly (Gilbert, in Brodsky & Hare-Mustin, 1980; Lerman, 1986; Lerman & Porter, 1990; Smith & Siegal, 1985; Sturdivant, 1980).

To view the therapist client relationship as **egalitarian** has involved an ethical imperative to empower the client and acknowledge the power of the therapist (Brodsky & Hare-Mustin, 1980; Lerman & Porter, 1990; Rosewater & Walker, 1985). This is done using various strategies.

- Encouraging the client to shop around for a therapist
- Encouraging the client to experience greater self-confidence and to be more self-directed and autonomous
- Encouraging self-nurturance
- Modeling by the therapist
- Facilitating expression of anger

- Encouraging "good" conflict
- Reclaiming power by renaming certain aspects of behavior as attempts to achieve goals of control and influence under given social constraints
- Redefining power and reducing guilt
- Encouraging clients to define their own reality
- Identifying internal and external costs and benefits of clients' past and present thoughts and actions
- Emphasizing responsibility for clients' own behavior

Addressing the "Personal Is Political" in the Helping Process. In recognition and emphasis of the first principle of feminist helping, that the personal is political, feminist helpers make use of various strategies. During the first stage of what Smith and Siegal (1985) identify as a three-stage process of feminist helping, helper and client work to identify those sociopolitical or interpersonal forces that may impact women and men differently. Clients differentiate between what they have been taught to accept as socially appropriate and what might actually be appropriate, if they were to self-define. Helpers encourage clients to evaluate the influence on their personal experience of social roles and norms and to see the relationship between sociological and psychological factors. As the helper validates the client's experience of rage at being shaped for second-class citizenship, the client learns she is not crazy. By a continual interweaving of childhood memories and current circumstances, helping facilitates the validation of past behavior and feelings and enables the woman to distinguish between behavior that was essential to her state as powerless and behavior that is appropriate to a more powerful position.

The second stage of helping (Smith & Siegal, 1985) is focused on those aspects of female development that become distorted through over- or underemphasis: power, dependency, and responsibility. Redefining earlier behavior as the best possible solution within the perceived environment, the client's guilt is reduced and perceptions of self begin to shift from victim to survivor. Understanding the purposes of both past and present behavior, clients recognize choices they had as children and different choices they may now have. In addition to encouraging clients to define their own behavior rather than to accept social definition, the helping relationship can serve as a model. By sharing personal experiences of oppression, struggles to overcome internalized fears, doubts, and anger, and growth toward present consciousness, the client begins to recognize a melting distinction between "sick" client and "healthy" helper. Rather than labeling the client's behavior, helpers engage in a dialogue that encourages the client to search collaboratively for the underlying purposes of her actions and choices.

During the third and final stage of feminist helping (Smith & Siegal, 1985), clients begin to synthesize what they have learned and practice new behavior. While the social and cultural etiology of the individual's personal difficulties are emphasized, helpers also emphasize personal responsibility for choice and change.

In feminist helping, change not only takes place through specific behavioral and cognitive-behavioral strategies and insight, but through the affective experience of the relationship between client and helper (Lerman & Porter, 1990; Rosewater & Walker, 1985; Sturdivant, 1980). The helping relationship provides the client with the opportunity to undo and rework past effects of oppression and abuse. The helper becomes, in Sturdivant's (1980) terms, an agent of resocialization. The client comes to attach herself to a significant other or others (as in group helping) and begins to model new behaviors. The equalizing relationship with the helper allows the client to reexperience oppression, but in a new context and with the potential for a more favorable resolution. Altering the experiential context, even by a factor of one, changes its meaning for the client and allows for the possibility that previous perceptions of power and dominance/subordination may be reexamined and restructured. Helping, then, provides an encouraging, compassionate, mutual empathy (Jordan, 1990; Jordan, Kaplan, & Surrey, 1985, 1990) and a controlled environment in which to examine, challenge, and restructure one's construct about one's own power and position, and the pursuant behaviors.

In addition to strategies that may be borrowed from more traditional therapies, feminist therapists have devised unique cognitive strategies (sex-role analysis and labeling, differential power analysis) and incorporated physical strategies (body work), spiritual strategies, emotional strategies (healing the child inside), and relationship strategies (using informational and referent power, rather than expert, coercive, or legitimate power) (Brody, 1984; Burman, 1990; Carter & Rawlings, 1977; Cox, 1981; Greenspan, 1983; Laidlaw & Malmo, 1990; Robbins & Siegal, 1985; Smith & Siegal, 1985; Sturdivant, 1980).

All of these strategies derive from the same basic principles described earlier. A feminist helper seeks to establish a relationship equal in power. While this does not deny the unequal power inherent in the helping relationship, it demands that the helper be cognizant of this power, recognize and name it, and move toward equalizing it.

RESEARCH

Since very little emphasis in feminist helping is on symptom reduction, it is not surprising that designing outcome research is a challenge for feminist helping models or that little controlled outcome research has been conducted on feminist helping. Further, feminist helping approaches have not typically been included in various meta-analyses on the effectiveness of helping. Although not entirely consistent (e.g., Orlinsky & Howard, 1980), some research has shown that female helping professionals, particularly those approaching helping from an androgynous or feminist perspective, and particularly when paired with female clients, appear to facilitate effective change (Beutler & Crago, 1991). Enhanced empathy and increased satisfaction appear to account for some of these results in same-gender dyads. Mary Ballou (1990) also reports that participants in consciousness-raising groups report significant changes in social/political awareness, vocational interests, attitudes, self-perceptions, sex-roles, and ego strength. Recent work by Judith Worell (2001) and Heather Frank (2002) calls for more careful and systematic attention to researching the effectiveness of feminist helping beyond symptom reduction.

CRITIQUING

Many problems may be understood in terms of power dynamics and cultural exigencies, and of socialization for dominant/subordinate roles. Many of women's problems may be best understood in these terms. For example, the most frequent reason that women give for seeking help is depression (McGrath, Keita, Strickland, & Russo, 1990). Depression can be easily understood in terms of helplessness, which is thought to be learned through a process in which one is exposed to an aversive environment over which she or he has no control (Seligman, 1975). In learning to dissociate effortful behavior from consequence, one learns helplessness and thereby clinical depression. Not only has this model of **learned helplessness** been used to describe laboratory aversive environments (Seligman, 1979), but also abusive situations (Walker, 1985, 1989, 1990) and women's depression (Walker, 1990).

In addition to understanding a common concern like depression, feminist theories of helping hold the potential to understand, interpret, and treat other behaviors that are the result of an unequal distribution of power. These include any symptom that reflects male or female sex-role stereotyping (e.g., men's difficulties in intimacy, bonding, or empathy or women's difficulties in self-nurturance, self-definition, dependence, and assertiveness).

Feminist theories of helping are specifically well-suited to addressing the effects (and perhaps the causes of) physical, sexual, and emotional abuses. In addition to the individual damage to victims of abuse, feminist helping theories suggest that abuse results from and serves to maintain the oppressive structure of dominance and subordination (Walker, 1993; Women Helping Women, 1990). Many programs now advocate addressing the needs of victims of battering, incest, rape, and sexual abuse from a feminist perspective (e.g., Goodman & Fallon, 1995; NiCarthy, Merriam, & Coffman, 1984; Poorman, 1993) and treating those who abuse from a feminist perspective (e.g., Edleson & Tolman, 1992; Poorman & Seelau, 2001). More broadly, feminist theories of helping hold the potential for helpful interpretation, assessment, and intervention into problems associated with any dominant-subordinate ascription (Ivey, Ivey, & Simek-Morgan, 1997). This includes racial, sexual, class, age, and sexual orientation oppression and their consequences to specific individuals. In fact, feminist helping theory has recently been challenged to expand its boundaries to accomplish just that.

Critics of feminist helping theories charge that not all problems can be conceptualized in terms of cultural exigencies, power or status dynamics, or sex-role socialization. Further, the criticism is well deserved that feminist helping theory has paid more attention to majority consumers (straight, white women) in developing theories of women's development, problems, and helping. Although this is slowly being remedied, until it is, feminist helping theory will be limited in its scope.

Another criticism of feminist helping is its implementation. Helpers are a part of a culture that may reflect the problems the client seeks to ameliorate. Helpers are a part of helping traditions that have oppressed women, people of color, differently abled people, aging people, gays and lesbians, and people of lower and working classes.

Further, helpers are necessarily in a dominant position. Many helpers may have sought helping as a profession precisely because it affords them status and power. To the extent that this is true for any individual helper, she or he may be in the difficult position of both trying to share power and trying to garner it.

Feminist helping is also limited by its relative newness and to some extent its lack of differentiation from other helping theories. Feminist helping theories have been criticized for being poorly differentiated, not really having a clear theory of helping. To the extent that there are at present numerous theories of feminist helping, this is true. While hardly atheoretical, the diffuseness and difficulties in differentiating feminist helping theories warrant ongoing efforts in developing and refining the theories.

Some traditional helping theories have held that a firm boundary exists between politics and helping and criticize feminist helpers whose basic premise is that the personal is political. Critics have raised concerns that feminist helpers engage in proselytizing (persuading another to convert to another philosophy of life, religion, party, and so forth). This is not a criticism unique to feminist helpers. Ellis's REBT helping theory and Haley's strategic family systems helping theory both rely on persuasion, as does one group of feminist helpers who advocate feminism as helping.

Despite the limitations, no other theory of helping addresses as extensive an explanation of cultural influences, power dynamics, and gender differences and the effects these have on both the dominant and the subordinate individually or in relationship to one another. Feminist helping theory has made a significant contribution to understanding human interactions with the recognition and exploration of power as a core dimension in relationships. Further, feminist helping, like no other theory of helping, expands client perspectives on the gendered social context in which they live.

14 Sociocultural Theories of Helping: Multicultural Theories

CONTEXT

Multicultural theories of helping are integrative sociocultural theories that emphasize both differences and similarities between people. Integrative theories blend together two or more theories or various viewpoints rather than being guided by a single theory. Integrative theories do not simply blend by selecting techniques isolated from their assumptions. Instead, integrative theories require an understanding of the foundation of many theories as they strive to blend theories based on compatibility and the empirical support for theories. As with other sociocultural theories of helping like feminist theories, multicultural theories of helping share an integrated focus on the social and cultural influences that shape and maintain human behavior and problems that humans encounter. Sociocultural theories are social psychological in that they examine social and cultural influences like ethnicity, culture, race, class, gender, orientation, ability, and religion on individual behavior, identity, and problems. Multicultural theories of helping are theories of helping that recognize the specific importance of differences and similarities in ethnic and cultural backgrounds in the ways that people develop and change.

Six influential propositions provide some of the background for understanding the multicultural theories of helping (Sue, Ivey, & Pedersen, 1996). The first proposition recognizes that an overemphasis on either differences or similarities predicts failure in understanding and helping. Second, multicultural theories propose that both helper and client form identities within multiple levels of experience and in multiple contexts. Third, cultural identity development is thought to be a major determinant of both the helper and client attitude toward self, others in the same group, others in a different minority group, and others in the dominant group. Fourth, multicultural theories posit that helping is enhanced when helpers set goals and use techniques and strategies that are consistent with the experiences and cultural values of the client.

Fifth, multicultural theories of helping, like feminist theories of helping, recognize the other three forces in helping theory (nature, nurture, and choice) and recommend going beyond an understanding of those forces to examine and change the social and cultural contexts that create problems. Further, multicultural theories of helping propose that helping processes must go beyond individual change to facilitate social and systemic interventions and changes that prevent problems.

Finally, liberation of consciousness about oppression constitutes a basic goal of multicultural helping. Multicultural theories of helping assist clients in developing and expanding their awareness of social, economic, and political oppression and its role in their identity and problems, and expanding awareness of themselves as relational beings and of families and organizations as embedded in other systems of influence. In short, like feminist theories, multicultural theories have a contextual orientation to the study of growth and development of human beings. While feminist theories of helping have explored contexts in which women and men grow, change, and develop, multicultural theories have emphasized the growth, change, and identity development of **people of color** and ethnic minorities and the political, social, economic, and interpersonal contexts in which humans grow, change, and develop. Multicultural theories of helping specifically focus on the development of a positive identity and a sense of awareness of oppression in the face of such oppression as mechanisms for changing both individuals and society.*

*The term *multicultural* when used in the context of theories of helping has often included all people of color and excluded other minority cultures like gays and lesbians and deaf and hearing impaired people. Gays, lesbians, and deaf people also have rich, complex cultures with distinct histories, music, literature, and language or language usage, as well as unique facets of oppression that warrant exploration. I use the term *multicultural* to be inclusive of gays, lesbians, and deaf people and *multiethnic* when I refer to people of color and ethnic minorities. In the same way that biracial people may share in the cultures and oppression of two (or more) racial or ethnic groups, bisexual people may share in the cultures and oppression of gays and lesbians.

Oppression

Being aware of, understanding, and taking action against oppression is at the heart of multicultural theories of helping. **Oppression** can take many forms, begins with a belief in the superiority of a particular difference, and results in attitudes, practices, and policies that use status, position, power, privilege, and institutions to impose restrictions or limitations on someone of difference. These beliefs, results, and restrictions reinforce the subordinate position. The following are examples of different types of oppression and the terms used to refer to each type.

> **Ethnocentrism** Belief that Western European cultural background is superior; assumption that European background is normative; use of one's position of power or position of privilege as someone of European cultural background to impose restrictions on, invalidate, or hold someone of another culture down.
>
> **Racism** Belief that white skin or Caucasian race is superior; assumption that white skin is normative; using one's power or privilege as someone with white skin to impose restrictions on, invalidate, or hold down someone of color.
>
> **Sexism** Belief that male gender is superior; assumption of male as normative; using one's power or privilege as a man to impose restrictions on, invalidate, or hold women down.
>
> **Ableism** Belief that full use of all original physical and biological functions is superior; assumption that a full range of abilities is the norm; using one's power or privilege as someone with a full range of abilities to impose restrictions on, invalidate, or hold down someone with a different ability or disability.
>
> **Heterosexism** Belief that a heterosexual orientation is superior; assumption that heterosexual is normative; using one's power or privilege as a heterosexual person to impose restrictions on, invalidate, or hold down someone whose orientation is gay, lesbian, or bisexual.*

---

*Oppression against transgendered and intersexed people is considered a complex variation of sexism and also represents confusion of orientation and gender identity that results from homophobia. Additional discussion can be found in Jones and M. J. Hill (2002) and Lombardi, Wilchins, Priesing, and Malouf (2001).

Oppression can be overt or covert, subtle or blatant, and has been built into governmental, religious, educational, and helping institutions. When the power of institutions (e.g., government, education) is used to reinforce the idea that one way of being is superior to another, to assume one demographic characteristic as normative, and to impose restrictions on, limit, or subordinate people of difference, we say that oppression has been institutionalized (Gelles & Levine, 1995). Many examples of **institutionalized oppression** exist in the United States. For example, African Americans were denied voting rights until the 1960s because of institutionalized racism. Women still do not have a constitutional protection of equal rights because of institutionalized sexism.

Cultural oppression occurs when language, values, symbols, history, and meanings are used to socialize humans to believe in the superiority of a particular difference and to maintain and reinforce the oppression. A good example of cultural oppression is recent discussion about whether to make English the official language of the United States, which would, of course, relegate the large percentage of people whose first language is Spanish to "unofficial" in the eyes of legal and educational institutions.

In addition to external forces, oppression can be internalized when those who are oppressed incorporate or take on the belief that their own specific difference is inferior, poses restrictions or limitations, or should keep them subordinated (Allport, 1958). Examples of **internalized oppression** include African Americans who believe that those of their own race are intellectually inferior and probably will not get into college or do well once there. A gay man who believes that hiding his identity or being beaten up by police is just the way it has to be because he is deviant, or a woman who takes for granted that she cannot walk alone at night are also examples of internalized oppression.

Oppression includes not seeing or acknowledging differences, as well as only seeing differences and feeling hatred, fear, disgust, pity, or tolerance (Riddle & Sang, 1978). Countering oppression occurs not simply as the result of believing in the equality of human differences, but by seeing, appreciating, nurturing, and even celebrating differences. Paolo Freire (1970, 1993) noted that oppression can be countered by *conscientização* which "refers to learning to perceive social, political, and economic contradictions, and to take action against the oppressive elements of reality."

Socialization

Socialization is the educational process that begins immediately with birth and includes those processes by which societies gradually teach their members what is expected of them and others. Socialization includes messages about one's social position in relation to others (**status**), patterns of behavior associated with a particular status (**role**), standards for behavior (**norms**), generalizations that are treated like truth (**stereotypes**), beliefs, and values. Families, peers, schools, organized religions, and mass media deliver the messages and are sometimes referred to as "agents of socialization." Socialization, like other learning processes, can be modified, although learning theory alone is insufficient to realize change. Creating social changes as a less tangible process requires not only awareness and a strong commitment, but also knowledge of how social changes occur. Nonetheless, multicultural approaches to helping advocate both individual and social change.

In addition to teaching humans about the dominant culture through socialization, different cultures are often assimilated or absorbed, thereby creating another potentially oppressive circumstance. When members of a different culture adopt the majority culture as their own and replace ancestral patterns in order to participate in the economic, political, educational, and community groups of that culture, we say they have experienced cultural assimilation. **Cultural assimilation** certainly involves inclusion, but it often results in the dilution or obliteration of the original cultural differences and feeds the idea that the dominant culture is superior. Take for example the family who immigrates to the United States. Parents often encourage their children to learn to speak the new language, dress as Americans do, and eat foods common to the American diet. The family may watch American television as a source of entertainment and cultural information. Although the family is likely to "fit in" better with their new culture, they may lose aspects of their original culture. As important aspects of that culture are lost and forgotten, they become relegated to the "old" culture, and their value may be minimized.

Multicultural theories of helping may not focus directly on understanding the dynamics of oppression as do feminist theories of helping, although they have emphasized consciousness-raising and dialogue about oppression as one means of countering its effects.

Neither do multicultural theories of helping directly investigate the processes of socialization or acculturation and assimilation. They do assume, however, that understanding these processes may provide a means of appreciating what is involved in the process of developing a conscious awareness of oppression and a positive identity.

A VIEW OF HUMAN NATURE AND THE DEVELOPMENT OF PROBLEMS

Sociocultural theories of helping look at humans as the product of social and cultural influences. People are assumed to have a contextual orientation, and it is these contexts that determine the development of human identity, growth, and development. Ethnic, racial, class, gender, orientation, ability, and religious traditions constitute elements of the social and cultural contexts in which growth and development occur for both helper and client. Differences in these elements of context have not been historically valued or appreciated, and people of color, lower socioeconomic classes, and/or different abilities, gays and lesbians, women, and those who are not Christian have been oppressed in the United States. Moreover, American helping traditions have also been influenced by these contexts, experiences, and oppression. Both helpers and clients have formed identities from multiple experiences and in multiple contexts.

The development of a sense of identity is considered by multicultural theories of helping to be a major determinant of both the helper's and the client's attitudes toward self, others, and each other. People are not assumed to enter the world with an identity, but to develop identity through their individual experiences with others in their intimate relationships, family relationships, and community and organizational relationships. Developing a positive identity in the face of centuries of oppression and cultural assimilation is no small task.

There are a number of minority identity development models that share considerable similarity and also evidence notable differences. William Cross's (1971) article "The Negro-to-Black Conversion Experience: Towards a Psychology of Black Liberation" is credited with beginning American theories about how someone subjected to oppressive circumstances can move toward the development of positive identity. In his article, Cross outlines the movement from a lack of awareness of one's difference to a full, rich awareness of and pride in one's self, evidenced by movement from seeing the self as "nigger" to seeing the self as "Black American." Charles Thomas (1971) continued this train of thought by examining black identity development. Derald Wing Sue and Stanley Sue (1972a) launched a similar approach to examining the identity development of Asian Americans. In their model, Sue and Sue outline stages of the development of a positive identity that move from a lack of awareness or denial of oppression to an encounter with oppressive situations or circumstances, to anger and immersion in cultural/ethnic uniqueness, and finally to a full awareness of self as multicultural. Szapocznik, Santisteban, Kurtines, Hervis, and Spencer (1982) and Aureliano Ruiz (1990) later adapted similar models to refer to the development of a positive identity among Latinos and Chicanos. Directly crediting both Cross and Sue and Sue with the framework they used to trace the steps from a lack of awareness of the differential treatment of women to an active, robust feminist commitment to change, Nancy Downing and Kristin Roush (1985) developed a model of positive feminist identity.

Vivienne Cass (1979) developed the first identity development model for gays and lesbians, a social-cognition model that examined the decision-making processes involved in coming to terms with a gay or lesbian identity. With more recognition of the oppressive circumstances of gays and lesbians, Eli Coleman's (1988) model of positive identity development for gays and lesbians more closely resembles Cross's original model in outlining movement from an identity based on definition by an oppressive other to self-definition and full cultural awareness.

Although all have been referred to as minority groups, the experiences of Black Americans, Asian Americans, Latino/Chicano Americans, Native Americans, female Americans, and gay and lesbian Americans are certainly not the same. Even within each group there is such diversity of experience that using the collective terms dilutes the richness and complexity of experience. For example, it is not accurate to refer to "Asian American" as though this included all of the many and complex experiences of all people whose backgrounds include an ethnic heritage influenced by the many different cultures found on a huge continent like Asia. Asian American includes those who come from Chinese, Japanese, Taiwanese, Korean, Pakistani, Hmong, and Thai backgrounds. Sometimes Pacific Islanders, like Hawaiians, Polynesians, and Maoris, are also included in this grouping, although the Pacific Rim is clearly not Asia nor are the cultures similar.

Black American includes those whose ancestors were brought to the United States from Africa as slaves and those who immigrated to the United States by choice. The countries and tribes that make up Africa are not only dissimilar, but often at vehement and lethal odds with one another. Assuming a connection between all Black Americans with an African heritage ignores the diversity of their pasts. Black Americans also include those whose ancestors immigrated from Carribean countries like Trinidad, Tobago, and Jamaica.

Those who made up the First Nation, now the geographical area called North and South America, were from many different tribes, but are now commonly referred to as Native Americans or American Indians. It should not be assumed that all Native Americans have the same language or cultural traditions.

No one group is really described by the terms Hispanic, Latino, or Chicano. People whose ancestors came from Spain are called Hispanic, and cultures indigenous to Central or South America or Mexico like the Aztecs and Mayans, who were later assimilated into Spanish culture, are also referred to as Hispanic. Cubans and Puerto Ricans are often tossed into this collective reference. Many of Spanish ancestry or assimilated indigenous groups prefer to refer to themselves as Latino, while others prefer Chicano (if they identify Mexico as their original culture), and some prefer the more radical *La Raza* ("The Race"). White or Anglo often refers collectively to those from both Eastern and Western European backgrounds, although obviously there are many differences between Western European cultures, such as England, Ireland, Spain, France, Belgium, and Germany, and Eastern European countries, such as Poland, Russia, Ukraine, and the Balkans.

Lesbians and gay men each share a common collective history and various elements of a common collective culture. In addition, gays and lesbians of color may share the histories and cultures of their ethnic backgrounds. To use "gay" as though the term includes all gay and lesbian people dilutes critical differences between lesbian and gay histories and cultures as well as other parts of their backgrounds and identities. Further, although frequently included in gay and lesbian issues or programs, bisexuals and transgendered people have different collective histories than gays and lesbians. Similarly, referring to deaf people as though this were one group fails to recognize ASL as a language quite different from BSL (British Sign Language) or JSL (Japanese Sign Language) or the richness and complexity of deaf cultures in America and elsewhere.

It does not show adequate complexity to refer to any minority group as a "minority" as though that covered all of the bases and captured the experience of any much less all oppressed groups. Minority is not even demographically accurate in all cases; some groups, like women, constitute a majority of the population. Taken together, women, people of color, gays, lesbians, and disabled people would certainly constitute the majority. When the term **minority** is being used, it refers to those who are underprivileged, subordinated, or regarded as of "minor" standing in a system of ethnic or cultural stratification. Minority, then, has come to refer to any group of people who have been oppressed or subordinated. People of color collectively refers to those people who face oppression and discrimination because of stereotypes associated with the color of their skin.

Although the people who constitute minorities are certainly not the same, the models that describe identity development are similar since many have been adapted from the same frameworks. To help compare and contrast each of these models, I have created a composite (Figure 14.1, on pages 250–251) to illustrate the stages that people who are members of oppressed groups are thought to go through in the development of a positive identity.

Both clients and helpers whose backgrounds include being from an oppressed group are thought to go through stages toward a positive sense of identity (Sue & Sue, 1990). Further, when they encounter one another in a helping relationship, each reacts to the other based not only on the stage they are in themselves, but also on the stage of development that the other is in or perceived to be in. So, for example, a helper who has just entered the encounter stage and is acutely aware of the dissonance of her or his previous denial of difference and experiences that refute this will be intensely uncomfortable with the denial of difference that the client who is in the preconscious stage will espouse. This helper may be a poor match for the client at that time. Or consider the angry client who is fully immersed in the exploration of her or his own oppression and cultural differences. This client will not react favorably to a helper who is not yet aware of the impact of differences.

In addition to the complexity of recognizing that helper and client may both come from oppressed backgrounds and may be at different stages in their development of a sense of positive identity, often clients and helpers come from different backgrounds. It is not uncommon for helpers to come from a majority or dominant background and clients to come from a minority or subordinate status. In fact, much of traditional helping theories were based on the assumption that this was the only configuration. More recently, ethical guidelines for professional helping organizations (e.g., **APA, ACA, NASW**) have clarified that it is imperative to view clients in more pluralistic terms.

Pluralism is the philosophical belief that reality is composed of multiple ultimate beings, principles, or substances; hence, there are multiple realities and multiple truths. Recognition of multiple realities or of the dynamics of oppression do not by themselves make a helper or client pluralistic. So coming from a dominant group background and simply saying you subscribe to a pluralistic worldview does not make it so. Helpers are encouraged to familiarize themselves with the guidelines for those who provide helping services to individuals from ethnically, linguistically, and culturally diverse populations like those from the Office of Minority Affairs of the American Psychological Association (APA, 1993).

In addition to minority identity development models, multicultural theories of helping also propose at least one model for development of a pluralistic identity and worldview among people who come from the dominant or majority culture and who are committed to developing a pluralistic worldview. Joseph Ponterotto (1988) adapted models of minority identity development to demonstrate the stages in developing a positive pluralistic identity for helpers and clients who come from dominant groups or majority culture backgrounds. Micael Kemp (1993) adapted Ponterotto's model, and I was fortunate to have had the opportunity to train with her. Based on this training, I have included descriptions of the stages that helpers and clients go through in coming to terms with the privilege of their dominant status as European American, heterosexual, male, Christian, conventionally able-bodied, and naturalized citizens of North America (Poorman, 1996).

FIGURE 14.1 Composite Identity Development Model

Stages	View of Self	View of Others (Same Oppressed Group)
Preconsciousness prefers majority standards; denies differences; denies oppression or discrimination	• self-deprecating • more different from majority is worse (darker, more different eyes, more "butch," "more nellie," etc.) • denial of differences	• negative majority stereo-types of others (blacks are lazy, women are bitches, lesbians are man-hating, etc.) • personal identity *not* the problem • incompetent
Encounter/Exposure/ Dissonance series of experiences that shake denial or pose dissonance; that is, encounters with oppression, trauma, hate crime, and so on	• wrestling with differences in identity • sees positive aspects of one's own culture • knowledge of own ethnicity, culture, gender, orientation, and so on	• growing sense of cama-raderie with others of similar ethnicity, culture, gender, orientation, and so on
Immersion increasing awareness of personal and collective differences immersion in values of one's own target group	• I am a . . . [oppressed group] • I don't want to feel ashamed of who/what I am • holding own cultural values in high esteem • guilt/shame at participa-tion in oppression • anger at oppressors	• bond with • empathy • complete endorsement of minority view and cul-ture; seen as ideal • reluctance to seek help even from oppressed others—the process of helping is viewed as an instrument of oppression
Contemplative Introspection Contemplative: who am I as an oppressed person?	• can I be a . . . [oppressed group] and still be different from that group? • recognition of individual differences • recognition of the oppres-siveness of oppressed group norms	• some discomfort with group expectations • need for autonomy • disagreement with rigidity
Integrative Awareness	• inner security • bicultural being • multicultural being	• appreciation of others who can understand or appreciate my worldview rather than only those sharing my specific background

Source: Composite adapted by Poorman, 1995; from Coleman, 1985; Cross, 1971; Downing & Roush, 1985; Ponterotto, 1988; Ruiz, 1990; Sue & Sue, 1972.

View of Others (Different Oppressed Group)	View of Majority Group
• seen in very unfavorable light • adopts majority stereotypes of others	• very positive • white, straight, males are very positive and superior • prefers majority helper/mentor
• intensely dislikes those who are in preconscious stage	• viewed with suspicion
• bond with • conflict: empathy for oppressed others and strong identification with own group as ideal • oppressed others who ally with majority are "sellouts," "oreos," "Toms"	• viewed with distrust, anger • active rejection of white, male, straight as enemies • only those in own group are trusted • hard to establish alliance with person of dominance • rejection of dominant culture
• beginning to see connecting points between oppressions • beginning appreciation of building alliances with others from different oppressed groups	• can view majority persons as allies/resources in the struggle to end oppression
• appreciation of differences that other oppressed peoples bring to my worldview	• appreciation of value in majority differences • risks asking: can you understand my worldview?

These stages can be described as follows.

Stage 1: Pre-exposure

- has not thought about helping as a cultural phenomena
- has minimal awareness of self as racial/ethnic, gendered, sexually oriented, or able being
- says "people are just people"; "differences are unimportant"
- seeks to treat all people the same
- evidences an underlying belief that values and norms are universal; "everyone wants . . ."
- has limited knowledge of "target" groups
- adheres to social stereotypes about "target" groups
- believes that she or he is not racist, sexist, homophobic, ableist, and so on
- believes that target group inferiority is what justifies discriminatory (or differences in) treatment
- believes that target group members are in some ways deviant or inferior
- uncomfortable with differences

Stage 2: Exposure

- begins to learn about cultural differences and realizes that previous education has been incomplete
- encounters information/experiences at odds with her or his denial of differences
- begins to see self and the privilege in her or his status
- begins to deal with inconsistencies in how people are treated
- may become confused and put off by the incongruities and seek refuge in denial again
- feels guilt, shame, anger, and depression at the full impact of systematic and institutionalized oppression
- believes that one person is powerless to make changes

Stage 3: Zealotry or Defensiveness

- begins to realize that racism, sexism, homophobia, ableism, and so on, are everywhere
- eyes are suddenly open; oppression is suddenly revealed
- feels guilty for having been a part of the oppression either through lack of awareness or actively discriminatory behavior
- actively advocates multiculturalism

- sometimes offends colleagues in their zeal without knowing it
- "white liberal syndrome":
  - wants to protect minorities from abuse or oppression
  - wishes to identify with minority groups to escape her or his own dominant group status
- separates self from oppressor—sometimes out of self-hatred at seeing oppressor within and sometimes to feel accepted by minorities
- may retreat into quiet defensiveness
- takes criticisms about the system, oppression, dominants, or majority culture personally
- feels unappreciated and rejected by target groups who do not recognize her or him as "other than oppressor"
- feels angry

Stage 4: Integration
- realizes that the standards used to judge one's identity cannot come from one group or the other; must be more autonomously and pluralistically defined
- realizes that the feelings of guilt or anger that motivated identification with either one group or the other are dysfunctional; although they may motivate for action, it is not guilt or anger that get things done
- begins an independent search for goals and direction
- ceases denial of majority group status; embraces both privilege and commitment to change
- reduces defensiveness and guilt associated with majority status
- keener awareness of, respect for, and appreciation of cultural differences
- awareness of self as cultural being and the impact of own culture on chosen discipline
- acceptance that one cannot know all dimensions of multiculturalism at once and plans are made for a lifetime of learning

From a multicultural standpoint, the root of problems people experience are social and cultural phenomena like oppression, discrimination, and a subordinate status, and countermeasures include developing a positive multicultural identity. Whether one is from a dominant or subordinate background, this process involves a series of changes motivated by increasing awareness of oppression, discrimination, and status as well as increasing awareness of one's own heritage and culture. Learning to take pride in, value, even celebrate one's self and others as multicultural beings is the essence of the helping process for multicultural helpers.

THE HELPING PROCESS

Goals

The goals of the helping process, from a multicultural helping perspective, are to facilitate client awareness of the impact of oppression, subordination, discrimination, and assimilation. The multicultural helper assists clients in developing or continuing a critical awareness of their social and cultural context and its impact on current behavior, personality, and problems. An implicit goal is to help people identify and stop cooperating in their own oppression. Finally, the multicultural helper facilitates recognition and actualization of strengths and sources of pride in a multicultural identity. She or he assists clients in examining, challenging, and changing dominant and subordinate roles in a variety of contexts, including the helping relationship. Consciousness-raising, positive identity development, and social action against oppression are considered countermeasures to problems created by a social and cultural context that subordinates many people.

The Helper's Role

The role of the multicultural helper is most like that of a collaborative mentor. The emphasis on consciousness-raising in multicultural theories of helping demands that the helper not only be knowledgeable about and sensitive to differences and similarities, but also must be able to engage clients in a dialogue that involves naming and reflecting on their oppression. To do so, helpers must critically examine their own identity-in-context and be open to views of experiences from the client's perspective.

Assessment

Little has been written about effective assessment through testing with people of color (PSYCHINFO, 2002). In the 1970s, a number of court cases about bias in intelligence tests spurred on researchers to study bias in testing. The many arguments against the use of intelligence tests included concerns that the tests demonstrated (1) cultural bias, (2) inappropriate norms for culturally and linguistically diverse groups, (3) cultural and linguistic handicaps in test-taking skills, (4) majority culture examiner effects, and (5) testing results that lead to inferior educational opportunities. The numerous studies conducted in the 1970s and 1980s have demonstrated little substantial evidence of bias in modern tests of intelligence (Kamphaus, 2001; Sattler, 1998, 2001).

In addition to research about intelligence tests as assessment tools, it has long been recognized that standard personality and psychopathology tests carry ethnic and cultural biases, and in recent years, efforts to correct these biases have accelerated (Dana, 2000). Numerous studies still caution about bias in assessment related issues including service delivery; moderator variables; modifications of standard tests; development of culturally specific tests; personality theory and cultural, racial, and identity description; cultural formulations for psychiatric diagnosis; and the use of findings, particularly in therapeutic assessment (Dana, 1998). Most personality tests were developed and standardized using participants who were predominantly white, Anglo-European, and middle class, and many such tests relied heavily on traditional-age college students as participant samples (Cuellar & Paniagua, 2000). The science of psychometric assessment has minimized group differences by assuming homogenization to be a fact, rather than the result of ethnocentrism (Cuellar & Paniagua, 2000; Dana, 1996, 1998; Suzuki, Ponterotto, & Meller, 2001).

It was precisely the finding that few significant differences could be found between heterosexual people and gays and lesbians on psychological tests (Hooker, 1958; see also Hooker, 1993 for a retrospective) and where differences did exist, psychological tests showed better mental health among gays and lesbians that finally resulted in the removal of homosexuality as a mental illness from the *Diagnostic and Statistical Manual of the American Psychiatric Association* in 1974. So, while there are certainly differences in the experiences of gays and lesbians and heterosexual people and there are differences in the incidence of certain mental health problems among gays and lesbians, few consistent differences have been demonstrated on standard psychological tests.

Several handbooks now advocate minimizing bias through the use of "culturally competent" assessments including culture-specific styles of service delivery; use of the client's first language; and evaluations of client's cultural orientation, assimilation, and acculturation prior to administration of standardized tests (Ponterotto, Casas, Suzuki, & Alexander, 1995). Ethical standards further demand a number of adaptations. Modification of tests through translation may precipitate other problems (Sattler, 1998, 2001), but many (e.g., Comunian & Gielen, 2000; Dana, 1996, 1998, 2000; Ephraim, 2000; Ponterotto et al., 1995; Reed, McLeod, Randall, & Walker, 1996; Sattler, 1998, 2001; Suzuki & Kugler, 1995) suggest that development of new, more culturally specific norms for such tests and scientific investigation of the construct validity and response sets among culturally diverse clients should be a priority for research in minimizing cultural bias.

Using a multicultural approach to helping means viewing assessment in a more general way. Rather than testing alone, assessment is a phase of helping in which a problem is being outlined. When working with ethnically or culturally diverse clients, this includes attention to the stresses of acculturation and assimilation, prejudice, and socioeconomic and class status. Assessing value orientations and stage of identity development will also assist the helper in identifying some of the critical dimensions of client strengths and limitations. Assessment becomes a part of helping in which a culturally specific plan is mapped based on a more "ecological assessment" (Okun, 2002).

Techniques and Process

Techniques for multicultural helping may be borrowed from other theories, but must be incorporated with care and attention to the basic assumptions, goals, and ethical guidelines of a multicultural model of helping. Although presenting all of the adaptations possible is beyond the scope of this book, readers are encouraged to see Freddy Paniagua (1994) for more. Eight general principles are offered here.

1. Generalizations cannot and should not be made about minorities.
2. The microskills of helping generally create a listening style conducive to creating an empathic and respectful connection with clients, although reflection alone may not always be well received across cultural and ethnic differences. For example, some Asian

Americans may wish for more direction and some Native American clients may require more silence.

3. Working in an office may not be as appropriate as joining clients within their communities. Multicultural helping may require that helpers be seen at community functions and as a part of the community. This enhances the trust of clients, although it challenges traditional notions about the boundaries between helping and living processes.

4. Concrete approaches are often regarded as more useful than abstract talk. A notable exception may be Native American clients' use of storytelling and metaphor to both delineate and solve problems.

5. Family and extended family work is often appropriate in multicultural helping, and more emphasis on family approaches is warranted in training programs.

6. Helpers must commit to continuous education because multicultural theories are new enough to be in flux and openness to change is valued highly.

7. Principles of egalitarian relationships are advocated for multicultural helpers.

8. Part of the content of helping must include the examination of oppression and social context.

Once integrated in such a way, a multicultural model of helping will change the appearance of even those compatible techniques borrowed from other theories of helping. Multicultural helpers must not only be well acquainted with many techniques, but with the underlying assumptions of those techniques in order to adapt only what is appropriate and in an appropriate way.

In addition to adapting traditional helping methods to serve the needs of clients of different ethnic or cultural backgrounds, multicultural professional helpers utilize unique cognitive strategies, physical strategies (body work), spiritual strategies, emotional strategies, and relationship strategies (Ivey, 1987a, 1987b, 1995; Ivey et al., 1997). Approaches like storytelling emphasize client narratives as unfolding constructions of life experiences (White & Epston, 1990, 1994). Life stages developmental mapping focuses on the network of relationships that develop over a lifespan and the tasks associated with each stage (Tamase, 1991). Naikan therapies focus on helping clients repair damaged relationships and discover meaning through connections

(Reynolds, 1990). L. Sunny Hansen's (1990, 1991) Integrative Life Patterns model of decisional helping facilitates a "lifelong process of identifying primary needs, roles, and goals and the consequent integration of these within ourselves, our work, and our family" (1990: 10). The model encourages clients to make decisions throughout a lifetime about total development and to recognize patterns in love, learning, labor, and leisure. Other approaches beside traditional helping strategies include meditation, which is now also commonly used in many stress-management and cognitive-behavioral helping models (Kabat-Zinn, 1990; Ram Dass, 1971; Suzuki, 1970), and networking, which may involve individual work, small group work, observation, support teams, family helping, state and government intervention, community intervention, and large group community network meetings (Attneave, 1969, 1974, 1982). These networking approaches are similar to those used to address child abuse (Ivey & Ivey, 1990) and the ecological approaches advocated for addressing domestic abuse (Edleson & Tolman, 1992).

Various dialogic techniques may also be used to facilitate awareness of oppression and focus on positive identity development. Paulo Freire's (1970) work has been influential in conceptualizing the technique and process of facilitating social, cultural, and political awareness and positive identity development. Freire, a Brazilian educator and political activist, began educating peasant workers and discovered in their process a pattern in which they moved from understanding their problems as *fatalismo* ("fate") or self-imposed, to recognizing and naming their oppressive situations and themselves in context. He noted five levels of consciousness: (1) naive consciousness, (2) identification with the oppressor, (3) discovery and naming the conditions, which is accompanied by anger, (4) reflection on self as a cultural being, and (5) development of a personal identity as a self-in-system that Freire thought necessitated action.

Many of the peasants Freire worked with could not read, so Freire used experiential techniques followed by listening to their storytelling to illustrate their experiences. It was Freire who helped them name the experiences, and, as more concrete storytelling ensued, the peasants eventually reflected together on similarities in their stories. Seeing their common oppression, they began to make plans for action. His work resembles that of early feminist consciousness-raising groups and other psychoeducational processes. Helping from Freire's perspective is conceptualized as liberation—liberation in thought, liberation of action, and liberation from internal and external forces that prevent development and growth. Oppression and its impact could be countered through dialogic interaction with the oppressed, and the divisiveness, manipulation, and cultural invasion that accompanied oppression could be countered through unity, self-directed organizing, active rejection of oppression, and synthesis of *conscientização* (Freire, 1970).

The process of multicultural helping involves using some of the microskills discussed in Part One, adapting techniques from other theories of helping described in Part Two, and training in additional approaches to helping. Multicultural helpers find focusing, following, and the ability to reflect the content of a client's stories useful (Ivey, Ivey, & Simek-Morgan, 1997) when integrated into the basic assumptions of a multicultural approach. For the white, Anglo-European helper working with a person of color, the process of helping poses some challenges. Growing up white rarely affords one the opportunity to know firsthand of racial or ethnic oppression and often does not demand knowledge of other cultures other than the dominant or majority culture. Helpers must allow for additional preparation to work with clients of different cultures. This work demands training and homework.

Sometimes the process of multicultural helping may involve some unique approaches, such as working with traditional healers like *curanderas* (Lee, 1996; Ponterotto et al., 1995) and *shaman* (Attneave, 1974) or asking extended family members to be a part of the helping (Attneave, 1969, 1982; Cheatham & Stewart, 1990). Also, providing minority clients with a pre-helping orientation may prepare them for what to expect of the helper and the process (Levine, Stolz, & Lacks, 1983; Lorion, 1978; Orlinsky & Howard, 1980, 1986).

RESEARCH

Research about the effectiveness of multicultural helping has often focused on utilization of mental health services, helper and client matches, and the benefit of therapy for clients of color. Utilization studies that examine who is using professional helping services have consistently found that mental health services are underutilized by racial and ethnic minority clients, but particularly by Asian Americans and Latinos (Sue, Zane, & Young, 1994). While this finding varies somewhat depending on ethnicity, the overall finding is that all ethnic groups use therapy and counseling less than whites. There may be many reasons for this pattern. Whites have been socialized to a more verbal approach to problem-solving, which is consistent with most helping models that draw on communication skills. Some minority groups have alternative methods of solving psychological and emotional problems. Traditional therapies have focused on examining *self* in some detail, which may be inconsistent with the *self-in-context* worldview of most groups of people who are not male, white, and heterosexual. Family helping models, community mental health, and ecological interventions may be more consonant with the view that self and problems develop within a context and that the context itself may be in need of change. Finally, helping itself has been a tool of the social status quo. In other words, rather than confronting the external realities of oppression and discrimination, helping models have often worked to facilitate adjustment to dysfunctional social norms.

Research shows that clients often prefer same-group therapists (Abramowitz & Murray, 1983; Atkinson, 1985), and people of color consistently prefer ethnically similar helpers to European American helpers (Coleman, Wampold, & Casali, 1995). Nonetheless, studies that have examined the match between helper and client have found no consistent differences in the outcomes of helping based on those matches (Atkinson, 1985; Beutler, Crago, & Arezmendi, 1986; S. Sue, 1988). So, although helping may be more comfortable with someone of a similar background, it may still be effective for helpers and clients of different backgrounds to work together. Client preferences about matches should not be ignored, but the effectiveness of the outcomes may not vary much based on the match. It is also possible that measuring helping outcomes itself cannot be conceptualized or measured in the same way with clients who are less focused on outcome than process. More study is clearly warranted.

Outcome research based on studying whether people of color benefit from professional helping varies somewhat by ethnic group, but generally demonstrates the need for additional research. A large meta-analytic study of Latinos yielded positive results especially when conducted in Spanish (Navarro, 1993), although Sue, Zane, and Young (1994) point out that controls were insufficient to draw many conclusions about the effectiveness of traditional helping with Latino clients. Sue et al. also suggest that it would be premature to draw conclusions about Asian Americans with only four studies. Research about the benefit of therapy for African American clients is as yet inconclusive. No study shows African Americans exceeding white Americans in terms of favorable helping outcomes. Some show no ethnic differences in terms of favorable outcomes, and some show less beneficial outcomes for Black Americans (Prochaska & Norcross, 1999).

Rather than focusing on whether people of color are helped more or less than white people or whether the traditional models of helping benefit people of color, future research might be more useful if focused on the comparative utility of different culturally specific strategies with clients of color. In other words, it might be far less important whether whites or people of color benefit more from helping processes than to establish what traditional or alternative strategies are most helpful in working with people of color.

CRITIQUING

Multicultural theories of helping are still relatively new and somewhat difficult to articulate. In addition, as integrative theories, multicultural theories of helping may be confusing to novice helpers. Multicultural theories of helping are criticized by many who subscribe to the traditional theories about the forces that shape human development. For example, some traditional psychodynamic thinkers view multicultural theories as little more than reflections of paranoid thinking about the many external forces oppressing and responsible for problems. Some rigid behaviorists, who perceive the goal of science to be universal laws, view multicultural theories of helping that embrace an emphasis on individual difference as nonscientific. Some humanists see multicultural theories as unnecessary, since an emphasis on individuality could also celebrate diversity. Nonetheless, multicultural theories have raised the consciousness of theorists and professional helpers alike and revealed external, contextual influences in human behavior and problems that may prepare the way for both individual and social change.

PART THREE

Applications of Microskills and Helping Theories

CHAPTER

15 Crisis Intervention and Suicide Prevention

In the Chinese written language, *crisis* is represented by two characters. One character is interpreted as "danger" or "hazard"; the other character is interpreted as "opportunity." The English translation then is that a crisis represents a dangerous or hazardous opportunity. The English word comes from the Latin *crisis* and Greek *krisis*—both mean "a separating decision; a serious or decisive state; a turning point in which something must terminate or suffer material change; a decisive or crucial time." It can be a state or an event, but it implies a crucial situation of which the outcome may be negative, damaging, or lethal. In medicine, for example, a health crisis is the turning point in the course of a disease indicating either recovery or death will be the outcome. **Crises** are crucial, dangerous, or hazardous situations that often represent emotional turning points in one's life. The outcomes of these emotional turning points hold opportunities. The opportunities that a crisis holds may be for mobilizing changes in basic life patterns, trying new coping strategies, or understanding one's role in a problem situation, or may be in seeing warning signals of future impending crises.

Crises are similar to other concepts with which students may be familiar. Emergencies, stress, and grief are often intertwined with crises and, because of their similarities, can complicate understanding crisis intervention and suicide prevention. These similar processes are addressed here as well.

In American Sign Language, the sign for "crisis" indicates an emergency situation. **Emergencies** are often confused with crises. Crises are both similar and dissimilar to emergencies. Emergencies are sudden, distressing events that require prompt or immediate action. Many kinds of actions can be undertaken to address an emergency. Some emergencies are also crises, but crises can also be less immediately compelling than emergencies. Crises also require a specific action—the search for alternative coping strategies—while emergencies may be addressed by various effective actions.

Many people also use *crisis* and *stress* interchangeably. Crises are both similar and dissimilar to stresses. **Stress** is any change that demands a response (Selye, 1936, 1956, 1976). Humans face stressors daily, even minute by minute. Any event that demands that we change constitutes a stressor. As life is filled with such events, the only way to avoid stress completely is to be dead. Life events can even be scored for the amount of stress or change they characteristically demand. The Holmes Rahe Social Readjustment Rating Scale (SRRS) is an example of a scale used to rate life stressors. Events that are evaluated positively can be categorized as *eu*stress, though it is *di*stress—those events evaluated negatively—that people often refer to when they talk about feeling stress. While both represent an opportunity to change, crises also represent an opportunity for growth that stress may not.

Since crises are almost always associated with a loss of some sort, it is easy to see that a crisis may also be similar to grief. Crises are also different from grief. Both may indicate a loss, but, more than grieving the loss, a crisis strains old coping strategies and has the potential for developing new ones.

CRISIS THEORY

Theories of crises are actually based on physiological principles of homeostatic balance. In physical terms, humans have a need to preserve the balance of electrolytes in order to sustain life. When this balance is disrupted, self-regulatory mechanisms are triggered that attempt to return balance. Crisis theory translates similar principles of homeostasis into psychological terms and assumes that humans require a certain balance in cognitive and emotional functioning. Normal, in this and other endeavors, is still relative. There is no absolute normal, either in physiological or psychological functioning. Crisis theory, while assuming a relative normal, indicates that painful affect should be minimized and that people should have enough cognitive skill for everyday problem-solving.

Everyone has experiences daily in which equilibrium is disrupted and from which uncomfortable affect can result. In fact, any shift or change in the environment that alters relationships or expectations of self can lead to a rise in stress and motivates one to find behaviors that reestablish homeostasis. Coping processes (a kind of psychological regulation) return us to homeostasis. Coping is critical to well-being and essential to functioning. Through coping, humans learn a repertoire of skills for regulating everyday stress. In addition, we have varying levels of awareness of those coping skills. Some operate outside of awareness, while others are conscious mechanisms employed for the purpose of managing or regulating life stresses. Coping skills themselves may be adaptive or maladaptive. At their best, coping strategies help us to master or transcend a problem situation, while at their worst, coping strategies help us to protect a vulnerable sense of self without mastery or transcendence. I find a continuum concept of adaptation is more useful than a dichotomy.

As each individual's coping mechanisms may be quite different, so also is tolerance for stress idiosyncratic or unique to each. What precipitates a crisis for any one individual may be different from what precipitates a crisis for anyone else. However, some common life events have been generally associated with crises.

Since humans are presumed always to be growing and developing and crises are associated with a need to grow or develop new coping strategies, anyone can be in crisis. There may be some people who imagine that they are or should have all of the coping strategies they will ever need, but crisis theory assumes that whenever there is a strain in these mechanisms, people need to figure out new ways to contend with demands. In the process of developing those new ways, people may experience a crisis.

Crises are less the product of encountering a singular risky event than they are a result of the perceived lack of resources. Crises result from encountering a hazardous or dangerous event and being unable to side step it, unable to utilize previous coping mechanisms, or finding that previous coping mechanisms do not work, resulting in the perception of a lack of resources.

It is important for helpers to remember that regardless of the eventual resolution, human tolerance for crisis is finite and self-limiting. Both good news and bad, crises are generally over in about four to six weeks. Some clients are reassured that the uncomfortable period of time will not last forever. For helpers, it is also important to note that the window of opportunity for facilitating effective or enhanced resolution is also relatively short. During a crisis, psychological defenses are weakened or absent, hence clients are very aware of difficulties at this time. Indeed, crises foster an enhanced capacity for cognitive and affective learning. When very aware of their difficulties, clients may use that awareness to learn something new.

Adaptive resolution of a crisis can be and frequently is a vehicle for resolving underlying conflicts, even those conflicts that may have determined or precipitated the crisis itself. This is part of what makes crisis intervention so powerful. Small external influences during a crisis state can produce disproportionate change in an even shorter period of time than counseling or therapy. It is the current social and psychological events that influence resolution and not necessarily character structure or previous experience, although certainly these can influence the client's abilities to resolve difficulties.

Many theorists suggest that inherent in each crisis is an actual or anticipated loss. Such losses include loss of sense of self, loss of another, loss of a valued possession, and loss of esteem. Helpers who know this can make a point of listening for the loss or sense of loss that the client may be experiencing. In the sense that crises in clients' lives represent the loss of significant people or their attention or approval, crises are interpersonal events. A crisis generally involves at least one other person who may be represented in the situation either directly, indirectly, or symbolically.

Effective crisis resolution can prevent future crises of a similar nature by removing vulnerabilities from the past and by increasing the repertoire of available coping strategies to be used in such situations. Resolution of any crisis may be adaptive or maladaptive. In an **adaptive resolution,** the client defines the issues, deals with feelings, makes the necessary decisions, and learns new problem-solving techniques. Any underlying conflicts that were reactivated are also identified and resolved. In short, resources are mobilized and discomfort is reduced. Crises can also be resolved in a maladaptive fashion. Maladaptive resolutions often result from inadequate help and support or the absence of help and support. A **maladaptive resolution** leaves the person without new coping mechanisms. Underlying conflicts are either unidentified or unresolved. In a maladaptive resolution, resources do not get mobilized and unpleasant, uncomfortable affect is only somewhat reduced or not appreciably reduced at all.

Following a crisis, clients' readjustment to their environment may also be adaptive or maladaptive. If they have made an adaptive resolution, clients will feel and be less vulnerable in other similar situations. They will have learned more skills for their repertoire of coping, confidence will increase, and general level of functioning will be improved. With general functioning improved, the probability that similar situations will trigger a crisis are also reduced. So, the effective resolution of one crisis actually better prepares each client for the next crisis she or he may encounter.

In a maladaptive resolution to a crisis, the client remains vulnerable, sometimes even more vulnerable in situations similar to the current crisis. In addition to resolving crises using maladaptive mechanisms, it is possible for the client to learn new maladaptive mechanisms in the resolution to a crisis. Take for example a client who may not have been a problem drinker previously but who, after the death of a loved one, resolves to avoid the uncomfortable emotion of the specific crisis by binge drinking for several weeks. The client will have dulled or reduced the discomfort she or he was feeling with alcohol. Subsequently, when the client returns to general functioning within a few weeks, she or he may return with binge drinking as a new skill for resolving crises. Utilizing this particular skill during a period of crisis serves to make the person more vulnerable to depression, leaves her or him with alcohol abuse as a coping mechanism, and will not serve the client well in future crises. It may even facilitate an alcohol abuse or dependency problem. In the face of a maladaptive resolution, a client's general level of functioning may be reduced and because of the real lack of internal resources, the probability of future hazardous events becoming crises is then increased.

New coping strategies may work to effectively address future crises that are unlike the crisis just resolved. In this way, crises not only increase the number of a client's coping strategies, but also add to a client's sense of confidence in being able to weather difficult situations.

EVOLUTION OF A CRISIS

Crises appear to follow a distinct pattern in their evolution (Baldwin, 1978). The first phase in any crisis can be thought of as *encountering the hazardous or dangerous event*. This phase occurs as clients become aware of new or renewed risks in the life events with which they are dealing. Again, it is helpful to remember that danger may be psychological, emotional, or interpersonal. The danger or hazard is generally accompanied by a rise in discomfort that signals disruption in personal homeostasis. Humans are motivated to reduce disruptions, so previously learned methods of reducing or regulating disruptions are generally drawn into play at this point. In most instances previously learned methods of coping with difficulty are successful and no crisis emerges. Crises emerge when previous methods have been tried but not found to be useful. As the person realizes that she or he is uncomfortable and that her or his usual mechanisms are not working to reduce the discomfort, unpleasant and uncomfortable affect intensifies and cognition often becomes disorganized. At this point, people are motivated to attempt novel methods and to seek help. This is the point at which someone in a crisis may present themselves to a professional helper. If the methods that they usually employ to address difficulty are working well, people do not feel the affective discomfort or cognitive disorganization that motivates them to seek out help.

Crisis resolution can be thought of as phases that involve both affective and cognitive tasks (Baldwin, 1978; Hoffman & Remmel, 1975; Morely, 1965; Okun, 2002; Rusk, 1971). In what has been called the *catharsis/assessment phase* of a crisis, a client's first task is to feel the impact and express the feelings about the crisis fully and to explore the meaning of the crisis for them. Take as an example a job loss. At the catharsis phase, a client should be focused on fully experiencing the feeling that the disruption of losing his job elicits. He may feel a kind of emptiness as he gets up each day and finds himself without his usual schedule; he may feel a sense of relief or freedom; he may feel anger at the company or supervisor who made the decision about the job loss. Without this activity to structure his days, he may feel lethargic and unmotivated or energized. He may wander about his home at loose ends or may do all of the things he had been putting off. He may just sit and feel empty for days. The helper's affective tasks are to help the client acknowledge the feelings by reflecting whatever feelings are generated by the crisis and exploring and defining the meaning of the precipitating event for that specific client. Catharsis for the client involves reflecting about feelings and assessing the current crisis in terms of the personal meanings attached to significant events. Did the loss of the job mean less structure, economic hardship, and a loss of self-esteem? On the contrary, did it mean a chance to do something different that may not have otherwise presented itself?

Clients in crisis are rarely in the best position to mobilize their own resources. If they were, they would not be in a crisis by definition. Clients in a crisis, then, are more dependent on a helper than at other times in their lives to help them find and access new resources. Helpers are called on to provide or facilitate resource mobilization. Advising clients about the exigencies of filing for unemployment benefits, launching a lawsuit, or registering with a temporary job service may be a part of the helper's role with a client who has just lost a job. Helpers are often reminded that being more directive when a client is in a crisis will not necessarily lead to ongoing client dependency.

In the catharsis/assessment phase of crisis resolution clients also have cognitive tasks to complete. Depending on the assessment of difficulties, helpers can assist in restoring realistic perspectives of a situation and defining options or courses of action. Helpers also facilitate clients' conceptualizing the precipitant or meaning that links past and present. It is important that helpers stay focused on obtaining limited but relevant information to the resolution of the crisis. Even though a crisis often precipitates the awareness of past events, the full exploration of those past events is less useful to a client in crisis than a focus on returning the client to equilibrium in the present.

In the second phase of a crisis, sometimes called the *focusing/contracting phase,* clients and helpers face affective tasks that involve helpers' facilitating awareness of feelings that impair the clients' use of coping strategies and building an alliance whose emphasis is on responsibility for change and resolution. Cognitive tasks include an agreement between the helper and client crafted through the helper's empathic paraphrasing, clarifying the content of the client's reports, and reflecting the client's affect and personal meaning about the core conflict or problem at hand. Client and helper work collaboratively to define a timeline and goal for the crisis resolution and then agree on a tentative strategy or plan.

The *intervention* or *resolution phase* (or third phase) of a crisis intervention involves the affective tasks of defining and supporting existing client strengths and adaptive coping strategies, working through any resistance the client may have to resolving the crisis, and facilitating direct and appropriate responses to the feelings and personal issues being raised by the crisis. The cognitive tasks of this phase involve teaching or helping clients to develop new, more adaptive strategies and then helping clients to define progress toward goals. Often helpers must prevent diffusion of the process away from the present goal. This may be a challenge for the helper who is aware of all the past events that have contributed to the current difficulties, but, in a crisis, it is essential for the client to return to a state of psychological equilibrium as soon as possible and feel the impact of being able to successfully effect that goal.

Once a client's resources have been mobilized sufficiently to design and then implement a strategy for resolving the crisis, the final phase of crisis resolution begins. The fourth phase, often called the *termination* or *integration phase,* also involves affective and cognitive tasks. Affective tasks for helpers include eliciting and responding to termination issues; avoiding prolonging the end of the helping relationship; and reinforcing the client's changes in affect and coping. Cognitively, the tasks for termination are to evaluate the client's goal attainment and offer the client anticipatory guidance to help her or him integrate the changes made. At this point, helpers also give information and facilitate direct referral to other resources.

TYPES OF CRISES

Different types of crises call for different helping responses. Knowing what type of crisis a client may be experiencing may assist the helper in responding appropriately. A problematic situation precipitates what is called a **dispositional crisis** (Baldwin, 1978). Such a crisis usually requires that the helper make appropriate referrals or take administrative action to facilitate intervention. A dispositional crisis indicates that something has changed in a client's status or disposition and that his or her usual resources are not helping to cope with the loss. A good example of this kind of crisis might be one in which a client has just been diagnosed with AIDS. The diagnosis of any disease process changes the client's life circumstance. An effective helper not only listens to and helps the client to fully explore her or his reactions to this diagnosis, but helps to pave the way for the client to seek further help from an AIDS response service accustomed to exactly the kinds of issues associated with such a diagnosis.

At various turning points, **life transitions crises** can also be anticipated. Leaving home for college is a common, albeit disruptive, life event that can precipitate a crisis. Sometimes students experience a crisis after getting to the college, sometimes before they have even left their parents' home. Another example might be what some faculty members refer to as "senior slump." Seniors in college often look ahead to leaving the relatively well-known, comfortable context of their colleges and entering unknown situations. Although this is a normal life transition from college to work or to graduate school, students may experience a crisis. It makes sense that usual coping strategies may be inadequate to deal with these different situations and that the students may need additional coping skills to face such crises.

In the case of an anticipated life transition that precipitates a crisis, an in-depth understanding of what has taken place or will take place is generally helpful to a client. In addition to exploring feelings about leaving home or graduating and entering the job market, a client experiencing such a crisis will need support from the helper for what they are about to do or have just done. They may need accurate information about what to expect. They may also need to map out adaptive responses they can make to the upcoming transition. Sometimes group helping approaches are beneficial in normalizing crises born of a life transition.

In the case of events that precipitate a **sudden trauma crisis,** helping responses are different than those used in helping clients who face normal life transitions or dispositional crises. Strong, externally imposed, unexpected, uncontrolled events like a death, a life-threatening natural disaster, or a violent incident often precipitate a crisis. Few of us have all of the coping strategies we need to face such circumstances and often people need additional mechanisms. During the period of time immediately following the trauma, sometimes called the *refractory period,* clients need support and acknowledgment of their negative affect, whatever that may include.

In the case of a death, a number of phases of adaptation have been outlined following Elisabeth Kubler-Ross's (1969) now famous work *On Death and Dying.* People facing a sudden death will first deny the loss and then when the realization breaks through will often become quite angry. Following the anger, many people begin bargaining with some perceived higher power like God or The Universe. "I will gladly give my life if you would only bring this person back." Out of guilt, they may say things like, "If only I had. . . ." Both represent a sort of bargaining to avert the loss. When the bargain can obviously not be met and the loss is beginning to become more real, most move on to feeling depressed. Following the depression, most people begin to accept the loss. All of these stages are normal approaches to a sudden death or even an anticipated death that require a helper to acknowledge and help a client express the negative affect. Though some may require additional intervention, support and acknowledgment of their feelings will assist most clients in resolving most grieving processes naturally.

In a **maturational** or **developmental crisis,** like one precipitated by evidence of aging, clients may need help to identify and conceptualize the underlying conflicts that the maturational or developmental crisis represents. In order to respond to the present more adaptively while weaving in past conflicts, helpers may use more skills aimed at exploring past events and interpreting the clients' personalized meanings of the events.

Some crises are the result of diagnosable psychological problems. In these cases, it is the fact of the psychological problem that constitutes the impetus for the current crisis. In other words, such crises are determined by the internal reactivation of unresolved past problems rather than of external stressors per se. Take for example a student who is generally anxious or has what psychologists call a generalized anxiety disorder. The student may face the end of a semester with a crisis that others might only experience if they were facing graduation. In this case, helpers can be most useful by supporting the client and taking a very strong problem focus. It is important to realize that focusing only on resolving the present crisis successfully will still offer long-term benefits. This is similar to Steven de Shazers's (1985) work on solution-focused helping. The emphasis remains on the current crisis even though other difficulties may be apparent.

When clients with preexisting mental health problems face crises, some care must be taken not to reinforce dependency on the helper. In general, helpers need not worry about client dependency in crisis intervention. As the crisis is short-lived and returns the client to pre-crisis functioning, the intense dependency on the helper is also short-lived and naturally abates once the client's own resources are successfully mobilized. However, when a client has preexisting mental health problems, helpers are more likely to lose the focus on the crisis itself, undertake too many problems, and address the problems in a manner that is useful for crisis intervention but fosters unnecessary dependency in the resolution of other problems. Helpers are advised to assess, but not address, long-standing problems and help stabilize client functioning in terms of the most immediate crisis.

Some emergencies involve a client whose general functioning is severely impaired or a client who is incapable of assuming personal responsibility for problem-solving. In these cases, rapid, accurate assessment; clarification of the situation; mobilization of any necessary resources; and arranging for follow-up and continuity of care must be undertaken with urgency by the helper. Crises requiring this type of helper response include alcohol or drug abuse, which not only impair client judgment but make client responses unpredictable and may render the client unhelpful. These crises also include psychoses. If a client is actively hallucinating or delusional, cognitive problem-solving is impaired, affect may be unreliable, and situations will be marked by less than complete information. In these cases, helpers may need to be more directive. In the case of suicidal or homicidal impulses, urgency is required to assess the lethality of the situation and to assist the client in making decisions to avert harm.

SUICIDE

Incidence

About 30,000 people each year commit suicide and approximately 10 times that number attempt to commit suicide (Andreasen & Black, 1991; National Institute of Mental Health, 2000). Attempts are more common in youth; suicide is the second leading cause of death among white 15- to 24-year-olds (car accidents are first) (Kaplan & Sadock, 1991). Completed suicides, on the other hand, increase at the age of 45 for men and 55 for women (Wilson, Nathan, O'Leary, & Clark, 1996). People over 65 years of age account for 25 percent of the suicides every year (United States Department of Commerce, 1993). Although suicidal thinking may affect anyone, whites and Native Americans are more likely than African Americans to attempt or commit suicide (Burr, Hartman, & Matteson, 1999; Hendin, 1995; Kaplan & Sadock, 1991). The strongest predictor of suicide is a sense of hopelessness coupled with a considered plan (Beck, Covacks, & Weissman, 1975; Schneidman, 1985). When this coincides with alcohol abuse, the suicide rate is 20 times higher than in the general population (Adams & Overholser, 1992; Merrill, Milner, Owens, & Vale, 1992).

Facts and Fictions

It is not true that people who *talk* about suicide do not *commit* suicide. Eight out of ten people who commit suicide announced their intentions to someone in some way. Sometimes those who hear someone talking about suicide do not know how to respond or feel uncomfortable or think it must be a joke or ignore it as a grab for attention. Some believe that talking about it will increase the likelihood of an attempt.

Most clients feel relieved when given an opportunity to discuss suicidal thoughts and often begin making plans to resolve the crisis underlying their suicidal thinking. If someone discusses suicidal thinking, helpers can safely assume that they are at least ambivalent about taking their own lives. If they were decided, they would not discuss it. People who are thinking about suicide are not necessarily consumed with a death wish; most are ambivalent right up until the end of their lives. Those who feel suicidal are often only going to feel suicidal during that particular short crisis in their lives and never again. If a client has made a previous suicide attempt, however, they are more likely to consider suicide or make a suicidal gesture at a later point (Litman, 1974). About half of all people who eventually kill themselves have made a previous attempt.

Ninety percent of the people who actually commit suicide have some diagnosable psychological problem. Almost half of the problems people experienced that preceded suicide would be identified as mood disorders (depression), although only 15 percent of those diagnosed with a mood disorder consider suicide (Henricksson et al., 1993). Just as perceived lack of resources predicts whether a person will experience a crisis in response to a hazardous event, the degree of helplessness predicts whether someone will make a suicide attempt.

The demographics of suicide victimology suggest that although women attempt suicide more frequently, men outnumber women three to one among those who complete suicides (Kushner, 1995; Moscicki, 1995; NIMH, 2000). In general, this is because the means that men choose for attempts are more lethal (e.g., firearms) (Canetto & Lester, 1995; Crosby, Cheltenham, & Sacks, 1999).

Assessing Lethality

A number of models are used to assess **lethality,** or likelihood that a given situation will result in death. All of the models for assessing suicidal lethality rely on actuarial data about who completes suicide attempts. While anyone can and many do think about suicide, only some people follow through and make a completed attempt.

The single most highly correlated factors placing a person at risk of completing a suicide have to do with the plans they have made. Someone with a specific and highly lethal plan and with access to the means to carry out that plan is at far greater risk than someone who is thinking about a vague wish to be dead or to escape their current situation. This does not mean that the person with a less lethal plan is not in pain. The helping professional, however, has more time and more options to intervene effectively.

Emotional and environmental factors have also been shown to increase risk. People who are depressed are more likely to feel a sense of hopelessness and this increases the risk that they will complete a plan for suicide. Isolation from relatives or friends increases risk, as does an absence of social support. Relatives' or friends' reactions, such as defensiveness, denial, punishment, or rejection, pose an increased risk that the person thinking about suicide will complete the thought with action. Someone who has previously attempted suicide has already crossed the line once into acting on this frightening impulse, and research shows that they will be more likely to follow through on a plan to do so again. Those with chronic physical or mental health problems are more likely to attempt suicide as are those who have recently experienced a particularly stressful event like divorce, unemployment, or abuse trauma.

While some advocate the use of a rating scale that assigns point values to suicidal risk factors (Cesnick & Nixon, n.d.; Cull & Gill, 1988; Holmes & Howard, 1980; Lewinsohn, Rohde, & Seeley, 1994), it is also possible to assess lethality without such a scale. Once an adequate assessment of the lethality of the situation has been made, helpers know how much urgency with which to respond to the client's situation and how directive their responses must be to effect safety for the client. It is the client's safety and empowerment that must guide helping responses in crises that involve suicidal thinking.

Intervention

Helping someone who is suicidal begins, as does any helping process, with a connection between helper and client. In a crisis situation in which a client is feeling suicidal, helpers must establish a much more immediate working alliance based on trust and confidence. Clients must trust that the helper wants to and is capable of helping. As suicide is the result of a sense of helplessness and believing that options do not exist, helpers are also called on to help establish a sense of hope for the future and must assist clients in finding options. Convincing the person to delay the suicidal act can rarely be successfully negotiated with reason, but rather with options for resolving the crisis that is underlying the suicidal thinking. The helper's primary concern with a suicidal client must be ensuring client safety. Again, it is helpful to remember that crises in general and suicides in particular result from a perceived lack of options. Helping clients generate options restabilizes client resources and lends a note of optimism about the future. Helpers must restrict client access to firearms and drugs and limit the amount of even prescription drugs available to clients until the person is no longer feeling suicidal. This simply takes away some of the opportunities for the person to harm her- or himself.

Many helpers (including myself) use a "No Harm Contract." This is a relatively simple piece of paper outlining a contract in which the client agrees not to harm her- or himself before she or he first contacts the helper. Clients cannot call and leave a message or have anyone else make the call. They must agree to make face-to-face contact in which the helper has at least one opportunity to discuss the suicide with the client. This has several effects. One is to ensure that the helper will have an opportunity to intervene one final time. Another is to reassure the client that there is always one more opportunity or option, thereby reducing some of the sense of helplessness. Helpers must obtain personal details, like telephone numbers for the client, family, and friends; license plate number and description of the client's car; name of the primary physician; and names and locations of places the client frequents. Likewise, the helper reciprocates with access information for the client. All of this reinforces a sense of future for the client and reiterates the message that options exist.

Helper concerns for a client's welfare should be discussed explicitly. Again, this has not been found to precipitate suicide attempts, but to relieve clients of the solitary burden of their own frightening thoughts. Helpers should also make clear that they will do whatever is necessary to prevent the suicide. Clients should be informed that although thinking about suicide can be confidential, suicidal intentionality is not a part of a confidential relationship. This is not only a legal consideration and a matter of professional ethical behavior, but again serves to reassure the client that even if she or he cannot see options or assume problem-solving responsibility, someone else can and will.

Finally, helpers are encouraged not to make moral judgments about suicide. Even if the client's own moral values preclude suicide, confronting the client with moral judgments is not generally a successful helping strategy. The reminder only serves to add to the feelings of guilt or shame already present, thereby increasing the very feelings that may be supporting her or his suicidal thoughts to begin with. In addition, confronting the client with moral judgments often confuses the client's thinking and makes it more difficult for the helper and client to work together effectively.

SUMMARY

Crises strain clients' resources and demand alternative coping mechanisms, because their usual coping strategies are not working to reduce discomfort. Crises are short-lived periods of time in which a client is very vulnerable and very motivated to find new ways to solve problems. This makes crises both an opportunity and a liability. The helper's challenge is to assist the client in fashioning as adaptive a response to the crisis as possible so as to facilitate growth and enhance future problem-solving capacity. Doing so requires that helpers attend to both the type of crisis a client is experiencing and a number of cognitive and affective tasks.

Some clients who are experiencing a crisis will also consider suicide and some may even attempt to kill themselves. A helper's responsibility is to try to prevent the client's death, and to do so involves rapid and accurate assessment of the likelihood that a given person will follow through on a suicidal thought and attempt or complete suicide. Following the lethality assessment, helpers must make rapid, effective connections that allow clients to see and implement options for resolving the current crisis without their death being the result.

Crisis intervention and suicide prevention are powerful tools for helping professionals. Both great benefit and great harm can result from these dangerous opportunities called crises. An effective helper recognizes and attends to both the hazards and the value of such situations and empowers clients to find strengthening responses that will not only address the present situation, but also position them well for the future.

CHAPTER

16 Interviewing as Research

Webster's Unabridged Dictionary (2001) shows that the word *research* comes from the Old French word *recherche,* which is made up of two words—*re,* meaning "again," and *cherche,* meaning "to seek." **Research** is defined as "a careful, patient, systematic, diligent inquiry or examination in some field of knowledge undertaken to establish facts or principles; the laborious, continuous, and ongoing search for truths." A second, rarely used definition of research comes from the study of music in which a *research* is an extemporaneous prelude used to introduce themes in a musical piece.

Donna Mertens, a professor at Gallaudet College, defines research as a way of knowing that uses systematic inquiry to collect, analyze, interpret, and use data to understand, describe, predict, or control a phenomena, but also as a way to empower individuals (Mertens, 1998). By this she means that gathering information can be a process not only of taking information from participants (i.e., the people being interviewed), but returning to individuals information that is necessary to improve their circumstances. The word *inquiry* comes from the Latin *inquirare* and is composed of *in,* meaning "into," and *quirare,* meaning "seek" or "search." To inquire means to look into or seek truth or information by asking questions or by investigation or examination. Inquiry, then, is the act of seeking information by asking questions. A researcher uses systematic methods of inquiry to acquire knowledge and understanding. A researcher seeks information by asking ongoing questions that may describe, predict, or control, but may also empower.

The different ways to ask and answer questions about human behavior can be categorized by two types of information being gathered. **Quantitative research** seeks information that involves accurate measurement of some phenomena or substance. **Qualitative research** seeks information about the characteristic elements, attributes, or qualities of some phenomena as its focus. Methods traditionally used in qualitative research include **ethnography, grounded theory, phenomenology, case study,** and **biography** (Creswell, 1998), and these qualitative traditions rely on many of the same microskills used by helping professionals. Observations, interviews, and interpretations are essential equipment for qualitative researchers. The microskills used to hear clients in effective helping can be used to hear data in effective qualitative research. Of course, the types of interviews, the questions asked, and the wording of the questions shifts from a focus on helping to a focus on gathering information. What remains at the heart of both processes is the importance of building a strong rapport in which an interviewer can accurately capture, reflect, and then report on the beliefs, feelings, and meanings of a client or a research participant.

TYPES OF QUALITATIVE INTERVIEWS

Many types of interviews are used in qualitative research. Michael Quinn Patton (2002), one of the United States' foremost researchers in qualitative research and evaluation, outlines four interview variations. The **informal conversational interview** is conducted without preset questions. The **general interview guide approach** is conducted using an outline of topics, but no preset questions. The **standardized, open-ended question interview** is conducted using a strict list of preset questions. The **closed, fixed-response interview** is conducted using both preset questions and preset answer options. A closer look at each interview type reveals other differences.

In an informal conversational interview, the researcher seeks to strike up a conversation with a specific person or group in order to gather information about some essential characteristic of the person or group, or their beliefs or experiences. Questions emerge from the immediate context and are asked in the natural course of a conversation. No decisions are made ahead of time about what questions will be asked or how they will be worded. This type of interview is customized to the individual or the circumstance by asking questions based only on spontaneous observation. Because questions actually emerge from the situation or observation, the questions are likely to be significant and appropriate to the interview. On the other hand, because different questions are asked of different people, systematic organization or analysis of the information can be quite difficult and generalizations to others are limited.

A general interview guide approach specifies topics or issues to be covered in advance in an outline. These constitute the general guide, although the researcher still makes spontaneous decisions about the order and wording of questions. The guide can enhance data organization and comprehensive coverage of the topic, while still permitting an approach that feels conversationally natural. At the same time, differences in sequencing and wording of the questions could result in different perspectives, thereby making comparisons and generalizations difficult.

In a standardized, open-ended interview, each person being interviewed is asked the same questions in the same order. The exact wording and sequencing of the questions are determined in advance. This interview type addresses concerns about comparing participant responses later in an organized fashion. It also makes it possible for a number of interviewers to work on the same question. At the same time, constraining the spontaneity of the interviewer may result in less relevant questions, and limiting the person being interviewed to answering only the preset questions may constrict and inhibit their responses.

Closed, fixed-response interviews set up not only the questions, but also the response possibilities in advance of the interview. People being interviewed choose from among a fixed set of responses. Fixed responses make analysis of the data simple and easy to summarize, even when compared to quantitative methods, and make it possible to interview many more people than the other interview designs. Fixing the types of responses that participants may give can also distort participant meanings or experiences by arbitrarily categorizing responses according to the interviewer's scheme rather than the respondent's intention.

In addition to Patton's four variations, interviews may be conducted with individuals or in groups. Individual interviews are often called *in-depth interviews* to indicate one of their acknowledged strengths. Interviewing an individual allows for in-depth exploration of participants' thoughts, feelings, experiences, and the meanings they attach to them. Group interviews, on the other hand, focus on the participants' interactions with one another and with the moderator for the development of ideas, perspectives, and meaning (Morgan, 1988, 1997). The group dialogue becomes a key source of information.

INTERVIEW QUESTIONS

Types of Questions

A number of different types of questions are used to gather information for research projects. Some of the more basic questions include general introducing questions, experience or behavior questions, and knowledge and sensory questions. Introducing questions introduce a topic to a research participant. "How much do you know about sexually transmitted diseases?" is an example of a question that also introduces the research topic. Experience or behavior questions request information about a specific behavior or experience. With this type of question, the interviewer wants to know what the participant actually does or has done in the past. An experience or behavior question might sound like, "When you worked as a longshoreman, what kinds of things did you do in a usual day?" When an interviewer wants to know what factual information a participant may have about a particular topic, they ask a knowledge question. "What do you think firefighters do when not fighting fires?" might allow a researcher to establish how much knowledge someone has about the job tasks of firefighters. Sensory questions establish what a participant has seen, heard, touched, tasted, or smelled. "When you've heard voices, what did they say to you?" would encourage a schizophrenic to report on a sensory experience.

Beginning interviewers often confuse opinion questions with feeling questions. Opinion or values questions ask the participant to report on the opinions or values they hold or what they think about some issue. "How do you think our new president is doing so far?" is an example of an opinion or values question. Feelings questions ask for a participant's emotional response to an experience or thought. "How do you feel when you stand up in front of a class to give a colloquium?" is an example of a feelings question. A beginning interviewer might confuse the two by asking, "How do you feel our new president is doing so far?" If the interviewer is seeking an opinion about the new president's job performance, using the word *think* or a synonym is critical. While we often use the word *feel* as a synonym for *think* in everyday conversation, one cannot be replaced by the other without changing the type of information being requested.

Other types of questions are more complex and require a higher level of interviewer skill or preplanning. Follow-up questions, exploratory questions, and interpretative questions fall into this category. Follow-up questions are used to pursue a topic already raised in the interview to see where it leads and elicit additional or clarifying information. Experienced researchers anticipate possible responses and have follow-up questions in mind. Good follow-up questions add depth to the interview data.

Exploratory questions are not unlike exploratory surgery. When physicians perform exploratory surgery, they do not have a clear diagnosis—they are cutting someone open to have a look around in an area they think could be implicated in the patient's symptoms. Exploratory questions serve a similar purpose. Researchers go looking in a general area they think may be implicated in understanding a particular phenomena or experience, but ask questions that will allow the participant to structure her or his responses.

As in helping interviews, research interviews include interpretive questions somewhat sparingly. An interpretation is the interviewer's view of what the participant has said, but framed in the interviewer's words or from the interviewer's frame of reference. To maintain research integrity, interviewers should be competent at paraphrasing and should paraphrase at Level 3 (see Chapter 3). Paraphrases should not venture too far beyond what the participant has said or the meaning the participant imposed on the situation, phenomena, behavior, or experience might be lost. In contrast to helping, which often subtly moves clients toward exploration, insight, or action, research seeks to capture accurately the participants' current experiences, beliefs, and perspectives.

Finally, background or demographic questions are used to gather information about the identifying characteristics of the person being interviewed. A common background question is "What is your birth date?" One way to allow participants to self-label is to ask "How do you refer to your ethnicity?" An advantage to asking this question in an interview rather than on a form is that participants can respond with multiple ethnicities and use the exact language with which they identify themselves.

Sequencing Questions

Sequencing questions to be asked in a research interview is important. Some questions are innocuous and where they appear in the interview sequence matters little. Some questions are volatile and best asked after rapport has been established. Some questions will preempt the possibility of asking other questions. In general, nonconversational questions about present behaviors, activities, and experiences should be asked first, followed by less concrete questions, such as interpretations, opinions, and feelings questions or knowledge and skills questions (Patton, 2002). Background questions tend to be pretty dry and boring. Keep background questions to a minimum and try to tie them to descriptive information about present experiences as quickly as possible.

Wording Questions

An effective research interview question is one that encourages the participant to tell more. More data are better. Interestingly, in both helping and research interviews, open-ended questions are the most effective. In a research interview as in a helping interview, an effective question is less like an interrogation, a pop quiz, or a multiple-choice exam, and more like the who, what, when, where, how, and how much that a journalist asks when investigating a news story. How, when, and where questions tend to be more effective than why questions, as why questions tend to evoke defensiveness.

Sometimes novice interviewers ask questions that are not truly open-ended or questions that are disguised as open-ended, but are not (see Chapter 5). Closed questions limit the possible responses a participant may make. Compare the possible responses between this example of a closed question, "Do your parents take care of your college expenses?" and this example of a more open question, "How do you pay for college?" The client could choose to answer the first question with a simple yes or no. While not a good replacement when an open-ended question is intended, closed questions have their uses. A closed question is a good option if the interviewer wants to summarize the responses across many participants and create a composite statement about how many believed this or experienced that.

Asking about a singular thought, perception, or topic is more useful than asking multiple questions within the same frame. Include no more than one idea in each question so that participants can fully explore that one before moving on to a new idea.

Although it may go without saying, questions should be clearly worded. Even in the case of a less structured interview, I find it useful to consider several ways of asking questions before entering the situation with the participant so that I can be certain that my questions are clear. Researchers should be clear about terms and language used by a participant. A good example is the word *bad,* which gained a positive definition late in the twentieth century along with its traditional negative definition. An interviewer unclear about its usage will at least spend more time than necessary and perhaps look foolish and fail to establish a necessary rapport with the participant.

It is more important for the participant to label her or his experience than for the interviewer to do so. Part of the purpose behind conducting an interview for research purposes is to ground a theory or story in the perspective of the participants who have been selected for their potential input. Avoid labeling the experiences of the interviewee so as not to impose the perspective of the researcher. Researchers who already have an opinion about the topic under investigation should "bracket" their opinion, that is, set it aside. Also, it might be better not to ask a question at all if the answer is already known. Follow-up questions can always be raised later. Interrupting participants may not only compromise rapport, but the process of their concept development.

INTERVIEWER SKILLS

The Importance of Silence

As in any kind of interview, silences are as important to the process as are the words chosen for a response and the order in which questions are asked (see Chapter 1). Silence allows a research participant to collect her or his thoughts, to process others' thoughts when in a group interview, and to organize or consider these thoughts. An effective interviewer is not only silent her- or himself, but leaves room for participant silences. As it is with helping microskills, reserving talk is a skill and involves more than simply waiting your turn to speak. It involves attending so closely to what a participant is saying that the interviewer could paraphrase the content—in this case, the data—that is important to the participant (see Chapter 3), hear what she or he is feeling and identify correctly what those feelings are (see Figure 4.1), or offer a glimpse of the participant through the eyes of the researcher (see Chapter 7). To be valid and reliable, data must be an accurate reflection of the participants that could even be replicated at a later time or in another context or by a different interviewer. When in doubt, listen rather than speak. In regard to research interviewing, I. E. Seidmann (1991) summarizes, "Listen more; talk less; ask real questions."

Rapport and Neutrality

Rapport is the ability to convey empathy and understanding. Letting research participants know that what they have to say is important will preserve not only the connection, but valuable data. Interviewers are advised to take a neutral stance about the content. In a helping interview, conveying a nonjudgmental approach to what clients say encourages them to continue to give more information. The same is true of participants in a research interview. If the researcher truly wants answers to questions from the perspective of participants, participants must feel comfortable that they can tell the researcher anything without engendering favor or disfavor.

Presuppositions can enhance participant responses if used properly. Asking clients for illustrative examples is often as critical to understanding their experience for research purposes as it is for helping. A well-placed question like, "How would that look?" gives clients and helpers a concrete example to illustrate the client perspective. Illustrations help to illuminate participant perspectives as well.

Role playing and simulations can sometimes also clarify participant perspectives. "Talk to me as though I were someone else" or "Tell me a story about . . ." may allow participants some distance on a topic that is too close or that makes them feel too vulnerable to continue. When conducting a research interview, just as when conducting a helping interview, summarizing can facilitate a smooth, seamless transition to the next topic. Summarizing gives the interview a more natural flow and makes it more like a conversation (see Chapter 3).

When students are first learning the art of asking questions, exploratory and follow-up questions can be difficult to create (see Chapter 5). Not only does the interviewer have to lose some of the self-consciousness that naturally comes with new skills, but experience teaches what to look for. The value of listening carefully to what is said and not said cannot be overstated. It is critical for the interviewer, whether helping a client or researching a participant's experience, to understand what the person being interviewed is saying.

Finally, interviewers should be sensitive to the feedback needs of the person being interviewed. Whether the person asking the questions is doing so because they seek information from a participant for a research project or to help a client, the person asking questions is controlling the conversation at the moment (see Chapter 5). She or he is controlling the topic being addressed, and participants often feel as though what constitutes satisfactory answers is also controlled by the interviewer. Many participants add phrases like "you know what I mean" or "you know" in their responses in order to get some feedback from the interviewer that they are being understood. Although tracking the participants' perspectives is crucial, it is still very important to offer neutral feedback in the form of minimal verbal responses to help make the participant feel heard and encourage elaboration (see Chapter 1).

I once had an assignment as a part of an undergraduate social psychology class. The goal was to give students some practice at field experimentation and to let us see firsthand the impact of minimal verbal responses. We were asked to conduct a brief interview in which we asked for a participant's perspectives on an arbitrarily chosen topic. In the first half of the interview, we sat absolutely stone-faced as we asked questions and gave no response to anything the participant said. In the second half of the same interview with the same participant, we made little sounds like "uh," "uh-huh," or "mm-hmm." We then recorded the amount of time the participant spent responding in the first half and compared it to the second half. No one was surprised to find that the minimal verbal responses resulted in more talk, more elaboration, and increased discussion about whatever had preceded the interviewer response. The responses of the interviewer seemed to act as reinforcements for continued speaking about a topic. This is, of course, a double-edged sword. Offering some encouragement can result in richer, more elaborate data, but researchers must be cautious not to contaminate findings by reinforcing only certain topical coverage. Researchers who ask for clarification of a particular response not only have more information for their later interpretations, but also continue to send a clear message to the participant that they are listening.

Support and Recognition

Before beginning with interview questions, most interviewers will convey their purpose in an opening statement that tells the participant what will be asked, who the information is for, how the information will be handled, what the purpose is of collecting the information, and how it will be used. This is part of the legally necessary, informed consent process of ethical research, but also an effective way to clear the air before heading into the purposeful data gathering. Once the interview has begun, it is important for the interviewer to use words of appreciation, support, and even praise for participating, but once again the interviewer should take care not to reinforce specific content. To do so can compromise the validity and reliability of the participant perspective. To maintain the flow of communication, research interviewers must maintain awareness of how the interview is going, how the participant is reacting to questions, and what kinds of feedback are appropriate and helpful. If this sounds like a lot to be thinking about while the research interview is taking place, that's because it is. New research interviewers may want to consider this yet another reason for utilizing more silence!

Structuring the Interview

Asking a clever initial question will not necessarily produce the data you require. By listening actively, the interviewer can assess the data and redirect the focus of the conversation respectfully if the data are off topic. In addition, the research interviewer must be able to intervene with a highly verbal respondent who gets off track, or data will get lost amidst unnecessary filler. This is sometimes hard to gauge as participants of different backgrounds may approach the task of a research interview quite differently. I have worked with enough Native American clients and research participants to know that often a direct response to a question begins with a narrative designed to tell their perspective. If I were someone who believed that participants should never get off the track and thought this was off-track behavior, I would lose valuable data.

Last-Ditch Question

Finally, at the end of a research interview, many researchers ask what has been called the "last-ditch, one-shot question." This is an all-encompassing question that allows the participant to launch a topic in any direction they choose. One example of a last-ditch question is, "Is there anything else you'd like me to know?" Such a question allows the participant or the interviewer to directly address something that has not been said. A broad, open-ended question is particularly important if the interview has been tightly focused and the researcher senses that something of value may be waiting in the wings, still unsaid. The last-ditch question allows the researcher to explore angles other than what might have been the intended focus of the interview.

SUMMARY

In summary, many of the same skills used in helping situations can be used to gather information for program evaluations or research. Certainly, the types of interviews vary, as do questions, sequencing of questions, and content. Nonetheless, helpers who are skilled at listening, reflecting, paraphrasing, summarizing, and interpreting are ahead of the curve in terms of learning to apply these skills to research projects involving interview and interpretation. Qualitative research is an excellent example of a type of research that requires good microskills. In fact, it is possible that the next generation of outcome research in helping will make additional use of this paradigm in evaluating the effectiveness of helping from the perspective of the client.

AFTERWORD

To my surprise, the process of writing this book paralleled the professional helping process at several points along the way. I had days when I felt motivated and empowered and entered each writing session with enthusiasm, excited by the momentum of new thoughts and connections and the experience of creation. I had days when I couldn't seem to picture what came next, and I felt bewildered and stalled. I even had days when I felt angry about having to work so hard with little or no reward. Even though it was my choice to write the book, I resisted getting down to business or found other "essential" activities to do, like doing the laundry or mowing the lawn or rewriting an already polished lecture or watching the movie *Sneakers* for the sixteenth time.

I noticed the closest similarities, however, when it came to finishing the book. I had developed a relationship with the writing of this book and its imagined readers. Although I was thoroughly ready to move on to other projects, I was reluctant to end this one. Not unlike the client who avoids ending a helping relationship by canceling or missing a scheduled termination session, I discovered months after completing the final draft that I had forgotten to write an ending. I have often thought that people pay much more attention to beginnings than they do to endings, and yet endings are equally important—maybe more so. Even recognizing the importance of endings, though, I can't say that I am very fond of them.

Endings and losses are a natural part of helping and teaching relationships, and I have learned that people say good-bye in many different ways. One way to create a more gentle closure process is by reviewing the journey and taking a look ahead. When I fashion terminations for classes or work with clients, I often use a past–present–future model, adapting the questions for different purposes:

- Where were you when you began this process? (What did you know about yourself? Your goals? Your skills? The process?)

291

- Where are you now? (What have you learned? What was different from what you expected?)
- Where are you going? (What would you still like to learn about yourself? The process? Other skills? What skills do you still want to refine?)

The questions encourage students and clients to reflect on their growth, development, and achievements and to think about future study and career goals. Exercise A.1 provides more examples of these exploratory questions.

As a professional helper and educator, I do not usually see how my clients' and students' lives continue to unfold or witness my impact. The same is true of the writer–reader relationship. In my roles of psychologist and professor, I have learned the importance of self-reflection to achieve a positive sense of closure.

The concept of this book developed from my own classroom needs. I wanted to teach beginning students the art and science of professional helping in a format that would foster an appreciation of how they were interrelated—by introducing both microskills and theories in one compact text.

In the Introduction, an overview of the training and education offered in the different helping disciplines, the nature of helping relationships, and our ethical standards were all intended to give some basic information to the beginner interested in exploring or entering the helping professions and some context for the chapters to come. The microskills chapters guided students through building helping communication skills—from basic nonverbal skills that create synchrony with clients to complex helping skills that advance clients' goals. The microskills exercises were designed to help raise awareness of students' verbal and nonverbal skills in listening and in building strong empathic relationships. If you practiced the microskills exercises, you may have noticed changes in your personal communication style as well as within your professional helping relationships.

The theory chapters explored the principles and methods that form the foundation of different approaches to helping—person-centered, behavioral, cognitive, cognitive-behavioral, psychodynamic, family systems, and sociocultural. These theoretical schools did not emerge or develop in isolation. Just as microskills build on previous microskills and interrelate with other microskills, theories build on previous theories and interrelate with other theories. A new theory

Closing

The following questions are designed to help you explore where you have been, where you are now, and where you want to go in your development as a professional helper. Write out your thoughts about the questions and share them with a friend, fellow student, or mentor.

1. Reflecting back:
   - What did you already know about professional helping before you began studying the subject?
   - What adjectives would you use to characterize or describe your experience with or your feelings about professional helping when you began your studies?
   - What did you expect learning about professional helping micro-skills and theories to be like?
   - What did you hope to learn about professional helping?
   - How was this subject the same as or different from what you expected?
   - How effective were your basic listening skills before you began studying the subject?

2. Considering the present:
   - What do you know now about professional helping?
   - What adjectives would you use to characterize or describe your experience with or your feelings about professional helping now?
   - What professional helping skills have you developed, begun to develop, or refined?
   - How effective are your basic listening skills now?
   - What do you wish you had done differently? More of? Better?
   - What topic areas did you find most interesting? Least interesting?
   - What topic areas did you find most valuable? Least valuable?
   - What are your strengths as a professional helper? Areas for improvement?

3. Looking ahead to the future:
   - What do you still need to learn about professional helping?
   - Which professional helping skills would you like to practice more?
   - Which theoretical concepts are still confusing or unclear to you?
   - Which theories would you like to study in more depth?
   - How do you anticipate that you will use what you have learned?
   - What adjectives would you use to characterize or describe your feelings about professional helping as you look into the future?
   - As you think about your career plans and your role in professional helping, what do you anticipate you will be doing in one year? In five years? In ten years? In thirty years?

sometimes develops to augment or extend an existing theory and sometimes to confront or oppose an existing theory, but helping theory development is always linked to practice. Practice and theory inform each other. The theory chapters were structured to help students to form a basic understanding of the web of theories that provide the foundation for professional helping and to begin to identify which theories they feel most comfortable with. If, as you studied the theory chapters, you considered them in relation to the microskills you were practicing, you may have noticed that the ostensibly simple exercises took on additional complexity with the additional layers of meaning.

Finally, the two applications chapters presented practice and theory in concert. I selected crisis intervention and research interviewing because students often first find employment, internships, or assistantships in these areas.

Just as microskills are not used in isolation and just as theories are not developed in isolation, neither should professional helpers work in isolation. As you enter the field of professional helping, build a personal network of supportive colleagues, consult with supervisors, and continue to read and take classes to increase and refine your knowledge and skills and to keep current with the developments in your field.

Just as you've learned to reflect a client's content and feelings to promote the process of building empathy, learn to reflect on your own thoughts and feelings to promote your development as a professional helper. Self-awareness and self-care are essential to maintaining healthy relationships with those you help and to achieving longevity in the field. Practice being gentle with yourself. You will make mistakes and have off days. If you don't, you're either not risking enough or not being human—both essential qualities of competent and engaged professional helpers.

Last, but not least, respect the need to acknowledge endings for both you and your client. Often therapists and clients each reenact their own habitually unsatisfying or problematic endings, or they avoid or minimize ending sessions because of their poor history with closure. Give endings as much thought, planning, and space as any other issue or session. Closure in professional helping involves recognizing successes, losses, new directions, fears, exhilaration, and power shifts. Ambivalence is inherent in endings and discomfort is normal. Novice helpers may be inclined to close abruptly so as not to feel this ambivalence or discomfort. Do not abandon microskills at the point of ending a helping relationship. Helpers need these skills just as much at an ending as during the course of the helping relationship—maybe more so. Professional helpers can use microskills to shape a positive ending by continuing to reflect feelings and content, build empathy, and advance client goals.

As I look ahead to the next edition of this text, I can already envision changes and refinements. I would welcome receiving suggestions about what worked for you, what did not work, and what you would like to see included in a future edition.

GLOSSARY

ABC model Albert Ellis's model, which suggests that activating events (A) are interpreted vis-a-vis a belief system (B), which leads to emotional and behavioral consequences (C). In this model, the client's beliefs cause the consequences. (D) represents disputing the irrational belief.

ableism the belief that full use of all physical or biological functions is superior; assumption that a full range of abilities is the norm; using one's power or privilege as someone with a full range of abilities to impose restrictions on, invalidate, or hold down someone with a different ability or disability.

ACA American Counseling Association.

acculturation the acquisition of complex social and cultural behaviors from social/cultural agents by a combination of all the learning mechanisms.

adaptive resolution a process of resolving a crisis in which the client defines the issues; deals with feelings; makes necessary decisions; learns new problem-solving techniques; reactivates, identifies, and resolves underlying conflicts; mobilizes resources; and reduces discomfort; contrasted with *maladaptive resolution.*

advising a helper's specific information about how to go about a particular behavior.

alignment the way members of a system or subsystem join with others and oppose each other.

AMA American Medical Association.

androgyny when used in psychology, refers to people who have abundant feminine and masculine qualities.

APA American Psychological Association.

approximation behavior that could be thought of as being close to a target behavior.

arbitrary inferences a form of dysfunctional thought caused by conclusions

and formed without any supporting or relevant evidence.

assertiveness training the use of modeling, rehearsal, and operant approaches to teach clients to express feelings and thoughts in a direct, honest, and socially appropriate manner, respecting the value of both their own and others' thoughts and feelings.

automatic thoughts irrational or dysfunctional ideas triggered by specific stimuli that lead to emotional responses.

avoidance learning behaviors acquired to avoid unpleasant or aversive situations or stimuli by responding before such situations or stimuli begin.

behavioral interview an interview process that focuses questions on the target behavior and includes specific questions about the circumstances of the behavior, the specific associations, the reinforcers, and the models that maintain the behaviors.

behavioral self-report or **behavioral rating scale** assessment tools (usually paper-and-pencil forms) used in behavioral theories of helping to gather more information about client behaviors targeted for acquisition, modification, or extinction.

biography a type of research that depicts one person's life story.

blamer term used by Virginia Satir to refer to those people who communicate their avoidance of responsibility for their actions. Accusing others of never doing well, the blamer sacrifices a sense of connection for an illusion of self-worth. Considered a complementary position to *placater.*

boundaries rules that limit types of interactions or relationships.

case study a type of research that emphasizes various methods to gather detailed information about one person or situation.

catastrophizing a form of arbitrary inference, specifically referring to thinking of the worst possible scenario or outcomes in a given situation.

chain a term used in behavioral theories of helping indicating the process of stringing together a number of behaviors that successively approximate the target behavior.

circumplex model a model that categorizes four levels of adaptability and four levels of cohesion to study how families address stresses and crises.

clarification gathering enough information about what the client is saying to make sure the helper is not confused.

classical conditioning the process by which a stimulus naturally producing a certain response becomes associated in time or location with another stimulus, and eventually the second stimulus elicits virtually the same response as the first one; also called "respondent conditioning" or "Pavlovian conditioning."

closed, fixed-response interview a type of interview in which not only the questions, but also the response possibilities are established in advance of the interview.

closed question a question that limits the possible responses a client may make (e.g., "yes," "no," or a fixed response, like a, b, c, or d).

coalition a connection born of opposition against another.

cognitive behavioral modification (CBM) a cognitive-behavioral theory of helping based on the idea that covert processes of thinking and internal dialogue can be observed and modified just as overt behaviors are: through association, operant conditioning, modeling, and rehearsal.

cognitive dissonance a state of discomfort that occurs whenever behavior, attitudes, or feelings contain discrepancies.

cognitive distortions automatic thoughts marked by "characteristic logical errors."

cognitive restructuring the process of disputing irrational beliefs clients make

about themselves, activating events, and others.

cognitive therapy (CT) a type of helping focused on correcting systematic errors in client thinking and reasoning that are believed to be underlying such psychological problems as depression.

collaborative empiricism a term used by cognitive-behavioral helpers to indicate that the professional helper is working together with the client to test thinking, feeling, and behavior.

computers term used by Virginia Satir to refer to people who use "ultrareasonable" words; a rigid, motionless, contained posture; deadpan expression; and lackluster voice to indicate that their emotions are tightly checked against the threat of vulnerability.

conditioned stimulus (CS) an originally neutral stimulus that has been paired with an unconditioned stimulus to produce the same response.

conditioned response (CR) a newly learned response to a conditioned stimulus.

conditions of worth term used by Carl Rogers to refer to beliefs and values that impose worth and limit the fullest expression of one's potential.

confrontation reflecting to a client any number of various discrepancies that can exist in the client's reports.

congruence term used by Carl Rogers to refer to the match between perceived self, ideal self, and real self.

conscientização term used by Paulo Freire; learning to perceive social, political, and economic contradictions and to take action against oppression.

conscious the part of a person's experience of which she or he is aware.

contingency management a term used in behavioral theories of helping to indicate modification of the antecedents or consequences of specific behaviors in order to manage, modify, or eliminate them.

continuous reinforcement a term used in behavioral theories of helping to refer to the process of administering reinforcements after every single response;

usually used to help facilitate the acquisition of a new behavior.

counterconditioning breaking the association between two or more stimuli; pairing the conditioned stimulus that elicits fear with an unconditioned stimulus that elicits positive emotion (see *unconditioned response*).

countertransference term used in psychodynamic helping that includes all of the helper's feelings toward the client, conscious or unconscious, transferred from significant others in the helper's life.

crises crucial, dangerous, or hazardous situations that often represent turning points in one's life, the outcomes of which hold opportunities.

cultural oppression a type of oppression in which language, values, symbols, history, and meanings are used to maintain or reinforce and to socialize humans to believe in the superiority of a particular cultural difference.

cultural assimilation a process by which members of a culture adopt a new culture as their own and replace ancestral patterns in order to participate in the economic, political, educational, and community group of the newly adopted culture.

Daily Thought Record (DTR) a record used in cognitive helping models in which the client keeps track of the dysfunctional thoughts he or she has each day.

deep-muscle relaxation a specific type of relaxation training used in behavioral theories of helping in which helpers focus on various muscle groups and teach clients to tense and then relax each one.

deterministic a philosophy that views behavior as being determined as opposed to chosen.

developmental crisis a type of crisis precipitated by maturing or aging; same as *maturational crisis.*

developmental lines Anna Freud's concept of the gradual development of various behaviors such as the movement from dependency to self-mastery and from an egocentric focus to an other-focus.

directing the process of telling the client how to, and perhaps when to, engage in a particular behavior.

disengaged family a family in which the boundaries are so rigid that there is little or no emotional contact between family members.

dispositional crisis a type of crisis in which something has changed in a client's life circumstance, or the client has lost some status that she or he has had, such that her or his usual resources are not helping the client to cope.

distractors a term used by Virginia Satir to refer to people who interject irrelevant words; people whose body postures are off balance from moving in so many different directions simultaneously; as a result of avoiding a clear position, they feel like no one knows or likes them and that there is no place for them.

dominant theme a recurring theme including both the content and feelings of what the client may be saying about her- or himself.

double-bind communication communication that is unclear and conveyed in such a way that the receiver cannot respond in any way without risk and cannot refuse the message.

dysfunctional thoughts illogical ideas maintained by self-defeating behaviors (i.e., overgeneralization, magnification).

eclectic combination, integration, or blend of several theories or strategies.

egalitarian a type of relationship based on equal distribution of power.

ego the personality structure that develops primarily to mediate conflicts between the *id* and *superego;* a conscious faculty for perceiving and dealing with reality.

Electra complex Freud's theory that girls in the phallic stage desire their fathers, experience penis envy, and identify with mothers in order to please and appease the powerful father and share in his phallus symbolically by being able to offer him a child.

emergency a sudden, distressing event that requires prompt or immediate action.

emotional cutoff one way to cope with unresolved triangulated attachments with parents (i.e., running away, denial).

empathy a cognitive and emotional skill that involves seeing the cognitive and affective world of others from their own perspective.

enmeshed family a family in which the boundaries are so diffuse or permeable that each is affected by and may be overinvolved in the business of the other.

Eros life force instincts, including the *libido*.

ethnocentrism the belief that Western European cultural background is superior; assumption that European background is normative; use of one's position of power or position of privilege as someone of European cultural background to impose restrictions on, invalidate, or hold someone of another culture down.

ethnography a type of research that seeks to depict a people or their culture.

evaluation a helper's comment about the value she or he places on a particular behavior, experience, feeling, or idea.

extinction a term used in behavioral theories of helping to indicate that a particular behavior or response no longer occurs.

family sculpting a technique created by Virginia Satir that consists of asking family members to physically position themselves according to her observations of their communication styles.

feedback the process of returning information to the source of a behavior with the intention of offering that person an opportunity to observe, improve, or refine a particular behavior.

feminism a belief that women and men are of equal value and women should have political, economic, and social power equal to men.

fixated to have left energy at an earlier stage of development or to have invested it in one or more defenses.

free association when the client relates anything and everything of which she or he is aware.

functional behavior analysis a detailed analysis of the antecedents (A), behaviors (B), and consequences (C) of the behaviors.

fusion a process that occurs when individuals are unable to adequately differentiate themselves from their families of origin or when rational thought is swamped by feeling.

general interview guide approach an approach to interviewing in which specific topics or issues to be covered in advance are outlined.

genogram a depiction of family members and the significant information about them.

"good enough mothering" Donald Winnicott's idea that mothers need not be perfect, but rather need to supply an adequate nurturing environment to facilitate maturation.

grounded theory a type of research that develops theories grounded in the perspectives of relevant participants.

guided discovery in cognitive helping models, a type of collaborative empiricism that may include role-playing, the three-question method, and testing beliefs to guide clients through the process of discovering fallacies in their thinking.

heterosexism the belief that a heterosexual orientation is superior; assumption that heterosexual is normative; using one's power or privilege as a heterosexual person to impose restrictions on, invalidate, or hold down someone whose orientation is gay, lesbian, or bisexual.

hierarchy an arrangement of people, things, ideas, and so on in order of rank, grade, class, or value.

holding environment an adequate nurturing environment in which humans could develop a sense of self.

homeostasis originally a term used to indicate a physiological balance of electrolytes; in psychological terms, a balance in cognitive and emotional functioning.

id the personality structure that includes instinctual urges demanding tension-discharge as quickly as possible without regard to values, ethics, logic, or concern for others.

imaginal flooding a term used in behavioral helping models to refer to the process of directing clients to imagine the most frightening stimuli possible.

immediacy helpers' comments on their own experience in the interaction with the client as the experience is occurring.

in vivo **desensitization** a process similar to systematic desensitization except that fearful or anxiety-provoking stimuli are introduced in reality rather than in imagination.

informed consent a term that refers to a prospective research participant being given information about the benefits and risks of the study and then asked to decide whether to participate.

informal conversational interview a type of interview in which a conversation with a specific person or group is initiated to gather information about some essential characteristic of the person or group, or their beliefs or experiences.

inquire the act of seeking information by asking questions.

institutionalized oppression a type of oppression in which the power of institutions is used to support oppressive beliefs or used to reinforce the idea that one way of being is superior to another; to impose restrictions on, limit, or subordinate people of differences.

instructing a longer, more intensive and extensive series of interactions than in advising that often involves some kind of assessment of the client's mastery of the ideas or behaviors.

interchangeable response a response that correctly identifies the general category and specific intensity, selects an accurate word to capture the experience of the client, and then delivers it while matching the client's affective tone and language well enough for the client to continue or modify it.

intermittent reinforcement the process of administering reinforcers at varying intervals; very resistant to extinction.

internalized oppression incorporating or taking on the belief that one's own specific difference is inferior or should pose restrictions or limitations or should keep one subordinated.

interpreting a helper's own perceptions of the meanings of a particular experience, behavior, feeling, or idea that the client has reported.

inter-rater reliability a term used in behavioral theories of helping and in research methods to indicate agreement between two or more observers who rate a particular behavior or response along a specific dimension.

labeling term used by cognitive helping theories to refer to allowing imperfections or mistakes made in the past to define oneself.

latent content the symbolic and unconscious motives represented in the dream material.

learned helplessness a process by which a person repeatedly exposed to an aversive environment over which she or he has no control learns to sever the association between effortful behavior and consequence, and exhibits changes in activity level, libido, eating, and sleeping synonymous with depression.

lethality the likelihood that a given situation will result in death.

libido term used by Sigmund Freud to refer to sexual and reproductive motives; life energy.

life transition crisis a type of crisis triggered by a common life event or change in one's status.

magnification perceiving an event in a more heightened light than it deserves.

maladaptive resolution resolving a crisis in such a way that the client's underlying conflicts remain unidentified or unresolved, resources do not get mobilized, and uncomfortable affect is reduced only somewhat or is not appreciably reduced; contrasted with *adaptive resolution*.

manifest content   what the client actually perceived during a dream.

maturational crisis   a type of crisis precipitated by maturing or aging; same as *developmental crisis*.

meta-analysis   statistical analysis of a number of previous statistical analyses.

microskills   the basic skill components that together form the common behaviors critical to the helping process.

minimal verbal responses   miniscule utterances made to encourage someone to continue with their report.

minimization   perceiving an event in a lesser light than it deserves.

minority   persons who are underprivileged, subordinated, or regarded as of minor standing in a system of ethnic, gender, orientational, or cultural stratification.

mislabeling   term used in cognitive helping models to refer to allowing imperfections or mistakes made in the past to define oneself.

modeling   refers to the helper or someone else demonstrating new behaviors for a client to observe and imitate.

naturalistic observation   a type of research or assessment tool in which a helper or researcher observes a behavior or response in the natural environment in which it occurs.

NASW   National Association of Social Workers.

negative punishment   a term used in behavioral theories of helping to indicate taking away something a person has as a consequence of behavior that serves to decrease the likelihood of the behavior.

NOHSE   National Organization of Human Services Education.

norms   standards for behavior.

Oedipal complex   Freud's theory that boys in the phallic stage develop in-

tense, erotic desires for their mother and competitive feelings toward their father and fears of castration. To resolve the conflict, boys identify with fathers and suppress feelings toward mothers.

open question   a question that requires more than a "yes" or "no" response. These questions usually begin with "who, "what," "when," "where," or "how."

operant conditioning   the acquisition of responses as a result of the consequences of the behavior; also called "instrumental conditioning."

operationalizing   to know in very specific terms how to measure success or how particular actions serve to realize a specific goal.

oppression   a belief in the superiority of a particular difference that results in attitudes, practices, and policies that use status, position, power, privilege, and institutions to impose restrictions or limitations on someone of difference, which reinforces a subordinate position.

overgeneralization   holding extreme beliefs on the basis of a single incident and then applying these to dissimilar events.

paradoxical tasks   tasks in family systems helping approach that ask a family to continue (or even increase) doing what they have sought help for in such a way that, paradoxically, positive change is produced.

paraphrasing   restating the content of a client's message in a brief comment.

parts parties   a technique used in Virginia Satir's family therapy that involves clients creating short enactments of different facets of themselves, giving each a name and interacting with others who are doing the same.

people of color   refers to people whose skin is not white and who face pervasive oppression and discrimination because of racial stereotypes associated with skin color.

personalization   a tendency to relate external events to oneself.

phenomenology a branch of any science that emphasizes classification and description rather than explanation; a type of research that seeks to describe a person's experience.

placater a term used by Virginia Satir to refer to those people who communicate by talking in an ingratiating way to please and accommodate others. Trying to be too many things to too many people, the placater feels worthless and loses a strong sense of self. Considered a complementary position to *blamer.*

pluralism the philosophical belief that since reality is composed of multiple views, ultimate beings, principles, or substances, there are multiple realities and multiple truths.

polarized thinking a term used in cognitive helping models to refer to interpreting events in an all-or-nothing fashion or categorizing experiences into either/or extremes.

positive punishment a term used in behavioral theories of helping to indicate the presentation of an aversive stimulus or condition as a consequence of a specific behavior that serves to decrease the likelihood of the behavior.

posttraumatic stress disorder (PTSD) a psychological problem following exposure to a traumatic event and characterized by reexperiencing the event, avoiding associations with the event, and increased autonomic nervous system arousal.

probe to search or investigate with great thoroughness in order to test or prove something.

problem-solving the process in which both client and helper engage to modify the behavior, correct the difficulty, or develop skills to offset limitations that the client is experiencing.

projective technique any technique in which an ambiguous stimulus is presented to a client who then responds, revealing something about her- or himself and her or his characteristic functioning. Primarily used by psychodynamic helpers.

psychological birth Margaret Mahler's term for the movement from an undifferentiated identity to a separate autonomous individual.

punishment any object, event, or response following a behavior that decreases the likelihood that the behavior will be repeated.

qualitative research a type of research that seeks information about the characteristic elements, attributes, or qualities of some phenomena as its focus.

quantitative research a type of research that seeks information that involves accurate measurement of some phenomena or substance.

racism the belief that white skin or Caucasian race is superior; assumption that white skin is normative; using one's power or privilege as someone with white skin to impose restrictions on, invalidate, or hold down someone of color.

rational-emotive behavior therapy (REBT) a cognitive-behavior technique of helping that emphasizes the impact of rational thinking on behavior and feelings.

reflection the process of returning to a client an image of her- or himself.

reinforcer any object, event, or response following a behavior that increases the likelihood that the behavior will be repeated.

research one way of knowing that seeks information by asking ongoing questions that may help bring understanding, may describe, predict, or control, but may also empower.

resistance a kind of client-imposed barrier to being helped.

role patterns of behavior associated with a particular status.

Rorschach test a projective assessment tool comprised of ten cards, each marked with an ink blot. Clients describe what they see. Helpers score responses along several dimensions. Primarily used by psychodynamic helpers.

selective abstraction a form of dysfunctional thinking; forming conclusions based on an isolated detail of an event and ignoring other information or the significance of the total context.

self theory Kohut's theory that self develops through an infant seeking and cueing surrounding caretakers to gratify her or his needs.

self-actualization the process of realizing and acting on one's potential.

self-differentiation a process through which intellectual processes are distinguished from feelings and emotions kept under rational control while objectively experiencing family life.

self-disclosure a glimpse of some part of the helper's experience that matches the client's experience and goals as an illustration.

self-downing term used by REBT helpers to indicate self-deprecating or putting oneself down.

sentence completion blanks relatively simple projective assessment devices that include the Incomplete Sentences Blank (ISB) and Rotter's Incomplete Sentences Blank.

sexism the belief that male gender is superior; assumption of male as normative; using one's power or privilege as a man to impose restrictions on, invalidate, or hold down women.

shaping see *successive approximations*.

socialization the educational process that begins immediately and by which any society gradually teaches its members what is expected behavior.

standardized, open-ended question interview a type of interview in which each person being interviewed is asked the same questions in the same order and the exact wording and sequencing of the questions are determined in advance.

status one's social position in relation to others.

stereotypes generalizations about a group of people that are treated like truth.

stimulus generalization a term used in behavioral theories to refer to the process in which a response to a stimulus comes to be extended to other like stimuli.

stress any change that demands response.

subjective units of disturbance (SUDS) an assessment used in systematic desensitization to measure a client's level of discomfort.

subsystems organizational structures marked by boundaries that define who participates in the subsystem, and when and how (e.g., parental and sibling subsystems).

successive approximations the gradual process of reinforcing some behavior that approximates a target behavior and then stringing together a number of behaviors that more and more closely resemble the target behavior. Reinforcements for each behavior are withheld until responses are closer, raising the criteria for getting the reinforcement over time.

sudden trauma crisis a type of crisis triggered by a strong, externally imposed, unexpected and uncontrollable or life-threatening trauma.

suggesting the process of offering an indication of possible options that a client may choose to pursue.

summarizing gathering together several paraphrases or reflections and offering someone a condensed version of them.

superego the personality structure that incorporates the ideals and values of both society and parents; largely unconscious.

system a set or consistent arrangement of things so related or connected as to form a unit or to operate as a whole.

systematic desensitization the breaking of the association between an anxious response and an anxiety-provoking stimulus by gradually introducing the associated fearful stimuli in a circumstance in which the response cannot occur (e.g., relaxation); uses an anxiety hierarchy.

target behavior a desired behavior.

technical eclecticism to draw from a theoretical view selected for a specific client or for a specific problem, or to draw techniques from many theoretical orientations without necessarily subscribing to the theories (i.e., multimodel theories).

tentafier a tentative phrase.

Thanatos a term used by Sigmund Freud to refer to the death force in humans; considered to be the seat of aggressive motives and behavior.

Thematic Apperception Test (TAT) a projective assessment tool composed of 31 ambiguous pictures. Clients create stories about the pictures following specific guidelines. Helpers interpret the stories.

theory a systematic statement (verified to some degree) of the underlying principles or the relationships between observed phenomena.

theory of use beliefs and assumptions helpers have about behavior that operate daily and affect our own interpersonal behavior.

transference neurosis a relationship that consists of a client attributing to the helper those qualities or characteristics of a significant person in her or his life, and then transferring early drive gratification difficulties to the helper.

transitional object concept developed by Donald Winnicott to refer to a familiar item that provides comfort, consolidation, and reassurance during difficult transitions (particularly from dependence to independence).

transtheoretical approach an approach to integrating theories that selects the conceptual and technical factors that effective helping approaches have in common.

triage the process of addressing patient or client difficulties in order of severity or lethality.

triangulation a process by which someone seeks involvement from a third party to bolster their own position within the dyad.

unconditioned response (UR) the response elicited by an unconditioned stimulus.

unconditioned stimulus (US) any stimulus capable of producing a reflexive or automatic response.

unconscious any material outside of a person's awareness or not readily available.

vicarious learning the acquisition of new behaviors by observing the behavior of others and the outcomes their actions produce; also called "imitative learning."

REFERENCES AND READING LIST

Abramowitz, S. L., & Murray, J. (1983). Race effects in psychotherapy. In J. Murray & P. Abramson (Eds.), *Bias in psychotherapy*. New York: Prager.

Adams, C. D., Kelley, M. L., & McCarthy, M. (1997). The Adolescent Behavior Checklist: Development and initial psychometric properties of a self-report measure for adolescents with ADHD. *Journal of Clinical Child Psychology, 26*(1), 77–86.

Adams, D. M., & Overholser, J. C. (1992). Suicidal behavior and history of substance abuse. *American Journal of Drug and Alcohol Abuse, 18,* 343–354.

Ainsworth, M. D. S. (1982). Attachment: Retrospect and prospect. In C. M. Parkes & J. Stevenson-Hinde (Eds.), *The place of attachment in human behavior* (pp. 3–30). New York: Basic Books.

Alagna, F. J., Whitcher, S. J., Fisher, J. D., & Wicas, E. A. (1979). Evaluative reaction to interpersonal touch in a counseling interview. *Journal of Counseling Psychology, 26,* 265–472.

Allen, W. D., & Olson, D. H. (2001). Five types of African-American marriages. *Journal of Marital and Family Therapy, 27*(3), 301–314.

American Psychological Association. (1992). Ethical principles of psychologists and code of conduct. *American Psychologist, 47,* 1597–1611.

Ammerman, R. T., & Herson, M. (Eds.). (1993). *Handbook of behavior therapy with children and adults.* Boston: Allyn and Bacon.

Anderson, E. M., & Lambert, M. J. (1995). Short-term dynamically oriented psychotherapy: A review and meta-analysis. *Clinical Psychology Review, 15,* 503–514.

Andreasen, N. C., & Black, D. W. (1991). *Introductory textbook of psychiatry* (2nd ed.). Washington, DC: American Psychiatric Press.

Arksey, H., & Knight, P. (1999). *Interviewing for social scientists: An introductory resource with examples.* London: Sage.

Arzin, N. H., & Holz, W. C. (1966). Punishment. In W. K. Honig (Ed.), *Operant behavior: Areas of research and application.* New York: Appleton-Century-Crofts.

Atkinson, D. R. (1985). A meta-review of research on cross-cultural counseling and psychotherapy. *Journal of Multicultural Counseling and Development, 13,* 138–153.

Atkinson, D. R., Morten, G., & Sue, D. W. (1989). A minority identity development model. In D. R. Atkinson, G. Morten, & D. W. Sue (Eds.), *Counseling American minorities* (pp. 35–52). Dubuque, IA: W. C. Brown.

Attneave, C. (1969). Therapy in tribal settings and urban network intervention. *Family Process, 8,* 192–210.

Attneave, C. (1974). Medicine men and psychiatrists in the Indian health service. *Psychiatric Annals, 4*(9), 49–55.

Attneave, C. (1982). American Indian and Alaskan native families: Emigrants in their own homeland. In M. McGoldrick, J. Pearce, & J. Giordano (Eds.), *Ethnicity and family therapy* (pp. 55–83). New York: Guilford.

Bachrach, H. M., Galatzer-Levy, R., Skolnikoff, A., & Waldron, S. (1991). On the efficacy of psychoanalysis. *Journal of the American Psychoanalytic Association, 39,* 871–916.

Baker, H. S., & Baker, M. W. (1987). "Heinz Kohut's self psychology: An overview." *American Journal of Psychiatry, 144*(1), 1–9.

Baldwin, B. A. (1978). A paradigm for the classification of emotional crises: Implications for crisis intervention. *American Journal of Orthopsychiatry, 48,* 538–552.

Ballou, M. B. (1990). Approaching a feminist-principled paradigm in the construction of personality theory. In L. S. Brown & M. P. P. Root (Eds.), *Diversity and complexity in feminist therapy* (pp. 23–40). New York: Hawthorne.

Ballou, M., & West, C. (2000). Feminist therapy approaches. In M. Biaggio & M. Hersen (Eds.), *Issues in the psychology of women* (pp. 273–297). New York: Plenum.

Bandura, A. (1962). Social learning through imitation. In M. R. Jones (Ed.), *Nebraska symposium on motivation*. Lincoln: University of Nebraska Press.

Bandura, A. (1965). Vicarious processes: A case of no-trial learning. In L. Berkowitz (Ed.), *Advances in experimental social psychology* (Vol. 2). New York: Academic.

Bandura, A. (1969). *Principles of behavior modification*. New York: Holt, Rinehart and Winston.

Bandura, A. (1975). Effecting change through participant modeling. In J. D. Krumboltz & C. E. Thoresen (Eds.), *Counseling methods*. New York: Holt, Rinehart and Winston.

Bandura, A. (1977). *Social learning theory*. Englewood Cliffs, NJ: Prentice-Hall.

Bandura, A., & Huston, A. C. (1961). Identification as a process of incidental learning. *Journal of Abnormal Social Psychology, 63,* 311–318.

Bandura, A., & Walters, R. H. (1963). *Social learning and personality development*. New York: Holt, Rinehart and Winston.

Barnett, M. A. (1987). Empathy and related responses in children. In N. Eisenberg & J. Strayer (Eds.), *Empathy and its development* (pp. 146–162). Cambridge, England: Cambridge University Press.

Baruch, G., & Barnett, R. (1975). Implications and applications of recent research on feminine development. *Psychiatry, 38*(4), 318–327.

Bateson, G., Jackson, D. D., Haley, J., & Weakland, J. (1956). Towards a theory of schizophrenia. *Behavioral Science, 1,* 251–264.

Batson, C. D. (1991). *The altruism question: Toward a social-psychological answer.* Hillsdale, NJ: Lawrence Erlbaum.

Beaver, B. R., & Busse, R. T. (2000). Informant reports: Conceptual and research bases of interviews with parents and teachers. In E. Shapiro & T. Kratochwill (Eds.), *Behavioral assessment in schools* (2nd ed.). New York: Guilford.

Beck, A. T. (1963). Thinking and depression: Idiosyncratic content and cognitive distortions. *Archives of General Psychiatry, 9,* 324–333.

Beck, A. T. (1967). *Depression: Clinical, experimental, and theoretical aspects.* New York: Harper & Row. (Republished as *Depression: Causes and treatment.* Philadelphia: University of Pennsylvania Press, 1972.)

Beck, A. T. (1976). *Cognitive therapy and the emotional disorders.* New York: International Universities Press.

Beck, A. T., Emery, G., & Greenberg, R. L. (1985). *Anxiety disorders and phobias: A cognitive perspective.* New York: Basic Books.

Beck, A. T., Kovacs, M., & Weissman, A. (1975). Hopelessness and suicidal behavior: An overview. *Journal of American Medical Association, 234,* 1146–1149.

Beck, A. T., Rush, A. J., Shaw, B. F., & Emery, G. (1979). *Cognitive therapy of depression.* New York: Guilford.

Beck, A. T., Steer, R. A., & Brown, G. K. (1996). *The BDI-II, Beck Depression Inventory Manual.* San Antonio: Harcourt Brace. (Original inventory published in 1978.)

Beck, A., & Weishaar, M. E. (1995). Cognitive therapy. In R. J. Corsini & D. Wedding (Eds.), *Current psychotherapies* (5th ed., pp. 229–261). Itasca, IL: F. E. Peacock.

Beck, J. S. (1995). *Cognitive therapy: Basics and beyond.* New York: Guilford.

Bednar, R. L., Burlingame, G. M., & Masters, K. S. (1988). Systems of family treatment: Substance or semantics? *Annual Review of Psychology, 39,* 401–434.

Belenky, M. F., Clinchy, B. M., Goldberger, N. R., & Tarule, J. M. (1986). *Women's ways of knowing: The development of self, voice, and mind.* New York: Basic Books.

Bem, S. (1975). Sex role adaptability: One consequence of psychological androgyny. *Journal of Personality and Social Psychology, 31*(4), 634–643.

Benjamin, A. (1987). *The helping interview* (4th ed.). Boston: Houghton Mifflin.

Bernard, J. (1976a). Sex role is major factor in depression of women. *Behavior Today,* September 7.

Bernard, J. (1976b). Homosociality and female depression. *Journal of Social Issues, 32*(4), 213–238.

Bernson, B. G., & Mitchell, M. M. (1978). *Confrontation for better or worse* (4th ed.). Athens, GA: Human Resource Development.

Bertalanffy, L., von. (1968). *General systems theory: Foundation, development, applications.* New York: Braziller.

Beutler, L. E., & Crago, M. (Eds.). (1991). *Psychotherapy research: An international review of programmatic studies.* Washington, DC: American Psychological Association.

Beutler, L. E., Crago, M., & Arezmendi, T. G. (1986). Research on therapist variables in psychotherapy. In S. L. Garfield & A. E. Bergin (Eds.), *Handbook of psychotherapy and behavior change* (3rd ed., pp. 257–310). New York: Wiley.

Binet, A., & Henri, V. (1896). Psychologie individuelle. *Annee Psychologie, 3,* 296–332.

Birdwhistell, R. L. (1970). *Kinesics and context.* Philadelphia: University of Pennsylvania Press.

Blechman, E. A. (1980). Behavior therapies. In A. M. Brodsky & R. T. Hare-Mustin (Eds.), *Women and psychotherapy: An assessment of research and practice* (pp. 191–215). New York: Guilford.

Block, J. (1973). Conceptions of sex role: Some cross-cultural and longitudinal perspectives. *American Psychologist, 28*(6), 512–526.

Bloom, C., Eichenbaum, L., & Orbach, S. (1982). A decade of women's oriented therapy. *Issues in Radical Therapy, 10*(4), 7–11.

Boukydis, K. (1981). *Existential/phenomenology as a philosophical base for a feminist psychology.* Paper presented at the Association for Women in Psychology Conference, Boston.

Bowen, M. (1961). The family as the unit of study and treatment. *American Journal of Orthopsychiatry, 31,* 40–60.

Bowen, M. (1972a). Being and becoming a family therapist. In A. Ferber, M. Mendelsohn, & A. Napier (Eds.), *The book of family therapy.* New York: Science House.

Bowen, M. (1972b). Family therapy and family group therapy. In H. I. Kaplan & B. J. Saddock (Eds.), *Group treatment of mental illness.* New York: J. Aronson.

Bowen, M. (1976a). Principles and techniques of multiple family therapy. In P. J. Guerin (Ed.), *Family therapy: Theory and practice.* New York: Gardner.

Bowen, M. (1976b). Theory in practice of psychotherapy. In P. J. Guerin (Ed.), *Family therapy: Theory and practice.* New York: Gardner.

Bowen, M. (1991). Family reaction to death. In F. Walsh & M. McGoldrick (Eds.), *Living beyond loss: Death in the family* (pp. 79–92). New York: Norton.

Brammer, L. M., & MacDonald, G. (1996). *The helping relationship: Process and skills* (6th ed.). Boston: Allyn and Bacon.

Brammer, L. M., Shostrom, E. L., & Abrego, P. J. (1989). *Therapeutic psychology: Fundamentals of counseling and psychotherapy* (5th ed.). Englewood Cliffs, NJ: Prentice-Hall.

Bretherton, I. (1987). New perspectives on attachment relations: Security, communication, and internal working models. In J. D. Osofsky (Ed.), *Handbook of infant development* (2nd ed., pp. 1061–1100). New York: Wiley.

Brill, N. I. (1998). *Working with people* (6th ed.). New York: Addison-Wesley.

Brodsky, A. M., & Hare-Mustin, R. T. (Eds.). (1980). *Women and psychotherapy: An assessment of research and practice.* New York: Guilford.

Brody, C. M. (Ed). (1984). *Women therapists working with women: New theory and process of feminist therapy.* New York: Springer.

Brown, L. S. (1990). The meaning of a multicultural perspective for theory-building in feminist therapy. *Women and Therapy, 1,* 1–21.

Brown, L. S. (1994). *Subversive dialogues: Theory in feminist therapy.* New York: Basic Books.

Brown, L. S., & Ballou, M. (Eds.). (1992). *Personality and psychopathology: Feminist reappraisals.* New York: Guilford.

Bugental, J. F. (1978). *Psychotherapy and process: The fundamentals of an existential-humanistic approach.* New York: Random House.

Burman, E. (Ed.). (1990). *Feminists and psychological practice.* London: Sage.

Burr, J. A., Hartman, J. T., & Matteson, D. W. (1999). Black suicide in U.S. metropolitan areas: An examination of the racial inequality and social integration-regulation hypotheses. *Social Forces, 77,* 1049–1081.

Burton, A. (1972). *Interpersonal psychotherapy.* Englewood Cliffs, NJ: Prentice-Hall.

Busse, R. T., & Beaver, B. R. (2000). Informant report: Parent and teacher interviews. In E. Shapiro & T. Kratochwill (Eds.), *Conducting school-based assessments of child and adolescent behavior.* New York: Guilford.

Butler, G., Fennell, M., Robson, P., & Gelder, M. (1991). Comparison of behavior therapy and cognitive behavior therapy in the treatment of generalized anxiety disorder. *Journal of Consulting and Clinical Psychology, 59,* 167–175.

Caddell, J. M., & Drabman, R. S. (1993). Post-traumatic stress disorder in children. In R. T. Ammerman & M. Hersen (Eds.), *Handbook of behavior therapy with children and adults* (pp. 219–235). Boston: Allyn and Bacon.

Cain, D. J. (Ed.). (1988). Roundtable discussion: Why do you think there are so few person-centered practitioners or scholars considering that literally thousands of persons throughout the world attest to the enormous impact Carl Rogers has had on their personal and professional lives? *Person-Centered Review, 3*(3), 353–390.

Canetto, S. S., & Lester, D. (1995). Gender and the primary prevention of suicide mortality. *Suicide and Life Threatening Behavior, 25,* 58–69.

Carkhuff, R. R. (1969). *Helping and human relations.* New York: Holt, Rinehart and Winston.

Carkhuff, R. R. (1977). *The art of problem solving.* Amherst, MA: Human Resource Development.

Carkhuff, R. R. (with Pierce, R. M., & Cannon, J. R.). (1978). *The art of helping* (3rd ed.). Amherst, MA: Human Resource Development.

Carkhuff, R. R. (1987). *The art of helping* (6th ed.). Amherst, MA: Human Resource Development.

Casas, M., & Pytluk, S. (1995). Hispanic identity development: Implications for research and practice. In J. G. Ponterotto, J. M. Casas, L. A. Suzuki, & C. M. Alexander (Eds.), *Handbook of multicultural counseling.* Thousand Oaks, CA: Sage.

Cashdan, S. (1988). *Object relations therapy.* Markham, Ontario: Penguin Books Canada.

Cass, V. C. (1979). Homosexual identity formation: A theoretical model. *Journal of Homosexuality, 4*(3), 219–235.

Cass, V. C. (1984). Homosexual identity formation: Testing a theoretical model. *Journal of Sex Research, 20*(2), 143–167.

Caudill, B. D., & Lipscomb, T. R. (1980). Modeling influences on alcoholics' rates of alcohol consumption. *Journal of Applied Behavior Analysis, 13,* 355–365.

Cesnick & Nixon. (n.d.). *Suicide lethality assessment.* Unpublished manuscript.

Chambless, D. L., & Gillis, M. M. (1993). Cognitive therapy of anxiety disorders. *Journal of Consulting and Clinical Psychology, 61,* 248–260.

Chambless, D. L., & Wenk, N. M. (1982). Feminist vs. nonfeminist therapy: The client's perspective. *Women and Therapy, 1*(2), 57–65.

Chapin, F. S. (1942). Preliminary standardization of a social insight scale. *American Sociological Review, 7,* 214–225.

Chapman, B. E., & Brannock, J. C. (1987). Proposed model of lesbian identity development: An empirical examination. *Journal of Homosexuality, 14*(3–4), 69–80.

Cheatham, H., & Stewart, J. (Eds.). (1990). *Black families: Interdisciplinary perspectives.* New Brunswick, NJ: Transaction.

Cheek, D. (1976). *Assertive Black . . . puzzled White.* San Luis Obispo, CA: Impact.

Chesler, P. (1972). *Women and madness.* New York: Avon.

Chodorow, N. J. (1978). *The reproduction of mothering: Psychoanalysis and the sociology of gender.* Berkeley, CA: University of California Press.

Chodorow, N. J. (1989). *Feminism and psychoanalytic theory.* New Haven: Yale University.

Coleman, E. (Ed.). (1988). *Integrated identity for gay men and lesbians: Psychotherapeutic approaches for emotional well-being.* New York: Harrington Park.

Coleman, H. L. K., Wampold, B. E., & Casali, S. L. (1995). Ethnic minorities' ratings of ethnically similar and European American counselors: A meta-analysis. *Journal of Counseling Psychology, 42,* 55–64.

Colligan, R. C., & Offord, K. P. (1985). Revitalizing the MMPI: The development of contemporary norms. *Psychiatric Annals, 15,* 558–568.

Combs, A. W. (1988). Some current issues for person-centered therapy. *Person-Centered Review, 3,* 263–276.

Comunian, A. L., & Gielen, U. P. (Eds.). (2000). *International perspectives on human development.* Lengerich, Germany: Pabst Science.

Condon, W. S., & Ogston, W. D. (1966). Soundfilm analysis of normal and pathological behavior patterns. *Journal of Nervous and Mental Disease, 143,* 338–347.

Corey, G. (1996). *Theory and practice of counseling and psychotherapy* (5th ed.). Pacific Grove, CA: Brooks/Cole.

Cormier, W. H., & Cormier, L. S. (1991). *Interviewing strategies for helpers: Fundamental skills and cognitive behavioral interventions* (3rd ed.). Pacific Grove, CA: Brooks/Cole.

Cornell, A. W. (1993). Teaching focusing with five steps and four skills. In D. Brazier (Ed.), *Beyond Carl Rogers* (pp. 167–180). London: Constable.

Corsini, R. J. (Ed.). (1981). *Handbook of innovative psychotherapies.* New York: Wiley.

Cox, S. (1981). *Female psychology: The emerging self.* New York: St. Martin's.

Craighead, L. W., Craighead, W. E., Kazdin, A. E., & Mahoney, M. J. (Eds.). (1994). *Cognitive and behavioral interventions: An empirical approach to mental health problems.* Boston: Allyn and Bacon.

Cresswell, J. W. (1998). *Qualitative inquiry and research design: Choosing among five traditions.* Thousand Oaks, CA: Sage.

Crits-Christoph, P. (1992). The efficacy of brief dynamic psychotherapy: A meta-analysis. *American Journal of Psychiatry, 149,* 151–158.

Crosby, A. E., Cheltenham, M. P., & Sacks, J. J. (1999). Incidence of suicidal ideation and behavior in the United States, 1994. *Suicide and Life-Threatening Behavior, 29,* 131–140.

Cross, W. E. (1971). The Negro-to-Black conversion experience: Towards a psychology of Black liberation. *Black World, 20,* 13–27.

Cross, W. E. (1978). The Thomas and Cross models of psychological nigrescence: A review. *Journal of Black Psychology, 5*(1), 13–31.

Cross, W. E. (1995). The psychology of Nigrescence: Revising the Cross model. In J. G. Ponterotto, J. M. Casas, L. A. Suzuki, & C. M. Alexander (Eds.), *Handbook of multicultural counseling.* Thousand Oaks, CA: Sage.

Cross, W. E., & Fhagen-Smith, P. (1996). Nigrescence and ego identity development: Accounting for differential Black identity patterns. In P. B. Pedersen & J. G. Draguns (Eds.), *Counseling across cultures* (4th ed., pp. 108–123). Thousand Oaks, CA: Sage.

Cross, W. E., Parham, T. A., & Helms, J. E. (1991). The stages of Black identity development: Nigrescence models. In R. L. Jones (Ed.), *Black psychology* (3rd ed., pp. 319–338). Berkeley, CA: Cobb and Henry.

Cuellar, I., & Paniagua, F. A. (Eds.). (2000). *Handbook of multicultural mental health.* San Diego: Academic Press.

Cull, J. G., & Gill, W. S. (1988). *Suicide probability scale*. Los Angeles: Western Psychological Services.

Dana, R. H. (1996). Culturally competent assessment practice in the United States. *Journal of Personality Assessment, 66*(3), 472–487.

Dana, R. H. (1998). Multicultural assessment of personality and psychopathology in the United States: Still art, not yet science, and controversial. *European Journal of Psychological Assessment, 14*(1), 62–70.

Dana, R. H. (Ed.). (2000). *Handbook of cross-cultural and multicultural personality assessment*. Mahwah, NJ: Lawrence Erlbaum.

Daniels, T. G., Rigazio-DiGilio, S. A., & Ivey, A. E. (1997). Microcounseling: A training and supervision paradigm for the helping professions. In C. E. Watkins, Jr. (Ed.), *Handbook of psychotherapy supervision* (pp. 277–295). New York: Wiley.

David, S. (1975a). Emotional self-defense groups for women. In D. Smith & S. David (Eds.), *Women look at psychology* (pp. 173–181). Vancouver: Press Gang.

David, S. (1975b). Becoming a non-sexist therapist. In D. Smith & S. David (Eds.), *Women look at psychology* (pp. 165–174). Vancouver: Press Gang.

Davis, M. H. (1980). A multidimensional approach to individual differences in empathy. *JSAS Catalog of Selected Documents in Psychology, 10*, 85.

Davis, M. H. (1983). Measuring individual differences in empathy: Evidence for a multidimensional approach. *Journal of Personality and Social Psychology, 44*, 113–126.

Davis, M. H. (1996). *Empathy: A social psychology approach*. Boulder, CO: Westview.

Davis, P. J., & Schwartz, G. E. (1987). Repression and the inaccessibility of affective memories. *Journal of Personality and Social Psychology, 52*, 155–162.

Deaux, K., & Major, B. (1987). Putting gender into context: An interactive model of gender-related behavior. *Psychological Review, 94*(3), 369–389.

Derlega, V. J., Catanzaro, D., & Lewis, R. J. (2001). Perceptions about tactile intimacy in same-sex and opposite-sex pairs based on research participants' sexual orientation. *Psychology of Men and Masculinity, 2*(2), 124–132.

de Shazer, S. (1985). *Keys to solutions in brief therapy*. New York: Norton.

de Shazer, S. (1986). An indirect approach to brief therapy. In S. de Shazer & R. Kral (Eds.), *Indirect approaches in therapy*. Rockville, MD: Aspen Systems.

de Shazer, S. (1988). *Clues: Investigating solutions in brief therapy*. New York: Norton.

DiGiuseppe, R., & Miller, N. J. (1977). A review of outcome studies on rational-emotive therapy. In A. Ellis & R. Grieger (Eds.), *Handbook of rational-emotive therapy* (pp. 72–95). New York: Springer.

Dobson, K. S. (1989). A meta-analysis of the efficacy of cognitive therapy for depression. *Journal of Consulting and Clinical Psychology, 57*, 414–419.

Doren, D. M. (1993). Antisocial personality disorder. In R. T. Ammerman & M. Hersen (Eds.), *Handbook of behavior therapy with children and adults* (pp. 263–276). Boston: Allyn and Bacon.

Downing, N. E., & Roush, K. L. (1985). From passive acceptance to active commitment: A model of feminist identity development for women. *The Counseling Psychologist, 13*, 695–709.

Doyle, R. E. (1998). *Essential skills and strategies in the helping process* (2nd ed.). Pacific Grove, CA: Brooks/Cole.

Duncan, S. P., Jr. (1972). Some signals and rules for taking speaking turns in conversations. *Journal of Personality and Social Psychology, 23*, 283–292.

Duncan, S. P., Jr. (1974). On the structure of speaker-auditor interaction during speaking turns. *Language in Society, 2*, 161–180.

Durham, R. C., & Turvey, A. A. (1987). Cognitive therapy vs. behavior therapy in the treatment of chronic general anxiety: Outcome at discharge and at six-month follow-up. *Behavior Research and Therapy, 25*, 229–234.

D'Zurilla, T., & Goldfried, M. R. (1971). Problem solving and behavior modification. *Journal of Abnormal Psychology, 78,* 107–126.

Eagle, M. (1984). Kohut's psychology of narcissism: A critical overview. In M. Eagle (Ed.), *Recent advances in psychoanalysis* (pp. 49–74). New York: McGraw-Hill.

Edleson, J. L., & Tolman, R. M. (1992). *Intervention for men who batter: An ecological approach.* Newbury Park, CA: Sage.

Egan, G. (1994). *The skilled helper* (5th ed.). Monterey, CA: Brooks/Cole.

Eichenbaum, L., & Orbach, S. (1983). *Understanding women: A feminist psychoanalytic approach.* New York: Basic Books.

Ekman, P., & Friesen, W. V. (1969). The repertoire of nonverbal behavior: Categories, origins, usage, and coding. *Semiotica: 1,* 49–98.

Elkin, I. (1994). The NIMH treatment of depression, collaborative research program: Where we began and where we are. In A. E. Bergin & S. L. Garfield (Eds.), *Handbook of psychotherapy change* (4th ed., pp. 114–139). New York: Wiley.

Elliott, R. (1985). Helpful and nonhelpful events in brief counseling interviews: An empirical taxonomy. *Journal of Counseling Psychology, 32,* 307–322.

Elliott, R., Hill, C. E., Stiles, W. B., Friedlander, M. L., Mahrer, A. R., & Marigison, F. R. (1987). Primary therapist response modes: Comparison of six rating systems. *Journal of Consulting and Clinical Psychology, 55,* 218–223.

Elliott, S. N., Busse, R. T., & Gresham, F. M. (1993). Behavior rating scales: Issues of use and development. *School Psychology Review, 22*(2), 313–321.

Ellis, A. (1962). *Reason and emotion in psychotherapy.* New York: Lyle Stuart.

Ellis, A. (1979). Rational-emotive therapy: Research data that support the clinical and personality hypotheses of RET and other modes of cognitive-behavior therapy. In A. Ellis & J. M. Whiteley (Eds.), *Theoretical and empirical foundations of rational-emotive therapy* (pp. 101–173). Pacific Grove, CA: Brooks/Cole.

Ellis, A. (1991). Achieving self-actualization. In A. Jones & R. Crandall (Eds.), *Handbook of self-actualization.* Corte Madera, CA: Select.

Ellis, A. (1994). *Reason and emotion in psychotherapy revised.* New York: Carol.

Ellis, A., & Bernard, M. E. (1986). What is rational-emotive therapy (RET)? In A. Ellis & R. Grieger (Eds.), *Handbook of rational-emotive therapy: Vol. 2* (pp. 3–30). New York: Springer.

Ellis, A., & Dryden, W. (1987). *The practice of rational-emotive therapy.* New York: Springer.

Ellis, A., & Grieger, R. (1977). *Handbook of rational-emotive therapy: Vol. 1.* New York: Springer.

Ellis, A., & Grieger, R. (1986). *Handbook of rational-emotive therapy: Vol. 2.* New York: Springer.

Ellis, A., & Harper, R. (1997). *A guide to rational living* (3rd ed.). North Hollywood, CA: Wilshire.

Ellis, A., & Whiteley, J. M. (Eds.). (1979). *Theoretical and empirical foundations of rational-emotive therapy.* Pacific Grove, CA: Brooks/Cole.

Ephraim, D. (2000). A psychological approach to TAT scoring and interpretation. In R. Dana (Ed.), *Handbook of cross-cultural and multicultural personality assessment* (pp. 427–445). Mahwah, NJ: Lawrence Erlbaum.

Erikson, E. H. (1950). *Childhood and society.* New York: Norton.

Erikson, E. H. (1968). *Identity: Youth and crisis.* New York: Norton.

Erikson, E. H. (1982). *The life cycle completed.* New York: Norton.

Evans, D. R., Hearn, M. T., Uhlemann, M. R., & Ivey, A. E. (1993). *Essential interviewing: A programmed approach to effective communication* (4th ed.). Pacific Grove, CA: Brooks/Cole.

Exner, J. E., Jr. (1974). *The Rorschach: A comprehensive system.* New York: Wiley.

Exner, J. E., Jr. (1993). *The Rorschach: A comprehensive system, Vol. 1. Basic foundations* (3rd ed.). New York: Wiley.

Falco, K. L. (1991). *Psychotherapy with lesbian clients: Theory into practice.* New York: Brunner/Mazel.

Festinger, L. (1957). *A theory of cognitive dissonance*. Stanford, CA: Stanford University Press.

Finch, J. A., Jr., Nelson, M. W., & Ott, E. S. (Eds.). (1993). *Cognitive-behavioral procedures with children and adolescents*. Boston: Allyn and Bacon.

Fonagy, P., & Target, M. (1996). Predictors of outcomes in child psychoanalysis: A retrospective study of 763 cases at the Anna Freud Centre. *Journal of the American Psychoanalytic Association, 44*, 27–77.

Foxx, R. M., & Hake, D. F. (1977). Gasoline conservation: A procedure for measuring and reducing the driving of college students. *Journal of Applied Behavior Analysis, 10*, 61–74.

Foy, D. W., Resnick, H. S., & Lipovsky, J. A. (1993). Post-traumatic stress disorder in adults. In R. T. Ammerman & M. Hersen (Eds.), *Handbook of behavior therapy with children and adults* (pp. 236–248). Boston: Allyn and Bacon.

Frame, C. L., & Cooper, D. K. (1993). Major depression in children. In R. T. Ammerman & M. Hersen (Eds.), *Handbook of behavior therapy with children and adults* (pp. 59–72). Boston: Allyn and Bacon.

Frank, H. M. (2002). *An exploratory study of feminist therapists' conceptualizations and uses of goals and outcomes in therapy*. Unpublished master's thesis, University of Rhode Island, Kingston.

Freedman, N. (1972). The analysis in movement behavior during the clinical interview. In A. W. Siegman & B. Pope (Eds.), *Studies in dyadic communication*. New York: Pergamon.

Freire, P. (1972). *Pedagogy of the oppressed*. New York: Herder and Herder.

Fretz, B. R., Corn, R., Tuemmler, J. M., & Bellet, W. (1979). Counselor nonverbal behaviors and client evaluations. *Journal of Counseling Psychology, 26*, 304–311.

Freud, A. (1936). *The ego and mechanisms of defense*. New York: International Universities Press.

Freud, A. (1965). Normality and pathology in childhood: Assessments of development. In *Writings* (Vol. 6). New York: International Universities Press.

Galton, F. (1879). Psychometric experiments. *Brain, 2*, 149–162.

Gardiner, J. (1987). Self psychology as feminist theory. *Signs: Journal of Women in Culture and Society, 12*(4).

Garfield, S. L., & Bergin, A. E. (1994). Introduction and historical overview. In A. E. Bergin & S. L. Garfield (Eds.), *Handbook of psychotherapy and behavior change* (4th ed., pp. 3–18). New York: Wiley.

Geller, E. S., Caffee, J. L., & Ingram, R. E. (1975). Promoting paper recycling on a university campus. *Journal of Environmental Systems, 5*, 39–57.

Gelles, R. J., & Levine, A. (1995). Social stratification. In *Sociology: An introduction* (5th ed., pp. 250–283). New York: McGraw-Hill.

Gendlin, E. T. (1981). *Focusing* (2nd ed.). New York: Bantam Books.

Gendlin, E. T. (1984). The client's client: The edge of awareness. In R. F. Levant & J. M. Shlien (Eds.), *Client-centered therapy and the person-centered approach: New directions in theory, research, and practice* (pp. 76–107). New York: Praeger.

Gendlin, E. T. (1990). The small steps of the therapy process: How they come and how to help them come. In G. Lietaer, J. Rombauts et al. (Eds.), *Client-centered and experiential psychotherapy in the nineties* (pp. 205–224). Leuven, Belgium: Leuven University Press.

Gendlin, E. T. (1996). *Focusing-oriented psychotherapy: A manual of the experiential method*. New York: Guilford.

Gielen, U. P., & Comunian, A. L. (Eds.). (1999). *International approaches to the family and family therapy*. Padova, Italy: Unipress.

Gilbert, L. A. (1980). Feminist therapy. In A. M. Brodsky & R. T. Hare-Mustin (Eds.), *Women and psychotherapy: An assessment of research and practice* (pp. 245–265). New York: Guilford.

Gillum, R. R., & Barsky, A. J. (1974). Diagnosis and management of patient noncompliance. *Journal of the American Medical Association, 12*, 1563–1567.

Goldfried, M. R., & Davison, G. (1994). *Clinical behavior therapy* (rev. ed.). New York: Wiley.

Goldfried, M. R., & D'Zurilla, T. G. (1973). Prediction of academic competence by means of the Survey of Study Habits and Attitudes. *Journal of Educational Psychology, 64*(1), 116–122.

Goldstein, K. (1959). *The organism: A holistic approach to biology derived from psychological data in man.* New York: American Book. (Original work published 1934.)

Goodman, M. S., & Fallon, B. C. (1995). *Pattern changing for abused women: An educational program.* Thousand Oaks, CA: Sage.

Gorall, D. M., & Olson, D. H. (1995). Circumplex model of family systems: Integrating ethnic diversity and other social systems. In R. H. Mikesell & D. D. Lusterman (Eds.), *Integrating family therapy: Handbook of family psychology and systems theory* (pp. 217–233). Washington, DC: American Psychological Association.

Gordon, R. L. (1992). *Basic interviewing skills* (7th ed.). Prospect Heights, IL: Waveland.

Gove, W., & Tudor, J. (1973). Adult sex roles, marital status and mental illness. *Social Forces, 51*(1), 34–44.

Grawe, K., Donati, R., & Bernauer, F. (1998). *Psychotherapy in transition.* Seattle: Hogrefe and Huber.

Greenberg, J. R., & Mitchell, S. A. (1983). *Object relations in psychoanalytic theory.* Cambridge, MA: Harvard University Press.

Greenberg, L. S., Elliott, R. K., & Lietaer, G. (1994). Research on experiential therapies. In A. E. Bergin & S. L. Garfield (Eds.), *Handbook of psychotherapy change* (4th ed., pp. 509–539). New York: Wiley.

Greenspan, M. (1983). *A new approach to women and therapy.* New York: McGraw-Hill.

Griffen, A. K., Wolery, M., & Schuster, J. W. (1992). Triadic instruction of chained food preparation responses: Acquisition and observational learning. *Journal of Applied Behavior Analysis, 25,* 193–204.

Gruen, R. J., & Mendelsohn, G. (1986). Emotional responses to affective displays in others: The distinction between empathy and sympathy. *Journal of Personality and Social Psychology, 51,* 609–614.

Gump, J. (1972). Sex role attitudes and psychological well-being. *Journal of Social Issues, 28*(2), 79–91.

Gurman, A. S., & Kniskern, D. P. (1981). *Handbook of family therapy.* New York: Brunner/Mazel.

Gurman, A. S., & Kniskern, D. P. (1992). The future of marital and family therapy. *Psychotherapy, 29*(1), 65–71.

Gurman, A. S., Kniskern, D. P., & Pinsof, W. M. (1986). Research on the process and outcome of marital and family therapy. In S. L. Garfield & A. E. Bergin (Eds.), *Handbook of psychotherapy and behavior change* (3rd ed.). New York: Wiley.

Haaga, D. A., Dyck, M. J., & Ernst, D. (1991). Empirical status of cognitive theory of depression. *Psychological Bulletin, 110,* 215–236.

Hacker, H. (1976). Women as a minority group. In S. Cox (Ed.), *Female psychology: The emerging self* (pp. 156–170). Palo Alto: Science Research Associates.

Hackney, H., & Cormier, L. S. (1994). *Counseling strategies and interventions* (4th ed.). Boston: Allyn and Bacon.

Haley, J. (1963). *Strategies of psychotherapy.* New York: Grune & Stratton.

Haley, J. (1971a). Approaches to family therapy. In J. Haley (Ed.), *Changing families: A family therapy reader* (pp. 227–236). New York: Grune & Stratton.

Haley, J. (1971b). Family therapy: A radical change. In J. Haley (Ed.), *Changing families: A family therapy reader* (pp. 272–284). New York: Grune & Stratton.

Haley, J. (1976). *Problem-solving therapy.* San Francisco: Jossey-Bass.

Haley, J. (1984). *Ordeal therapy.* San Francisco: Jossey-Bass.

Hall, C. S., & Lindzey, G. (1970). *Theories of personality* (2nd ed.). New York: Wiley.

Hampson, R. B., Hulgus, Y. F., & Beavers, W. R. (1991). Comparisons of self-report measures of the Beavers systems model and Olson's circumplex model. *Journal of Family Psychology, 4,* 326–340.

Hansen, S. (1990, July). *Work and family roles: An integrated context for career planning.* Paper presented at the International

Round Table for the Advancement of Counseling, Helsinki, Finland.

Hansen, S. (1991). Integrative life planning: Work, family, community. *Futurics, 15,* 80–86.

Hare-Mustin, R. T. (1984). Resource collaboration, feminist therapy, and models. *American Psychologist, 39*(2), 185.

Harper, R. G., Wiens, A. N., & Matarazzo, J. D. (1978). *Nonverbal communication: The state of the art.* New York: Wiley.

Harran, S. M., & Ziegler, D. J. (1991). Cognitive appraisal of daily hassles in college students displaying high or low irrational beliefs. *Journal of Rational-Emotive and Cognitive-Behavioral Therapy, 9,* 265–271.

Hartmann, H. (1958). *Ego psychology and the problem adaptation.* New York: International Universities Press.

Hartmann, H. (1964). *Essays on ego psychology: Selected problems in psychoanalytic theory.* New York: International Universities Press.

Hazelrigg, M. D., Cooper, H. M., & Borduin, C. M. (1987). Evaluating the effectiveness of family therapies: An integrative review and analysis. *Psychological Bulletin, 101,* 428–442.

Hendin, H. (1995). *Suicide in America.* New York: Norton.

Henggeler, S. W., Borduin, C. M., & Mann, B. J. (1993). Advances in family therapy: Empirical foundations. *Advances in Clinical Child Psychology, 15,* 207–241.

Henriksson, M. M., Aro, H. M., Marttunen, M. J., Heikkinen, M. E., Isometsa, E. T., Kuoppasalmi, K. I., & Lonnqvist, J. K. (1993). Mental disorders and suicide. *American Journal of Psychiatry, 150,* 935–940.

Henry, W. P., & Strupp, H. H. (1991). Vanderbilt University: The Vanderbilt Center for Psychotherapy Research. In L. E. Beutler & M. Crago (Eds.), *Psychotherapy research: An international review of programmatic studies.* Washington, DC: American Psychological Association.

Hertzberg, J. F. (1990). Feminist psychotherapy and diversity: Treatment considerations from a self psychology perspective. *Women and Therapy, 1,* 275–297.

Hill, C. E. (1978). Development of a counselor verbal response category system. *Journal of Counseling Psychology, 25,* 461–468.

Hill, C. E., & Gormally, J. (1977). Effect of reflection, restatement, probe, and nonverbal behaviors on client affect. *Journal of Counseling Psychology, 24,* 92–97.

Hill, C. E., Helms, J. E., Spiegel, S. B., & Tichenor, V. (1988). Development of a system for categorizing client reactions to therapist interventions. *Journal of Counseling Psychology, 35,* 27–36.

Hill, C. E., Helms, J. E., Tichenor, V., Spiegel, S. B., O'Grady, K. E., & Perry, E. S. (2001). Effects of therapist response modes in brief psychotherapy. In C. E. Hill (Ed.), *Helping skills: The empirical foundation* (pp. 61–86). Washington, DC: American Psychological Association.

Hill, C. E., & O'Brien, K. M. (1999a). *Helping skills: Facilitating exploration, insight, and action.* Washington, DC: American Psychological Association.

Hill, C. E., & O'Brien, K. M. (1999b). *Helping skills test booklet.* Washington, DC: American Psychological Association.

Hill, C. E., Siegelman, L., Gronsky, B., Sturniolo, F., & Fretz, B. R. (1981). Nonverbal communication and counseling outcome. *Journal of Counseling Psychology, 28,* 203–212.

Hill, M. (1986). Reflections of an experiential feminist therapist. *Women and Therapy, 5*(1), 27–32.

Hill, M. (1990). On creating a theory of feminist therapy. *Women and Therapy, 1,* 53–65.

Hill, M., & Ballou, M. (1998). Making feminist therapy: A practice survey. *Women and Therapy, 21,* 1–16.

Hjelle, L. A., & Ziegler, D. J. (1992). *Personality theories* (3rd ed.). New York: McGraw-Hill.

Hoberman, H. M., & Clarke, G. N. (1993). Major depression in adults. In R. T. Ammerman & M. Hersen (Eds.), *Handbook of behavior therapy with children and adults* (pp. 73–90). Boston: Allyn and Bacon.

Hoffman, D. L., & Remmel, M. L. (1975). Uncovering the precipitant in crisis intervention. *Social Casework, 56,* 259–267.

Hoffman, M. L. (1984). Interaction of affect and cognition in empathy. In C. E. Izard, J. Kagan, & R. B. Zajonc (Eds.), *Emotions, cognition, and behavior* (pp. 103–131). Cambridge, England: Cambridge University Press.

Hoffman, M. L. (1987). The contribution of empathy to justice and moral judgment. In N. Eisenberg & J. Strayer (Eds.), *Empathy and its development* (pp. 47–80). Cambridge, England: Cambridge University Press.

Holdstock, T. L., & Rogers, C. R. (1977). Person-centered theory. In R. J. Corsini (Ed.), *Current personality theories* (pp. 125–152). Itasca, IL: Peacock.

Hollon, S. D., & Beck, A. T. (1994). Cognitive and cognitive-behavioral therapies. In A. E. Bergin & S. L. Garfield (Eds.), *Handbook of psychotherapy change* (4th ed., pp. 428–466). New York: Wiley.

Holmes, C. B., & Howard, M. E. (1980). Recognition of suicide lethality factors by physicians, mental health professionals, ministers, and college students. *Journal of Consulting and Clinical Psychology, 48*(3), 383–387.

Hooker, E. (1956). A preliminary analysis of group behavior of homosexuals. *Journal of Psychology, 42,* 217–225.

Hooker, E. (1957). The adjustment of the male overt homosexual. *Journal of Projective Techniques, 21,* 18–31).

Hooker, E. (1958). Male homosexuality in the Rorschach. *Journal of Projective Techniques, 22,* 33–54.

Hooker, E. (1959). Symposium on current aspects of the problems of validity: What is a criterion? *Journal of Projective Techniques, 23,* 278–286.

Hooker, E. (1962). The homosexual community. In G. Nielson (Ed.), *Proceedings of the XIV International Congress of Applied Psychology: Vol. 2. Personality research* (pp. 40–59). Ann Arbor, MI: University Microfilm International.

Hooker, E. (1992). The adjustment of the male overt homosexual. In W. R. Dynes & S. Donaldson (Eds.), *Homosexuality and psychology, psychiatry, and counseling* (pp. 142–155). New York: Garland.

Hooker, E. (1993). Reflections of a 40-year exploration: A scientific view on homosexuality. *American Psychologist, 48*(4), 450–453.

Horney, K. (1937). *The neurotic personality of our time.* New York: Norton.

Horney, K. (1967). On the genesis of the castration complex in women. In K. Horney, *Feminine psychology* (pp. 37–53). New York: Norton.

Horvath, A., & Greenberg, L. (1989). Development and validation of the Working Alliance Inventory. *Journal of Counseling Psychology, 36,* 223–232.

Hubble, M. A., Noble, F. C., & Robinson, S. E. (1981). The effect of counselor touch in an initial counseling session. *Journal of Counseling Psychology, 28,* 533–535.

Hughes, D. E., & Roberts, L. E. (1985). Evidence of a role for response plans and self-monitoring in biofeedback. *Psychophysiology, 22*(4), 427–439.

Hutchinson, R. R. (1977). By-products of aversive control. In W. K. Honig & J. E. R. Staddon (Eds.), *Handbook of operant behavior.* Englewood Cliffs, NJ: Prentice-Hall.

Hyde, J. S. (1996). *Half the human experience: The psychology of women* (5th ed.). Lexington, MA: D. C. Heath.

Israel, J. (1984). Feminist therapy. *Women and Therapy, 3*(3–4), 157–161.

Ivey, A. E. (1987a). Cultural intentionality: The core of effective helping. *Counselor Education and Supervision, 26*(3), 168–172.

Ivey, A. E. (1987b). The multicultural practice of therapy: Ethics, empathy, and dialectics. *Journal of Social and Clinical Psychology, 5*(2), 195–204.

Ivey, A. E. (1991). *Developmental strategies for helpers: Individual, family, and network interventions.* Pacific Grove, CA: Brooks/Cole.

Ivey, A. E. (1994). *Intentional interviewing and counseling: Facilitating client development in a multicultural society* (3rd ed.). Pacific Grove, CA: Brooks/Cole.

Ivey, A. E. (1995). Psychotherapy as liberation: Toward specific skills and strategies in multicultural counseling and therapy. In J. Ponterotto, M. Cass, L. Suzuki, & C. Alexander (Eds.), *Handbook of multicultural counseling* (pp. 53–72). Thousand Oaks, CA: Sage.

Ivey, A. E., & Authier, J. (1978). *Microcounseling: Innovations in interviewing, counseling, psychotherapy, and psychoeducation* (2nd ed.). Springfield, IL: Charles C. Thomas.

Ivey, A., E., & Ivey, M. B. (1990). Assessing and facilitating children's cognitive development: Developmental counseling and therapy in a case of child abuse. *Journal of Counseling and Development, 68,* 299–306.

Ivey, A. E., Ivey, M. B., & Simek-Morgan, L. (1997). *Counseling and psychotherapy: A multicultural perspective* (4th ed.). Boston: Allyn and Bacon.

Izard, C. E. (1977). *Human emotions.* New York: Plenum.

Jakubowski, P. A. (1977). Assertion training for women. In E. I. Rawlings & D. K. Carter (Eds.), *Psychotherapy for women* (pp. 147–190). Springfield, IL: Charles C. Thomas.

Johnson, W. G., & Boggess, J. T. (1993). Obesity in adults. In R. T. Ammerman & M. Hersen (Eds.), *Handbook of behavior therapy with children and adults* (pp. 393–412). Boston: Allyn and Bacon.

Jones, B. E., & Hill, M. J. (Eds.). (2002). *Mental health issues in lesbian, gay, bisexual, and transgender communities.* Washington, DC: American Psychiatric Publishing.

Jordan, J. V. (1990). *Courage in connection.* (Available from The Stone Center, Wellesley College, Wellesley, MA 02181-8293).

Jordan, J. V., Kaplan, A. G., Miller, J. B., Stiver, I. P., & Surrey, J. L. (1991). *Women's growth in connection: Writings from the Stone Center.* New York: Guilford.

Jordan, J., Kaplan, A., & Surrey, J. (1990). *Empathy revisited.* (Available from The Stone Center, Wellesley College, Wellesley, MA 02181-8293.)

Jordan, J., Surrey, J., & Kaplan, A. (1985). *Women and empathy.* (Available from The Stone Center, Wellesley College, Wellesley, MA 02181-8293.)

Kabat-Zinn, J. (1990). *Full catastrophe living.* New York: Delta.

Kamphaus, R. W. (2001). *Clinical assessment of child and adolescent intelligence* (2nd ed.). Boston: Allyn and Bacon.

Kantrowitz, R. E., & Ballou, M. (1992). A feminist critique of cognitive-behavioral therapy. In L. S. Brown & M. Ballou (Eds.), *Personality and psychopathology: Feminist reappraisals* (pp. 70–87). New York: Gilford.

Kapelovitz, L. H. (1987). *To love and to work: A demonstration and discussion of psychotherapy.* North Vale, NJ: J. Aronson. (Original work published in 1976.)

Kaplan, H. I., & Sadock, B. J. (1991). *Synopsis of psychiatry. Behavioral sciences and clinical psychiatry* (6th ed.). Baltimore: Williams and Wilkins.

Kaplan, H. I., & Sadock, B. J. (1993). *Pocket handbook of psychiatric drug treatment.* Baltimore: Williams & Wilkins.

Kazdin, A. E. (1985a). The role of meta-analysis in the evaluation of psychotherapy. *Clinical Psychology Review, 5,* 49–61.

Kazdin, A. E. (1985b). Selection of target behaviors: The relationship of the treatment focus to clinical dysfunction. *Behavioral Assessment, 7,* 33–47.

Kazdin, A. E. (1985c). The token economy. In R. Turner & L. M. Asher (Eds.), *Evaluating behavior therapy outcome.* New York: Springer.

Kazdin, A. E. (1994a). Antisocial behavior and conduct disorder. In L. W. Craighead, W. E. Craighead, A. E. Kazdin, & M. J. Mahoney (Eds.), *Cognitive and behavioral interventions: An empirical approach to mental health problems* (pp. 267–299). Boston: Allyn and Bacon.

Kazdin, A. E. (1994b). *Behavior modification in applied settings* (5th ed.). Pacific Grove, CA: Brooks/Cole.

Kazdin, A. E. (1994c). Methodology, design, and evaluation in psychotherapy research. In A. E. Bergin & S. L. Garfield (Eds.), *Handbook of psychotherapy and behavior change* (4th ed., pp. 19–71). New York: Wiley.

Kazdin, A. E. (1994d). Psychotherapy for children and adolescents. In A. E. Bergin & S. L. Garfield (Eds.), *Handbook of psychotherapy and behavior change* (4th ed., pp. 543–594). New York: Wiley.

Kazdin, A. E., Moser, J., Colbus, D., & Bell, R. (1985). Depressive symptoms among physically abused and psychiatrically disturbed children. *Journal of Abnormal Psychology, 94*(3), 298–307.

Keith, K. (Ed.). (1985). *Behavior: Practical strategies for human service workers.* Omaha, NE: Meyer Children's Rehabilitation Institute.

Kemp, M. (1993). *Ally identity development model.* Educational Program Increasing Racial Awareness (EPIRA) Training, University of California at Santa Barbara.

Kleinke, C. L. (1986). Gaze and eye contact: A research review. *Psychological Bulletin, 100,* 78–100.

Klopfer, W. G., & Taulbee, E. S. (1976). Projective tests. In M. R. Rosenzweig & L. W. Porter (Eds.), *Annual review of psychology.* Palo Alto, CA: Annual Reviews.

Kerr, M. E., & Bowen, M. (1988). *Family evaluation: An approach based on Bowen theory.* New York: Bowen.

Kerr, W. A., & Speroff, B. G. (1954). Validation and evaluation of the empathy test. *Journal of General Psychology, 50,* 369–376.

Knapp, M. L. (1978). *Nonverbal communication in human interaction* (2nd ed.). New York: Holt, Rinehart and Winston.

Knight, R. P. (1941). Evaluation of the results of psychoanalytic therapy. *American Journal of Psychiatry, 98,* 434–436.

Kohler, W. (1929). *Gestalt psychology.* New York: Liveright.

Kohut, H. (1966). Forms and transformations of narcissism. In P. Ornstein (Ed.), *The search for self: Selected writings of Heinz Kohut: 1950–1978* (pp. 427–460). New York: International Universities Press.

Kohut, H. (1971). *The analysis of the self.* New York: International Universities Press.

Kohut, H. (1977). *The restoration of the self.* New York: International Universities Press.

Kohut, H. (1984). *How does analysis cure?* New York: International Universities Press.

Kübler-Ross, E. (1969). *On death and dying.* New York: Macmillan.

Kushner, H. I. (1995). Women and suicidal behavior: Epidemiology, gender and lethality in historical perspective. In S. S. Canetto & D. Lester (Eds.), *Women and suicidal behavior.* New York: Springer.

LaFrance, M., & Mayo, C. (1976). Racial differences in gaze behavior during conversations: Two systematic observational studies. *Journal of Personality and Social Psychology, 33,* 547–552.

Laidlaw, T. A., Malmo, C., et al. (1990). *Healing voices: Feminist approaches to therapy with women.* San Francisco: Jossey-Bass.

Lavee, Y., & Olson, D. H. (1991). Family types and response to stress. *Journal of Marriage and the Family, 53,* 786–798.

Lazarus, A. A. (1971). *Behavior therapy and beyond.* New York: McGraw-Hill.

Lazarus, A. A. (1974). Women in behavior therapy. In V. Franks & V. Burtle (Eds.), *Women in therapy: New psychotherapies for a changing society* (pp. 217–229). New York: Brunner/Mazel.

Lazarus, A. A. (1981/1989). *The practice of multimodel therapy.* Baltimore: Johns Hopkins University Press.

Lecomte, C., Bernstein, B. L., & Dumont, F. (1981). Counseling interactions as a function of spatial-environmental conditions. *Journal of Counseling Psychology, 28,* 536–539.

Lee, C. (1996). Implications for indigenous healing systems. In D. Sue, A. Ivey, & P. Pederson (Eds.), *A theory of multicultural counseling and therapy.* Pacific Grove, CA: Brooks/Cole.

Lerman, H. (1985). Some barriers to the development of a feminist theory of personality. In L. B. Rosewater & L. E. A. Walker (Eds.), *Handbook of feminist therapy: Women's issues in psychotherapy* (pp. 5–12). New York: Springer.

Lerman, H. (1986). From Freud to feminist personality theory: Getting here from there. *Psychology of Women Quarterly, 19*(1), 1–18.

Lerman, H. (1987). *A note in Freud's eye: From psychoanalysis to the psychology of women.* New York: Springer.

Lerman, H. (1992). The limits of phenomenology: A feminist critique of the humanistic personality theories. In L. S. Brown & M. Ballou (Eds.), *Personality and psychopathology: Feminist reappraisals.* New York: Guilford.

Lerman, H., & Porter, N. (Eds.). (1990). *Feminist ethics in psychotherapy.* New York: Springer.

Levine, J. L., Stolz, J. A., & Lacks, P. (1983). Preparing psychotherapy clients: Rationale and suggestions. *Professional Psychology: Research and Practice, 14,* 317–322.

Lewinsohn, P. M., Rohde, P., & Seeley, J. R. (1994). Psychosocial risk factors for future adolescent suicide attempts. *Journal of Consulting and Clinical Psychology, 62,* 297–305.

Lewis, J. M., Beavers, W. R., Gossett, J. T., & Phillips, V. A. (1976). *No single thread: Psychological health in family systems.* New York: Brunner/Mazel.

Linehan, M. M. (1993a). *Cognitive-behavioral treatment of borderline personality disorder.* New York: Guilford.

Linehan, M. M. (1993b). *Skill training manual for treating borderline personality disorder.* New York: Guilford.

Lipps, T. (1905). Das Wissen von fremden Ichen. *Psychologische Untersuchungen, 4,* 694–722.

Lipps, T. (1926). *Psychological studies.* Baltimore: Williams and Wilkens.

Litman, R. E. (1974). Models for predicting suicide risk. In C. Neuringer (Ed.), *Psychological assessment of suicidal risk.* Springfield, IL: Charles C. Thomas.

Lombardi, E. L., Wilchins, R. A., Priesing, D., & Malouf, D. (2001). Gender violence: Transgender experiences with violence and discrimination. *Journal of Homosexuality, 42*(1), 89–101.

Lorion, R. P. (1978). Research on psychotherapy and behavior change with the disadvantaged: Past, present, and future directions. In S. L. Garfield & A. E. Bergin (Eds.), *Handbook of psychotherapy and behavior change* (2nd ed.). New York: Wiley.

Luborsky, L., & Crits-Christoph, P. (1990). *Understanding transference.* New York: Basic Books.

Luborsky, L., Crits-Christoph, P., Mintz, J., & Auerbach, A. (1988). *Who will benefit from psychotherapy? Predicting therapeutic outcomes.* New York: Basic Books.

Luiselli, J. K. (1993). Pervasive development disorder. In R. T. Ammerman & M. Hersen (Eds.), *Handbook of behavior therapy with children and adults* (pp. 279–294). Boston: Allyn and Bacon.

Lyons, L. C., & Woods, P. J. (1991). The efficacy of rational-emotive therapy: A quantitative review of the outcome research. *Clinical Psychology Review, 11,* 357–369.

Maccoby, E. (1966). Sex differences in intellectual functioning. In E. Maccoby (Ed.), *The development of sex differences.* Stanford, CA: Stanford University Press.

Mahler, M. (1968). *On human symbiosis and the vicissitudes of individuation.* New York: International Universities Press.

Maracek, J. (1976). Powerlessness and women's psychological disorders. *Voices, 12*(3), 50–60.

Marx, M. H., & Goodson, F. E. (Eds.). (1976). *Theories in contemporary psychology* (2nd ed.). New York: Macmillan.

Masson, J. M. (1984). *The assault on truth: Freud's suppression of the seduction theory.* New York: Farrar Straus and Giroux.

Master, S. M., & Miller, S. M. (1991). A test of rational-emotive theory using a mood induction procedure: The rationality of thinking rationally. *Cognitive Therapy and Research, 15,* 491–502.

Matlin, M. W. (2002). *The psychology of women* (4th ed.), South Melbourne, Victoria, Australia: Wadsworth Thompson Learning.

Maultsby, M. C. (1984). *Rational behavior therapy.* Englewood Cliffs, NJ: Prentice-Hall.

Maurer, R. E., & Tindall, J. H. (1983). Effect of postural congruence on client's perception of counselor empathy. *Journal of Counseling Psychology, 30,* 158–163.

Mayhew, G. L., & Harris, F. C. (1978). Some negative side effects of a punishment procedure for stereotyped behavior. *Journal of Behavior Therapy and Experimental Psychiatry, 9,* 245–251.

McGovern, T. E., & Silverman, M. S. (1984). A review of outcome studies of rational-emotive therapy from 1977–1982. *Journal of Rational Emotive Therapy, 2,* 7–18.

McGrath, E., Keita, G. P., Strickland, B. R., & Russo, N. F. (Eds.). (1990). *Women and depression: Risk factors and treatment issues: Final report of the American Psychological Association's National Task Force on Women and Depression.* Washington, DC: American Psychological Association.

McMurtry, C. A., & Williams, J. E. (1972). The evaluation dimension of the affective meaning system of the preschool child. *Developmental Psychology, 6,* 238–246.

Mead, G. H. (1934). *Mind, self, and society.* Chicago: University of Chicago Press.

Mehrabian, A. (1976). *Public places and private spaces.* New York: Basic Books.

Meichenbaum, D. (1977). *Cognitive-behavior modification: An integrative approach.* New York: Plenum.

Meichenbaum, D. (1985). *Stress inoculation training.* New York: Pergamon.

Meichenbaum, D. (1986). Cognitive behavior modification. In F. H. Kanfer & A. P. Goldstein (Eds.), *Helping people change: A textbook of methods* (pp. 346–380). New York: Pergamon.

Meichenbaum, D. (1996). Stress inoculation training for coping with stressors. *The Clinical Psychologist, 49,* 4–10.

Meichenbaum, D. H. (1997). *Cognitive behavior modification: An integrative approach.* New York: Plenum.

Meissner, W. W. (1988). Theories of personality. In A. M. Nicholi (Ed.), *The new Harvard guide to psychiatry* (pp. 171–199). Cambridge, MA: Belknapp.

Merril, J., Milner, G., Owens, J., & Vale, A. (1992). Alcohol and attempted suicide. *British Journal of Addiction, 87,* 83–89.

Mertens, D. M. (1998). *Research methods in education and psychology: Integrating diversity with qualitative and quantitative approaches.* Thousand Oaks, CA: Sage.

Miller, J. B. (1982). Women and power. *Work in Progress* (Monograph of The Stone Center for Developmental Services and Studies), *82*(1).

Miller, J. B. (1986). *Toward a new psychology of women* (2nd ed.). Boston: Beacon.

Miller, K. L. (1975). *Principles of everyday behavior analysis.* Monterey, CA: Brooks/Cole.

Minuchin, S. (1974). *Families and family therapy.* Cambridge, MA: Harvard University Press.

Mitchell, J. (1974). *Psychoanalysis and feminism: Freud, Reich, Laing and women.* New York: Random House.

Moradi, B., Fischer, A. C., Hill, M. S., Jome, L. M., & Blum, S. A. (2000). Does "feminist" plus "therapist" equal "feminist therapist"? *Psychology of Women Quarterly, 24*(4), 285–296.

Morely, W. E. (1965). Treatment of the patient in crisis. *Western Medicine, 3,* 1–10.

Morely, W. E., Messick, J. M., & Aguilera, D. C. (1967). Crisis: Paradigms of intervention. *Journal of Psychiatric Nursing, 5,* 531–544.

Morgan, C. D., & Murray, H. A. (1935). A method for investigating fantasies: The Thematic Apperception Test. *Archives of Neurology and Psychiatry, 34,* 289–306.

Morgan, D. L. (1986). Personal relationships as an interface between social networks and social cognitions. *Journal of Social and Personal Relationships, 3,* 403–422.

Morgan, D. L. (1988). *Focus groups as qualitative research.* Newbury Park, CA: Sage.

Morgan, D. L. (1997). *Focus groups as qualitative research* (2nd ed.). Thousand Oaks, CA: Sage.

Morrison, R. L., & Sayers, S. (1993). Schizophrenia in adults. In R. T. Ammerman & M. Hersen (Eds.), *Handbook of behavior therapy with children and adults* (pp. 295–310). Boston: Allyn and Bacon.

Moscicki, E. (1995). Epidemiology of suicidal behavior. *Suicide and Life-Threatening Behavior, 25,* 22–35.

Mowbray, C. T., Lanir, S., & Hulce, M. (Eds.). (1985). *Women and mental health: New directions for change.* New York: Harrington Park.

Murray, H. A. (1938). *Explorations in personality: A clinical and experimental study of fifty men of college age.* New York: Oxford University Press.

Murray, H. A. (1943). *Thematic Apperception Test manual.* Cambridge, MA: Harvard University Press.

Myer, R. A. (2001). *Assessment for crisis intervention.* Toronto: Wadsworth.

National Institute of Mental Health. (1986). *Useful information on suicide.* Rockville, MD: US Department of Health and Human Services.

National Institute of Mental Health. (2000). *Suicide facts.* Washington, DC: Author. Retrieved January 26, 2000 from the World Wide Web: http://www.nimh. nih.gov/genpop/su_fact.htm.

Navarro, A. M. (1993). Effectividad de las psicoterapias con latinos en los estados unidos: Una revision meta-analitica. *Interamerican Journal of Psychology, 27,* 131–146.

NiCarthy, G., Merriam, K., & Coffman, S. (1994). *Talking it out: A guide to groups for abused women.* Seattle: Seal.

Nichols, M. P., & Schwartz, R. C. (1984). *Family therapy: Concepts and methods.* (4th ed.). Boston: Allyn and Bacon.

Nolen-Hoeksema, S. (2001). *Abnormal Psychology* (2nd ed). Boston: McGraw Hill.

Norcross, J. C. (1985). In defense of theoretical orientations for clinicians. *The Clinical Psychologist, 38*(1), 13–17.

Nwachuku, U. T., & Ivey, A. E. (1991). Culture-specific counseling: An alternative training model. *Journal of Counseling and Development, 70*(1), 106–111.

O'Donohue, W., & Krasner, L. (1995). *Theories of behavior therapy.* Washington, DC: American Psychological Association.

Office of Ethnic Minority Affairs. (1993). Guidelines for the providers of psychological services to ethnic, linguistic, and culturally diverse populations. *American Psychologist, 48,* 45–48.

Okun, B. F. (2002). *Effective helping: Interviewing and counseling techniques* (6th ed.). Pacific Grove: Brooks/Cole.

O'Leary, K. D., & Wilson, G. T. (1975). *Behavior therapy application and outcome.* Englewood Cliffs, NJ: Prentice-Hall.

Olson, D. H. (1986). Circumplex model VII. Validation studies and FACES III. *Family Process, 25*(3), 337–351.

Olson, D. H. (1990). Family circumplex model: Theory, assessment and intervention. *Japanese Journal of Family Psychology, 4,* 55–64.

Olson, D. H. (1993). Circumplex Model of Marital and Family Systems: Assessing family functioning. In F. Walsh (Ed.), *Normal family processes* (2nd ed., pp. 104–137). New York: Guilford.

Olson, D. H. (1996). Clinical assessment and treatment interventions using the family circumplex model. In F. W. Kaslow (Ed.), *Handbook of relational diagnosis and dysfunctional family patterns* (pp. 59–80). New York: Wiley.

Olson, D. H. (1997). Family stress and coping: A multisystem perspective. In S. Dreman (Ed.), *The family on the threshold of the 21st century: Trends and implications* (pp. 259–280). Mahwah, NJ: Lawrence Erlbaum.

Olson, D. H. (2000). Circumplex Model of Marital and Family Systems. *Journal of Family Therapy, 22*(2), 144–167.

Olson, D. H., & DeFrain, J. (2000). *Marriage and the family: Diversity and strengths* (3rd ed.). Mountain View, CA: Mayfield.

Orlinsky, D. E., & Howard, K. I. (1976). The effects of sex of therapist on the therapeutic experience of women. *Psychotherapy: Theory, Research, and Practice, 13* (1), 82–88.

Orlinsky, D. E., & Howard, K. I. (1980). Gender and psychotherapeutic outcome. In A. M. Brodsky & R. T. Hare-Mustin (Eds.), *Women and psychotherapy.* New York: Guilford.

Orlinsky, D. E., & Howard, K. I. (1986). Process and outcome in psychotherapy. In S. L. Garfield & A. E. Bergin (Eds.),

Handbook of psychotherapy and behavior change (3rd ed.). New York: Wiley.

Osborne, J. G., & Powers, R. B. (1980). Controlling the litter problem. In G. L. Martin & J. G. Osborne (Eds.), *Helping in the community: Behavioral applications.* New York: Plenum.

Paniagua, F. (1994). *Assessing and treating culturally diverse clients.* Thousand Oaks, CA: Sage.

Patton, M. Q. (2002). *Qualitative evaluation and research methods* (3rd ed.). Newbury Park, CA: Sage.

Peterson, C. (1996). *The Psychology of Abnormality.* Fort Worth, TX: Harcourt Brace.

Pettijohn, T. F. (1989). *Psychology: A concise introduction* (2nd ed.). Guilford, CT: Dushkin.

Piaget, J. (1932). *The moral judgment of the child* (trans.). London: Kegan Paul, Trench, Trubner.

Pinto, A., & Francis, G. (1993). Obsessive-compulsive disorder in children. In R. T. Ammerman & M. Hersen (Ed.), *Handbook of behavior therapy with children and adults* (pp. 156–166). Boston: Allyn and Bacon.

Polk, B. (1974). Male power and the women's movement. *Journal of Applied Behavioral Science, 10*(3), 415–431.

Pollack, D., & Shore, J. H. (1980). Validity of the MMPI with Native Americans. *The American Journal of Psychiatry, 137,* 946–950.

Ponterotto, J. G. (1988). Racial consciousness development among white counselors' trainees: A stage model. *Journal of Multicultural Counseling and Development, 16,* 146–156.

Ponterotto, J. G., Casas, J. M., Suzuki, L. A., & Alexander, C. M. (Eds.). (1995). *Handbook of multicultural counseling.* Thousand Oaks, CA: Sage.

Poorman, P. B. (1992). *Psychoeducational groups for abused women: A feminist theoretical framework and model.* Unpublished manuscript.

Poorman, P. B. (1992). *Toward a more unified feminist theory of therapy: Foundation and application.* Unpublished manuscript, Colorado State University, Fort Collins, CO.

Poorman, P. B., & Seelau, S. M. (2001). Lesbians who abuse their partners: Assessing interpersonal characteristics using FIRO-B. *Women and Therapy, 23*(3), 87–106. Also in E. Kashchak (Ed.), *Intimate betrayal: Domestic violence in lesbian relationships.* New York: Haworth.

Pope, K. S., & Velquez, M. J. T. (1998). *Ethics in psychotherapy and counseling: A practical guide* (2nd ed.). San Francisco: Jossey-Bass.

Prochaska, J. O., & Norcross, J. C. (1999). *Systems of psychotherapy: A transtheoretical analysis* (4th ed.). Pacific Grove, CA: Brooks/Cole.

Ram Dass, Baba. (1971). *Be here now.* New York: Crown.

Rawlings, E. I., & Carter, D. K. (Eds.). (1977). *Psychotherapy for women: Treatment toward equality.* Springfield, IL: Charles C. Thomas.

Reed, M. K., McLeod, S., Randall, Y., & Walker, B. (1996). Depressive symptoms in African-American women. *Journal of Multicultural Counseling and Development, 24*(1), 6–14.

Reynolds, D. (1990). Morita and Naikan therapies: Similarities. *Journal of Morita Therapy, 1,* 159–163.

Riddle, D. I., & Sang, B. (1978). Psychotherapy with lesbians. *Journal of Social Issues, 34*(3), 84–100.

Rigazio-DiGilio, S. A., Daniels, T. G., & Ivey, A. E. (1997). Systemic cognitive-developmental supervision: A developmental-integrative approach to psychotherapy supervision. In C. E. Watkins, Jr. (Ed.), *Handbook of psychotherapy supervision* (pp. 223–245). New York: Wiley.

Rigazio-DiGilio, S. A., Goncalves, O. F., & Ivey, A. E. (1996). From cultural to existential diversity: The impossibility of psychotherapy integration within a traditional framework. *Applied and Preventive Psychology, 5,* 235–247.

Rigazio-DiGilio, S. A., & Ivey, A. E. (1995). Individual and family issues in intercultural therapy: A culturally centered perspective. *Canadian Journal of Counseling, 29,* 244–261.

Rimm, D. C., & Masters, J. C. (1974). *Behavior therapy.* New York: Academic.

Robbins, J. H., & Siegal, R. J. (Eds.). (1985). *Women changing therapy: New assessments, values and strategies in feminist therapy.* New York: Harrington Park.

Roberts, L. E., Birbaumer, N., Rockstroh, B., Lutzenberger, W. et al. (1989). Self-report during feedback regulation of slow cortical potentials. *Psychophysiology, 26*(4), 392–403.

Robinson, L. A., Berman, J. S., & Neimeyer, R. A. (1990). Psychotherapy for the treatment of depression: A comprehensive review of controlled outcome research. *Psychological Bulletin, 108,* 30–49.

Rockland, L. H. (1989). *Supportive therapy: A psychodynamic approach.* New York: Basic Books.

Rogers, C. R. (1939). *The clinical treatment of the problem child.* Boston: Houghton Mifflin.

Rogers, C. R. (1942). *Counseling and psychotherapy.* Boston: Houghton Mifflin.

Rogers, C. R. (1951). *Client-centered therapy: Its current practice, implications, and theory.* Boston: Houghton Mifflin.

Rogers, C. R. (1957). The necessary and sufficient conditions of therapeutic personality change. *Journal of Consulting Psychology, 21,* 95–103.

Rogers, C. R. (1959). A theory of therapy, personality, and interpersonal relationships as developed in the client-centered framework. In S. Koch (Ed.), *Psychology: A study of science: Formulations of the person and the social context* (pp. 184–256). New York: McGraw-Hill.

Rogers, C. R. (1961). *On becoming a person.* Boston: Houghton Mifflin.

Rogers, C. R. (1969). *Freedom to learn: A view of what education might become.* Columbia, OH: Charles E. Merrill.

Rogers, C. R. (1970). *Carl Rogers on encounter groups.* New York: Harper and Row.

Rogers, C. R. (1975). Empathic: An unappreciated way of being. *Counseling Psychologist, 5,* 2–10.

Rogers, C. R. (1977). *Carl Rogers on personal power: Inner strength and its revolutionary impact.* New York: Delacorte.

Rogers, C. R. (1980). *A way of being.* Boston: Houghton Mifflin.

Rogers, C. R. (1986). Carl Rogers on the development of the person-centered approach. *Person-Centered Review, 1,* 257–259.

Rogers, C. R. (1987a). Comments on the issue of equality in psychotherapy. *Journal of Humanistic Psychology, 27,* 38–40.

Rogers, C. R. (1987b). Rogers, Kohut, and Erickson: A personal perspective on some similarities and differences. In J. K. Zeig (Ed.), *The evolution of psychotherapy* (pp. 179–187). New York: Brunner/Mazel.

Rogers, C. R. (1987c). Steps toward world peace, 1948–1986: Tension reduction in theory and practice. *Counseling and Values, 32,* 38–45.

Rohrbaugh-Bunker, J. (1979). *Women: Psychology's puzzle.* New York: Basic Books.

Rorschach, H. (1921). *Psychodiagnostik.* Bern, Switzerland: Huber.

Rose, C. (1975). Women's sex role attitudes: A historical perspective. *New Directions for Higher Education, 11,* 1–31.

Rosewater, L. B. (1982). *The development of an MMPI profile for battered women.* Doctoral dissertation, The Union for Experimenting Colleges and Universities.

Rosewater, L. B. (1985). Schizophrenic, borderline, or battered? In L. B. Rosewater & L. E. A. Walker (Eds.), *Handbook of feminist therapy: Women's issues in psychotherapy* (pp. 215–225). New York: Springer.

Rosewater, L. B. (1986). *Advocacy and the DSM-III-R.* Paper presented at the annual meeting of the American Psychological Association, Washington, DC.

Rosewater, L. B. (1987). The clinical and courtroom application of battered women's personality assessments. In D. E. Sonkin (Ed.), *Domestic violence on trial* (pp. 86–94). New York: Springer.

Rosewater, L. B. (1990). Diversifying feminist theory and practice: Broadening the concept of victimization. *Women and Therapy, 1,* 299–311.

Rosewater, L. B. (1990). Public advocacy. In H. Lerman & N. Porter (Eds.), *Feminist ethics in psychotherapy* (pp. 229–238). New York: Springer.

Rosewater, L. B., & Walker, L. E. A. (Eds.). (1985). *Handbook of feminist therapy: Women's issues in psychotherapy.* New York: Springer.

Rossi, A. S. (1964). Equality between the sexes: An immodest proposal. In R. J. Lifton (Ed.), *The woman in America.* Boston: Beacon.

Rossi, A. S. (1972). The roots of ambivalence in American women. In J. Bardwick (Ed.), *Readings on the psychology of women* (pp. 125–127). New York: Harper and Row.

Rothenberg, P. S. (1998). *Race, class, and gender in the United States: An integrated study* (4th ed.). New York: St. Martin's.

Ruiz, A. S. (1990). Ethnic identity: Crisis and resolution. *Journal of Multicultural Counseling and Development, 18,* 29–40.

Rusk, T. N. (1971). Opportunity and technique in crisis psychiatry. *Comprehensive Psychiatry, 12,* 249–263.

Saley, E., & Holdstock, L. (1993). Encounter group experiences of black and white South Africans in exile. In D. Brazier (Ed.), *Beyond Carl Rogers* (pp. 201–216). London: Constable.

Santos de Barona, M., Dutton, M. A., Ackerman, R. J., Balou, M., Culbertson, F., Peck, T., & Laurenti, A. M. (1997). Feminist perspectives on assessment. In J. Worell & N. G. Johnson (Eds.), *Shaping the future of feminist psychology: Education, research, and practice* (pp. 37–56). Washington, DC: American Psychological Association.

Sarafino, E. P. (1996). *Principles of behavior change.* New York: John Wiley.

Satir, V. M. (1967). *Conjoint family therapy* (rev. ed.). Palo Alto, CA: Science and Behavior.

Satir, V. M. (1972). *Peoplemaking.* Palo Alto, CA: Science and Behavior.

Satir, V. M. (1983). *Conjoint family therapy* (3rd ed.). Palo Alto, CA: Science and Behavior.

Satir, V. M. (1988). *The new peoplemaking.* Palo Alto, CA: Science and Behavior.

Satir, V. M., & Bitter, J. R. (1991). The therapist and family therapy: Satir's human validation process model. In A. M. Horne & J. L. Passmore (Eds.), *Family counseling and therapy* (2nd ed., pp. 13–45). Itasca, IL: F. E. Peacock.

Sattler, J. M. (1998). *Clinical and forensic interviewing of children and families: Guidelines for the mental health, education, pediatric, and child maltreatment fields.* San Diego: Author.

Sattler, J. M. (2001). *Assessment of children: Cognitive applications* (4th ed.). San Diego: Author.

Schafer, R. (1954). *Psychoanalytic interpretation in Rorschach testing: Theory and application.* New York: Grune and Stratton.

Scherzinger, M. F., Keogh, D. A., & Whitman, T. L. (1993). Mental retardation in adults. In R. T. Ammerman & M. Hersen (Eds.), *Handbook of behavior therapy with childen and adults* (pp. 331–348). Boston: Allyn and Bacon.

Schloss, P. J., & Smith, M. A. (1994). *Applied behavior analysis in the classroom.* Boston: Allyn and Bacon.

Schneidman, E. S. (1985). *Definition of suicide.* New York: Wiley.

Seidmann, I. E. (1991). *Interviewing as qualitative research: A guide for researchers in education and the social sciences.* New York: Columbia University Teachers College.

Seligman, M. E. P. (1975). *Helplessness: On depression, development, and death.* San Francisco: W. H. Freeman.

Selye, H. (1936). A syndrome produced by diverse nocuous agents. *Nature, 138,* 32.

Selye, H. (1956). *The stress of life.* New York: McGraw-Hill.

Selye, H. (1976). *The stress of life* (rev. ed.). New York: McGraw-Hill.

Shadish, W. R., Montgomery, L. M., Wilson, P., Wilson, M. R., Bright, I., & Okwumakua, T. (1993). The effects of family and marital psychotherapies: A meta-analysis. *Journal of Consulting and Clinical Psychology, 61,* 61.

Shapiro, D. A., & Shapiro, D. (1982). Meta-analysis of comparative therapy outcome studies: A replication and refinement. *Psychological Bulletin, 92,* 581–604.

Sharf, R. S. (1996). *Theories of psychotherapy and counseling: Concepts and cases.* Pacific Grove, CA: Brooks/Cole.

Shroyer, E., & Shroyer, S. (1982). *Signs across America.* Washington, DC: Gallaudet University Press.

Silverman, M. S., McCarthy, M. L., & McGovern, T. (1992). A review of outcome studies of rational-emotive therapy from 1982–1989. *Journal of Rational-Emotive and Cognitive-Behavioral Therapy, 10,* 111–186.

Skinner, B. F. (1938). *The behavior of organisms.* New York: Appleton-Century-Crofts.

Skinner, B. F. (1948). *Walden Two.* New York: Macmillan.

Skinner, B. F. (1953). *Science and human behavior.* New York: Macmillan.

Skinner, B. F. (1954). The science of learning and the art of teaching. *Harvard Educational Review, 24,* 86–97.

Sloane, R. B., Staples, F., Cristol, A., Yorkston, N., & Whipple, K. (1975). *Psychotherapy versus behavior therapy.* Cambridge, MA: Harvard University Press.

Smith, A. J., & Siegal, R. F. (1985). Feminist therapy: Redefining power for the powerless. In L. B. Rosewater & L. E. A. Walker (Eds.), *Handbook of feminist therapy: Women's issues in psychotherapy* (pp. 13–21). New York: Springer.

Smith, M. L., & Glass, G. V. (1977). Meta-analysis of psychotherapy outcome studies. *American Psychologist, 32,* 752–760.

Smith, M. L., Glass, G. V., & Miller, T. I. (1980). *The benefits of psychotherapy.* Baltimore: Johns Hopkins University Press.

Spiegler, M. D., & Guevremont, D. C. (1998). *Contemporary behavior therapy* (3rd ed.). Pacific Grove, CA: Brooks/Cole.

Spitzer, R. L., Williams, J. B. W., Gibbon, M., & First, M. (1992). The Structured Clinical Interview for DSM-III-R (SCID): I. History, rationale, and description. *Archives of General Psychiatry, 49,* 624–636.

St. Clair, M. (1986). *Object relations and self psychology: An introduction.* Monterey, CA: Brooks/Cole.

St. Clair, M. (1996). *Object relations and self psychology: An introduction* (2nd ed.). Pacific Grove, CA: Brooks/Cole.

Sterman, M. B. (1996). Physiological origins and functional correlates of EEG rhythmic activities: Implications for self-regulation. *Biofeedback and Self Regulation, 21*(1), 3–33.

Stewart, C. J., & Cash, W. B., Jr. (1997). *Interviewing principles and practices* (8th ed.). Madison, WI: Brown and Benchmark.

Stock, W., Graubert, J., & Birns, B. (1982). Women and psychotherapy. *International Journal of Mental Health, 11*(1–2), 135–158.

Stotland, E. (1969). Exploratory investigations of empathy. In L. Berkowitz (Ed.), *Advances in experimental social psychology* (Vol. 4, pp. 271–314). New York: Academic.

Stotland, E., Sherman, S., & Shaver, K. (1971). *Empathy and birth order: Some experimental explorations.* Lincoln: University of Nebraska Press.

Strauss, M. (1977). Wife-beating: How common and why? *Victimology: An International Journal, 2*(3–4), 443–458.

Sturdivant, S. (1980). *Therapy with women: A feminist philosophy of treatment.* New York: Springer.

Sue, D. W. (1977a). Barriers to effective cross-cultural counseling. *Journal of Counseling Psychology, 24,* 420–429.

Sue, D. W. (1977b). Counseling the culturally different: A conceptual analysis. *Personnel and Guidance Journal, 55,* 422–424.

Sue, D. W., Carter, R. T., Casas, J. M., Fouad, N. A., Ivey, A. E., Jensen, M., LaFrombiose, T., Manese, J. E., Ponterotto, J. G., & Vasquez-Nutall, E. (1998). *Multicultural counseling competencies: Individual and organizational development.* Thousand Oaks, CA: Sage.

Sue, D. W., Ivey, A. E., & Pedersen, P. (1996). *A theory of multicultural counseling and therapy.* Pacific Grove, CA: Brooks/Cole.

Sue, D. W., & Sue, S. (1972a). Counseling Chinese-Americans. *Personnel and Guidance Journal, 50,* 637–644.

Sue, D. W., & Sue, S. (1972b). Ethnic minorities: Resistance to being researched. *Professional Psychology, 2,* 11–17.

Sue, D. W., & Sue, S. (1990). *Counseling the culturally different* (2nd ed.). New York: Wiley.

Sue, S. (1988). Psychotherapeutic services for ethnic minorities: Two decades of research findings. *American Psychologist, 43,* 301–308.

Sue, S., Zane, N., & Young, K. (1994). Research on psychotherapy with culturally diverse populations. In A. E. Gerfin & S. L. Garfield (Eds.), *Handbook of psychotherapy and behavior change* (4th ed., pp. 783–817). New York: Wiley.

Sullivan, H. (1953). *Conceptions of modern psychiatry.* New York: Norton.

Suzuki, L. A., & Kugler, J. F. (1995). Intelligence and personality assessment: Multicultural perspectives. In J. G. Ponterotto, J. M. Casas, L. A. Suzuki, & C. M. Alexander (Eds.), *Handbook of multicultural counseling* (pp. 493–515). Thousand Oaks, CA: Sage.

Suzuki, L. A., Ponterotto, J. G., & Meller, P. J. (Eds.). (2001). *Handbook of multicultural assessment: Clinical, psychological, and educational applications* (2nd ed.). San Francisco: Jossey-Bass.

Suzuki, S. (1970). *Zen mind, beginner's mind.* New York: Weatherhill.

Svartberg, M., & Stiles, T. C. (1991). Comparative effects of short-term psychodynamic psychotherapy: A meta-analysis. *Journal of Consulting and Clinical Psychology, 5,* 704–714.

Szapocznik, J., Santisteban, D., Kurtines, W. M., Hervis, O. E., & Spencer, F. (1982). Life enhancements counseling: A psychosocial model of service for Cuban elders. In E. E. Jones & S. J. Korchin (Eds.), *Minority mental health* (pp. 296–329). New York: Praeger.

Tamase, K. (1991, April). *The effects of introspective-developmental counseling.* Paper presented at the American Association of Counseling and Development, Reno, NV.

Tharp, R. G., & Wetzel, R. J. (1969). *Behavior modification in the natural environment.* New York: Academic.

Thomas, C. (1971). *Boys no more.* Beverly Hills, CA: Glencoe.

Thomas, V., & Olson, D. H. (1993). Problems families and the Circumplex Model: Observational assessment using the Clinical Rating Scale (CRS). *Journal of Marital and Family Therapy, 19*(2), 159–175.

Thorne, B. (1992). *Carl Rogers.* London: Sage.

Tiesel, J. W., Miller, B., & Olson, D. H. (1995). Systemic intervention with stepfamilies using the Circumplex Model. In D. K. Huntley (Ed.), *Understanding stepfamilies: Implications for assessment and treatment* (pp. 35–55). Alexandria, VA: American Counseling Association.

Todd, J., & Bohart, A. C. (1999). *Foundations of clinical and counseling psychology* (3rd ed.). New York: Longman.

Truax, C. B., & Carkhuff, R. R. (1971). *Toward effective counseling and psychotherapy.* Chicago: Aldine.

Truax, C. B., & Mitchell, K. M. (1971). Research on certain therapist interpersonal skills in relation to process and outcome. In A. E. Bergin & S. L. Garfield (Eds.), *Handbook of psychotherapy and behavior change: An empirical analysis* (pp. 299–344). New York: Wiley.

Trull, T. J., & Phares, E. J. (2001). *Clinical psychology: Concepts, methods, and profession* (6th ed.). Belmont, CA: Wadsworth.

United States Department of Commerce. (1993). *Statistical abstract of the United States* (113th ed.). Washington, DC: Author.

Velasquez, R. (1984). An atlas of MMPI group profiles on Mexican Americans. *Spanish Speaking Mental Health Research Center, 19,* 1–45.

Venn, J. R., & Short, J. G. (1973). Vicarious classical conditioning of emotional responses in nursery school children. *Journal of Personality and Social Psychology, 28,* 249–255.

Walker, L. E. A. (1979). *The battered woman.* New York: Harper & Row.

Walker, L. E. A. (1980). Battered women. In A. Brodsky & R. Hare-Mustin (Eds.), *Women and psychotherapy*. New York: Guilford.

Walker, L. E. A. (1985). Feminist therapy with victim/ survivors of interpersonal violence. In L. B. Rosewater & L. E. A. Walker (Eds.), *Handbook of feminist therapy: Women's issues in psychotherapy* (pp. 203–214). New York: Springer.

Walker, L. E. A. (1986). *Diagnosis and politics: Abuse disorders*. Paper presented at the annual meeting of the American Psychological Association, Washington, DC.

Walker, L. E. A. (1989, April). Psychology and violence against women. *American Psychologist*, 695–702.

Walker, L. E. A. (1990). Feminist ethics with victims of violence. In H. Lerman & N. Porter (Eds.), *Feminist ethics in psychotherapy* (pp. 214–226). New York: Springer.

Wallerstein, R. S. (1985). The concept of psychic reality: Its meaning and value. *Journal of the American Psychoanalytic Association, 33*(3), 555–569.

Wallerstein, R. S. (1986). *Forty-two lives in treatment*. New York: Guilford.

Wallerstein, R. S. (Ed.). (1992). *The common ground of psychonanalysis*. North Vale, NJ: J. Aronson.

Wallerstein, R. S. (1996). Outcomes of psychoanalysis and psychotherapy at termination and at follow-up. In E. Nersessian & R. G. Kopff, Jr. (Eds.), *Textbook of psychoanalysis* (pp. 531–573). Washington, DC: American Psychiatric Press.

Wallerstein, R. S. (2001). The generations of psychotherapy research: An overview. *Psychoanalytic Psychology, 18*(2), 243–267.

Wallerstein, R. S., & Weinshel, E. M. (1989). The future of psychoanalysis. *Psychoanalytic Quarterly, 58,* 341–373.

Watson, J. B. (1913). Psychology as the behaviorist views it. *Psychological Review, 20,* 158–177.

Watson, J. B. (1930). *Behaviorism*. New York: Norton.

Webster's unabridged dictionary. (2001). New York: Random House.

Westen, D. (1996). *Psychology: Mind, brain, and culture*. New York: Wiley.

Whaley, D. L., & Malott, R. W. (1971). *Elementary principles of behavior*. New York, NY: Meredith.

White, M., & Epston, D. (1990). *Narrative means to therapeutic ends*. New York: Norton.

White, M., & Epston, D. (1994). *Experience, contradiction, narrative, and imagination*. Adelaide, South Australia: Dulwich Centre.

Whorf, B. L. (1956). Language, thought, and reality. In J. B. Carroll (Ed.), *Selected writings of Benjamin Lee Whorf*. New York: Wiley.

Wiebe, D. J. (1991). Hardiness and stress moderations: A test of proposed mechanisms. *Journal of Personality and Social Psychology, 60*(1), 89–99.

Wiebe, D. J., & McCallum, D. M. (1986). Health practices and hardiness as mediators in the stress-illness relationship. *Health Psychology, 5*(5), 425–438.

Williams, J. H. (1977). *Psychology of women*. New York: Norton.

Williams, R. J., & Roberts, L. E. (1988). Relation of learned heart rate control to self-report in different task environments. *Psychophysiology, 25*(3), 354–365.

Wilson, G. T., Nathan, P. E., O'Leary, K. D., & Clark, L. E. (1996). *Abnormal psychology: Integrating perspectives*. Boston: Allyn and Bacon.

Wispé, L. (1986). The distinction between sympathy and empathy: To call forth a concept, a word is needed. *Journal of Personality and Social Psychology, 50,* 314–321.

Wispé, L. (1991). *The psychology of sympathy*. New York: Plenum.

Wolfman, B. R. (1983). *Women and their many roles*. (Available from The Stone Center, Wellesley College, Wellesley, MA 02181-8293.)

Wolpe, J. (1958). *Psychotherapy by reciprocal inhibition*. Palo Alto, CA: Stanford University Press.

Wolpe, J. (1973). *The practice of behavior therapy* (2nd ed.). New York: Pergamon.

Wolpe, J. (1990). *The practice of behavior therapy* (4th ed.). Elmsford, NY: Pergamon.

Women Helping Women. (1990). *Women helping battered women: Working together to change the way we think about violence* (vols. 1–3). Burlington, VT: Author.

Woods, P. J., Silverman, E. G., & Bentilini, J. M. (1991). Cognitive variable related to suicidal contemplation in adolescents with implications for long range prevention. *Journal of Rational-Emotive and Cognitive-Behavior Therapy, 9,* 215–245.

Worell, J. (2001). Feminist interventions: Accountability beyond symptom reduction. *Psychology of Women Quarterly, 25*(4), 335–343.

Worthington, R. L. (n.d.). *Education 165L: Introduction to counseling psychology skills training laboratory: A manual for teaching assistants.* (Available from the Office of Instructional Development, University of California, Santa Barbara, CA 93101.)

Wyckoff, H. (1977). *Solving women's problems through awareness, action and contact.* New York: Grove.

INDEX

oppression, awareness of, 241, 242–243, 244, 254, 257
oppression, cultural, 243, 299
oppression, institutionalized, 243, 301
oppression, internalized, 243, 301
outcome research (effectiveness), 259–261
pluralistic identity development model, 249, 252–253
race and ethnicity, 241
socialization, 244–245, 304
Sue, Derald Wing, and Sue, Stanley, 246
terminology for minority groups (language), 246–248
and traditional theories, 261

NASW (National Association of Social Workers), 21, 302
National origin
and ethical standards, 22
Nature or nurture, 142
No Harm Contract, 278
NOHSE (National Organization of Human Services Employees), 21, 302
Nonverbal communication, 27–48, 148. *See also* Kinesics; Paralanguage; Proxemics; Time
client difference (multicultural), 30–31
dyssynchrony, 28, 33, 41–42, 130–137
feedback, 60–61, 300
feelings, reflection of, 75
mirroring, 75
rating guideline for students, 46–47 (Exercise 1.3)
relaxed helper, 45–46
synchrony, 40–42, 63
voice, 29
Nurses, psychiatric. *See* Psychiatric nurses

Object relations theories, 15, 182, 190–192, 194, 195, 198. *See also* Psychodynamic theories
development of, 190–192
and ego psychology theories, 190
Fairbairn, W. R. D., 190–191
and feminist theories, 221
and Freud's drive theories, 190, 191
and immediacy, 124
and interpersonal theories, 190
Klein, Melanie, 190
Mahler, Margaret, 191–192

transitional object, 191, 305
Winnicott, Donald, 191
Okun, Barbara, 12
On Becoming a Person (Rogers), 143
Open questions, 92–93, 282, 302
Operant conditioning, 154, 302
Oppression, 302
awareness of, 241, 242–243, 244, 254, 257
cultural, 243, 299
institutionalized, 221, 243, 301
internalized, 243, 301
Orientation. *See* Emotional orientation; Sexual orientation; Theoretical orientation
Outcome research. *See under specific theories*

Paralanguage (paralinguistics), 29–30, 42–43
fluency, 29, 30, 42
minimal verbal responses, 44, 302
silence, 27–28, 43–44
voice characteristics, 29, 42
Paraphrasing, 64–67, 73, 302
Patton, Michael Quinn, 282–283. *See also* Research, qualitative
Pavlov, Ivan, 154, 157
Perls, Frederick, 27
Personal context, 86–87, 104–105
Person-centered theory, 16, 141–152. *See also* Existential theory; Humanistic theories; Phenomenological psychology; Rogers, Carl
assessment, 147–148
and clarifying, 148, 298
conditions of worth, 144, 298
and confrontation, 148
and content, restatement of (reflection of), 148
and culture, 150, 151
development of, 143–144
and empathy, 147, 150
and feelings, reflection of, 148
and feminist theories, 221, 222
and gender, 151–152
and interpreting, 148, 149
and nonverbal communication, 148
outcome research (effectiveness), 149–150
and paraphrasing, 148